The Possible
and the Actual

The Possible
and the Actual

READINGS IN THE METAPHYSICS OF MODALITY

EDITED BY

Michael J. Loux

CORNELL UNIVERSITY PRESS
Ithaca and London

First published 1979 by Cornell University Press
First printing, Cornell Paperbacks, 1979

ISBN-13: 978-0-8014-9178-8 (pbk.:alk.paper)
ISBN-10: 0-8014-9178-9 (pbk.:alk.paper)
Library of Congress Catalog Card Number 79-7618
Printed in the United States of America

Cornell University Press strives to use environmentally responsible suppliers and materials to the fullest extent possible in the publishing of its books. Such materials include vegetable-based, low-VOC inks and acid-free papers that are recycled, totally chlorine-free, or partly composed of nonwood fibers. For further information, visit our website at www.cornellpress.cornell.edu.

Paperback printing   10 9 8 7

TO NEIL DELANEY
BEST OF ALL POSSIBLE CHAIRMEN

Contents

Preface

In these days, an anthology on the topic of possible worlds hardly needs justification. No issue has given rise to as much literature in the past couple of decades. It has, of course, been the central focus of discussions in philosophical logic and ontology; but the framework of possible worlds has played a prominent role in other areas of philosophy, such as epistemology, philosophy of religion, philosophy of science, aesthetics, and philosophy of mind. Theorists have insisted that talk of alternative possible worlds illumines philosophical issues as diverse as the nature of belief and knowledge, the ontological argument, the problem of evil, the nature of lawlike statements, the concept of causation, the nature of fictional discourse, and the mind-body problem. Such applications of the framework of possible worlds are of great philosophical interest, but obviously their success hinges on the legitimacy of the framework itself. Consequently, in this anthology, I have included only writings that bear on foundational questions about possible worlds. I have arranged the papers chronologically; and apart from my introductory essay, "Modality and Metaphysics," only two of the papers appearing here (David Kaplan's "Transworld Heir Lines" and William Lycan's "The Trouble with Possible Worlds") have not been published previously.

The papers I have selected tend to fall into two thematic groups. Eight of the papers are primarily concerned with the nature and status of possible worlds. David Lewis' "Possible Worlds" is a defense of the view that possible worlds and their contents are all equally real; Lewis takes these worlds to be primitives and insists that his realistic interpretation of possibilia is merely a formalization of our common-sense thinking about modality. In "Modal Realism" Fabrizio Mondadori and Adam Morton try to counter Lewis' approach by arguing that modal notions can be understood independently of any reference to possible worlds or possible objects. The remaining six papers in this group all defend a possible worlds interpretation of modal discourse, but attempt to show how we can embrace an ontology of possible worlds within the context of an actualist ontology, that is, an ontology that holds that only the actual world and its contents are real. Robert Stalnaker (in "Possible Worlds") proposes that we identify possible worlds with certain actually existing but uninstantiated properties. Robert M. Adams (in "Theories of Actuality") takes the notion of a proposition as primitive and construes worlds as maximally consistent sets of propositions. In "Actualism and Possible Worlds" Alvin Plantinga tells us that possible worlds are maximally possible states of affairs and insists that talk about nonexistent possibles is to be understood as talk about unexemplified individual essences. William Lycan's "The Trouble with Possible Worlds" represents a defense of a view like that of Stalnaker, Adams, and Plantinga. He suggests that if we take some category of intensional abstract entities as basic we can provide a coherent account of unrealized possibility. In "The Ontology of the Possible" Nicholas Rescher adopts a conceptualist approach to possibility, contending that the existence of unactualized possibilia is grounded in human conceptual activity. Finally M. J. Cresswell's "The World Is Everything That Is the Case" represents a combinatorialist approach to possible worlds. Cresswell argues that possible worlds are alternative set theoretical constructs of the nonmodal atoms making up the actual world.

The second group of papers deals with the problem of transworld identity. In "Identity through Possible Worlds: Some Questions" Roderick Chisholm tries to show how an ontology of possible worlds generates this problem. David Kaplan's "Transworld Heir Lines" is a defense of the view that this problem can be handled only if we suppose that some relation weaker than that of strict identity ties objects in different worlds. In "Counterpart Theory and Quantified Modal Logic" David Lewis tries to give a formal representation of this weaker relation; he calls it the counterpart relation and argues that it is strong enough to accommodate our ordinary modal intuitions. In "Transworld Identity or Worldbound Individuals?" Alvin Plantinga criticizes Lewis' counterpart theory; he argues that the relation will not support our prephilosophical views about modality and attempts to show that transworld identity provides no serious problem for the defender of possible worlds. Finally, in "How to Russell a Frege-Church" David Kaplan returns to the problem of transworld identity; he suggests that we understand the problem in terms of questions about the structure of singular propositions and argues that, when understood in these terms, transworld identity does not warrant the sort of skepticism we meet in the papers by Chisholm and Lewis or in his own earlier work on the problem.

I was unable to obtain permission to publish two papers I had originally intended to include in the anthology, Saul Kripke's "Semantical Considerations on Modal Logic" and his paper "Identity and Necessity." The latter can be found in Stephen P. Schwartz's collection *Naming, Necessity, and Natural Kinds* (published by Cornell University Press). The former provides an account of the semantics of modal logic; a slightly different treatment of the same material can be found in Jaakko Hintikka's "The Modes of Modality," which appears herein. My introductory essay provides an informal outline of Kripke-type semantics.

A number of people deserve my special thanks for their distinctive contributions to the anthology. I want to thank David Kaplan for his willingness to let his early paper "Transworld Heir Lines" appear in print and William Lycan for contributing his helpful essay. Alvin Plantinga was extremely generous both in helping me with the selection of papers and in discussing the metaphysical issues at work in the debate over possible worlds. Robert M. Adams, David Solomon, James Garson, and Michael Duffy read my introductory essay and provided many helpful suggestions. Ann, Laurie, Joey, Chris, Sandy, and Julie Loux all lived with me during the often trying period in which the manuscript for the anthology was being put together; for that alone, but also for their loving patience, they deserve a lifetime of appreciation. Ryan Welsh gave her expert help in the preparation of the manuscript; she deserves my thanks as well as a high-paying job with the Secret Service, in which her uncanny ability to decipher even the most obscure codes would doubtless do much to enhance our national security. Finally, I want to thank Neil Delaney; his kindness, encouragement, and help were given in even greater abundance than the dedication suggests.

MICHAEL J. LOUX

Notre Dame, Indiana

The Possible
and the Actual

1

Introduction:
Modality and Metaphysics

MICHAEL J. LOUX

University of Notre Dame

Although the idea that reality has a modal structure is prominent in traditional metaphysics, it has not been popular in Anglo-American philosophy. Hume vigorously attacked the view that modality is an objective feature of the world, and his philosophical descendants in the analytic tradition tended to assume that Hume's attack here was decisive. Modal notions, they argued, either are illegitimate or are mere reflections of our decisions to use words in certain ways; there is no modality out in the world. In the past couple of decades, however, the venerable idea that reality has a modal structure has taken on a new life in analytic philosophy. Results in the semantical analysis of modal logic and reflection on a variety of forms of modal discourse have conspired to bring to the center of the philosophical arena the Leibnizian idea that our world is not the only possible world, that there are other possible worlds, and that it is the various possible worlds that constitute the subject matter of modal discourse. In this introductory essay, I want to provide a general survey of this renewed interest in the traditional thesis about modality. In the first section, I try to show how the Leibnizian idea came back into philosophy by discussing in an informal way the results of recent work on the semantics of modal logic. In the second section, I try to show how these results hook up with our preanalytic intuitions about modality and to indicate how the framework of possible worlds might be thought to provide the machinery for clarifying a host of problematic forms of discourse; and in the last three sections, I discuss the metaphysical issues raised by the appeal to that framework.

I

Traditional logic viewed the systematization of modal inference as a central part of the logician's enterprise. In the *Prior Analytics,* Aristotle provided a painstaking analysis of the special problems raised by modal inference, and medieval logic books regularly included a detailed presentation of the doctrine of the modal syllogism. But despite its impressive historical credentials, the notion of a modal logic was regarded with suspicion by logicians in the first half of this century. In part, their suspicions can be traced to the typically empiricist orientation of early twentieth-century analytic philosophy, which embraced a kind of skepticism about the modalities; and in part, they can be traced to the general belief that the extensional system formalized in the *Principia Mathematica* represents a paradigm of logic. This is not to say that there was no important work in modal logic in the first half of the century. C. I. Lewis and others, convinced that the material conditional of the Russell-Whitehead system fails to capture our prephilosophical notion of implication, did important work in the formalization of modal inference. Despite its ultimate significance, however, their work did more to harm than to help the cause of modal logic, for their investigations showed the possibility of constructing a large number of nonequivalent theories of modal inference.

To show how this work might have deepened existing suspicions about modal logic, I want to focus on the case of propositional (as opposed to quantified) modal logic; and I want to point to four nonequivalent propositional modal systems. All four incorporate the various symbols of nonmodal propositional logic as well as the symbols $\square$ (or L) and $\lozenge$ (or M) which express, respectively, necessity and possibility.[1] The weakest of the four systems is called M (sometimes, T); it takes as its axioms all the truth-functional tautologies and the following two modal formulas:

(1) $\square (A \supset B) \supset (\square A \supset \square B)$
(2) $\square A \supset A$

and has two underived rules: modus ponens and the rule of necessitation, which tells us that if a formula, A, is a thesis of M (i.e., an axiom or theorem of M), then $\square A$ is also a thesis of M. A system stronger than M is

1. $\square$ and $\lozenge$ are read, respectively, as 'Necessarily...' or 'It is necessary that...' and 'Possibly...' or 'It is possible that....' The two operators are taken to be interdefinable; usually one is taken as primitive and the other defined in terms of it. Thus, if $\square$ is taken as primitive, $\lozenge$ is introduced as follows: $\lozenge A = $ df. $\sim \square \sim A$.

called the Brouwer system. It contains M (i.e., all the theses of M are theses of the Brouwer system) but adds to the axioms of M the following formula:

(3) $A \supset \Box \Diamond A$.

Another system (S-4) is built on M by adding to the axioms of M not (3), but

(4) $\Box A \supset \Box \Box A$.

What is interesting about S-4 is that the following two formulas are derivable in it:

(5) $\Box A \equiv \Box \Box A$
(6) $\Diamond A \equiv \Diamond \Diamond A$.

They allow us to take any formula incorporating a string of iterated modal operators (i.e., a string of more than one occurrence of a single modal operator, e.g., $\Box\Box\Box\Box\Box P$) and to substitute for it a formula in which the relevant string is replaced by a single occurrence of the modal operator in question. Finally, there is a system (S-5) which contains both the Brouwer system and S-4. We could obtain this system by adding to the axioms of M both (3) and (4); but we can effect this more economically by adding to the axioms of M the single formula

(7) $\Diamond A \supset \Box \Diamond A$.

The interesting feature of S-5 is that among its theorems are

(8) $\Diamond A \equiv \Box \Diamond A$

and

(9) $\Box A \equiv \Diamond \Box A$.

They allow us to take a formula prefaced by a string of two or more modal operators, whether the same or different (e.g., $\Diamond\Box\Box\Diamond\Box\Diamond p$), and replace it by the same formula prefaced by the last operator in the string (in the example just given, $\Diamond p$).

There are, of course, other propositional modal systems; but reflection on these four is sufficient to show why the diversity of modal logics should have been thought problematic. What we want is a theory that systematizes modal inference. We want a theory that will enable us to determine which modal inferences are legitimate and which not, but the four systems just outlined give us four different answers to the question: which propositional modal inferences are legitimate? Just which system, then, are we to take as *the* correct theory of propositional modal inference?

It might be thought that there is a straightforward strategy for coming up with an answer here. We simply look to the axioms of the different systems and compare them with our considered intuitions about matters modal. Pretty clearly, (1) and (2) are acceptable. (1) tells us that a necessary truth entails (i.e., necessarily implies) only necessary truths, and that seems correct. (2), on the other hand, tells us that if a proposition is necessarily true, then it is true, and that seems as certain as anything. Things become a bit more complicated when we confront the more complex axioms generating the Brouwer system, S-4, and S-5; but even here, it might be thought, a careful consideration of our modal intuitions will enable us to decide one way or the other. Consider (3). What (3) tells us is that if a proposition is true, then it is not just possible; its possibility is a matter of necessity. Now, if we think that the possibility attaching to a true proposition is not just a matter of contingency, that a true proposition does not just happen to be possible, but that it is necessarily possible, then we will want to claim that the inferences licensed by the Brouwer system are all legitimate modal inferences. If, on the other hand, we think, in line with (4), that a proposition is necessarily true only if its necessity is a matter of necessity, then we will take the inferences licensed by S-4 to be one and all legitimate. Finally, if we think that both (3) and (4) represent the formalization of correct modal inference (i.e., if we think that the modal status of a proposition, no matter what that status, is a matter of necessity), then we commit ourselves to the view that S-5 provides a correct systematization of legitimate modal inference.

This line of thinking has a certain plausibility to it, but there are two problems. First, the assumption that everyone interested in the systematization of modal inference has clear-cut intuitions about (3), (4), and (7) is likely hazardous. Philosophers frequently claim to have no firm intuitions at all on these matters: they claim that it is just not intuitively clear what we are to say about the modal status attaching to modal propositions. But even if they are wrong about this, there is a second difficulty. If we take our intuitions to be decisive in determining our choice of a modal logic, then we must remember that our original intuitions about the axioms generating the Brouwer system, S-4, and S-5 have to be tested, in turn, by our intuitions about the formulas derivable from those axioms. But when we reflect on the formulas derivable in these different systems, we are confronted with strings of symbols about which no one, I think, has any clear-cut intuitions. Consider

(10) $\Diamond\Box p \supset \Box\Diamond\Diamond\Box\, p$

(11) $\sim (\Diamond\Diamond\Diamond\Diamond\Diamond q) \vee (\Diamond\Diamond q)$

(12) $\sim ((\Box\Diamond\Box\Diamond\Box\Box\Diamond\Diamond r) \;\&\; \sim (\Box\Diamond\Diamond r)).$

(10) is derivable in the Brouwer system; (11), in S-4; and (12), in S-5. But what are we to say about these formulas? Do they represent the symbolization of true modal principles? No one, I think, can answer this question simply by reading out the formulas; and the problem is not just that we are unsure whether 'If possibly necessarily p, then necessarily possibly possibly necessarily p' is a correct modal principle. Few, if any, of us have even the faintest idea what this sentence means.

It is not surprising, then, that the diversity of modal systems should have been thought problematic in the first half of this century. The different systems yield different answers to the question: which modal inferences are legitimate? and our intuitions fail to carry us very far in determining which answer to this question is correct. There is, however, another reason why logicians had doubts about the notion of a modal logic. Lewis and other early figures in twentieth-century modal logic were successful in giving axiomatic presentations of the various modal systems; but while they succeeded in specifying the syntax for those systems, they failed to come up with anything like a thoroughgoing semantics for the various modal systems. They failed, that is, to identify models for those systems, sets of objects in terms of which the formulas of the systems could be interpreted. The result was that modal logicians were incapable of defining the notion of a *valid* formula of a modal system and so were incapable of providing completeness proofs for the systems.

This second difficulty is not unrelated to the first; for in the absence of a semantics, modal logicians lacked anything more than the ordinary language renderings of $\Box$ and $\Diamond$ as 'Necessarily . . . ' and 'Possibly . . . ' A clear-cut semantics for the various systems would provide us with models for the systems, sets of objects we could take the bare formulas of the system to be about; and presumably that would provide us with some clear-cut intuitions as to what a choice from among the various nonequivalent calculi actually involves.

The status of modal logic, then, was precarious in the first half of the century. The logician surveying the field in the early fifties found a variety of nonequivalent systematizations of legitimate modal inference, all of them lacking the kind of perspicuous semantics associated with purely extensionalist systems of logic. In the late fifties and early sixties, however, there were important breakthroughs in the study of modal systems. A number of different logicians (more or less concurrently) came up with a strategy for providing a semantics for modal logic. The intuitive core of this strategy was the Leibnizian idea that necessary truth is truth across all possible worlds. The idea that we can provide a Leibnizian interpretation of modal logic was not altogether novel. In the forties, Rudolf Carnap had tried to work out the implications of the Leibnizian theme for modal logic by reference to what he called *state descriptions*.[2] For Carnap, a state description is a maximally consistent set of atomic sentences, that is, a consistent set of sentences such that for every atomic sentence, S, either S is a member of the set or the negation of S is a member of the set. Carnap's idea was that the notion of a state description enables us to explain what necessary (in the sense of logical) truth amounts to; for, given this notion, we can say that a sentence is necessarily (logically) true just in case it is true in every state description. The attempt to understand modal logic in Leibnizian terms, then, was not new in the late fifties and early sixties. What was new in the semantical investigations of that period was the adaptation of the Leibnizian notion of necessity across worlds to the diversity of modal systems. Those investigations showed how we could give a uniform reading of the modal operators in Leibnizian terms while accommodating the fact that those symbols function as operators in diverse, nonequivalent modal systems.

As I have indicated, a number of logicians worked out a Leibnizian semantics for modal logic; but rather than generalize about their work, I shall focus on the work of just one of these writers, Saul Kripke,[3] and I shall try to spell out the precise way in which he accommodated the Leibnizian theme in providing a semantics for the four modal systems I have outlined. I shall first discuss the case of propositional modal logic;

2. See Rudolf Carnap, *Meaning and Necessity* (Chicago: University of Chicago Press, 1947).

3. Other names here are Richard Montague, Stig Kanger, Dana Scott, and Jaakko Hintikka. For Kripke's approach, see "Semantical Considerations on Modal Logic" *Acta Philosophica Fennica*, 16 (1963), 83–94 (reprinted in Leonard Linsky, *Reference and Modality* [Oxford: Clarendon Press; New York: Oxford University Press, 1971]; for Hintikka's, see "The Modes of Modality," Chapter 2 of this anthology.

then, I shall try to indicate the strategy required for extending the semantics to cover the case of quantified modal logic, and I shall begin by examining the semantics required for the propositional modal system M. Toward providing a semantics for M, Kripke defines what he calls an M-model structure, telling us that "this is an ordered triple (G, K, R),"[4] where K is a set of objects, G is one of the objects belonging to K, and R is a relation defined over the members of K. Intuitively, Kripke tells us, we are to think of K as the set of all possible words; G is to be thought of as the actual world; and R represents a relation which Kripke calls *relative possibility* and others have called *accessibility*. Intuitively, we are to understand this relation in such a way that a world, W, is possible relative to or accessible to a world, W', just in case every situation that obtains in W is possible in W'. Now, we are to suppose that R is defined over K in advance; that is, we are to suppose that it is antecedently fixed just which worlds are possible relative to which. To get an M-model structure, the specification is subject to just one restriction: the relation of accessibility has to be reflexive; it has to be the case that every world is accessible to or possible relative to itself.

Having defined the notion of an M-model strcture, Kripke defines the notion of a model by telling us that a model is a binary function from the atomic sentences of M and the various possible worlds to the truth values. Informally, the idea is that a model assigns to each atomic formula of M a truth value in each world. Given a model, we can determine the truth value that any nonatomic sentence of M has in any possible world on that model; we need merely invoke the following rules and the assumption that every formula is either true or false:

(a) $\sim A$ is true in W if and only if A is false in W.

(b) $(A \lor B)$ is true in W if and only if either A is true in W or B is true in W.

(c) $\Diamond A$ is true in W if and only if there is at least one possible world, W', such that W' is accessible to W and A is true in W'.

(d) $\Box A$ is true in W if and only if for every world, W', such that W' is accessible to W, A is true in W'.

Rules (a) and (b) gives us recipes for determining the truth value of formulas embedding the truth-functional connectives $\sim$ and $\lor$; since all

4. "Semantical Considerations on Modal Logic," p. 84.

other truth-functional connectives can be defined in terms of those two, (a) and (b) provide us with the resources for determining the truth value of formulas embedding $\&$, $\supset$, and $\equiv$. Rules (c) and (d), on the other hand, invoke the Leibnizian notion that necessity is truth across all possible worlds and that possibility is truth in some possible world; but given the antecedently defined notion of relative possibility, they restrict the Leibnizian idea by specifying that the calculation of truth values for formulas embedding $\Box$ and $\Diamond$ need only consult the worlds accessible to the world with respect to which we are assigning truth values to those formulas.

There are, of course, many different models for M, as many as result from assigning different truth values to the atomic formulas of M in each of the various possible worlds. Kripke defines the notion of *validity-in-M* by telling us that a formula is M-valid just in case it comes out true in all models on an M-model structure. Informally, what this comes to is that a formula is M-valid just in case, when we restrict the accessibility relation only by specifying that it be reflexive, the formula comes out true in all possible worlds under all assignments of truth value to its atomic constituents in those worlds. Given this definition of validity-in-M, Kripke was able to prove the completeness of M, to show, that is, that every formula that is M-valid can be derived by successive applications of the rules of M.[5]

What is significant in the definition of validity-in-M, then, is the idea that relative possibility must be reflexive. That the relation must be reflexive comes out when we reflect on the axiom

$$(2) \ \Box A \supset A.[6]$$

We want this axiom to be valid, that is, to come true in every world, W, under every assignment of truth value to A in W. Now, take any arbitrary world, W; $\Box A \supset A$ comes out false in W in only one case, viz., the case where $\Box A$ is true in W, but A is false in W. But for $\Box A$ to be true in W, A must be true in all worlds accessible to W. Thus, if $\Box A \supset A$ is to come out false in W, A must be true in all worlds accessible to W, but false in W itself; and this can happen only if W is not possible relative to itself.

5. Kripke's strategy here involves the use of semantic tableaux which provide diagrammatic tests for validity in the various systems; the completeness proofs show that every formula which passes the diagrammatic test for validity in a given system is provable in that system; but the details of the actual proofs go beyond the informal presentation given here.

6. Axiom (1) (i.e., $\Box \ (A \supset B) \supset (\Box \ A \supset \Box \ B)$) is weaker than (2) in not requiring that any restrictions be placed on the accessibility relation.

Hence, to ensure validity for (1) (as well as for all formulas derivable from it), we need merely make the relation of accessibility reflexive.

In defining the notion of validity-in-the Brouwer system, Kripke introduces the notion of a B-model structure, where a B-model structure is like an M-model structure except that the relation of accessibility is further restricted. It is not simply reflexive, but symmetrical as well; that is, in a B-model structure the relation of relative possibility is so defined over the various possible worlds that each world is possible relative to itself and for any worlds, W and W', if W is possible relative to W', then W' is, in turn, possible relative to W. Then, Kripke tells us that a formula is B-valid just in case it comes out true in all models on a B-model structure (i.e., just in case it comes out true in all possible worlds under all interpretations of its atomic constituents when the relation of accessibility is taken to be both reflexive and symmetrical). That reflexivity is required here is obvious when we recall that the Brouwer system contains M, but that symmetry also is required becomes clear when we reflect on the additional axiom required to generate the Brouwer system:

(3) $A \supset \Box \Diamond A$.

Again, we want (3) to be valid, to come out true in all possible worlds under all interpretations of A. So, take any arbitrary world, W; $A \supset \Box \Diamond A$ comes out false in W in only one case, the case where A is true in W, but $\Box \Diamond A$ is false in W. Now, $\Box \Diamond A$ is false in W only if there is a world accessible to W for which there is no accessible world in which A is true. But since we are assuming that A is true in W, this can happen only if W is not accessible to all the worlds accessible to it. To ensure, then, that (3) never comes out false in a possible world, we need only require that accessibility be symmetrical.

Kripke similarly defines validity-in-S-4 in terms of truth in every model on an S-4 model structure, where an S-4 model structure is like an M-model structure except that relative possibility is stipulated to be both reflexive and transitive, i.e., to be such that each world is possible relative to itself and if a world, W_1, is possible relative to a world, W_2, and another world, W_3, is possible relative to W_1, then W_3 is possible relative to W_2. As in the case of the B-model structure, the S-4 model structure has to be reflexive since S-4 contains M; but transitivity is required as well. Consider the axiom generating S-4:

(4) $\Box A \supset \Box \Box A$.

We want (4) to come out true in every possible world on every assignment of truth value to A. But again consider an arbitrary world, W. (4) comes out false in W in only one case, the case where $\Box A$ is true in W and $\Box\Box A$ is false in W; and this requires that A be true in all worlds accessible to W, but false in some world accessible to a world accessible to W. If, however, we insist that relative possibility be transitive, this cannot happen; for since every world accessible to any world accessible to W will be accessible to W itself, $\Box A$ will be true in W only if $\Box\Box A$ is true as well.

Finally, Kripke defines validity-in-S-5 in terms of truth in every model on an S-5 model structure, where this is as before, except that relative possibility is taken to be an equivalence relation; that is, it is a relation that is reflexive, symmetrical, and transitive. All of these properties are required since S-5 contains both the Brouwer system and S-4, for which the accessibility relation is reflexive-symmetrical and reflexive-transitive respectively. Given the definitions of validity-in-the Brouwer system, validity-in-S-4, and validity-in-S-5, Kripke went on to prove the completeness of these systems, showing that every formula that is valid in one of these systems is provable in that system.

Now, corresponding to each of the four propositional modal systems I have discussed, there is a system of quantified modal logic.[7] Each contains

7. Certainly the most influential critic of modal logic over the past few decades has been W. V. O. Quine, who has tried to show that the defender of quantified modal logic is committed to what he calls Aristotelian essentialism. Quine asks the defender of quantified modal logic to existentially generalize a claim like

(a) Necessarily, nine is greater than seven

to get

(b) ($\exists x$)   (Necessarily, x is greater than seven).

Since

(c) Nine is the number of planets

is true, Quine claims that we ought to be able to instantiate (b) by way of

(d) Necessarily, the number of planets is greater than seven.

Quine, however, argues that if we settle for a linguistic interpretation of modal sentences, where the necessity of property-attributions to objects depends on the linguistic devices we employ in identifying those objects, (d) is false. According to Quine, the only way of preserving the truth of (d), and with it the legitimacy of quantification into modal contexts, is by denying that modality is a matter of language and claiming that "an object, of itself and by whatever name or none," has "some of its traits necessarily and others contingently, despite the fact that the latter traits follow just as analytically from some ways of specifying the object as the former traits do from other ways of specifying it" (Quine, "Reference and Modality," all of the theses of the propositional modal logic in question, all of the theses of first order predicate logic, and modal formulas involving the apparatus of quantification. Toward defining validity for each of these systems, Kripke introduces the notion of a quantificational model structure, which is a model structure of one of the four sorts we have considered together with a function that assigns to each world a set of objects. Intuitively, Kripke tells us, we are to think of each such set as the set of objects existing in a particular possible world. He calls these sets domains for the various possible worlds and symbolizes the union of these domains as $\mathcal{U}$; we can think of $\mathcal{U}$ as the set of all possible objects. Next, Kripke defines the notion of a quantificational model, telling us that this is binary function from predicate expressions and possible worlds to sets of n-tuples of objects. Informally, what a quantificational model does is provide an interpretation for the predicate expressions of our systems; for each predicate and each possible world, it assigns a set of ordered n-tuples of objects (sets of singletons for one place predicates, sets of ordered pairs for two place predicates, etc.). We are to think of these sets as the extensions of the predicates in the various worlds, the sets of n-tuples which in each world satisfy the various predicates. Using the notion of a quantificational model, Kripke gives us directions for determining the truth value that each formula in the various systems has in the different worlds on a given quantificational model. We have already seen how to determine the truth value of formulas incorporating propositional connectives and modal operators. What we need are directions for determining the truth value of formulas incorporating predicate expressions and the apparatus of quantification. In giving these directions, Kripke begins with the case of unquantified atomic formulas of the form $Fx_1, \ldots, x_n$. He tells us that to determine the truth

---

in Linsky, *Reference and Modality*, p. 30). But Quine takes a dim view of this claim: "To defend Aristotelian essentialism . . . is no part of my plan. . . . And in conclusion I say . . . so much the worse for quantified modal logic" (ibid., p. 31). Initially, Quine's criticisms were taken very seriously, and a large number of philosophers tried to show that quantified modal logic does not commit its proponents to Aristotelian essentialism. But with the development of a semantics for modal logic, attempts to answer Quine became less and less frequent. Philosophers came to see (as I shall try to show in a few pages hence) that if we take a realistic interpretation of possible-worlds semantics, we have a perfectly coherent framework for expressing the content of an essentialist metaphysics. Since Quine's difficulties with modal logic have tended to play a less central role in recent discussions, I do not deal with them in the body of my essay. In any case, Leonard Linsky's anthology *Reference and Modality* contains most of the pivotal papers concerned with Quine's objections to quantified modal logic, and the interested reader is directed to that anthology.

value that a formula of this form has in a world, W, on a chosen quantificational model, we must assign objects from $\mathcal{U}$ to the variables $x_1, \ldots, x_n$;
if the n-tuple of objects assigned these variables belongs to the set of
n-tuples which the model in question assigns 'F' in W, then $Fx_1, \ldots, x_n$
is true in W on that model; otherwise, it is false in W. Combining this
account with Kripke's account of the truth-functional connectives and the
modal operators, we have the tools for determining the truth value of an
unquantified formula of any degree of complexity. Now, if we bear in
mind that ascriptions of truth value to a formula are always made relative to
a quantificational model and relative to an assignment of objects in $\mathcal{U}$ to the
formula's free variables, we can summarize Kripke's treatment of quantified formulas by saying that where $Fx, y_1, \ldots, yn$ is a formula with x,
$y_1, \ldots, yn$ as free variables, (i) $(\forall x)(Fx, y_1, \ldots, y_n)$ is true in a world,
W, just in case $Fx, y_1, \ldots, y_n$ comes out true in W regardless of how we
readjust the value of x with objects from W and (ii) $(\exists x)(Fx, y_1, \ldots, y_n)$
is true in a world, W, just in case there is at least one object in W which,
when construed as the value of x, makes $Fx, y_1, \ldots, y_n$ come out true in
W. These rules provide us with the resources for determining the truth
conditions that any formula from one of our four systems of quantified
modal logic has in a possible world on a quantificational model, so that
with these rules before him, Kripke can say that a formula is valid (in the
quantificational version of M, B, S-4, or S-5) just in case it comes out true
in all quantificational models on a (M-, B-, S-4, or S-5) quantificational
model structure; and using this definition, he can go on to prove the
completeness of each of these systems.[8]

I have focused on Kripke's version of the Leibnizian strategy for dealing
with modal logic; but as I indicated earlier, other logicians developed
alternative versions of essentially the same strategy, and what their combined effort gives us is a semantics for modal logic. It takes the purely
syntactical treatments of modal inference found in the work of logicians
like Lewis and shows how we can define validity for the bare formulas of
the different modal systems. Thus, their work serves to handle the second
difficulty we pointed to in our original discussion of modal logic; but their

---

8. My discussion of the semantics for quantified modal logic is necessarily oversimplified.
One crucial issue I do not discuss concerns the population of the various worlds. Are possible
worlds other than G to be populated with objects not found in G? Are world populations
constant? One's answers to such questions have important consequences for one's quantified
modal logic. In particular, one's answers determine whether or not the Barcan formula $(\forall x)$
$\square\ Fx \supset \square\ (\forall x)Fx)$ and its converse $(\square(\forall x)\ Fx \supset (\forall x)\ \square\ Fx)$ come out valid.

Leibnizian strategy also seems to provide a framework for handling the first difficulty, that of deciding just which among the many nonequivalent systems provides the correct account of the range of legitimate modal inference. What their work suggests is that in all the systems we have considered the modal operators function as something like quantifiers over possible worlds. $\Box$ functions as a kind of universal quantifier; its application to a formula, A, yields a second formula that is true in a world, W, just in case the original formula, A, is true in every world that is possible relative to W; whereas $\Diamond$ functions as a kind of existential quantifier; the result of applying it to a formula, A, is a formula true in a world, W, just in case there is at least one world accessible to W in which A is true. The different systems agree, then, in that their modal formulas are to be understood in terms of quanitification over accessible worlds; they differ in that each places different restrictions on the accessibility relation. In M, the relation is merely reflexive; in the Brouwer system, reflexive and symmetrical; in S-4, reflexive and transitive; and in S-5, reflexive, symmetrical, and transitive. The Leibnizian strategy, then, gives us something like a picture of what the various modal systems are about and provides an account of how the differences in those systems depend on the various restrictions we place on the accessibility relation. But, then, our choice of a modal system need not be dictated by our very shaky intuitions about the complex formulas of those systems. We can rather ask ourselves which picture best conforms to our notions of modal inference. Suppose that our concern is with metaphysical (as opposed, say, to physical or causal) necessity and possibility.[9] Invoking the Leibnizian account of the various modal systems, we can answer this question by asking another: Do we think that what is metaphysically necessary or possible can vary across possible worlds? If we answer the question affirmatively, then we commit ourselves to the view that M, the Brouwer system, or S-4 provides a

9. Metaphysical modality is what Alvin Plantinga calls broadly logical modality. The notion of metaphysical possibility is narrower than that of strictly logical possibility (where a proposition is possible just in case it is not the negation of a thesis of, say, first order logic) and broader than that of causal or physical possibility (where a proposition is possible just in case it is not incompatible with the laws of nature). It is the sense of possibility at work in each of the following:

(i) It is possible that this page be red;
(ii) It is possible that Jimmy Carter run a two minute mile;
(iii) It is possible that there be no human beings.

Metaphysical necessity and possibility will concern us in the remainder of this essay.

complete systematization of legitimate inference of the metaphysically modal variety; for, in all these systems, what is necessary or possible varies as we move from one possible world to another. If, however, we reject this sort of "situationalism" with regard to metaphysical modality, if, that is, we hold that what is metaphysically possible or necessary does not vary as we move from one possible situation or state of affairs to another, then we join most philosophers in thinking that it is S-5 that provides us with the correct theory of inference bearing on metaphysical modality; for it is only an S-5 model structure, where accessibility is an equivalence relation, that allows us to construe every world as accessible to every other.[10] Only S-5 accommodates the Leibnizian idea that necessity is truth across all possible worlds, so that if we take metaphysical modality to be fixed or invariant, the Leibnizian strategy suggests that we construe S-5 as the correct theory of legitimate modal inference.

II

The development of a semantics for modal logic represented an important breakthrough in the study of modal inference. It did little to alter the views of those empiricist skeptics who insisted that no sense can be made of modal notions or of those diehard extensionalists who simply identified the notion of a logic with the notion of an extensional system. But for the philosopher who took seriously distinctions between propositions that are necessary and contingent, possible and impossible, it provided modal logic with a solid foundation. Furthermore, the semantical strategy developed by Kripke and others proved to have applications beyond the field of modal logic, for it was discovered that by adapting the semantical apparatus of possible worlds to the special contexts of tense logic, epistemic logic, and deontic logic, each of these nonextensional systems could also be provided with a clear-cut semantics.

But while the Leibnizian strategy may give clarity to the study of nonextensional systems, it might be thought that the price the account exacts is too great; for the clarity the account gives to modal logic (and other inten-

10. Actually, not all worlds need be possible relative to each other in an S-5 model structure. An S-5 model structure can partition the various worlds into equivalence classes, so that worlds in one equivalence class are not accessible to worlds in another. What makes S-5 the appropriate logic for an antisituationalist interpretation of modality is the fact that one can provide the semantics for S-5 by referring to just one of the relevant equivalence classes.

sional systems) seems to hinge on the notion of a possible world. If we are to make sense of the various modal systems, we have to suppose that in some sense there really are possible worlds other than our own and that in some sense there really are possible objects not found in the actual world. This at least is what my account of Kripke's version of Leibnizian semantics suggests, but here one might object that my presentation is misleading. The criticism would be that while Kripke and other propnents of the Leibnizian strategy informally talk of possible worlds and possible objects, they are careful to distinguish this informal, intuitive picture from the set theoretical machinery employed in their semantics. It is the latter and not the former, the critic contends, that is essential to the Leibnizians project.

The critic here would have us think of the various modal systems as completely uninterpreted systems of inscriptions incorporating a primitive vocabulary and two kinds of rules: (1) rules that license the construction of strings of inscriptions out of the primitive vocabulary and (2) rules that license the derivation of certain strings of inscriptions (the theorems of the system) from certain antecedently chosen strings (the axioms of the system). Viewed in these terms, the various systems are not about anything, so that if we are to define the notion of validity for these systems, we need to interpret the systems, to construe them as languages about some set of objects in terms of which we can give sense to the concept of a true or false formula in the system. But, the critic claims, no one set of objects is privileged here; focusing on Kripke's version of the Leibnizian strategy, the critic will insist that any sets of objects which satisfy the formal constraints imposed by Kripke's account, can play the role of K and $\mathcal{U}$. Thus, while we can, for heuristic purposes, choose to think of K as the set of possible worlds and $\mathcal{U}$ as the set of all possible objects, nothing in Kripke's semantics commits us to this choice; and our critic will insist that the same point holds for the accounts provided by other proponents of the Leibnizian strategy. Viewed aright, he will claim, their semantics commits us to the existence of no peculiar objects whatsoever.

There is surely something right in this criticism. To the extent that we take the formulas of the various modal systems to have no antecedent meaning, the task of defining validity for these systems does not require us to think of Kripke's K and $\mathcal{U}$, for example, as sets of possible worlds and possible objects. Any objects that can be construed as having the formal properties specified by the semantics will do as members of K and $\mathcal{U}$. But the question is: Can we really think of the modal systems in the way suggested? The answer, I think, is that we cannot if we are to take them to be systems of *modal* logic, systems that provide theories of legitimate *modal* inference. The point here is that as long as we take M, the Brouwer system, S-4, and S-5 as systems of uninterpreted inscriptions with no connections at all with the sentences of ordinary discourse, we can, as the critic suggests, invoke any formally adequate sets of objects in defining validity for those systems. But if we take them as *modal* logics, theories of *modal* inference, then we have to suppose that the objects making up the models for those systems are things that are plausibly thought of as constituting the subject matter of modal discourse; and while the idea that there are possible worlds other than the actual may initially appear problematic, it is not difficult to be convinced both that the idea is perfectly respectable and that it encapsulates a compelling account of the subject matter of modal discourse.

The trouble with possible worlds, we want to say, is that they represent an exotic piece of metaphysical machinery, the armchair invention of a speculative ontologist lacking what Bertrand Russell called "a robust sense of reality." But the fact is that reflection on some of our most deep-seated intuitions suggests that the appeal to possible worlds is nothing more than a formalization of generally held prephilosophical views about matters modal. All (or at least most) of us think that things might have gone otherwise, that there are different ways things might have been, alternative ways things might have gone; and we tend to think that these different ways things might have been constitute the touchstones for determining the truth value of sentences prefaced by modal operators. Thus, we think of the claim 'It is necessary that two plus two equals four' as the claim that no matter how things might have been, no matter how things might have differed from the way they actually are, two plus two would have equaled four; and this suggests that in ordinary discourse we take the necessity-operator to be the kind of universal quantifier the semantics of Kripke and others suggests it is. We do not, of course, talk of "possible worlds"; that is the philosopher's name for the different ways things might have been. Nonetheless, we seem to recognize that there are such things, and it is with respect to them that we take ourselves to be talking when we say 'Necessarily. . . . ' In the same way, when we say that it might have turned out or it could have happened that Jimmy Carter is secretary of state, we seem to be saying that there is at least one way things might have gone, such that had they gone that way, Jimmy Carter would have been secretary of state; and here we seem to be taking 'It might have turned out that . . . ' or 'It might have happened that . . . ' (our ordinary language counterparts to the logician's 'It is possible that . . . ') as a kind of existential quantifier over possible worlds and to be construing those worlds as the things that make our possibility-claims true or false.[11]

So far our discussion has focused on the notion of modality *de dicto,* the notion of necessity and possibility as it applies to propositions; and we have found the idea that modal discourse is discourse about possible worlds to have a real plausibility here. But there are other forms of discourse for which a possible worlds interpretation seems equally plausible. Consider the case of what is called modality *de re.* Whereas *de dicto* modality attaches to propositions, an ascription of *de re* modality specifies the modal status of an object's exemplification of an attribute. Thus, we think that the number three *necessarily* or *essentially* exemplifies the property of being prime but only *contingently,* the property of being fascinating to Quine. Likewise, we distinguish between Jimmy Carter's exemplifying the property of being a person and his exemplifying the property of being president of the United States; the former, we say, is *necessary* or essential; the latter, only *contingent* or *accidental.* In all these cases, what we say involves an appeal to the notion of *de re* modality. We can get at the difference between *de dicto* and *de re* modality if we suppose that Kripke is now thinking about the number three and then reflect on

(13) Necessarily, the thing Kripke is thinking about is prime

and

(14) The thing Kripke is thinking about is necessarily prime.

(13) involves an ascription of *de dicto* modality and (14) an ascription of *de re* modality. Whereas it is, subject to our supposition about Kripke, plausible to think that (14) is true, there are compelling reasons for thinking that (13) is false. (13) tells us that a certain proposition, the proposition that the thing Kripke is thinking about is prime, is necessarily true, that it could not have been false. But this is implausible, for surely it could have turned out that Kripke is thinking of something else, say Quine; but had things turned out that way, the proposition that the thing Kripke is thinking about is prime would have been false. (14), however, makes no claim at all about the modal status of a proposition. It simple tells us that the thing Kripke is thinking about has and has necessarily the property of being prime; it tells

11. This is the view argued for in David Lewis' "Possible Worlds," Chapter 9 of this anthology.

us, that is, that the thing in question could not have existed without being prime. But when we recall that Kripke is, in fact, thinking about the number three, that claim seems true enough.[12]

But while ascriptions of *de re* modality are not to be identified with ascriptions of *de dicto* modality, it is plausible to think that the former, like the latter, involve a reference to possible worlds other than the one that is actual. Thus, when we say that Jimmy Carter has the property of being a person necessarily or essentially (that Jimmy Carter could not have failed to be a person), we seem to be saying something of the following sort: take this individual we call Jimmy Carter; as things have actually gone, he has the property of being a person; but no matter how things might have gone, provided the individual in question were to exist, he would have had the property of being a person. Likewise, when we say that Jimmy Carter is only contingently president ("He's president all right; but he needn't have been!" Ford might say to console himself), we seem to be saying that while this individual is, in fact, president, things might have turned out differently, so that he would, say, have lost the election of 1976. In both cases, then, our *de re* claims are plausibly construed as claims about possible worlds. We seem to be claiming, in the first case, that Jimmy Carter has the property of being a person in the actual world and in every other possible world in which he exists, and, in the second, that while Jimmy Carter is president in the actual world, there are possible worlds where he exists but fails to achieve that distinction.[13]

The idea that possible worlds are elements in the ontology to which we

---

12. This is not to say that there is no connection between *de re* and *de dicto* assertions of modality. Indeed, a familiar theme in recent literature is that we can provide *de dicto* counterparts for *de re* modal assertions. We might, for example, say that an object, x, exemplifies a property, P, necessarily just in case x exemplifies P and

either
    (a) the proposition that if x exists, then x exemplifies P (where 'x' and 'P' deputize for proper names) is necessarily true

or
    (b) there is an object, z, and a property, Q, such that x is identical with z and P is identical with Q and z exemplifies Q necessarily in the sense of (a)

and that an object, x, exemplifies a property, P, contingently just in case x exemplifies P, but x does not exemplify P necessarily. For a detailed elaboration of this approach to *de re* modality, see Alvin Plantinga, "*De Re et De Dicto,*" *Noûs*, 3 (1969), 235-258.

13. The connection between *de re* modality and possible worlds is argued for in Plantinga's "Transworld Identity or Worldbound Individuals?" Chapter 7 of this anthology and "Actualism and Possible Worlds," Chapter 14 of this anthology.

commit ourselves in our nonphilosophical discourse is likewise supported by reflection on counterfactual discourse. While the propositions expressed by

> (15) If Nixon had not resigned, there would have been a constitutional crisis

and

> (16) If the Blue Jays were to win the pennant, Toronto would go wild

are not explicitly modal, it is notorious that they are like explicitly modal propositions in resisting analysis in terms of the machinery afforded by a strictly extensionalist logic. And when we reflect on the fact that claims of the form 'If it were (had been) the case that *p*, it would be (would have been) the case that *q*' are not claims about how things have actually gone, we are likely to conclude that the similarity here is no accident, that counterfactual discourse resists an extensionalist analysis for precisely the reason explicitly modal discourse does: counterfactual claims are about things (possible worlds other than the actual world) that go beyond the ontology required for standard extensional discourse. In recent years, a growing number of philosophers have tried to give substance to these intuitions.[14] Counterfactual discourse, they have argued, is indeed discourse about possible worlds; but they have insisted that while counterfactual discourse agrees with explicitly modal discourse on this score, there is an important difference. Ascriptions of modality (whether *de dicto* or *de re*) involve quantification over *all* possible worlds; but when we make some particular counterfactual claim, the reference to possible worlds is more narrowly circumscribed. When I say that if the Blue Jays were to win the pennant, Toronto would go wild, I am not saying that in every possible world where the Blue Jays win the pennant, Toronto goes wild; for there obviously are possible worlds where the Blue Jays win the pennant and few, if any, of the citizens of Toronto find the event very interesting. My claim, these theorists suggest, has its eye to just one possible world, a world that is very "close" to, very similar to the actual world. I am talking about that possible world which is as like the actual world as is compatible

---

14. Two central figures in the possible-worlds approach to counterfactuals are Robert Stalnaker ("A Theory of Conditionals," in *Studies in Logical Theory,* ed. by Nicholas Rescher [Oxford: Basil Blackwell, 1968]) and David Lewis (*Counterfactuals* [Cambridge, Mass.: Harvard University Press, 1973]).

with the Blue Jays' winning the pennant in it, and I am saying that in that world, Toronto goes wild. More generally, these theorists have proposed that a counterfactual of the form 'If it were the case that p, then it would be the case that q' is a claim about that world which resembles the actual world as closely as is compatible with P's being true in it, the claim that in that world q is true.[15] It is difficult not to find this proposal attractive, for it captures the insight that when we talk or think counterfactually we are concerned with ways things might have gone but did not; and it does this while accommodating our intuition that there is a difference between counterfactual and explicitly modal discourse.

Another area of discourse that has of late been claimed to be about possible worlds is talk about meaning. Philosophers of an extensionalist bent have always found meaning-talk troublesome. The problem with meanings, they have told us, is that they lack straightforward principles of individuation and clear-cut criteria of identity. Some of these thinkers have proposed that we simply give up talk about meaning; but others, unwilling to engage in such drastic conceptual revision, have tried to elucidate the notion of meaning in terms of the more transparent concept of reference. In its most extreme form, this approach identifies the meaning of a nonlogical expression with its extension: singular terms are said to take their referents as their meanings, the meanings of predicate-terms are identified with the sets of n-tuples which satisfy them, and sentences are said to have as their meanings the truth values. But while it may appear to make meaning-talk respectable, this extreme form of the referential theory of meaning fails to give a sufficiently fine-grained account of meanings: coreferential singular terms turn out to be synonymous, as do coextensive predicates and sentences with the same truth value. Defenders of the referential theory have usually recognized the short comings of the theory of its extreme form and have tried to express its central insight in ways that avoid these difficulties of coextensionality. It is notorious, however, that their attempts have not been very successful.

These coextensionality problems might lead one to conclude that the referentialist's strategy is a philosophical dead end and to tempt one either to follow the skeptics and reject talk of meaning or to bite the bullet and

---

15. My account here is oversimplified in a number of ways. For one thing, the account needs to be supplemented to handle counterfactuals whose antecedents are necessary falsehoods; for another, it needs to be filled in to accommodate the fact that, perhaps, no single world (but rather a variety of worlds) will turn out to be "closest to" the actual world.

take as primitive the occult entities extensionalists have had so much fun deriding. Nevertheless, there is something attractive in the idea that the concept of meaning can be understood in terms of the notion of extension. What makes the idea attractive is the insight that to know the meaning of a term is to be able to fix its extension. To know the meaning of a predicate-term, for example, is to be able to determine which objects or n-tuples of objects satisfy it, and to know the meaning of a declarative sentence is to know under which conditions it comes out true.

A growing number of writers have been arguing that we can preserve this insight while avoiding the difficulties associated with standard referential theories.[16] Those theories go wrong, they argue, not in claiming that meaning can be explicated in referential terms, but in supposing that the referential force of a term can be identified simply by reference to actual objects. They point out that we use linguistic expressions not merely in talking about how things actually are, but in talking about how they might have been; and what this shows, they claim, is that the referential force of an expression extends beyond objects in the actual world to objects in other possible worlds. Meaning is a referential concept and so must be analyzed in terms of the notion of an extension; but it is also a modal notion and, hence, is to be explicated in possible-worlds terms. Toward accommodating these two facets of the notion of meaning, defenders of "modal referentialism" usually tell us that the meaning of a nonlogical expression is a set theoretical entity, a function from possible worlds to extensions; it is a function that assigns to each possible world the extension the expression has when we use it in talking about that world. Thus, singular terms have as their meanings functions from worlds to objects; the meaning of an n-place predicate is a function from worlds to sets of ordered n-tuples; and the meaning of a declarative sentence is a function from worlds to truth values.

Another area of discourse that has traditionally proved problematic for the extensionalist is talk about things like properties, relations, individual concepts, and propositions. Extensionalists have typically attempted to analyze this talk in set theoretical terms, but their attempts have invariably given rise to extensionality difficulties analogous to those infecting stan-

---

16. See M. J. Cresswell's "The World Is Everything That Is The Case," Chapter 6 of this anthology, and David Kaplan's two papers, "Transworld Heir Lines" and "How to Russell a Frege-Church," Chapters 4 and 11 of this anthology. Again, let me warn the reader that my account of this approach to meaning is oversimplified in a number of ways.

dard referential theories of meaning. The modal referentialist finds the analogy here telling and proposes that we invoke the strategy at work in his theory of meaning in providing analyses of these recalcitrant notions. Individual concepts, he tells us, are functions from worlds to individuals; properties are functions from worlds to sets of objects; relations, functions from worlds to sets of ordered pairs, triples, quadruples, etc.; and propositions, functions from worlds to truth values. The advantages of this approach should be obvious. Since it identifies abstract objects of the problematic kinds with set theoretical entities, the approach provides a straightforward account of their identity conditions; but since it insists that the relevant set theoretical constructs incorporate possible as well as actual objects, it preserves the modal features of those abstract objects. Finally, the account accommodates the intuition (often noted, but never cogently developed) that things like properties and propositions are meanings, for on this approach, the meanings of singular terms just are certain individual concepts; the meanings of predicates, certain properties and relations; and the meanings of declarative sentences, certain propositions.

III

The suggestion, then, is that a variety of forms of discourse can be accommodated within the framework of possible worlds: discourse involving ascriptions of modality (both *de re* and *de dicto*), counterfactual discourse, discourse about meanings, and discourse about intentional abstract entities. Two things make the suggestion attractive: first, these are all forms of discourse that have proved intractable within the nonmodal framework of the extensionalist; and second, it can be plausibly argued that in each case the appeal to the framework of possible worlds represents no exotic departure from prephilosophical thinking. Possible worlds, one wants to say, were there all along as part of the ontology of common sense playing just the roles the possible-worlds theorist attributes to them.

But despite its explanatory power and apparent connections with prephilosophical thinking, the appeal to the framework of possible worlds has been severely criticized. Two criticisms have proved especially significant in recent philosophical literature. The first is based on the vexing problem of transworld identity; the second, on the problem of possible but nonactual objects. I want to discuss each of these issues in detail. The first will provide the subject matter of this section; the second will dominate the remaining two sections of the essay.

As I have presented the framework of possible worlds, it seems clear that the proponent of this framework is committed to the idea that one and the same individual exists in different possible worlds. The proponent of the framework insists that our ordinary modal discourse has as its subject matter different possible worlds; but he will surely want to hold, for example, that Jimmy Carter could have been secretary of state. According to the possible-worlds theorist, what this means is that in some other possible world, Jimmy Carter is secretary of state; but of course this presupposes that Jimmy Carter exists in more than one possible world, that Jimmy Carter is a transworld individual. Critics, however, argue that the notion of a transworld individual is incoherent and conclude that the possible-worlds framework is itself objectionable. They have invoked a number of different arguments to convince us that the concept of a transworld individual is genuinely problematic. I want to consider three of them.

The first urges that the notion of a transworld individual violates the *indiscernibility of identicals,* the principle that for any object x and any object y, if x is identical with y, then every property of x is a property of y, and vice versa.[17] The argument goes as follows: Suppose a person, P, exists in a pair or worlds, W_1 and W_2; then, regardless of who P is and what W_1 and W_2 are like, there will be properties exemplified by P-existing-in-W_1 that P-existing-in-W_2 fails to exemplify and vice versa. This is obvious where W_1 and W_2 are worlds in which things go quite differently for P. But even if things go much the same for P in W_1 and W_2, it remains the case that P-in-W_1 and P-in-W_2 have different properties; for obviously if W_1 and W_2 are to be genuinely different worlds, they will differ in some way. Suppose the only difference is that whereas in W_1 pigs have tails, in W_2 they do not; then, there is at least one property that P-in-W_1 has that P-in-W_2 lacks, the property a thing has just in case it is a person and pigs have tails. The doctrine of transworld individuals, then, is incompatible with the Indiscernibility of Identicals. But since this principle is as true as any, we are forced to reject the idea that a single individual exists in several possible worlds; and since it would seem to be an essential ingredient in the framework of possible worlds, we seem forced to reject that framework itself.

A second argument against the notion of transworld individuals con-

---

17. For a statement of this argument, see Roderick Chisholm's "Identity through Possible Worlds: Some Questions," Chapter 3 of this anthology and David Kaplan's "Transworld Heir Lines," Chapter 4 of this anthology.

cedes, for dialectical purposes, that the possible-worlds theorist can handle
the tension between the Indiscernibility of Identicals and the view that a
single individual exists in several worlds and seeks to show the doctrine of
transworld individuals to be incompatible with the view that identity is
transitive.[18] The proponent of this line of argument asks us to take a pair of
objects, x and y, both of which exist in a world, W_1, and which in W_1
differ in a variety of ways. We are supposed, then, to focus our attention on
a different world, W_2, in which each of x and y remain much as they were
in W_1 but exchange, say, their sizes, so that x-in-W_2 has the size that y has
in W_1 and y-in-W_2 has the size that x has in W_1. Since problems with the
Indiscernibility of Identicals have been waived, we are all willing to grant
that this interchange of sizes does nothing to change the identity of x and y;
despite their different sizes, x-in-W_2 is identical with x-in-W_1 and y-in-W_2
is identical with y-in-W_1. But now we are supposed to move to a new
world, W_3. Once again the properties x and y respectively have in W_3 are
much the same as the properties they had in W_2, but once again we are to
suppose that a slight interchange of properties takes place in the move from
W_2 to W_3: x-in-W_3 has the color of y-in-W_2 and vice versa. Again, we want
to say that the shift from W_2 to W_3 does nothing to alter the identity of x
and y: x-in-W_3 is identical with x-in-W_2, and y-in-W_3 is identical with
y-in-W_2. Now, we are supposed to continue moving in the same way from
world to world and with each move to engage in a single interchange of
properties. With each move, we preserve identity; since our changes in
property are slight, x in any world is identical with x in the world before it
and similarly for y. The problem, however, is that ultimately we will come
to some world, W_n, where the accumulating interchanges result in x's
having in W_n all the properties of y in our original world, W_1, and y's
having in W_n all the properties that x had in W_1; and this seems to entail
that x-in-W_n is identical with y-in-W_1 and that y-in-W_n is identical with
x-in-W_1; but since identity is transitive, this cannot be the case. Conclusion? Individuals cannot be identical across worlds, and since the
possible-worlds theorist is commited to the idea that they can, the
framework he embraces is unsatisfactory.

The first two arguments take formal properties of identity—its being
subject to the Indiscernibility of Identicals and transitivity—and argue that
the doctrine of transworld individuals forces us to reject these properties.

18. This argument is presented in Chisholm's "Identity through Possible Worlds: Some
Questions," Chapter 3 of this anthology.

The last argument I want to consider takes a slightly different line, contending that since we have no criteria for settling issues of identity and difference across worlds, talk of identity in this context can only be incoherent.[19] The idea here is straightforward. Take some individual in our world, say, Jimmy Carter; and now move to some world, W, where Jimmy Carter is supposed to exist. The question is: how are we to determine just which individual in W is Jimmy Carter? We cannot rely on any of the properties we normally use in picking out Jimmy Carter: his characteristic look, his gait, his personality, his background, etc., for, of course, there is no guarantee that anyone in W will have these properties; and if someone does, there is no guarantee that it is Jimmy Carter. Maybe someone else in W bears the name 'Jimmy Carter', looks like our Jimmy Carter, talks like him, etc. There is, to use Alvin Plantinga's useful expression, no "empirically manifest property" we can appeal to in determining just which object in W is Jimmy Carter, and that means that we have no criteria for settling the issue; but in the absence of criteria, questions of identity and difference make no sense. The claim, then, that individuals exist in different possible worlds only appears to be intelligible; it takes our concepts of identity and difference and employs them in contexts where they cannot intelligibly be applied.

I have suggested that these arguments against the doctrine of transworld individuals all call the framework of possible worlds into question. In fact, this is not quite right, for the philosopher who endorsed any one of these arguments could grant that there are alternative possible worlds, alternative ways things might have gone. But it is important to see that in the hands of the proponent of "worldbound" individuals, the framework of possible words loses much of its attractiveness. Initially we found the framework of possible worlds appealing because it accommodates our prephilosophical intuitions that things might have been other than they actually are. The proponent of "worldbound" individuals can concede this claim, but for him it has a force quite alien to our prephilosophical modal intuitions. What he means is that it might have turned out that a completely different set of individuals populate the world; whereas our prephilosophical intuitions about the different ways things might have gone typically bear on the very individuals found in the actual world, and it is hard to see how the critic of transworld individuals could accommodate those intuitions. In-

19. This theme recurs in almost all the literature on transworld identity, although it is seldom presented as a formal argument but rather as a kind of puzzle or perplexity.

deed, his central claim (viz., that no individual exists in more than one world) seems to commit him to the very counterintuitive claim that it is impossible for things to have gone differently for individuals like Richard Nixon and Jimmy Carter; every property of an individual, it would seem, turns out to be essential to that individual.

But perhaps one could steer a middle course here, rejecting both the doctrine of transworld individuals and the extreme essentialism that we have just encountered. This, at least, is the contention of defenders of what has come to be known as *counterpart theory*. A number of writers have suggested such an approach, but the title "counterpart theory" and the detailed development of this approach are associated with the work of David Lewis.[20] Lewis wants to deny that individuals exist in more than one world, while insisting that he can accommodate all of the prephilosophical intuitions motivating the doctrine of transworld individuals. The strategy here is to hold that while each individual is worldbound, an object existing in one possible world can have a counterpart in some other world. As Lewis puts it, an individual's counterparts are things that resemble it "closely in both content and context in important respects"; they resemble the object "more closely than do other things in their worlds." What Lewis wants to claim is that talk about alternative ways things might have gone for individuals in our world can be understood as talk about the counterparts of those individuals. To say of Jimmy Carter, for example, that he might have been secretary of state is to say that in some other possible world there is an individual that resembles Jimmy Carter in significant ways and that that individual is secretary of state. Likewise, to say that Jimmy Carter is essentially (could not have failed to be) a person is not to imply that Jimmy Carter exists in other worlds; it is to claim, on the contrary, that all of Jimmy Carter's counterparts are persons.

But while Lewis' approach may strike one as a promising compromise, the view has met with a good deal of criticism; and, for the most part, this criticism has attempted to show that, contrary to Lewis' claims, counterpart theory fails to accommodate our ordinary modal intuitions. Kripke argues this point in an informal way, focusing on the case of counterfactual discourse.[21] He asks us to suppose that

20. See Lewis' "Counterpart Theory and Quantified Modal Logic," Chapter 5 of this anthology.

21. "Identity and Necessity," in Milton Munitz, *Identity and Individuation* (New York: New York University Press, 1971).

(17) If Nixon had bribed a certain senator, he would have gotten Carswell through

is true, and he points out that the truth of (17) gives Nixon grounds for regret. "If only I had offered the bribe!" Nixon might say. But Kripke contends that the counterpart theorist can make no sense of Nixon's regret here, for on his account, (17) isn't a claim about Nixon or Carswell at all, but a claim about their counterparts; and, according to Kripke, how things go for people distinct from himself and Carswell, however like them they might be, can hardly be a source of regret for Nixon.

Plantinga criticizes Lewis' approach in a more formal way, arguing that there are cases of *de re* modality that resist treatment in terms of counterpart theory.[22] According to Plantinga, one property that Jimmy Carter exemplifies essentially or necessarily is the property of being identical with Jimmy Carter; but, on the counterpart theorist's rendition of *de re* modality, this property cannot be exemplified essentially; for since Jimmy Carter is numerically different from all of his counterparts, no one of them exemplifies the property of being identical with Jimmy Carter. Nor does this represent an isolated counterexample to the counterpart theorist's claim to accommodate all our modal intuitions; for a sentence like

(18) Jimmy Carter is secretary of state

is plausibly thought of as expressing the proposition that the property of being identical with Jimmy Carter and the property of being secretary of state are coexemplified; but, then, the counterpart theorist fails to provide an adequate account of

(19) It is possible that Jimmy Carter be secretary of state.

As he reads it, (19) is a claim about some other possible world; but since, on his account, no object in any other possible world is identical with Jimmy Carter, the counterpart theorist seems committed to the view that (19) is false, but, of course, there is a general point here. Since the interpretation we placed on (18) holds for all subject-predicate sentences ascribing properties to individuals, the counterpart theorist of Lewis' persuasion seems to fail to accommodate any of our modal intuitions about alternative ways things might have gone for individuals in the actual world. His view seems no closer to our ordinary way of thinking about matters modal than that of the extreme essentialist considered a couple of pages back; on

22. "Transworld Identity or Worldbound Individuals?" Chapter 7 of this anthology.

Lewis' view, things could indeed have gone otherwise, but they could not have been different for any of the individuals existing in our world.

But not only do such philosophers as Kripke and Plantinga argue that Lewis' view fails to accommodate our modal intuitions; they insist that the very appeal to counterpart theory is misguided, for they contend that none of the arguments meant to cast doubt on the notion of transworld individuals succeed. The first argument, we have seen, tries to show that the doctrine of transworld individuals is incompatible with the indiscernibility of identicals, but defenders of transworld individuals insist that the argument proves too much. The same form of argument, they claim, could be used to establish the impossibility of identity through change, for presumably, as a result of change, an object has properties at one time that it lacks at another. This fact does not, however, cast doubt on identity through time; it merely shows that either our notion of a property or our notion of indiscernibility in properties is more complicated than it might initially appear. What the phenomenon of change shows is that we must either suppose that properties are temporally indexed (so that where an object is P at t and *not-P* at t', it has two distinct, yet compatible properties—the property of being-P-at-t and the property of being not-P-at t') or introduce a temporal quantifier into the Indiscernibility of Identicals and formulate it as follows:

> For any object, x, and any object, y, if x is identical with y, then for any property, P, and any time, t, x has P at t if and only if y has P at t.

We can, then, show the compatibility between transtemporal individuals and the indiscernibility of identicals in either of these two ways; but, proponents of transworld individuals urge, parallel moves in the transworld case enable us to accommodate the intuitively appealing idea that there are alternative ways things might have gone for one and the same individual without rejecting the Indiscernibility of Identicals. We can either take properties to be world-indexed (so that a single individual has the distinct yet compatible properties of being-P-in-W and being-not-in P-in-W'), or we can take the indiscernibility of identicals to require both world and time quantifiers, reading it as follows:

> For any object, x, and any object, y, if x is identical with y, then for any property, P, any world, W, and any time, t, x has P in W at t if and only if y has P in W at t;

and in either case identity across worlds turns out to be no more problematic than the idea of identity across times.[23]

The second argument asks us to take a pair of distinct objects, x and y, and an ordered series of worlds, $W_{,1} \ldots W_n$, and to make successive identity-preserving interchanges of properties in x and y as we move from one world in the series to its successor; the argument contends that the ultimate result of these interchanges is an interchange in identity itself, which is supposed to be incompatible with the transitivity of identity. Proponents of transworld individuals, however, insist that the argument fails to recognize a pair of properties that cannot intelligibly he thought of as interchanged—the individual essences or haecceities of x and y. In the initial world, W_1, x has the property of being identical with x and y has the property of being identical with y. But a requirement of preserving identity as we move from any world, W_i, to its successor-world, W_{i+1}, is that x have its identity-property in both W_i and W_{i+1} and similarly for y; but, then, x must have the property of being identical with x in the last world in the series, W_n, and y must have the property of being identical with y in that world; but that, defenders of transworld individuals argue, is sufficient to ensure that x-in-W_n is identical with x-in-W_1 and similarly for y. Our interchanges may show that many of the properties of x can be properties of y and vice versa, but they fail to show that the defender of transworld individuals is committed to denying the transivitity of identity.[24]

But, of course, this appeal to individual essences or haecceities plays directly into the hands of the third argument, for even if the appeal to haecceities enables the defender of transworld individuals to preserve the distinctness of x and y across the series of adjacent worlds, he seems forced to deny that we can consult any "empirically manifest property" in determining which object is which in a given world. Pretty clearly, the properties of being identical with x and being identical with y are not empirically manifest properties by appeal to which we can make any noncircular headway in resolving questions of identity; but, then, x in one world can be empirically indiscernible from y in another, and vice versa. And that seems to mean that we have no workable criteria of identity and difference here, so that talk of identity and difference would appear to be, as the third argument contends, unintelligible in the transworld case.

23. See Chisholm's "Identity through Possible Worlds: Some Questions," Chapter 3 of this anthology, and Plantinga's "Transworld Identity or Worldbound Individuals?" Chapter 7 of this anthology.

24. See Plantinga's "World and Essence," *Philosophical Review*, 79 (1970), 461–492.

The last argument, then, is epistemological. Urging that we lack any effective criteria for settling questions about the identity of individuals across worlds, it concludes that the notion of transworld identity for individuals is incoherent. But, here, the proponent of transworld individuals argues that the critic has been misled by a picture.[25] He supposes that the various possible worlds are spread out before us in all their infinite detail and that before we can talk about a specific individual in one of those worlds, we have to determine, first, whether the individual really exists in the world, and, second, just which individual among the objects existing in the world is the one we wish to talk about. But according to the defender of transworld individuals, this account is misleading on two counts. First, it assumes that our epistemic access to different possible worlds involves their being given to us for some kind of investigation, as things we can somehow look into. According to proponents of transworld individuals, our access to possible worlds is effectively stipulative; we stipulate just which world is to function as the subject of our counterfactual discourse; but, second, our stipulation settles questions of identity. We say, for example, "Suppose Plato had lived ten years longer." In saying this, we fasten on a world; but our very way of characterizing the world ensures that it is one in which Plato exists and that it is he, among the objects in that world, that we are talking about. Transworld identity, then, presents a problem only if we think of worlds as things given us with the identities of their inhabitants as yet unsettled; worlds aren't given us; we stipulate just which world we mean to talk about, and our stipulation ensures that the individual we are concerned with is the object of our reference.

IV

The critic of transworld individuals will, of course, try to rebut these rejoinders; but lest our discussion trail off into rejoinders to rejoinders to . . . , let us turn to the second problem confronting the defender of a possible-worlds ontology.[26] As I indicated earlier, this problem bears on

25. See Plantinga's "Transworld Identity or Worldbound Individuals?" Chapter 7 of this anthology.

26. As regards the rejoinder to the first argument, David Lewis seems to suggest that identity through change is itself problematic (see "Counterpart Theory and Quantified Modal Logic," Chapter 5 of this anthology). The skeptic about transworld identity will have doubts about the appeal to haecceities in the rejoinder to the second argument, contending either that in the strict sense of 'property' there are no properties of the relevant sort or that the appeal to

the notion of nonactual objects. The contention here is that the defender of a possible-worlds ontology is committed to the existence of nonactual objects and that the notion of a nonactual object is incoherent or contradictary. That the defender of the possible-worlds framework is committed to the existence of nonactuals seems clear when we reflect on his contention that there are possible worlds other than the one that is actual; but it would seem that, on his view, worlds do not exhaust the category of the nonactual. The following is pretty clearly true:

> (20) It is possible that there exists an object distinct from every actually existent object;

for surely there could have been more dogs, more human beings, more trees, and more electrons than there actually are. However, as the possible-worlds theorist understands it, (20) is the claim that some possible world has among its inhabitants at least one object that does not inhabit our world, the actual world. But, then, worlds are not the only nonactual objects to which the possible-worlds theorist is committed; he appears to be committed as well to the existence of nonactual objects of familiar kinds—nonactual but possible dogs, nonactual but possible human beings, nonactual but possible trees, nonactual but possible electrons, and so on.

But where is the contradiction in the claim that there are things— possible worlds and their inhabitants—that are not actual? Just below the surface, the critic claims. What the defender of the possible-worlds framework is saying is that there exist things—possibilia—that do not actually exist; and, according to the critic, the contradiction involved in this claim becomes obvious when we translate it into the language of quantification, for what the possible worlds theorist is claiming is the following:

$$(\exists x) \sim (\exists y) (x = y);$$

---

identity-properties in dealing with questions about transworld identity simply begs the question in favor of transworld individuals (see, e.g., Chisholm's "Identity through Possible Worlds: Some Questions," Chapter 3 of this anthology). The rejoinder to the last argument involves an appeal to the notion of rigidity of reference; it assumes that there are referring devices which are such that when used in talking about possible worlds other than the actual, they pick out the same objects they do when used in discourse about the actual world. This idea involves controversial assumptions about the semantics of referring devices. For discussions of these assumptions, see Stephen Schwartz, ed., *Naming, Necessity, and Natural Kinds* (Ithaca, N.Y.: Cornell University Press, 1977).

he is claiming, that is, that there exist things that do not exist; and a more blatant contradiction is hard to find.[27]

This is a serious charge. How exactly does the defender of nonactual possibilia handle it? David Lewis, whose possibilism is as extreme as any in the literature, argues that the charge of inconsistency is based on a confusion.[28] The critic, he tells us, just assumes that the possibilist is using the expression 'exist' in one and the same sense when he claims that there exist things that do not actually exist; but according to Lewis, there are really two different quantifiers at work in this claim. One is an unrestricted quantifier, a quantifier that ranges over all possible objects, both those that are actual and those that are not; the other is a restricted quantifier, one whose range is limited to the actual world and its contents. We can, of course, mark this distinction symbolically, stipulating that the familiar $(\exists \ldots)$ express unrestricted quantification and some other symbol (e.g., $(\underset{\alpha}{\exists} \ldots)$, restricted quantification; and when we do, the claim of the defender of unactualized possibilia comes out as

$$(\exists x) \sim (\underset{\alpha}{\exists} y)\ (x=y),$$

which, according to Lewis, is consistent.

This is a promising strategy, but pretty clearly the possibilist owes us some sort of account of the distinction between these two quantifiers. Lewis, as I understand him, wants to take the unrestricted quantifier as primitive and to define the restricted quantifier in terms of it. Thus,

$$(\underset{\alpha}{\exists} x)(\phi x) = \text{df.} \quad (\exists x)(\phi x\ \&\ x \text{ is actual}).$$

But, of course, this definition only pushes the problem back one step: "What is it to be actual?" we want to ask. Now, the recalcitrant possibilist might insist here that the predicate 'actual', like the unrestricted quantifier, has to be taken as an unanalyzable primitive. Such an approach is consistent, but not very illuminating. Lewis realizes this and tries to clarify the concept of actuality at work in the definition by way of his indexical theory of actuality. According to Lewis, the term 'actual' is first and foremost applied to possible worlds and secondarily to their inhabitants; and, as he explains it, application of the predicate 'actual' to a possible world does not involve the ascription of some property that distinguishes that world in any

---

27. See Plantinga's "Actualism and Possible Worlds," Chapter 14 of this anthology, and William Lycan's "The Trouble with Possible Worlds," Chapter 15 of this anthology.

28. "Possible Worlds," Chapter 9 of this anthology.

absolute way from other possible worlds. 'Actual' is, on the contrary, an indexical expression; "it depends for its reference on the circumstances of utterance, to wit the world where the utterance is located."[29] When I say that our world is actual, then, I am not singling out that world as one having come special ontic status; I am merely identifying it as the world in which my utterance takes place. And when I say that some object in our world is actual, I am not pointing to some nonrelational characteristic which that object has but objects in other worlds lack. I am, on the contrary, pointing to a relation between that object and my utterance; I am saying that the object inhabits the world in which my utterance takes place.

On Lewis' view, then, all possible worlds are equally real, and all the objects populating the various possible worlds are equally existent. Lewis takes this extreme possibilism in deadly earnest. He insists that the notion of a possible world cannot be reduced to more basic notions; he contends that if we are to explain to someone what a possible world is, we "can only ask him to admit that he knows what sort of thing our actual world is, and then explain that other worlds are more things of *that* sort, differing not in kind but only in what goes on at them."[30] Other possible worlds, then, are things like our own world—concrete objects or spatiotemporal spreads of concrete objects; and each is equally real, equally existent. Against the background of this picture of possible worlds, it is intuitively easy to see why Lewis is so anxious to deny that a single individual can exist in more than one world and to endorse counterpart theory. If all possible worlds are equally real and all possible objects equally existent, then you and I can exist in but a single world; we cannot, so to speak, inhabit two worlds at once.

Now, some philosophers claim that Lewis' extreme possibilism is unintelligible; or better, they claim to have no understanding of what Lewis is saying when he tells us that in the basic or primary sense of 'exist' all possibilia exist. They contend that the only use of the term they can understand is as a quantifier over the actual world and its contents. I, for one, do not have these problems. I think I understand what Lewis is saying. Indeed, apart from his commitment to worldbound individuals and his appeal to counterpart theory (which I shall return to later), I find Lewis' view both intelligible and internally consistent. But even if it is coherent, Lewis' approach saddles us with a Meinongion ontology few philosophers

29. Ibid.
30. Ibid.

will find attractive. What Lewis is claiming is that the various possible worlds and their inhabitants are all really "out there" and that, absolutely considered, all possibilities are realized. This is, to say the least, a bizarre picture, one that smacks of science fiction; and if embracing Lewis' extreme possibilism were the price exacted by acceptance of the possible-worlds framework, one couldn't blame philosophers for concluding that the price is just too great.

In fact, most defenders of the possible-worlds framework have wanted to argue that acceptance of the framework does not commit us to the ontology Lewis proposes. They have argued that we can accommodate the framework of possible worlds within the context of an ontology that recognizes no quantification over nonactual objects. The proponent of this view (it is usually called *actualism*) contends, then, that the only things that exist are objects that exist in the actual world; and he wants to claim that an actualist ontology is sufficiently rich to accommodate the idea that ours is not the only possible world. On his view, possible worlds can be identified with actually existing objects or with constructions out of actually existing objects. One version of actualism is grounded in the Platonic insight that there are objects—things like properties, relations, kinds, and states of affairs—for which there is a clear-cut distinction between existence and instantiation. This version of actualism goes on to identify possible worlds with instantiable entities of one of these categories. Robert Stalnaker, for example, identifies possible worlds with certain properties, total ways things might be.[31] Claiming that the notion of an actually existent but unexemplified property is intelligible, he contends that possible worlds all actually exist, but only one of them—the actual world—is exemplified. In a similar vein, Alvin Plantinga takes possible worlds to be certain obtainable states of affairs. As such, they are all actual existents, but only one among them obtains—our world, the actual world.[32]

Both Stalnaker and Plantinga, then, take possible worlds to be actually existing abstract entities; both construe the possibility of these abstract objects to consist in some variant of the generic notion of instantiability, and both hold that what distinguishes the actual world is that it is the only object from the set of possible worlds that has the property of being instantiated. Since both hold that abstract entities can be actually existent without

---

31. "Possible Worlds," Chapter 12 of this anthology.
32. "Actualism and Possible Worlds," Chapter 14 of this anthology.

being instantiated, both count as actualists; but it is important to notice that both Stalnaker and Plantinga are what I shall call *modal actualists*. That is, while both hold that the framework of possible worlds can be accommodated within the context of a thoroughgoing actualism, both take modal notions as essential to an adequate characterization of the actual world, for both hold that among the contents of the actual world there are modal or intensional entities—properties for Stalnaker and states of affairs for Plantinga—and both hold that the framework of possible worlds is grounded in the fact that these modal entities have a modal property or characteristic, that of *being possibly instantiated* or *instantiability*. Furthermore, both are *de re modal actualists*, since both take as primitive modal *entities* and a modal property of those entities.

Since both Plantinga and Stalnaker invoke notions that are modal in explicating the notion of a possible world, neither succeeds in providing a framework that has quite the explanatory scope of Lewis' extreme possibilism. Lewis takes the notion of a world to be unqualifiedly primitive and, consequently, can invoke the framework of possible worlds in explaining all the forms of modal discourse I discussed two sections back. There are things, however, which Stalnaker and Plantinga cannot, on pain of circularity, explain by appeal to the framework of possible worlds. Neither of them can explain the generic notion of *de re* modality in this way; and while Stalnaker cannot explain the generic notion of a property in possible-worlds terms, Plantinga is unable to invoke the framework of possible words in explaining what a state of affairs is.

Of course, the *de re* modal actualist will readily admit that his account has a narrower explanatory scope than Lewis', but he will insist that any loss of explanatory power is more than compensated for by the ontological gains involved in rejecting Lewis' extreme possibilism. Here, though, the accounts of Stalnaker and Plantinga differ, for given the way each explains the notion of a possible world, Stalnaker's version of modal actualism would seem to have an explanatory scope outstripping that of Plantinga's approach. While Stalnaker involves the notion of a property and the *de re* modal property of exemplifiability in explaining the notion of a possible world, he refuses to see the apparently very complex properties he identifies with possible worlds to be reducible to what would appear to be more elementary notions. The properties that are possible worlds, he insists, are to be taken as primitive or basic; and concepts of apparently "simpler" or less complex properties, the concept of a proposition, etc. are to defined in terms of them.[33] Thus, while Stalnaker cannot invoke the framework of possible worlds to explain in general terms what a property is or what *de re* modality is, he can use the framework in explaining what any property "less complex" than a possible world is and in making sense of any ascription of *de re* modality short of that involving the attribution of instantiability to a world.

Plantinga, on the other hand, takes a less holistic approach to possible worlds, claiming that possible worlds are constructions out of less complex states of affairs. He begins with the notions of a state of affairs and obtainability and defines two notions, that of state-of-affairs-inclusion and state-of-affairs-preclusion. Roughly, a state of affairs, *S*, includes a state of affairs, *S'*, just in case *S* has the property of not possibly obtaining without *S'*'s obtaining, and a state of affairs, *S*, precludes a state of affairs, *S'*, just in case *S* has the property of not possibly coobtaining with *S'*. Then, he tells us that a maximal state of affairs, *S*, is one such that for any state of affairs, *S'*, *S* either includes *S'* or *S* precludes *S'*; and he identifies possible worlds with maximal obtainable states of affairs.[34]

There is an obvious advantage to Plantinga's approach: it provides us with a picture of the structure of possible worlds. It takes familiar notions (notions of ordinary states of affairs) and shows how possible worlds can be thought of as built out of these; but while Plantinga's approach gives us a clear picture of the structure of worlds, it pays a price in explanatory scope for this clarity. His constructivism requires that a wide range of modal phenomena be taken as primitive or unanlyzable. Not just the notion of a state of affairs as applied to possible worlds and not just ascriptions of *de re* modality to maximal states of affairs, but all talk of states of affairs and all talk about their obtainability resist analysis on Plantinga's constructivist account. But there is a further restriction on the explanatory scope of Plantinga's account. To appreciate this, we need only reflect on the connection between the concepts of a state of affairs and a proposition. The connection here is close. Some philosophers have even insisted that propositions just are states of affairs; but whether this is so or not, it is unlikely that one could have the concept of some particular state of affairs (say, that of Jimmy Carter's being president) without having the concept of the corresponding proposition (here, the proposition that Jimmy Carter is president). Likewise, it is difficult to see how one could have the notion of a

---

33. "Possible Worlds," Chapter 12 of this anthology.
34. "Actualism and Possible Worlds," Chapter 14 of this anthology.

state of affairs consisting in an object's exemplifying a property (e.g., Socrates' being pale) without understanding what properties are. The notions of state of affairs, proposition, property, then, are all intimately related, so that it is hard to see how anyone who took familiar states of affairs as basic in the analysis of the notion of a possible world could go on and use the resulting notion in providing an account of what properties and propositions are.

Plantinga's version of *de re* modal actualism, then, would seem to have a more restricted explanatory scope than one like Stalnaker's. Plantinga recognizes this fact, but he insists that it represents no weakness in his account. Indeed, he argues that attempts to provide set theoretical accounts of notions like that of a property or a proposition in terms of a possible-worlds framework one and all break down.[35] They tell us that properties are functions from worlds to sets of n-tuples and that propositions are functions from worlds to truth values; but according to Plantinga, the proponent of this sort of approach is committed to the idea that necessarily coexemplified properties are identical and that logically equivalent propositions cannot be distinct. Triangularity and trilaternality, for example, are coexemplified across possible worlds, so that on the set theoretical approach they come out identical; but, according to Plantinga, this result is counterintuitive. Likewise, we want to hold that there can be distinct necessarily true propositions and distinct necessarily false propositions, but, on the set theoretical approach, we cannot. According to Plantinga, then, the explanatory superiority of an account like Stalnaker's is only apparent; the concept of abstract entities like properties and propositions cannot be defined in set theoretical modal terms, and so it counts as no objection against a version of actualism like his own to point out that the account forces us to take these notions as primitive.[36]

In any case, the accounts of Stalnaker and Plantinga represent two versions of what I have called *de re* modal actualism. But the insight (just noted) that there is an intimate connection between states of affairs and propositions suggests a different form of modal actualism, one that takes the notion of a proposition as basic and tries to elaborate the framework of possible worlds in terms of it. One such account is that outlined by Robert Adams, who tells us that a possible world is a set, S, of propositions such

---

35. Ibid.
36. Stalnaker bites the bullet here, suggesting that our intuitions are misguided. See "Possible Worlds," Chapter 12 of this anthology.

that (1) for every proposition, p, either p is a member of S or the contradictory of p is a member of S and (2) it is possible for the conjunction of all of the members of S to be true.[37] For Adams, then, possible worlds are maximal sets of propositions, all of whose members might have been true, and the actual world is that maximal set of propositions the conjunction of whose members is, in fact, true. This view represents a version of actualism since presumably the existence of propositions (and consequently sets of propositions) does not require their truth. It is also a version of modal actualism since it takes both the notion of a modal entity, a proposition, and the notion of the *possible* truth of a conjunction of propositions as primitive; but since the possibility invoked here is a feature of propositions, the account represents a version of what we might call *de dicto* modal actualism.

Initially, one might find Adams' view puzzling; for it was in the interests of clarifying discourse involving ascriptions of modality *de dicto* that we originally appealed to the framework of possible worlds. It was its success in clarifying that brand of modality that gave the framework its initial respectability. A view like Adams' which uses the very concept of *de dicto* modality in explicating the notion of a possible world would seem, then, to cut the framework from its intuitive roots; and in his hands the framework would lose much of its original charm. Adams, however, could insist that much else besides *de dicto* modality requires explanation, and his approach allows us to invoke the framework in handling much of that residue. In any case, most ascriptions of *de dicto* modality can be explained noncircularly on his account. Admittedly, we cannot invoke the possible-worlds framework, as Adams presents it, in explaining what it is for a conjunction of propositions consituting one of the sets he identifies with a possible world to be possible or possibly true; but any *de dicto* ascription of modality which does not bear on one of those infinitely long conjunctions has a noncircular analysis on Adams' account. Thus, where p is a proposition short of one of those conjunctions, we can say that p is possible just in case p is a member of some maximally possible set of propositions, that p is necessary just in case it is a member of every such set, and that p is impossible just in case it is a member of none.[38]

But despite its explanatory power, this approach gives rise to two problems which Adams quite candidly admits are serious and must be resolved

37. "Theories of Actuality," Chapter 10 of this anthology.
38. Ibid.

if his version of *de dicto* modal acutalism is to be genuinely satisfactory. The first bears on the semantic paradoxes. Adams tells us that a possible world is a set such that for every proposition, p, either p or its contradictory is a member of the set. But this sort of approach to possible worlds would seem to run into problems when it confronts the proposition that says of itself that it is false. To allow either this proposition or its contradictory into the sets in question will generate the result that there are no *possible* worlds at all, for, given the contradictions generated by either one of those propositions, no conjunction having either among its conjuncts is possibly true. The second problem associated with Adams' approach bears on the cardinality of the sets he identifies with possible worlds. The difficulty here is that where we have a set, S, the power set of S (i.e., the set whose members are all of the subsets of S) has a cardinality greater than S. Take, then, some maximally consistent set of propositions which, on Adams' account, is to be identified with a possible world. The power set of that set will have a cardinality greater than that of the set itself. Unfortunately, for each member of the power set, there will be a proposition—the proposition, say, that the member in question is distinct from Richard Nixon; but, then, it turns out that there is a set, presumably a consistent set, of propositions which has a greater cardinality than what was supposed to be a *maximally* consistent set of propositions; and of course if we change our minds and decide that the union of our original set and this new set is a *maximal* set, we find ourselves able to construct once again a consistent set of propositions with a cardinality greater than it, so that the very notion of a *maximally* consistent set of propositions would seem to be incoherent.[39]

To avoid at least the second of these two problems, the defender of *de dicto* modal actualism might try to provide a formulation of the view that does not invoke set theoretical notions. One might, for example, appeal to the notion of a world-proposition, where a proposition, p, is world-proposition just in case (1) p is possible and (2) for any proposition, q, either p entails q or p entails the negation of q, and then claim, that

---

39. The first difficulty could be handled by claiming that since the assumption that the sentence 'This proposition is false' expresses a proposition gives rise to a contradiction, there is no proposition that ascribes falsity to itself. The second difficulty may appear less tractable; but in conversation, Plantinga (whose world-books would seem to be essentially the same thing as Adams' possible worlds) has indicated doubts about Cantor's proof here. If I understand him, he finds the view that there is a universal set more intuitively plausible than the premises at work in Cantor's proof that there can be none. He seems to think that the universal set and its power set have precisely the same cardinality.

possible worlds can be understood as world-propositions with the actual world being that world-proposition which is not merely possible, but true.[40] Such a view has certain explanatory deficiencies as compared with Adams' approach, for since it takes as primitive a wider range of ascriptions of *de dicto* modality (those bearing on the possibility of world-propositions *and* those bearing on the entailment relations which tie world-propositions to propositions generally), the approach just outlined will result in a framework capable of accommodating a much narrower range of cases of *de dicto* modality; but of course the fact that it enables us to provide an actualist account of possible worlds without catching us up in cardinality problems will recommend the approach to anyone who wants to take the notion of *de dicto* modality as primitive or basic.

The four approaches I have been discussing all represent different versions of modal actualism. I have been stressing the differences in these approaches, but it is important to recognize that they all agree in taking possible worlds to be actually existent objects or constructions of such and in holding that the contents of the actual world cannot be characterized in nonmodal terms. Before I conclude my discussion of this general view, I want to consider an apparent problem for this approach. The difficulty here is that certain prephilosophical intuitions which are nicely accommodated in a possibilist ontology seem to resist treatment within the modal actualist's framework. These are intuitions of the sort we confronted at the beginning of this section, intuitions of the sort encapsulated in the following two claims:

(23) There could have been more human beings that there are.

(24) There could have been more electrons then there are.

Now, (23) and (24) appear to be claims about things that do not actually exist, claims to the effect that objects not found in our world inhabit or populate some other possible world. But, then, how can the philosopher who embraces actualism and denies that there are things over and above actual existents make any sense of such claims?

Modal actualists, who have addressed this difficulty, have suggested a number of strategies for handling claims like (23) and (24). I shall discuss just one, a strategy defended by Plantinga.[41] The central idea behind this

40. See Kit Fine, "Prior on the Construction of Possible Worlds and Instants," in Arthur Prior and Kit Fine, *Worlds, Selves, and Times* (London: Duckworth, 1977).

41. See Plantinga's "Actualism and Possible Worlds," Chapter 14 of this anthology.

strategy is that sentences like (23) and (24) are misleading; they appear to express propositions about familiar, concrete objects, but really express propositions about something else—the individual essences or haecceities we encountered in our discussion of transworld identity. Individual essences, we are told, are properties (like that of being identical with Socrates) such that if they are exemplified at all, they are exemplified (1) essentially, (2) uniquely, and (3) necessarily uniquely. As properties, they are all actual existents; but only some of them are instantiated—those that are essences of individuals which actually exist. The modal actualist who takes this strategy, however, wants to claim that had things gone differently, i.e., had some other world been actualized, other individual essences would have been instantiated. Claims like (23) and (24), he tells us, are to be understood as claims about those uninstantiated, but instantiable, individual essences. (23), then, is not a claim about nonactual but possible human beings; it is rather a claim about certain individual essences, the claim that in at least one possible world some uninstantiated but instantiable individual essence is coexemplified with the property of being human. Likewise, for (24); it is not a claim about electrons other than those that actually exist, but rather a claim about things that make up part of the furniture of the actual world, certain individual essences; it is the claim that in some world they are coexemplified with the property of being an electron.

Modal actualism, then, represents one alternative to the extreme possibilism of Lewis, an alternative that will prove attractive to the philosopher who has no difficulties with things like properties, states of affairs, or propositions. Taking things of one or more of these kinds along with some additional modal machinery (such as the *de re* notion of instantiability or the *de dicto* notion of possible truth) as primitive, one can make intelligible the idea that our world is not the only possible world. But to the philosopher who has qualms about properties, states of affairs, and propositions, the Platonism of the modal realist is likely to seem only a slight improvement over the ontological extravagance of Lewis' extreme possibilism; and the philosopher who has doubts about the idea that the world is irreducibly modal is unlikely to find the modal actualist's contention that modal notions (whether *de re* or *de dicto*) are required for a complete description of the world very attractive. But while skeptics of either sort (the two forms of skepticism, of course, tend to coincide) have often been content to consign modal discourse to the philosophical junk heap, some have wanted to take our language at its face value and to provide analyses of ascriptions of modality, counterfactual discourse, meaning-talk, and talk about abstract entities of the intensional variety. Skeptics of this non-revisionist sort might well find the framework of possible worlds a natural and powerful device for providing the requisite analyses. What they will demand, however, is an actualist reconstruction of the framework that invokes no modal notions whatsoever. There is, of course, much to recommend the strategy they insist on, for if successful, this sort of approach to possible worlds (predictably, I shall call it *nonmodal actualism*) would take all of the mystery out of modal discourse; modal discourse would have as its subject matter possible worlds all right, but possible worlds would turn out to be perfectly respectable nonmodal constructions out of actually existent nonmodal entities.

But just how are we to effect the reconstruction demanded here? One strategy is suggested by Carnap's work on modal logic, which might be interpreted as the attempt to identify possible worlds with certain sets of sentences, what we earlier called state descriptions. A state description, we said, is a set, A, such that (1) for every atomic sentence, S, either S belongs to A or the negation of S belongs to A, and (2) the conjunction of all the sentences in A is consistent. But just what sort of thing are we to count as a sentence here? A tough line would take possible worlds to be sets of sentence-tokens, the individual vocables issuing from human mouths and the individual marks inscribed on paper. The theoretical economy of this proposal makes it attractive; but, pretty clearly, this interpretation of the notion of a sentence will fail to provide us with sets that are plausibly identified with possible worlds. There won't even be enough sentences to express all that is required if we are to do justice to the actual world. There is a noncountable infinity of real numbers, and we will need a sentence for each, specifying that the number in question exists; but, even viewed tenselessly, there are only countably many sentence-tokens, each finite in length, so not even that part of the actual world consisting in the existence of the real numbers can be expressed by sets of sentences in the sense of tokens.

Obviously, the nonmodal actualist cannot handle this difficulty by appealing to the notion of possible sentence-tokens; but neither, I think, will the appeal to sentence-types do. For one thing, talk about maximally consistent sets of sentence-types will generate difficulties like those we encountered in our discussion of Adams' attempt to construe worlds as maximally possible sets of propositions—semantic difficulties and cardinality difficulties; but, for another, the appeal to sentence-types is too close to the appeal to abstract entities of an intensional or modal sort to conform to the non-modalist's avowed program of reducing the modal to the nonmodal. Sentence-types can have tokens, and the relationship between a type and its token would seem to be just one case of the relationship between a universal and its instance. Types are properties *exemplified* by all and only their tokens or kinds to which all and only their tokens *belong*.

But even if the defender of the Carnapian line could come up with a satisfactory rendering of 'sentence' here, there are difficulties with the suggestion that the merely syntactical notion of consistency is sufficient to reconstruct all of our modal notions. David Lewis has argued this point persuasively.[42] Just when, he asks, is a sentence consistent? One might respond by saying that a sentence is consistent when it comes out true under some interpretation; but, as Lewis points out, there are impossible interpretations, e.g., one that identifies the extensions of the predicates 'round' and 'square'. To explain consistency as truth under some interpretation, we have to qualify our definition by restricting it to *possible* interpretations; and, of course, that sort of qualification is not an option for the nonmodal actualist. A different proposal here is to say that a sentence is consistent just in case it is not the negation of a theorem of some specified formal system; but, according to Lewis, this proposal also fails since, as Kurt Gödel has shown, there is no way of axiomatizing arithmetic that is at once consistent and complete. Thus, this account of consistency will either fail to give us all the sentences we need for generating sets completely representing the various possible worlds, or it will yield sentences that we do not want in those sets; for either some sentences expressing arithmetical possibilities will be excluded from the sets, or some sentences expressing arithmetical impossibilities will be included.

The approach to possible worlds suggested by Carnap's work bears interesting affinities to the approach to the problem of universals called nominalism. Just as the nominalist (at least, under one venerable use of that term) identifies universals with linguistic expressions, the defender of the Carnapian approach takes worlds to be set theoretical constructs out of linquistic expressions. The analogy here suggests a different strategy for carrying out the nonmodal actualist's program. When philosophers found difficulties in nominalism, they sought refuge in conceptuatism. Similarly, the difficulties with Carnapian actualism suggest the view that the framework of possible worlds could be accommodated by reference to talk

42. ''Possible Worlds,'' Chapter 9 of this anthology.

about conceptual thinking. This sort of strategy has of late been defended by Nicholas Rescher.[43] Rescher wants to claim that possible worlds other than the actual world exist only "as the objects of certain intellectual processes."[44] Their existence is rooted in human acts of conceiving, entertaining, hypothesizing, supposing, and the like.

The defender of possible-worlds conceptualism will have to fill in this proposal with a general account of conceptual activity, one that accommodates the intentionality of the conceptual without reference to nonactual objects, for, notoriously, one of the phenomena that has led philosophers (like Alexius Meinong) to embrace a possibilist ontology is that involving conceptual acts which "take as their objects" things that do not exist. But even if he succeeds here, the possible-worlds conceptualist will find himself confronted with a difficulty analogous to that pointed to in our discussion of the austere version of possible-worlds nominalism. Just as there are not enough sentence-tokens to yield the complete framework of possible worlds, there are not enough actual conceivings to generate the full range of possibilities, for not only is the notion of a possible state of affairs that no human being has ever conceived of coherent, reflection once again on the case of the real numbers is sufficient to convince us that there are uncountably many such states of affairs. Rescher addresses this difficulty, telling us that existence of the possible depends not upon their being conceived, but upon their conceivability. One wants to object, however, that such a response is not open to the nonmodal actualist like Rescher, since conceivability is pretty clearly a modal notion. Rescher anticipates the objection and responds by claiming that his account succeeds in eliminating the notion of a possible *state of affairs* in terms of the notion of possible conceptual *functions*.[45] It is not altogether clear that this response will do, however, for even supposing that Rescher could succeed in showing us how possible intellectual activities or functions do not represent possible

43. "The Ontology of the Possible," Chapter 8 of this anthology. It could be that Kripke's view is also a version of possible-worlds conceptualism. His talk about stipulating rather than discovering possible worlds suggests that possible worlds have an objective existence only in the conceptual activities of thinking counterfactually. But while there clearly are conceptualist overtones in his work, there are strong modalist strains as well; and so I am not certain how one is to categorize his views about the ontic status of the modal.

44. Ibid.

45. Ibid. Some of these difficulties are discussed in Rescher's *A Theory of Possibility* (Pittsburgh: University of Pittsburgh Press, 1975).

states of affairs, at least one kind of modality remains uneliminated; and that, it might be argued, is sufficient to show that the nonmodal actualist's program has not been carried out.

One could, however, preserve the central insight underlying possible-worlds conceptualism while accommodating the difficulty presented by unconceived possibilia by insisting that possible worlds are grounded in divine conceptual activity, for presumably God's conceptual activity is not subject to the restriction imposed on the thinking of finite intellects. The idea that the existence of possibilia is rooted in God's thought seems to have enjoyed some popularity in medieval philosophy; it may represent Leibniz's considered views on the reality of possible worlds other than the actual; and it is suggested by some remarks of Robert Adams.[46] But while this approach does provide the nonmodal actualist with sufficient resources for constructing the various possible worlds in their entirety, it has its own problems. The suggestion here is that possibilia exist as objects of God's intellectual activity; but impossible states of affairs are also open to God's ken, so that the defender of this version of possible-worlds conceptualism owes us a further characterization of the nature of possibilia. One suggestion here is that what distinguishes possibilia from impossibilia is that the former but not the latter are objects or states of affairs that (at least once) it was within God's power to realize or actualize. But of course this cannot be the end of the matter, since reference to divine *power* leaves us with a modal notion; nor is it obvious that we can eliminate the reference to divine power here by saying that a situation, S, is one that was within God's power to actualize just in case if God had willed to actualize S, S would have been realized; for this analysis of the notion of divine power makes use of a counterfactual, and the avowed aim of the nonmodal actualist is one of reconstructing the framework of possible worlds without reference to modal machinery of any sort.

But even if the defender of this view were to succeed in reducing the notion of God's creative power to nonmodal notions, it is difficult to believe that his account provides a really satisfactory theory of modality. The root idea is that an object, situation, or state of affairs is possible *because* its actualization was (at least once) within God's power; but this idea seems to have things backward. One wants to say that things are not possible or impossible because their actualization is or is not within God's

46. "Theories of Actuality," Chapter 10 of this anthology.

power. Quite the contrary; it is because they are possible or impossible that their actualization is or is not within God's power; and that suggests that we need an account of possibility that is independent of what God could or could not have done.

Nominalistic and conceptualistic approaches to modality are well entrenched in the philosophical tradition. A more novel form of nonmodal actualism is one defended by M. J. Cresswell and endorsed in the writings of others.[47] The central idea here is that possible worlds other than the actual world can be construed as alternative combinations of entities populating the actual world. The proponent of this approach (which has appropriately been called "combinatorialism"[48]) identifies some set of entities which he takes to be the basic building blocks of the actual world, and he tells us that alternative possible worlds can be represented as alternative arrangements of those basic entities. Thus, the combinatorialist might insist that it is certain elementary physical particles that constitute the "stuff" out of which our world is constructed, telling us that the world is as it is because those particles have some particular spatiotemporal arrangement. Talk about alternative ways the world might have been, he will claim, is talk about alternative ways those same particles (or, perhaps, some of them) might have been arranged; and he will insist that those alternative arrangements can be identified in nonmodal terms. Here, set theory comes to rescue; alternative possible worlds are simply sets of ordered n-tuples, where the relevant n-tuples assign spatiotemporal locations to the various particles. The example here is materialistic; but presumably the defender of a dualistic ontology could endorse the combinatorialist strategy, insisting that both material entities and Cartesian spirits constitute the "atoms" out of which possible worlds are constructed; and similarly for the hard-core phenomenalist, who would insist that certain actually existing sense-impressions constitute the stuff out of which worlds are built. The combinatorialist strategy, then, leaves the choice of "atoms" open. Committing us to no particular ontology, it merely dictates that we take alternative possible worlds to be set theoretical constructs of those entities we take to be basic in our characterization of the actual world.

This is an appealing approach. Its firm commitment to actualism, its

___

47. See Cresswell's "The World Is Everything That Is the Case," Chapter 6 of this anthology. See also W. V. O. Quine, "Propositional Objects," in *Ontological Relativity and Other Essays* (New York: Columbia University Press, 1968).

48. The label is due to William Lycan.

promise as a genuinely nonmodal account of possible worlds, and the freedom it affords the ontologist all make it attractive. But attractive as it is, the combinatorialist approach to modality has a serious and obvious drawback. It fails to generate what, intuitively at least, would appear to be the full range of possibilities.[49] Suppose, for example, the combinatorialist takes elementary physical particles of some specified kind to be basic. Then, he is committed to the idea that all of the various possible worlds can be constructed out of those particles of the relevant kind that are found in the actual world and no others, but it seems at least intuitively plausible to suppose that there might have been more particles of the relevant sort than there actually are. The defender of this materialistic version of combinationalism must, however, reject our intuitions here. He has to say that it is impossible that there be more particles than there actually are. In the same way, both the Cartesian combinatorialist and his phenomenalist counterpart are committed to the view that there could not have been more minds or sense-impressions than there actually are, and this seems highly implausible.[50]

One might try to handle this difficulty by denying that it is individual physical particles, individual spirits, or individual sense-impressions that are basic. One might follow Cresswell, for example, and hold that it is space-time points and the generic notion of being-occupied-by-matter that are to be taken as primitive and claim that possible worlds are sets of ordered n-tuples, where the n-tuples specify just which space-time points are occupied by matter. If we make plausible assumptions about the infinity of space and time, then this form of combinationalism would seem to avoid the difficulty we have just formulated; and perhaps the defender of a dualistic or phenomenalistic ontology could introduce parallel modifications in his view to achieve the same end. But having warded off the difficulty as I stated it in the previous paragraph, the combinatorialist who invokes a Cresswell-type strategy will, in the end, find himself confronted with a difficulty of a similar sort. The difficulty derives from the intuitively plausible idea that there is nothing necessary about the contents of the actual world. It surely seems possible that the world be "made out of" objects of radically different sorts or kinds from the objects, whatever

49. These difficulties are discussed in Lycan's "The Trouble with Possible Worlds," Chapter 15 of this anthology.

50. Note that since the combinatorialist is a nonmodalist, he cannot invoke the strategy of a modalist like Plantinga and appeal to uninstantiated individual essences in handling this difficulty.

they turn out to be, that make up the actual world, or at least that there be *some* things not reducible to or constructible out of the "atoms" making up our world. In taking the basic "stuff" of our world as the "stuff" out of which all possible worlds are constructed, the combinatorialist is committed to denying that this is so. His possible worlds, we want to say, constitute a subset of the set of all possible worlds; but our intuitions about how things might have been suggest that they constitute only a proper subset.

V

There may, of course, be other forms of nonmodal actualism that one might want to defend, but the difficulties we have encountered in the most popular versions of this reductionist approach suggest that nonmodal actualism is not a very promising strategy for reconstructing the framework of possible worlds. Philosophers who find the nonmodal actualist's approach the only strategy for making that framework respectable will take those difficulties to spell disaster for the framework itself; and to the extent that they find modal discourse an indispensable feature of our conceptual framework, they will look to other quarters in their attempts to make sense of ascriptions of modality, counterfactual thinking, talk about meaning, and talk about things like properties and propositions. It is surely possible that their efforts here will generate interesting and significant results;[51] but whatever the outcome of their investigations, it is important to notice a serious shortcoming in the approach they recommend. Any approach to the topic of modality that refuses to relate modal discourse to the framework of possible worlds fails to accommodate certain important features of our prephilosophical modal thinking; for, as the discussions of earlier sections in this essay urge, the idea that there are possible worlds other than our world is not the invention of the modal logician or speculative metaphysician. Possible worlds are incorrectly thought of as postulated entities introduced into our logical or ontological theories to explain independently identifiable features of modal discourse. Possible worlds are anchored in prephilosophical thinking. As philosophers like David Lewis remind us, it is one of our prephilosophical beliefs that there *are* ways things might have

51. One such approach to modality is outlined in Mondadori and Morton, "Modal Realism: The Poisoned Pawn," Chapter 13 of this anthology. Another approach is suggested in Bas van Fraasen's "Meaning Relations among Predicates," *Noûs*, 1 (1967), 161–179, and "Meaning Relations and Modalities," *Noûs*, 3 (1969), 155–157, as well as in his "The Only Necessity Is Verbal Necessity," *Journal of Philosophy* (1977), 71–85.

gone but did not and that these different ways things might have gone represent the touchstones for assessing the truth value of modal discourse. The term 'possible world', then, is just the philosopher's name for things which we, as nonphilosophers, have recognized all along. But, then, it would seem that no theory that refuses to countenance the framework of possible worlds can be a really satisfactory account of modality. Something central to modal thinking will be left out.

If this is correct, barring new developments from the nonmodal actualist's camp, the philosopher seeking to understand the phenomenon of modal discourse is forced to choose between the extreme possibilism of a philosopher like David Lewis and some version of modal actualism. He is forced, that is, to embrace the venerable theme discussed at the beginning of the essay and to hold that reality is irreducibly modal, either because all possibilia are really "out there" or because the actual world incorporates irreducibly modal entities with irreducibly modal characteristics.

As I have indicated, the great strength of Lewis' possibilism is its explanatory power. Since he takes possible worlds and their contents to be unqualifiedly primitive, he can invoke the possible-worlds framework in explicating all modal phenomena. His account has precisely the same explanatory power that would attach to a successful version of nonmodal actualism. Since the modal actualist has to take certain modal notions as primitive in constructing the possible-worlds framework, however, the framework, as he presents it, has a more restricted explanatory scope. This, of course, speaks in favor of Lewis' possibilism. But most philosophers would prefer to settle for the weaker theory rather than embrace the account Lewis recommends. As we have seen, some find his appeal to the unrestricted quantifier unintelligible; and almost all of his critics are uncomfortable with the extravagance of Lewis' contention that absolutely speaking all possibilities are realized. I have already indicated that I find complaints about the intelligibility of the unrestricted quantifier more rhetorical than genuine. I do, however, have sympathy with the worry that Lewis' view runs roughshod over our desire for a theory with at least a minimal degree of parsimony. But my ultimate doubts about Lewis' view are really quite different. I am not convinced that Lewis' account successfully accommodates the prephilosophical intuitions it claims to accommodate. My difficulties bear on the issue of counterpart theory. As I see it, Lewis' appeal to counterpart theory is not a merely incidental feature of his account. It seems to me that if one holds that the various possible worlds are really "out there" as concrete objects, sums of concrete objects, or spatiotemporal spreads of concrete objects (as things like myself "and all my surroundings"), then the idea that one and the same individual exists in more than one possible world verges on the incoherent. We would have to suppose that absolutely speaking one and the same individual *realizes* different and incompatible life-histories. I suspect that Lewis agrees here. Toward accommodating our intuitions that things might have been different for the individuals surrounding us, he settles on the machinery provided by the counterpart relation; but here I find the arguments of philosophers like Kripke and Plantinga compelling. Although counterpart theory represents an ingenious attempt to avoid the extreme essentialism resulting from the doctrine of worldbound individuals, it fails; and in this connection I find our prephilosophical modal intuitions decisive. They require transworld individuals; and since the idea of a transworld individual has no place within the context of Lewis' extreme possibilism, that account would seem to be an unsatisfactory theory of modality.

I would conclude, then, that some version of modal actualism provides us with the most satisfactory theory of modality. Which one? Here, I have no strong convictions. One's choice among the various versions of modal actualism will have to be dictated by one's intuitions about the primacy of *de re* or *de dicto* modality and by one's judgments as to which phenomena are genuinely analyzable in terms of possible worlds.[52] There are, as we have seen, serious difficulties with some of those theories. Set theoretical versions of modal actualism like Adams' will have to confront the cardinality difficulties discussed in the previous section, and versions of *de dicto* modal actualism will have to confront problems associated with the semantic paradoxes. Barring successful resolutions of these problems, some nonset-theoretical version of *de re* modal actualism like Stalnaker's or Plantinga's[53] would seem to be our only recourse. Pretty clearly, however, much hard work remains to be done here toward articulating the various alternatives the strategy of modal actualism allows, exploring their relationships to each other, and comparing them with our considered modal intuitions; but if I am right in thinking that it is this strategy which is most promising, the hard work will be repaid by a clarification of modal discourse generally.

52. For example, does one side with Plantinga or with Stalnaker on the question of whether a set theoretical approach to intensional abstract entities succeeds? One's answer to this question will determine just which things one is willing to take as primitive in explicating the notion of a possible world.

53. Without Plantinga's appeal to world-books as maximally possible sets of propositions.

2

The Modes of Modality

JAAKKO HINTIKKA

Florida State University

By the modes of modality, I do not mean the changing fashions that prevail or have prevailed in the study of modal logics, although I would be tempted to comment on them, too.[1] I am referring to those modes or modifications which have given modal logic its name. In other words, I have in mind the variety of systems of modal logic and the variety of philosophically interesting interpretations which can often be given of them. The point of my paper is to recommend a specific method for the study of this variety, which to my mind constitutes a veritable embarrassment of riches. This embarrassment also affects my paper, I am afraid; the major part of it is a series of sketches for applications of my methods rather than a continuous argument.

These methods have been outlined in a recent paper [12]. I shall begin by recapitulating their essentials. They are based on the notion of a *model set*

Originally published in *Acta Philosophica Fennica*, 16 (1963), 65-79; reprinted here with permission of the author and the Philosophical Society of Finland.

1. In [1], Gustav Bergmann has presented interesting criticisms of earlier treatments of modal logic. As far as the situation at the time of the writing of Bergmann's article is concerned, I agree with what I take to be his main point, viz., the failure of all the earlier deductive systems of modal logic to be based on a satisfactory semantical (or, if you prefer, combinatorial) characterization of validity (logical truth). It seems to me, however, that in this respect the situation is now radically different. I am convinced that in the writings of Stig Kanger [14]-[17], of Saul Kripke [18], of Richard Montague [19] and Donald Kalish [20], of myself and of still others we have the beginnings of the kind of foundation for modal logics which Bergmann missed.

(m.s.). A model set is a set of formulas—say μ—satisfying the following conditions:

(C.$\sim$)   If μ contains an atomic formula or an identity, it does not contain its negation.

(C.&)   If $(F \ \& \ G) \in \mu$, then $F \in \mu$ and $G \in \mu$.

(C.v)   If $(F \ v \ G) \in \mu$, then $F \in \mu$ or $G \in \mu$.

(C.E)   If $(Ex)F \in \mu$, then $F \ (a/x) \in \mu$ for at least one free individual symbol a. (Here $F \ (a/x)$ is the result of replacing x everywhere by a in F.)

(C.U)   If $(Ux)F \in \mu$ and if b is a free individual symbol which occurs in at least one formula of μ, then $F(b/x) \in \mu$.

(C.self$\neq$) μ does not contain any formulas of the form $\sim (a = a)$

(C.=)   If $F \in \mu$, $(a = b) \in \mu$, and if G is like F except for the interchange of a and b at some (or all) of their occurrences, then $G \in \mu$ provided that F and G are atomic formulas or identities.

In addition to these conditions, we need either corresponding conditions for negated formulas or else some way of reducing negated (nonatomic) formulas to unnegated ones. Both courses are very easy.

In the absence of logical constants other than sentential connectives, quantifiers, and identity, a m.s. may be thought of as a partial description of a possible state of affairs or a possible course of events ("possible world"). Although partial, these descriptions are large enough to show that the described states of affairs are really possible: in quantification theory the *satisfiability* of a set of formulas may be equated with its imbeddability in a m.s., as I have shown in [7]-[8].

This approach may be extended to modal logic by using certain configurations of m.s.'s, called *model systems*. A model system is a set of m.s.'s on which a dyadic relation has been defined. This relation will be called the relation of alternativeness, and the sets bearing it to some given set μ will be called the *alternatives* to μ. Intuitively, they are partial descriptions of those states of affairs which could have been realized instead of the one described by μ. On the basis of this idea, it is seen at once that the following conditions have to be satisfied by each model system Ω and by its alternativeness relation:[2]

2. As I shall proceed to point out, however, there are many ways of modifying these conditions. A modification of (C.N$^+$) is sometimes necessary; see [12, pp. 124–125].

(C.N)   If $NF \in \mu \in \Omega$, then $F \in \mu$.

(C.M*)   If $MF \in \mu \in \Omega$, then there is in Ω at least one alternative to μ which contains F.

(C.N$^+$)   If $NF \in \mu \in \Omega$ and if ν is an alternative to μ in Ω, then $F \in \nu$.

Of course, we must also set up similar conditions for negated formulas, or else reduce them to unnegated ones. Both these things are easy to accomplish.

The content of (C.M*) and (C.N$^+$), relatively, may be expressed fairly accurately by saying that whatever is possible must be true in some alternative world and that whatever is necessary must be true in all the alternative worlds. What we have here therefore is a slightly modified version of the traditional idea that possibility equals truth in some "possible world" while necessity equals truth in all "possible worlds". Apart from using the notion of a m.s. as an explication of the notion of a description of a possible world, our only departure from the traditional idea lies in rejecting the presupposition that all "possible worlds" are on a par. We have assumed that not every possible world (say P) is really an alternative to a given possible world (say Q) in the sense that P could have been realized instead of Q. We have assumed, moreover, that only these genuine alternatives really count. Each statement has to be thought of as having been made in some "possible world"; and nothing can be said to be possible in such a world which would not have been true in some world realizable in its stead. Hence the use of the alternativeness relation and the consequent appearance of the phrases "some *alternative* possible world" and "all *alternative* possible worlds" where you probably expected the simpler phrases "some possible world" and "all possible worlds", respectively.

Here we already have a theory of modal logic in a nutshell. The *satisfiability* of a set of formulas may be defined as its imbeddability in a member of a model system. (This, it is seen, is a natural generalization of the corresponding definition for quantification theory.) Even more generally, the satisfiability of an arbitrary set of sets of formulas which has an arbitrary dyadic relation (we shall call that, too, an "alternativeness relation") defined on it may be defined as the possibility of mapping it homomorphically into a model system so that each element is included in its image (both are of course sets). Other notions, for instance, those of validity, inconsistency, and logical consequence, may be defined in terms of satisfiability in the usual way.

Because of the prominence of the notion of satisfiability in this approach it may perhaps be called *semantical*. It is not very difficult to obtain a kind of *syntactical* treatment of modality, too, from the same basic ideas. Given a set of formulas, how can we hope to show that it is satisfiable? An answer is immediately suggested by the form of the conditions which define a m.s. and a model system. With the sole exception of (C. ~), they are all closure conditions or very much like closure conditions. (The exceptional condition (C. ~) may be considered as a kind of consistency condition.) In other words, whenever a set Σ of sets (on which an alternativeness relation has been defined) violates one of the conditions which define a model system (other than (C. ~)), this violation may be removed by adjoining a new formula to one of the members of Σ or (in the case of (C.M*)) by adjoining a new member of the form $[F]$ to Σ to serve as an alternative to one of the old members. It can be shown without difficulty that adjunctions of this kind preserve the satisfiability of a satisfiable Σ. (In the case of (C.v) at least one of the two adjunctions which may satisfy it preserves its satisfiability.) One natural way of trying to see whether Σ is satisfiable is therefore to carry out successive adjunctions of this kind so as to try to build a model system which would show that Σ is satisfiable. If all the alternative ways of trying to do so end up in a violation of (C. ~), then we know that Σ is *not* satisfiable. It is also possible to show that every proof of a formula in a suitable system of modal logic can be thought of as such an abortive attempt to build a counterexample to it, i.e., to build a model system which would show that its negation is satisfiable.[3]

It is not immediately obvious that every inconsistent set of formulas can be shown to be inconsistent by means of an abortive model system con-

3. Given a set of formulas for which we are trying to construct a model system, it does not usually suffice to consider just one m.s. together with suitable alternatives to it. Normally, we have to consider alternatives to these alternatives, and so on. In fact, for every finite integer k we can easily find a set of formulas (and even a single formula) such that more than k m.s.'s have to be considered in order to show that it is satisfiable (or that it is not satisfiable). Since each m.s. may be thought of as describing a "possible world" in which sentences are true or false, it is to be expected that no set of truth-table-like matrices with only a finite number of truth values serves to define such concepts as satisfiability and validity for our system. Small wonder, therefore, that the corresponding result for provability has in fact been proved for a number of Lewis's modal systems by James Dugundji in [2] (cf. also [4]). I fail to see why his results should show that a satisfactory semantical theory of modal logic is impossible, as has been alleged. On the contrary, it would seem quite unnatural if we could fix once and for all a finite upper limit to the number of the possible worlds we have to consider in a semantical theory of modal logic.

struction of this kind. It can be proved, however, that this is always possible if we conduct the attempt in a suitable way (essentially, if we do not forget any possibility of adjunction for good). This result, which will not be proved here, constitutes an interesting *completeness theorem*.

All this gives us but one system of modal logic, albeit one of the most natural systems. If we look away from its quantificational aspects, it turns out to be a semantical counterpart to that deductive system of modal logic which is perhaps best known as von Wright's system M (see [25]), although it was suggested much earlier by Gödel in [5]. (We shall call the corresponding semantical system "system M", too.) The natural way in which we have arrived at this system constitutes, in my opinion, a very strong argument for its interest and importance. There are other interesting systems of modal logic, however, and we must therefore be able to modify the defining conditions of our system M so as to be able to cope with them.

There are several widely different possibilities of modification. Some of the systems which result from these modifications are semantical counterparts to well-known deductive systems; others are important for the interpretation of modal logics. Among the relevant possibilities of modification there are the following:

(1) The alternativeness relation may be assumed to have properties additional to those imposed on it by the above conditions. Conversely, it may lack some of these. For instance, it is seen that (C.N) is, in the presence of (C.N$^+$) or some similar condition, tantamount to the requirement that the alternativeness relation be reflexive. This requirement may be given up. Then it is often advisable to adopt a weaker condition which ensures that the necessity-operator N is at least as strong as the possibility-operator M, e.g., as follows:

(C.n*) If $NF \in \mu \in \Omega$, then there is in Ω at least one alternative to μ which contains F.

Conversely, we may require that the alternativeness relation be not only reflexive but also symmetric or transitive or both. Thus transitivity gives rise to a semantical counterpart to Lewis's S-4, and the combined requirement of symmetry and transitivity (plus reflexivity, of course) to a counterpart to S-5. These modifications have been briefly commented on in [12].

A remark on the semantical counterpart of S-5 may have some philosophical interest. A transitive and symmetric relation is sometimes known as an equivalence relation: it effects a partition of its field into "equivalence classes" in such a way that two different members of the same class always bear this relation to each other while members of different classes never bear it to each other. In the case of our semantical version of S-5, we may for certain purposes require that there is but one such equivalence class. (For instance, this requirement does not affect the satisfiability of any sets of formulas.) And if we do so, the situation will begin to seem rather familiar: every m.s. is an alternative to every other m.s. This is indeed the situation presupposed by the traditional identification of possibility with truth in some possible world and of necessity with truth in every possible world. The fact that the traditional idea thus yields only a very special kind of a modal system perhaps serves to explain why the traditional idea was not very fruitful in the theory of modal logic for a long time, and motivates our departure from the tradition.

(2) We may modify the assumptions which pertain to quantification. Modifications of this kind are sometimes independent of the presence of modal notions. But even so, they are made desirable by the interplay of modality and quantification. The most fundamental modification of this kind is the elimination of what I have called *existential presuppositions*; see [11] and [13, pp. 129-131]. They are presuppositions to the effect that all our singular terms refer to some actually existing individual, i.e., that empty singular terms are excluded from the discussion. In an uninterpreted system, this of course means that free individual symbols must not behave like empty singular terms.

Presuppositions of this kind are made, usually tacitly, in all the traditional systems of quantification theory. In terms of our model set technique, they are especially easy to eliminate. All we have to do is to modify (C.E) and (C.U) as follows:

(C.E$_0$) If $(Ex)F \in \mu$, then $F(a/x) \in \mu$ and $(Ex)(x=a) \in \mu$ for at least one free individual symbol a.

(C.U$_0$) If $(Ux)F \in \mu$ and $(Ey)(y=b) \in \mu$ (or $(Ey)(b=y) \in \mu$), then $F(b/x) \in \mu$.

Explanation: The formula $(Ex)(x=a)$ naturally serves as the formalization of the phrase "*a* exists." (Cf. Quine's dictum "to be is to be a value of a bound variable" which for our purposes might be expanded to read "to be is to be identical with one of the values of a bound variable.") Accordingly, the new condition (C.U$_0$) says that whatever is true of all actually existing individuals is true of the individual referred to by b

provided that such an individual really exists. If empty singular terms are admitted to our systems, the italicized provided-clause is obviously needed. Similarly, the additional force of (C.E$_0$) over and above that of (C.E) is seen to lie in the requirement that the term a, which serves to represent one of those individuals which are being claimed to exist by $(Ex)F$, really refers to some actually existing individual (or, if we are dealing with an uninterpreted system, behaves as if it did). This strengthening is made necessary by the admission of empty singular terms.

The system obtained by eliminating the existential presuppositions is weaker than our original system M. All those inferences, exemplified by the existential generalization, which turn on the exclusion of empty singular terms, are now invalid. They are restored, however, by means of contingent extra premises of the form $(Ey)(y=b)$. For instance, although the formula $F(a/x) \supset (Ex)F$ is not valid any more, the closely related formula $(F(a/x) \ \& \ (Ex)(x=a)) \supset (Ex)F$ is valid.

(3) This does not yet solve the much-discussed problems of combining modality with quantification. There is a way out of these difficulties, however, for which I have argued (in a particular case) in [13, pp. 138–158]. Here we shall consider only sentences with no iterated modalities. In this case, our way out is completely analogous to the elimination of existential presuppositions which we just accomplished. All we have to do is to give the formula $(Ex)N(x=a)$ a role similar to the role which the formula $(Ex)(x=a)$ plays in the elimination of existential presuppositions: Whenever there are occurrences of x within the scope of modal operators in F we modify (C.E)(or (C.E$_0$)) by making the presence of $(Ex)F$ in μ imply the presence of $(Ex)N(x=a)$ in μ; and we modify (C.U)(or (C.U$_0$)) by making its applicability conditional on the presence of a formula of the form $(Ey)N(y=b)$ or $(Ey)N(b=y)$ in μ.

These modifications effect a further weakening of our system. The critical inferences whose feasibility was at issue will now depend on contingent premises of the form $(Ex)N(x=a)$ or $(Ex)N(a=x)$.

It may be argued that these modifications give us a way of meeting the objections of those logicians who have doubted the feasibility (or the advisability) of quantifying into modal contexts. (See e.g. [22]–[24] and cf. [3].) The gist of these objections has been, if I have diagnosed them correctly, that a genuine substitution-value of a bound individual variable must be a singular term which really specifies a well-defined individual, and that an ordinary singular term may very well fail to do so in a modal context. For instance, from

(i) the number of planets is nine but it is possible that it should be larger than ten

(which may be assumed to be true for the sake of argument) we cannot infer

(ii) (Ex) $(x=9$ & it is possible that $x > 10)$,

for insofar as (ii) makes sense, it appears to be obviously false.

The reason for this failure is connected with the fact that the singular term "the number of planets" in (i) does not specify any well-defined number such as is asserted to exist in (ii). (Is this number perhaps 9? But 9 cannot possibly be larger than 10. If it is not 9, what is it?) Yet the inference from (i) to (ii) is justified by our conditions (C.E) and (C.U). Hence there is something wrong with our system, and it is easily seen that the elimination of existential presuppositions does not help us.

It seems to me that these objections are entirely valid, and that they must be met by anybody who presumes to work out a system of quantified modal logic. A way of meeting them is perhaps seen by asking: Why do some terms fail in modal contexts to have the kind of unique reference which is a prerequisite for being a substitution-value of a bound variable? An answer is implicit in our method of dealing with modal logic. Why does the term "the number of planets" in (i) fail to specify a well-defined individual? Obviously because in the different states of affairs which we consider possible when we assert (i) it will refer to different numbers. (In the actual state of affairs it refers to 9, but we are also implicitly considering other states of affairs in which it refers to larger numbers.) This at once suggests an answer to the question as to when a singular term (say a) really specifies a well-defined individual and therefore qualifies as an admissible substitution-value of the bound variables. It does so if and only if it refers to one and the same individual not only in the actual world (or, more generally, in whatever possible world we are considering) but also in all the alternative worlds which could have been realized instead of it; in other words, if and only if there is an individual to which it refers in all the alternative worlds as well. But referring to it in all these alternatives is tantamount to referring to it *necessarily*. Hence $(Ex)N(x=a)$ formulates a necessary and sufficient condition for the term a to refer to a well-defined individual in the sense the critics of quantified modal logic seem to have been driving at, exactly as I suggested.

Other modal logicians have preferred to let all the free individual symbols of a logical system be admissible subsitution-values of bound individual variables. Then they have had to restrict the class of singular terms which in an interpretation may be substituted for free individual symbols to those which have the desired kind of unique reference. This procedure is certainly feasible, but it seems to me to restrict the applicability of our logical system far too much. These limitations are especially heavy in areas where even proper names might fail to have the required sort of well-defined reference and hence might not qualify as substitution-values of free individual symbols. This seems to happen in epistemic logic. In [13, pp. 148–154] I have argued that in epistemic logic the well-defined reference with which we are here concerned is tantamount to *known* reference. If so, proper names may certainly fail to have it, for one may very well fail to know to whom a certain proper name refers. And if proper names fail us, what does not?

(4) We may also attempt modifications in an entirely different direction. We may, or we may not, assume that individuals existing in one state of affairs always exist in the alternative states of affairs. Conversely, we may, or we may not, assume that individuals existing in one of the alternatives to a given state of affairs always exist in this given state itself. In a system *without* existential presuppositions these assumptions may be formalized very simply by assuming the transferability of formulas of the form $(Ex)(x=a)$ or $(Ex)(a=x)$ from a model set to its alternatives or vice versa. In systems *with* existential presuppositions the situation is more complicated. The simplest and most flexible system is the one in which no transferability assumptions are made. In order to reach such a system, we must in fact modify $(C.N^+)$ so as to make its applicability conditional on the occurrence of each free individual symbol of F in at least one formula of μ. The rationale of this modification is straightforward: From $(C.U)$ it is seen that in systems with existential presuppositions the mere presence of a free individual symbol in the members of a m.s. presupposes that it refers to an actually existing individual. In order not to assume that individuals always transfer from one possible world to its alternatives, we must therefore avoid assuming that free individual symbols may be transferred from a m.s. to its alternatives.

The ways in which such transferability assumptions may be formulated in systems with existential presuppositions have been briefly discussed in [12].

(5) Thus far, we have been concerned with ways of obtaining new systems of modal logic. There are other methods of variation, however,

viz., methods of formulating the assumptions of any given system in different ways, some of which may often be more useful or more illuminating for certain particular purposes than others. An especially useful strategy in this connection is to replace "global" conditions pertaining to the alternativeness relation at large by "local" ones governing the relation of a m.s. to its alternatives. A typical example of global conditions is the requirement of transitivity. It is not very difficult to show (cf. [13, pp. 46–47]) that this condition can be replaced (unless further conditions are present in addition to those of M) by the following local condition:

(C.NN^+) If $NF \in \mu \in \Omega$ and if ν is an alternative to μ in Ω, then $NF \in \nu$.

If this condition is fulfilled and if the other conditions are those of M, the effect of the requirement of symmetry may be obtained by adding the following condition which is again of the "local" type:

(C.NN_+) If $F \in \nu \in \Omega$ and if ν is an alternative to μ in Ω, then $NF \in \mu$.

It is fairly obvious, in fact, that this condition should give us the effects of symmetry. We have assumed that the only other conditions regulating the relation of all alternatives are (C.NN_1) and (C.N_1). The latter, however, is a consequence of the former and (C.N). Hence the only relevant condition is (C.NN^+), and (C.NN_+) is its mirror image.

We may also combine two or more conditions into one. For instance, part of the combined power of the conditions (C.M*) and (C.N^+) can obviously be obtained by using the following condition:

$(\text{C.M\&N}^+)$ If $MG \in \mu \in \Omega$, $NF_1 \in \mu$, $NF_2 \in \mu$, $\ldots$, $NF_k \in \mu$, then there is an alternative to μ in Ω which contains all the formulas G, F_1, F_2, $\ldots$, F_k.

In a sense, even the whole power of (C.N^+) is obtained by means of this rule, viz., in the sense that every set of formulas which is satisfiable remains satisfiable when $(\text{C.M\&N}^+)$ replaces (C.N^+), and vice versa. This is not obvious. In case some m.s. μ contains an infinity of formulas of the form NF, it follows from (C.N^+) that all its alternatives likewise contain an infinity of formulas. Our new condition $(\text{C.M\&N}^+)$ only guarantees that there are alternatives to μ which contain any given finite subset of the infinity of formulas which (C.N^+) squeezes into each alternative of μ. That the weaker-looking condition $(\text{C.M\&N}^+)$ nevertheless suffices is suggested, although not quite proved yet, by the completeness theorem mentioned above. It says that every set of formulas which is not satisfiable may be shown to be so by trying to construct a model system for it; if we proceed in a suitable way, all the possible ways of trying to construct one end up in a violation of $(C.\sim)$ after some finite number of steps. Now because of this finitude only a finite number of applications of $(C.N^+)$ are needed in the argument. And any such finite number of applications of $(C.N^+)$ can be shown to be replaceable by an application of $(C.M\&N^+)$.

If the requirement of transitivity is added to our basic system M, the condition $(C.M\&N^+)$ must be replaced by the following condition:

$(C.M\&N^+)$ If $MG \in \mu \in \Omega$, $NF_1 \in \mu$, $NF_2 \in \mu$, . . . , $NF_k \in \mu$, then
there is in Ω at least one alternative to μ which contains all the formulas G, NF_1, NF_2, . . . , NF_k.

Such variations of our original conditions might be produced almost indefinitely. They are sometimes of technical interest. More importantly, they often help us in the interpretation of the different systems of modal logic, and in finding systems of modal logic to formulate the structure of the various philosophically interesting notions to the analysis of which we may wish to apply our industry. I shall give you a few instances of such formulations.

If we are doing tense-logic, more explicitly, if we read "M" as "it is or will be the case that," then our "possible worlds" may be given a clear-cut meaning: they are the states of the world at the different moments of the future. Each m.s. is a set of true statements that can all be made at one and the same moment of (future) time. A m.s. is an alternative to another if and only if the moment of time thus correlated with the former is later than that correlated with the latter. Then it is readily seen that a formulation of this tense-logic is obtained by taking our basic system M and adding to its defining conditions the requirement that the alternativeness relation must effect a *linear* ordering.[4]

More accurately, what we obtain in this way is a tense-logic which goes together with classical physics. If we do not want to tie our logic to old-fashioned physics, we are undoubtedly wiser if we interpret each m.s. as a set of true statements that can all be made in one and the same

4. Hence S-4 is not yet a satisfactory system of this kind of tense-logic, for in S-4 the alternativeness relation need not yet be linear; it is only required to be transitive. Cf. [21] and [10].

world-point (point-instant) and read "*M*" as "it will be the case some-where that." Then we can no longer require that the alternativeness rela-tion (in this case it could perhaps be more appropriately termed "futurity relation") effect a linear ordering. At the relativistic best, we seem to have only transitivity. Hence S-4 is perhaps not so inappropriate as a system of tense-logic after all.

We can also see which system of modal logic recommends itself as the formalization of *logical* possibility and *logical* necessity. It seems to me obvious that whatever is logically necessary here and now must also be logically necessary in all the logically possible states of affairs that could have been realized instead of the actual one. (It is logically possible that this Colloquium had not been held; but no logical truths would undoubtedly have been destroyed as a consequence.) But this is exactly what (C.NN⁺) says. Conversely, it also seems fairly clear that no new logical necessities can come about as the result of the realization of any logical possibility. In short, it seems to me that whatever is logically necessary in one logically possible world must also be logically necessary in others. But this presup-poses that (C.NN₊) is also satisfied. Together with (C.NN⁺), this condi-tion imposes the structure of Lewis's S-5 on our modal logic. The system S-5, then, seems to be the best formalization of our logic of *logical necessity and logical* possibility.

An important qualification is in order here, however. In the argument I just gave no reference was made to any way of actually finding out which sentences are logically necessary or logically possible. This is essential for the correctness of the argument. In fact, we obtain entirely different results if we consider, not logical truths "by themselves", but such logical truths as can be actually proved by means of some definite class of arguments, e.g., in some given deductive system. Then "*NF*" will say that *F* can be proved by means of the arguments in question, and "*MF*" will say that *F* cannot be disproved by their means. But if so, a formula like

(iii) *MF* ⊃ *NMF*

is not likely to be valid, for what it would amount to is to say that if *F* cannot be disproved by means of a certain class of arguments, then it can be proved by means of those very arguments that we cannot disprove it. And this is in most cases false. Nevertheless, (iii) is valid in S-5, as you can verify without any difficulty. Hence S-5 cannot really serve as a formaliza-tion of *provable* logical truth. It may even be doubted whether all the laws of S-5 are valid in this case, as witness by Gödel's comments on the

formula $N(NF \supset F)$ in [5]. If so, Halldén's conclusions in [6] may have to
be modified.

Further interpretations are indicated in earlier works of mine. In [9] I
have discussed along these lines (albeit in a slightly different terminology)
the conditions which our normative notions must satisfy. In [13, pp.
16–22, 23–29] I have examined our principal epistemic notions, viz., those
of knowledge and belief, in the same respect. The former of these is simple
enough to be discussed here. Suppose someone makes a number of statements on one and the same occasion, including the following: "it is possible, for all that I know, that G"; "I know that F_1", "I know that
F_2," ..., "I know that F_k." When is he consistent? It seems clear that if it
is really possible, for all that he knows, that G should be the case, then it
must be possible for G to turn out to be the case while everything he says
he knows is also true. On the interpretation "N" = "I know that," "M"
= "it is possible, for all that I know, that," this is exactly what (C.M&N$^+$)
says. But this is not enough. If our man really knows what he claims he
knows, i.e., knows it in the sense in which knowledge is contrasted to true
opinion, then it must be possible for G to turn out to be the case while he
continues to know everything he claims to know. In other words, the
realization of whatever is possible, for all that he knows, must not force
him to give up any of his claims to knowledge, if he is to be as much as
self-consistent. But this is exactly what the condition (C.M&NN$_1$) requires. And the satisfaction of this condition means, we have seen, that the
logic of knowledge is at least as strong as Lewis's S-4. (It is, as far as I can
see, exactly tantamount to S-4, provided that we forget a number of qualifications which I have considered in some detail in [13] and also forget the
fact that epistemic notions are normally relative to a person.)

On the other hand, if our man only aspires to true opinion, the situation
is different. There is no inconsistency in his giving up one of his opinions
when something which may be true according to his (true) opinion turns
out to be the case. In other words, the logic of true belief is not that of S-4,
although the logic of "real" knowledge is. Hence our approach suggests
an interesting, albeit partial, answer to the time-honoured question concerning the difference between "genuine" knowledge and "mere" true
opinion. If I am right, the two notions even have different logics.

Since this is a very interesting point, it may be worth elaborating further.
With more justification than perhaps meets the eye, the import of
(C.M&N$^+$) may be said to consist in the requirement that if μ is satisfiable
and if $MG \in \mu$, $NF_1 \in \mu$, $NF_2 \in \mu$, ..., $NF_k \in \mu$, then the set $\{G, F_1,$

$F_2. \ldots, F_k$} is also satisfiable. The latter set is satisfiable if an only if the implication

$$G \supset (\sim F_1 \text{ v } \sim F_2 \text{ v} \ldots \text{ v } \sim F_k)$$

is *not* valid (logically true). When used in connection with the epistemic notions, the import of (C.M&N$^+$) may thus be said to consist in the requirement that nothing that is compatible with what somebody knows may qualify as a destructive objection to *what he says he knows.*

Likewise, the import of the stronger condition (C.M&NN$^+$) in epistemic contexts may be said to consist in the requirement that nothing that is compatible with what somebody knows may amount to a destructive objection to *his claim to know* what he says he knows. For its gist may be shown to lie in the requirement that the satisfiability of μ (of the kind mentioned in (C.M&NN$^+$)) entails that the implication

$$G \supset (\sim NF_1 \text{ v } \sim NF_2 \text{ v} \ldots \text{ v } \sim NF_k)$$

is not valid. From this it is seen that if we are dealing with genuine knowledge and not just with true opinion, (C.M&NN$^+$) has to be fulfilled. For somebody's claim to knowledge in this sense of the word can be criticized not only by showing that the facts are not as he claims to know they are but also by showing that *he does not really know* (is not in the position or in the condition to know it, or whatnot) that they are as they are. By the same token, mere true opinion does *not* satisfy (C.M&NN$^+$), although it satisfies (C.M&N$^+$). (Of course, much of what passes as knowledge in ordinary discourse is, in the sense of our artificially precise distinction, mere true opinion.)

REFERENCES

[1] GUSTAV BERGMANN, "The Philosophical Significance of Modal Logic," *Mind,* 69 (1960), 466–485.
[2] JAMES DUGUNDJI, "Note on a Property of Matrices for Lewis and Langford's Calculi of Propositions," *Journal of Symbolic Logic,* 5 (1940), 150–151.
[3] DAGFINN FØLLESDAL, "Referential Opacity and Modal Logic," Ph.D. dissertation, Harvard University, 1961; deposited in Widener Library, Harvard University.
[4] KURT GÖDEL, "Zum Intuitionistischen Aussagenkalkül," *Akademie der Wissenschaften in Wien, Mathematisch-Naturwissenschaftliche Klasse,* 69 (1932), 65–66.

[5] KURT GÖDEL, "Eine Interpretation des Intuitionistischen Aussagenkalküls," *Ergebnisse eines Mathematischen Kolloquiums,* 4 (1933), 39-40.

[6] SÖREN HALLDÉN, "A Pragmatic Approach to Modal Logic," in *Filosofiska Studier Tillägnade Konrad Marc-Wogau 4 April 1962,* ed. by Ann-Mari Henschen-Dahlquist and Ingemar Hedenius (Uppsala, 1962), pp. 82-94.

[7] JAAKKO HINTIKKA, "Form and Content in Quantification Theory," *Acta Philosophica Fennica,* 8 (1955), 7-55.

[8] JAAKKO HINTIKKA, "Notes on Quantification Theory," *Societas Scientiarum Fennica, Commentationes Phys.-Math.,* 17, no. 12 (1955).

[9] JAAKKO HINTIKKA, "Quantifiers in Deontic Logic," *Societas Scientiarum Fennica, Commentationes Humanarum Litterarum,* 23, no. 4 (1957).

[10] JAAKKO HINTIKKA, "Review of Prior's *Time and Modality,*" *Philosophical Review,* 67 (1958), 401-404.

[11] JAAKKO HINTIKKA, "Existential Presuppositions and Existential Commitments," *Journal of Philosophy,* 56 (1959), 125-137.

[12] JAAKKO HINTIKKA, "Modality and Quantification," *Theoria,* 27 (1961), 119-128.

[13] JAAKKO HINTIKKA, *Knowledge and Belief: An Introduction to the Logic of the Two Notions* (Ithaca, N.Y.: Cornell University Press, 1962).

[14] STIG KANGER, *Provability in Logic* (Stockholm: Almquist and Wiksell, 1957).

[15] STIG KANGER, "The Morning Star Paradox," *Theoria,* 23 (1957), 1-11.

[16] STIG KANGER, "A Note on Quantification and Modalities," *Theoria,* 23 (1957), 133-134.

[17] STIG KANGER, "On the Characterization of the Modalities," *Theoria,* 23 (1957), 152-155.

[18] SAUL A. KRIPKE, "A Completeness Theorem in Modal Logic," *Journal of Symbolic Logic,* 24 (1959), 1-14.

[19] RICHARD MONTAGUE, "Logical Necessity, Physical Necessity, Ethics, and Quantifiers," *Inquiry,* 3 (1960), 259-269.

[20] RICHARD MONTAGUE AND DONALD KALISH, " 'That,' " *Philosophical Studies,* 10 (1959), 54-61.

[21] ARTHUR N. PRIOR, *Time and Modality* (Oxford: Clarendon Press, 1957).

[22] W. V. O. QUINE, *From a Logical Point of View,* 2d ed. (Cambridge, Mass.: Harvard University Press, 1961).

[23] W. V. O. QUINE, "Quantifiers and Propositional Attitudes," *Journal of Philosophy,* 53 (1956), 177-187.

[24] W. V. O. QUINE, *Word and Object* (Cambridge, Mass.: MIT Press, 1960).

[25] G. H. VON WRIGHT, *An Essay on Modal Logic* (Amsterdam: North Holland, 1951).

3

Identity through Possible Worlds: Some Questions

RODERICK M. CHISHOLM

Brown University

> It is now easy to see a simple way of avoiding undesirable existential generalizations in epistemic contexts. Existential generalization with respect to a term—say *b*—is admissible in such contexts if *b* refers to one and the same man in all the "possible worlds" we have to consider.
>
> —Hintikka[1]

In an article on Hintikka's *Knowledge and Belief,* I suggested that certain difficult questions come to mind when we consider the thought that an individual in one possible world might be identical with an individual in another possible world.[2] The present paper is written in response to the invitation of the editor of *Noûs* to be more explicit about these questions.

Let us suppose, then, that the figure of an infinity of possible worlds makes good sense and let us also suppose, for simplicity of presentation, that we have a complete description of this one. We may consider some one of the entities of this world, alter its description slightly, adjust the descriptions of the other entities in the world to fit this alteration, and then ask ourselves whether the entity in the possible world that we thus arrive at

Reprinted from "Identity through Possible Worlds: Some Questions," *Noûs,* 1 (1967), 1–8, by Roderick Chisholm, by permission of the Wayne State University Press. © 1967 by Wayne State University Press.

1. Jaakko Hintikka, *Knowledge and Belief: An Introduction to the Logic of the Two Notions* (Ithaca, N.Y.: Cornell University Press, 1962), p. 152.

2. "The Logic of Knowing," *Journal of Philosophy,* 60 (1963), 773–795; see especially pp. 787–795.

is identical with the entity we started with in this world. We start with Adam, say; we alter his description slightly and allow him to live for 931 years instead of for only 930; we then accommodate our descriptions of the other entities of the world to fit this possibility (Eve, for example, will now have the property of being married to a man who lives for 931 years instead of that of being married to a man who lives for only 930); and we thus arrive at a description of another possible world.[3]

Let us call our present world "W^1" and the possible world we have just indicated "W^2". Is the Adam of our world W^1 the same person as the Adam of the possible world W^2? In other words, is Adam such that he lives for just 930 years in W^1 and for 931 in W^2? And how are we to decide?

One's first thought might be that the proposition that Adam is in both worlds is incompatible with the principle of the indiscernibility of identicals. How could our Adam be identical with that one if ours lives for just 930 years and that one for 931? Possibly this question could be answered in the following way:

"Compare the question: How can Adam at the age of 930 be the same person as the man who ate the forbidden fruit, if the former is old and the latter is young? Here the proper reply would be: it is not true that the old Adam has properties that render him discernible from the young Adam; the truth is, rather, that Adam has the property of being young when he eats the forbidden fruit and the property of being old in the year 930, and that these properties, though different, are not incompatible. And so, too, for the different possible worlds: It is not true that the Adam of W^1 has properties that render him discernible from the Adam of W^2; the truth is, rather, that Adam has the property of living for 930 years in W^1 and the property of living for 931 in W^2, and that these properties, though different, are not incompatible."

I think it is clear that we must deal with the old Adam and the young Adam in the manner indicated; but in this case, one could argue, we know independently that the same Adam is involved throughout. But are we justified in dealing in a similar way with the Adam of W^1 and the Adam of W^2? In this latter case, one might say, we do not know independently that

---

3. It should be noted that the possible world in question is not one that Hintikka would call *epistemically* possible, for it could be said to contain certain states of affairs (Adam living for 931 years) which are incompatible with what we know to hold of this world; hence it is not one of the worlds Hintikka is concerned with in the passage quoted above. But it is *logically* possible, and that is all that matters for purposes of the present discussion.

the same Adam is involved throughout. Here, then, is one of the questions that I do not know how to answer. Let us suppose, however, that we answer it affirmatively.

The Adam of this world, we are assuming, is identical with the Adam of that one. In other words, Adam is such that he lives for only 930 years in W^1 and for 931 in W^2. Let us now suppose further that we have arrived at our conception of W^2, not only by introducing alterations in our description of the Adam of W^1, but also by introducing alterations in our description of the Noah of W^1. We say: "Suppose Adam had lived for 931 years instead of 930 and suppose Noah had lived for 949 years instead of 950." We then arrive at our description of W^2 by accommodating our descriptions of the other entities of W^1 in such a way that these entities will be capable of inhabiting the same possible world as the revised Noah and the revised Adam. Both Noah and Adam, then, may be found in W^2 as well as in W^1.

Now let us move from W^2 to still another possible world W^3. Once again, we will start by introducing alterations in Adam and Noah and then accommodate the rest of the world to what we have done. In W^3 Adam lives for 932 years and Noah for 948. Then moving from one possible world to another, but keeping our fingers, so to speak, on the same two entities, we arrive at a world in which Noah lives for 930 years and Adam for 950. In that world, therefore, Noah has the age that Adam has in this one, and Adam has the age that Noah has in this one; the Adam and Noah that we started with might thus be said to have exchanged their ages. Now let us continue on to still other possible worlds and allow them to exchange still other properties. We will imagine a possible world in which they have exchanged the first letters of their names, then one in which they have exchanged the second, then one in which they have exchanged the fourth, with the result that Adam in this new possible world will be called "Noah" and Noah "Adam." Proceeding in this way, we arrive finally at a possible world W^n which would seem to be exactly like our present world W^1, except for the fact that the Adam of W^n may be traced back to the Noah of W^1 and the Noah of W^n may be traced back to the Adam of W^1.

Should we say of the Adam of W^n that he is identical with the Noah of W^1 and should we say of the Noah of W^n that he is identical the Adam of W^1? In other words, is there an x such that x is Adam in W^1 and x is Noah in W^n, and is there a y such that y is Noah in W^1 and y is Adam in W^n? And how are we to decide?

But let us suppose that somehow we have arrived at an affirmative answer. Now we must ask ourselves: How is one to tell the difference between the two worlds W^1 and W^n? Shall we say that, though they are diverse, they are yet indiscernible from each other—or, at any rate, that the Adam of W^1 is indiscernible from the Adam of W^n (who is in fact the Noah of W^1) and that the Noah of W^1 is indiscernible from the Noah of W^n (who is in fact the Adam of W^1)? There is a certain ambiguity in "discernible" and in "indiscernible." The two Adams could be called "discernible" in that the one has the property of being Noah in the other world and the other does not, and similarly for the two Noahs. But in the sense of "indiscernible" that allows us to say that "Indiscernibles are identical" tells us more than merely "Identicals are identical," aren't the two Adams, the two Noahs, and the two worlds indiscernible? Could God possibly have had a sufficient reason for creating W^1 instead of W^n?

If W^1 and W^n are two different possible worlds, then, of course, there are indefinitely many others, equally difficult to distinguish from each other and from W^1 and W^n. For what we have done to Adam and Noah, we can do to any other pair of entities. Therefore among the possible worlds which would seem to be indiscernible from this one, there are those in which you play the role that I play in this one and in which I play the role that you play in this one.[4] (If this is true, there may be good ground for the existentialist's *Angst;* since, it would seem, God could have had no sufficient reason for choosing the world in which you play your present role instead of one in which you play mine.)

Is there really a good reason for saying that this Adam and Noah are identical, respectively, with that Noah and Adam? We opened the door to this conclusion by assuming that Adam could be found in more than one possible world—by assuming that there is an x such that x is Adam in W^1 and lives here for 930 years and x is also Adam in W^2 and lives there for 931. If it is reasonable to assume that Adam retains his identity through the relatively slight changes involved in the transition from W^1 to W^2, and so, too, for Noah, then it would also seem reasonable to assume that each retains his identity through the equally slight changes involved in all the other transitions that took us finally to W^n. (These transitions, of course, may be as gradual as one pleases. Instead of it being a year that we take

4. "She [Ivich] looked at the glass, and Mathieu looked at her. A violent and undefined desire had taken possession of him; a desire to *be* for one instant that consciousness . . . to feel those long slender arms from within. . . . To be Ivich and not to cease to be himself." Sartre, *The Age of Reason.* Compare N. L. Wilson, "Substance without Substrata," *Review of Metaphysics,* 12 (1959), 521–539, and A. N. Prior, "Identifiable Individuals," *Review of Metaphysics,* 13 (1960), 684–696.

away from Noah in our first step and give to Adam, it could be only a day, or a fraction of a second.) But identity is transitive. And therefore, one might argue, once we allow Adam to exist in more than one possible world, we commit ourselves to affirmative answers to the puzzling questions we have encountered.

Is there a way, then, in which we might reasonably countenance identity through possible worlds and yet avoid such extreme conclusions? The only way, so far as I can see, is to appeal to some version of the doctrine that individual things have essential properties. One possibility would be this:

For every entity x, there are certain properties N and certain properties E such that: x has N in some possible worlds and x has non-N in others; but x has E in every possible world in which x exists; and, moreover, for every y, if y has E in any possible world, then y is identical with x. (If "being identical with x" refers to a property of x, then we should add that E includes certain properties other than that of being identical with x.) The properties E will thus be *essential* to x and the properties N *non-essential, or accidental.*[5]

To avoid misunderstanding, we should contrast this present use of "essential property" and with two others.

(1) Sometimes the "essential properties" of a thing are said to be just those properties that the thing has *necessarily*. But it is not implausible to say that there are certain properties which are such that *everything* has those properties necessarily; the properties, for example, of being either red or non-red, of being colored if red, and of being self-identical.[6] Thus the Eiffel Tower is necessarily red or non-red, necessarily colored if red, and necessarily self-identical; and so is everything else.[7]

(2) And sometimes it is said (most unfortunately, it seems to me) that

---

5. We could put the doctrine more cautiously by saying that the distinction between the two types of property holds, not for *every* entity x, but only for *some* entities x. But what reason could there be for thinking that it holds of some entities and not of others?

6. Sometimes these properties are called "analytic properties" or "tautological properties"; but the property of being colored if red should not be so-called if, as some have argued, "Everything that is red is colored" is not analytic.

7. From the proposition that the Eiffel Tower is red and necessarily colored if red, it would be fallacious to infer that the Eiffel Tower is necessarily colored; this is the fallacy of inferring *necessitate consequentis* from *necessitate consequentiae*. And from the proposition that the Eiffel Tower is necessarily red or non-red, it would be fallacious to infer that the proposition that the Eiffel Tower is red or non-red is a necessary proposition; the proposition could hardly be necessary, for it implies the contingent proposition that there is an Eiffel Tower. This latter fallacy might be called the fallacy of inferring *necessitate de dicto* from *necessitate de re*.

each individual thing is such that it has certain properties which are essential or necessary to it "under certain descriptions of it" and which are not essential or necessary to it "under certain other descriptions of it." Thus "under one of his descriptions," the property of being president is said to be essential to Mr. Johnson whereas "under that description" the property of being the husband of Lady Bird is not; and "under another one of his descriptions," it is the other way around. Presumably *every* property P of every individual thing x is such that, "under some description of x," P is essential or necessary to x.

But if E is the set of properties that are essential to a given thing x, in the sense of "essential" that we have defined above, then: E will not be a universal property (indeed, *nothing* but x will have E); some of the properties of x will not be included in E; and E will not be such that there are descriptions of x "under which" E is not, in the sense defined, essential to x.

If we accept this doctrine of essential properties, we may say, perhaps, that the property of living for just 930 years is not essential to Adam and therefore that he may inhabit other possible worlds without living for just 930 years in each of them. And so, too, perhaps, for having a name which, in English, ends with the letter "m." But, we may then go on to say, somewhere in the journey from W^1 to W^n, we left the essential properties of Adam (and therefore Adam himself) behind. But where? What *are* the properties that are essential to Adam? Being the first man? Having a name which, in English, begins with the first letter of the alphabet? But why *these* properties? If we can contemplate Adam with slightly different properties in another possible world, why can't we think of him as having ancestors in some possible worlds and as having a different name in others? And similarly for any other property that might be proposed as being thus essential to Adam.

It seems to me that even if Adam does have such essential properties, there is no procedure at all for finding out what they are. And it also seems to me that there is no way of finding out whether he *does* have any essential properties. Is there really a good reason, then, for supposing that he does?

The distinction between essential and non-essential properties seems to be involved in one of the traditional ways of dealing with the problem of *knowing who.*[8] If this way of dealing with that problem were satisfactory,

---

8. Compare Aristotle, *De Sophisticis Elenchis,* 179 b 3; Petrus Hispanus, *Summulae Logicales,* ed. I. M. Bochenski (Turin, 1947), 7.41; Franz Brentano, *Kategorienlehre* (Leipzig, 1933), p. 165.

then the doctrine of essential properties might have a kind of independent confirmation. But I am not sure that is satisfactory. The problem of *knowing who* may be illustrated in this way. I do not know who it was who robbed the bank this morning, but I do know, let us assume, that there is someone who robbed the bank and I also know that that person is the man who drove off from the bank at 9:20 A.M. in a Buick Sedan. For me to know *who* he is, therefore, it is not enough for me to have information enabling me to characterize him uniquely. What kind of information, then, *would* entitle me to say that I know who he is? The essentialistic answer would be: "You *know who* the bank robber is, provided that there is a certain set of properties E which are essential to the x such that x robbed the bank and you know that x has E and x robbed the bank." But if my doubts about essential properties are well-founded, this solution to the problem of knowing who would imply that the police, though they may finally "learn the thief's identity," will never know that they do. For to *know that one knows who* the thief is (according to the proposed solution) one must know what properties are essential to the thief; and if what I have said is correct, we have no way of finding out what they are. How are the police to decide that they know who the thief is if they have no answer to the metaphysical question "What are the essential properties of the man we have arrested?"[9]

It is assumed, in many writings on modal logic, that "Necessarily, for every x, x is identical with x" implies "For every x, necessarily x is identical with x," and therefore also "For every x and y, if x is identical with y, then necessarily x is identical with y." But is the assumption reasonable? It leads us to perplexing conclusions: for example, to the conclusion that *every* entity exists in *every* possible world and therefore, presumably, that everything is an *ens necessarium*.

Why assume that necessarily the evening star is identical with the evening star? We should remind ourselves that "The evening star is identical with the evening star" is not a logical truth, for it implies the contingent

---

9. Hintikka says that we know who the thief is provided that there exists an x such that we know that the thief is identical with x (*op. cit.*, p. 153). But under what conditions may it be said that there exists an x such that we know that the thief is identical with x? Presumably, if ever, when we catch him in the act—when we *see* him steal the money. But the teller saw him steal the money and *she* doesn't know who he is. I have suggested elsewhere a slightly different way of looking at these questions; compare *op. cit.*, pp. 789–791, and "Believing and Intentionality," *Philosophy and Phenomenological Research*, 25 (1964), 266–269, esp. p. 268.

proposition "There is an evening star," and that its negation is not "The evening star is diverse from the evening star." Wouldn't it be simpler to deny that "Necessarily, for every x, x is identical with x" implies "For every x, necessarily x is identical with x?" Then we could deny the principle *de dicto*, "Necessarily the evening star is identical with the evening star," and also deny the principle, *de re*, "The evening star is necessarily identical with the evening star."[10] We could still do justice to the necessity that is here involved, it seems to me, provided we continued to affirm such principles, *de dicto*, as "Necessarily, for every x, x is identical with x" and "Necessarily, for every x and y, if x is identical with y then y is identical with x," and such principles, *de re*, "The evening star, like everything else, is necessarily self-identical."

10. I have discussed this possibility in "Query on Substitutivity," in *Boston Studies in the Philosophy of Science*, Vol. II, ed. by Robert S. Cohen and Marx W. Wartofsky (New York: Humanities Press, 1965), pp. 275–278.

If we deny that "Necessarily, for every x, x is F" implies "For every x, necessarily x is F," then presumably we should also deny that "It is possible that there exists an x such that x is F" implies "There exists an x such that it is possible that x is F." But isn't this what we should do? One could hold quite consistently, it seems to me, that though it is possible that there exists something having the properties that Christians attribute to God, yet nothing that does exist is such that it is possible that *that* thing has the properties that Christians attribute to God.

4

Transworld Heir Lines

DAVID KAPLAN

University of California, Los Angeles

A certain kind of linguistic context has come in for increasing attention over the past several years. The occurrences of the word "nine" in

It is provable in arithmetic that nine is the square of three;
It is possible that the number of planets is nine;
It is permissible that the number of occupants exceed nine;
It is probable that the number of enrolled students will be less than nine;

Copyright © 1978 by David Kaplan. This paper was presented at a joint symposium of the American Philosophical Association and the Association for Symbolic Logic in Chicago in May 1967. The commentators were Jaakko Hintikka and Terence Parsons. The paper was written to be heard, not read, which accounts for its stylistic deviation from the stately prose of my other publications. This version is essentially unaltered except for the addition of the footnotes, all of which are 1978 postscripts. The appearance of the paper at this time may seem anachronistic. It is anachronistic. Most of its truths are now well known, and most of its errors are now rarely repeated. Furthermore, I no longer champion the antihaecceitist viewpoint (as I called it in "How to Russell a Frege-Church," *Journal of Philosophy*, 72 [1975]; Chapter 11 of this anthology). Why, then, allow it to appear at this time? Primarily because it has been called a "classic" by the leading modal logician of our time, and I would not wish to be accused of suppressing classical sources. (To be more exact, the paper is described as a "*locus classicus*" of a certain philosophical mistake. I suppose one must learn to take the bitter with the better.) A second reason for permitting publication at this time is that in its easy, naive way, the paper does focus on what I still take to be the fundamental metaphysical ideas that underlie various common logical constructions in intensional logic. The research was supported by the National Science Foundation.

It is desirable that symposia be limited to nine;

and,

It is believable that nine is prime

illustrate such contexts. These occurrences of the word "nine" are neither so vulgar as that in

Nine is larger than five

nor so accidental as that in

Canines are larger than felines.

Presumably there are no logical or semantical problems concerned with vulgar or accidental occurrences. Vulgar occurrences of "nine" denote a certain number, are open to substitution and generalization, and contribute to the meaning of the containing sentence. Accidental occurrences are irrelevant to all such concerns. But analysis of the intermediate contexts produced by "provable," "possible," "permissible," "probable," "believable," and "desirable" is neither trivial nor pointless.

Gottlob Frege, who tried to assimilate such intermediate occurrences to the vulgar ones by means of a doctrine about ambiguity and indirect denotation, called such contexts "oblique" or "indirect." W. V. O. Quine, who often seems to want to assimilate the intermediate occurrences to accidental ones by means of a doctrine of indissolubility, calls such contexts opaque.

Frege's way is the more sanguine, for it suggests the possibility of developing a nontrivial logic for such contexts. And indeed our intuitions suggest that such arguments as

It is probable that the number of enrolled students will exceed nine. Therefore it is probable that the number of enrolled students will exceed six

are valid, and valid in view of logical form.

Frege did not link his doctrine of indirect denotation with any particular kind of entity indirectly denoted. But he emphasized cases in which what was indirectly denoted was the ordinary sense.

A number of different proposals have been advanced for conditions under which two sentences, say, would be said to have the same ordinary sense. The most liberal of these, proposed by both Rudolf Carnap and

Alonzo Church, is that the sentences should be logically equivalent. The most restrictive of these, proposed by Benson Mates, is that distinct sentences never have the same sense. In between lie two alternatives, discussed by Church, and Carnap's Intensional Isomorphism. I believe it best to think of these proposals as suggesting different senses of the word "sense". In terms of these proposals, we can form a useful classification of oblique contexts by seeking the most liberal sense of "sense" according to which we can interchange the component sentences in a given oblique context without affecting the truth value of the whole compound.

Following Carnap, let us call the sense of "sense" according to which logically equivalent sentences have the same sense *intension*. And let us call the oblique contexts within which sentences with the same intension can be interchanged *intensional contexts*. These contexts form a large and important class of oblique contexts. Of our original examples, those associated with "provable", "possible", "permissible", "probable", and "desirable" are all rather clearly intensional, and "believable" (or better just "believe") is thought by some to be intensional in at least one of its senses. But in their primary senses the psychological oblique contexts, what Bertrand Russell called *propositional attitudes,* form a second important group whose specific logic has been little investigated.

For the remainder of the paper I will discuss only intensional contexts.

So far I have spoken of intensions only by way of the phrase "have the same intension". But, as Frege noted in the case of "have the same number", to determine conditions under which two classes have the same number is not yet to say what *the number of a class* is, let alone what numbers in general are. Frege, of course, thought of senses as definite entities of a certain kind which could be combined and decomposed, and if we are to develop an intensional logic it would certainly be helpful to have some notion of at least the structure of these entities.

A very natural and simple proposal about the nature of intensions has been advanced by Carnap. He proposes to understand the category of intensions appropriate to sentences (which intensions he calls *propositions*) as sets of possible worlds. The intension of a particular sentence, i.e., the proposition expressed by the sentence, is then taken as the set of all possible worlds in which the sentence is true. This immediately yields the desired consequence that two sentences will express the same proposition if and only if they are logically equivalent.[1]

---

1. At least if all logically possible states are represented by possible worlds.

I prefer to think of propositions as what might be called characteristic functions of sets of possible worlds, that is, as functions which assign to each possible world one of the two truth values. I prefer this way of thinking about the intensions of sentences because one sees quickly and easily how to generalize the idea. We have rather general agreement now as to what kind of entity the *extension* of an expression of a given grammatical category should be. Thus, the extension of a term is the individual named or described by that term (if there is one; otherwise it has no extension), the extension of a one-place predicate is the class of individuals to which the predicate applies, the extension of a sentence is its truth value, the extension of a truth-functional sentential connective is a certain truth function, etc. We can even provide an analogous extension for variable binding operators. Without going into the matter at this time, let me just mention that it is possible to give arguments showing that in each of these cases the expression bears a similar relation to its extension.[2] So the general notion of the extension of an expression is not just an arbitrary union of some semantical property of terms, some semantical property of predicates, some semantical property of sentences, etc., but really has a kind of validity (as a notion) of its own.

Carnap's simple idea for constructing intensions of arbitrary expressions is just this. Let the intension of an expression be that function which assigns to each possible world the extension of the expression in that world. Intensions, so understood, are independent of expressions, in that we can identify (i.e., define) the class of intensions independently of their being expressed by any particular expression. In fact, if there are at least ω possible worlds, there are at least 2^ω propositions, and for most languages this would exceed the number of sentences available to express them.

We will now have a one-minute quiz to make sure that you have been paying attention. Let us call the intension of a name an *individual concept*. What kind of an entity is an individual concept? All those who mumbled something like "a function which assigns to each possible world an individual in the universe of that world", pass. But there is a little problem here. Suppose we have a name which has an extension in some worlds but not in all. "Hamlet" has no extension in the actual world, and I like to think that there are other worlds in which "Reagan" has no extension. You

---

2. I had in mind here arguments like those given in my dissertation to show that it is natural, if extending the notion of *denotation* from names to sentences, to take the denotation of a sentence to be its truth value.

can probably think of a number of ways of handling this problem. One very simple way is to treat such names as if their extension in such a world were the whole world itself or some other entity so chosen that could not be in the universe of that world, which is the prime desideratum. A slightly more flexible method is to imagine the universe of a world divided into two parts: the individuals which *exist* in the world and those which do not. Then we can stick to the notion of an individual concept as a function which assigns to each possible world an element of its universe, without the consequence that the function always assign something which exists in the possible world.

So to determine the intension of an expression it suffices to determine its extension in each possible world. And if we are given for each possible world the extension of each *atomic* expression in that world and the range of each style of variable in that world, we should be able to determine for each world the extension of an arbitrary compound expression by using the familiar method developed by Alfred Tarski. But there is a hitch.

A special problem arises when the expression in question contains free variables. Suppose we ask for the intension of "x is bald". One way of treating this is to assume implicit universal closure and take "x is bald" as synonymous with "For all x, x is bald." But this avoids the real question. The notion we need is not just the *intension of* Φ but *the intension of* Φ *with respect to a given assignment of values to the free variables of* Φ. Another way of putting it is to say that what we need is not just the proposition expressed by a closed sentence, but the function expressed by an open sentence. Where such a function would yield a proposition for every set of values of the free variables and for different values of the variables, we might get different propositions. Russell called such functions, from individuals to propositions, *propositional functions*. He drove poor Frege to despair by also calling *expressions* like "x is bald" propositional functions. But let's forget that and adopt the terminology "propositional function" to describe the intension of "x is bald". For us, the importance of propositional functions appears in connection with expressions in intensional contexts containing free variables bound to quantifiers outside the intensional contexts. For in such situations the truth conditions of the whole depend in part upon how the proposition expressed by the formula changes as the variable takes different values.

The more subtle among you will have noted that this coining of the phrase "propositional function" does nothing to clarify the notion. Let me review: we are clear on *the proposition expressed by the closed sentence*

Γ—it is that function which assigns to each world W, the truth value of Γ in W, and we are also clear on the simpler notion of a *proposition*—any function from worlds to truth values. We are clear on the simple notion of a *propositional function*—a function from individuals to propositions (and we know what propositions are). But we are *unclear* on the notion *the propositional function expressed by the open formula* Φ.

When we hit this problem about propositional functions, I was saying that to determine the intension of an expression it suffices to determine the extension in all possible worlds. So to determine the propositional function expressed by "x is bald" it suffices to determine for each value of the variable "x" the extension of "x is bald" in each possible world. That of course means each actual value, each individual of the actual world.

Let us try in a simple case. Let the value of "x" be Bobby Dylan. Now we must determine the truth value of "x is bald" in each possible world. That is, for each world W does "x is bald" hold of Bobby Dylan in W? First, consider the actual world at the present moment[3] (I'll come to change over time shortly). Clearly "x is bald" fails of Bobby Dylan in this world. Now consider another possible world, the one which would have currently obtained if I had taken my black pen to Chicago and left my red pen in Los Angeles rather than taking my red pen and leaving my black pen as I in fact did. I am fairly confident that "x is bald" fails of Bobby Dylan in that world too. Now how about the world in which the Germans win the Second World War and immediately issue an edict that the only public musical performances allowed will be Wagner and polkas. Call this world "G". I don't want you to focus on the counterfactuals, "would Bobby Dylan have shaved his head if . . . " That is not the problem. I'll even let you peep in at this other world through my Jules Verne-o-scope. Carefully examine each individual, check his fingerprints, etc. The problem is: which one, if any, is Bobby Dylan? That is, which one is *our* Bobby Dylan—of course he may be somewhat changed, just as he will be in our world in a few years. In that possible world which ours will become in, say, thirty years, someone may ask "What ever happened to Bobby Dylan?" and set out to locate him. Our problem is to similarly locate him in G (if he exists there). Although I will continue to speak of *identification,* there are reasons, to which I will return, for claiming that the Bobby Dylan in G is not strictly identical with our Bobby Dylan but related to him in a way something like descendant to ancestor, what Kurt Lewin called *gen-identity.* So I call the

3. That is, May 1967.

task of locating individuals in other worlds the problem of determining transworld heir lines.

I will flatly assert that this problem is the central problem of philosophical interest in the development of intensional logic. The other problems are all technical. (For the general treatment of oblique contexts, there remains the pressing problem of a development, corresponding to that given for the notion of intension, of a sense of "sense" appropriate to the propositional attitudes.)

I know that I have not yet sorted out in detail all our different intuitions related to the transworld identification problem. But I would like to outline three kinds of response. I call them (1) the skeptical, (2) the metaphysical, and (3) the relativistic.

The skeptical response is that it just can't be done. Everyone to his own world. This position may be elaborated by an attempt to show how the idea that we can locate Bobby Dylan in another world arises from confusion of mention and use. Thus the skeptic may claim that it is perfectly reasonable to attempt to locate an individual-under-a-description in another world. So we may try to find Bobby Dylan-under-the-description-"Bobby Dylan" in some other world by, say, looking him up in the telephone book. Or we may seek Bobby Dylan-under-the-description-"the composer of 'Blowin' in the Wind' " in another world by looking him up in the ASCAP registry. But these endeavors may well lead to different results. (We are all aware of the consequence of looking up nine-under-the-description-"the number of planets.") And why take one description rather than another? It would be more enlightening to break the "x-under-the-description-α" nomenclature down into its two components: (a) the intension of α (this is some individual concept, and it does the transworld identification), and (b) the fact that α actually describes x (in our world). The skeptic feels that such talk as

> Bobby Dylan-under-the-description-"the composer of 'Blowin' in the Wind' " is necessarily a musician

is like saying that

> Professor Marcus-under-the-description-"Ruth" is monosyllabic.

Being monosyllabic attaches directly to the name "Ruth" and only in a most remote and indirect way to Professor Marcus. And, similarly, being *necessarily* a musician attaches directly to the individual concept expressed by "the composer of 'Blowin' in the Wind' ", and only indirectly, by way of that particular concept, to Bobby Dylan. Another way of putting the skeptic's point about "why select one description rather than another" is to say that he sees no favored way of making the identification. Now you may feel that at least we can eliminate some possibilities, namely, any individual of another world who shares *no* description with our Bobby Dylan. But if there is any sentence true in the other world and false in our own and any description whatsoever which applies to the other individual in his world, then by a logician's trick we can construct a description which describes Bobby Dylan in our world and the given individual in his.[4]

To retrace briefly: the skeptic says there are no favored transworld heir lines; we wanted the transworld heir lines in order to make sense of quantification into intensional contexts, that is, quantification over *individuals* into intensional contexts. Back at the problem of quantifying-in, the skeptic might offer a kind of antiseptic (perhaps "sterile" is a better word) version as follows: Replace such formulations as

> Necessarily x is bald

with free "x", by either

> For *all* descriptions α which in fact describe x the proposition expressed by $\ulcorner \alpha$ is bald$\urcorner$ is necessary.

or

> For *some* description α which in fact describes x the proposition expressed by $\ulcorner \alpha$ is bald$\urcorner$ is necessary.

These two make sense, according to the skeptic, but nothing in between. In view of the logician's trick, however, the first virtually reduces to

> Necessarily everything is bald,

and the second reduces to

> Necessarily something is bald

Among proponents of the skeptical view, I would count William Kneale, Church, half of Quine, and myself at times. I count only half of Quine because, although he is skeptical about quantifying into modal contexts, and I believe for pretty much the reasons I have indicated, he appears

---

4. Let α describe the other individual in the world in which Φ is true. Then, $\ulcorner$The $x((x = $ Bobby Dylan $\wedge \sim\phi)$ v $(x = \alpha \wedge \phi))\urcorner$ is the required description.

to have no qualms about quantifying into epistemological contexts such as "Wyman believes that x is bald". Of course, his discussions don't reach the point of talking about possible worlds and transworld identifications so he might just reject our whole way of looking at these problems.[5]

I turn now to the second response, the metaphysical position. This is the typical view of logicians. Let me tell the philosophers how logicians think about possible worlds. They identify a possible world with a certain construct which they call a *model*. This construct will depend in an essential way on some language L which might be used to describe the possible world. The model is usually a function or an ordered n-tuple or something of that sort. It has two main features. First, for each style of variable in L, the model provides a set (usually nonempty) as universe of discourse for that style of variable. Distinct styles of variables represent distinct grammatical categories, so we might say that the model provides a set of entities which forms the ontology for each grammatical category of L. Second, the model provides an extension for each nonlogical constant of L, an extension chosen from the ontology corresponding to the grammatical category of the constant. The model, so to speak, gives us the extension of all the atomic expressions of L, and from this we can obtain the extension of any compound expression of L, in particular, the truth value of any sentence of L.

There are two interesting reasons for calling these things "models." First, the primary use of logicians, is in the sense of "exemplar" as in "he is the very model of a modern major general". In this sense we speak of a model as being a model *of* any set of sentences which correctly describe the possible world represented by the model. The second reason for calling these things models is that they *represent* possible worlds. It is reasonable to say that every possible world is represented by some model and that, assuming that there are no unexpressed logical dependencies among the nonlogical constants of L, every model represents some (logically) possible world.

As long as we relied only on a syntactical criterion—being able to derive an explicit contradiction—to tell us when a sentence was logically consistent, we ran the danger that a sentence which under the intended interpretation could not be true in any possible circumstances still would not yield an

---

5. In 1968, I undertook a more detailed examination of Quine's views on quantifying into epistemological contexts ("Quantifying In," *Synthese* [December 1968]). It, too, I fear, is a *locus classicus* of a philosophical mistake. At least it is a different mistake.

explicit contradiction. This could come about if axioms or rules were not formulated in a sufficiently strong way. And without some independent notion of truth in a possible world there was little to say about the adequacy of such formulations. Insofar as we are satisfied that models represent all possible worlds, and no impossible worlds, they provide the independent criterion against which to check our formulations of axioms and rules. This idea of using models to represent possible worlds was really quite clever. I think it is fair to say that it is due mainly to Tarski and that about 37 percent of the work in logic over the past thirty years is based on it.

In fact, the use of models as representatives of possible worlds has become so natural to logicians that they sometimes take seriously what are really only artifacts of the model. In particular, they are led almost unconsciously to adopt a *bare particular metaphysics*. Why? Because the model so nicely separates the bare particular from its clothing. The elements of the universe of discourse of a model have an existence which is quite independent of whatever properties the model happens to tack onto them. Suppose we want a model for the sentence of L which asserts that there is exactly one thing and that it is a unicorn. A model for such a sentence must have a universe with only one element, and the extension assigned to the predicate "is a unicorn" must be the set consisting of that single element. And that is *all* that is required of the model. It is certainly *not* required that the single element of the universe of the model really be a unicorn. That would make the whole idea of the models unworkable (since there are no unicorns). The single element of the universe of the model may be Jaakko Hintikka, or more likely, because logicians like their entities to exhibit a maximum degree of purity, it may be the null set, or singleton null. But, at any rate, it will be some definite entity which, in this model, is dressed as a unicorn.

Let me refer in a loose way to this kind of situation by saying that the entity in question is *intrinsically* Professor Hintikka or the null set or whatever, and *extrinsically* a unicorn. Most of the time logicians recognize a certain lack of significance in the intrinsic nature of the elements of the universe of a model (except, of course, with respect to identity and difference, i.e., how *many* of them there are) and focus their attention on isomorphism classes of models (two models being isomorphic if their universes can be put into a one-to-one correspondence in such a way that corresponding elements differ only intrinsically). But there is a kind of confusion as to whether we should think about isomorphic models as distinctive representatives of the same possible world, or as representatives of distinct possible worlds which differ only as to individuals (i.e., bare particulars). The last is in violation of the law of the identity of indiscernibles (that law becomes interesting primarily in these transworld situations).[6]

I hope you see how taking the intrinsic nature of the elements of the universe of a model seriously is connected with the bare particular metaphysics. If we adopt this metaphysical view, we have a simple solution to the transworld identification problem: we identify by bare particulars. If our worlds are represented by models and we take the elements of the universe of the models to be (or represent) bare particulars, individuated by their intrinsic characteristics, then there is no difficulty from the point of view of the metalanguage in making such identifications. A metalanguage in which we talk explicitly about models provides us with a kind of meta-x-ray of the bare particular lurking beneath each individual. For example, let us take our earlier model, call it M_1, of "There is exactly one thing and it's a unicorn". To identify that unicorn in some other model M_2, say, of "Everything wears sandals", we ignore the extrinsic characteristics of the unicorn and the hippies and check instead to see if Professor Hintikka who appeared in M_1 as a unicorn reappears in M_2 as, say, Timothy Leary.[7]

This metaphysical conception is at the heart of much of the extremely interesting work that has been done on the semantics of modal logic in the last twenty years. It appears most explicitly in Saul Kripke's work, but occurs also in Carnap's pioneering article of 1946, "Modalities and Quantification."

The distinction between intrinsic and extrinsic characteristics is somewhat blurred in Carnap's article because his systems were intended to have *abstract* entities such as space-time positions as the values of the variables. Thus he was not faced with the problem of finding entities to appear as unicorns. He did have to find space-time positions to appear as occupied-by-a-unicorn, but the conception of a space-time position separable from its occupant still seems to me some distance from that of a bare particular separable from all its properties. (Maybe not.) I think this is an interesting and even relevant problem, but I won't pursue it here.

---

6. I wish I hadn't said this.

7. That is, reappears in M_2 "clothed" in the predicates known to apply to Timothy Leary, a notorious sandal wearer of the sixties.

Now I want to move on to the third position on transworld identifications: the relativistic. This position might be associated with the bundle-of-qualities metaphysics insofar as it is associated with any particular metaphysical view. We so-to-speak look only at the clothes, and we identify individuals in terms of their strikingly similar manner of dress, i.e., their sharing of a large number of prominent qualities. Our view of individuals in different worlds is through the Jules Verne-o-scope, which, you recall, enables us to compare fingerprints, ASCAP registries, and even CIA files, but does not allow us to see into any underlying bare particular as does the meta-x-ray machine of the previous position. Now let us go back to some of the cases considered earlier; first, the world in which I brought my other pen to Chicago, call that world "p". [Note that I have actually introduced this world in terms of a transworld identification of myself, but let's neglect that. Given sufficient time or technical skill I might have introduced it by reading its complete book of history or showing you transcriptions from the Verne-o-scope.] I think we would have no difficulty in deciding with what individual of that world to connect Terence Parsons. Let's call that individual "Parsons-in-p". In the terminology of my colleague David K. Lewis, Parsons-in-p is a *counterpart* of our Parsons.[8] He is not *identical* with our Parsons, because *he* is sitting next to a man carrying a black pen, whereas our Parsons is sitting next to a man without one.[6] And whatever you may think about the identity of indiscernibles, *no* sensible person would deny the indiscernibility of identicals. We call Parsons-in-p and our Parsons counterparts, in spite of this difference, because we regard the difference as inessential, especially in view of the overwhelming similarities. Our world and p are very much alike, and that makes the transworld identifications quite easy. But as the disparity grows, these identifications become more difficult. And we find ourselves forced to make finer and finer discriminations between what is essential to Professor Parsons (being named "Terence Parsons"? being a philosopher? being rational?) and what is only accidentally true of him (sitting next to a man carrying a red pen? having lived in California? being bearded?). What we are searching for is his *essence,* that which identifies an individual of any possible world W as Parsons-in-W, or more exactly: as being the counterpart in w of our Professor Parsons.

---

8. David K. Lewis, "Counterpart Theory and Quantified Modal Logic," *Journal of Philosophy,* 65 (1968); Chapter 5 of this anthology.

Don't get confused here. I'm not talking about anything so prosaic as the intension of some particular name, say, the name "Professor Terence Parsons"; I'm talking about a counterpart of *him* (pointing).

I prefer to think of an essence in this way (as a transworld heir line) rather than in the more familiar way (as a collection of properties) because the more familiar way too much suggests the idea of a fixed and final essential *description,* and that the essence should somehow be expressible, whereas my way of thinking of essences seems to me to accord better with our intuitions and the ordinary practices of scientists. When geographers decide whether the Missouri-Mississippi is one river or two, demographers whether Los Angeles and Ventura form one metropolitan area or two, and jurists whether bludgeoning the victim with the spent rifle constitutes a second attempted murder or a continuation of the first, they are neither searching for a metaphysical oneness (a common bare particular) nor are they applying a previously fixed formula for, say, the individuation of rivers and the Mississippi in particular. Instead they make a determination based on a careful examination of all the facts of the case and aimed at the discovery of especially prominent characteristics relevant to the particular science. Typically, each case is judged on its merits (within certain broad guidelines) and at no point is a fixed and final principle of individuation, or essence, offered.

From here on out, when I speak of "transworld identifications" you should understand that I am not speaking of identities in the strict sense, but of counterparts. Since each transworld heir line corresponds to an individual concept, the essences are some subset of the individual concepts, namely, those which link counterparts. Remember that we admit individual concepts that are not the intension of any singular term, and some essences may be of this form.

I believe we all have at least partial intuitions about many essences. If you will allow a momentary indulgence in the subjective, I might remark that I have the feeling that some things are so unremarkable that they have no essence, which is to say more than that they have no counterparts. (The latter might hold of an extremely vivid person whose remarkable qualities were somehow specific to this world.) And that other persons, for example Da Vinci, seem to me to have more than one essence.

It may help to clarify this idea of an essence if I make explicit what is implicit in the analogy to the decisions of geographers, demographers, and jurists, namely, that any choice of essences (from among *all* the individual concepts) is *relative* to certain interests. Thus the constant appearance in my earlier formulations of such adjectives as "relevant", "prominent", etc. We can acknowledge the skeptic's point regarding the plentitude of definite descriptions of a single object, where each description expresses a different individual concept (i.e., a different candidate for the object's essence), and still maintain that relative to certain interests, one description may be more relevant or pertinent than another. If we inquire after the unique essence of Sir Lancelot, Lady Guinevere, King Arthur, and Lancelot's mother would no doubt each answer differently to the question: "What makes this knight different from all other knights?"

Suppose I spend twelve hours in the hospital, go home, spend a few days feeling lousy, and return to the hospital for another twelve hours. How many periods of confinement and of what length have I spent? My insurance company, which only wants to pay for certain medical charges when connected with a *serious* illness, restricts such payments to cases involving a single period of hospital confinement lasting at least eighteen hours. But they count interrupted confinements as single periods provided that I do not return to work during the interruption. So from their point of view I was confined to the hospital for a single period of twenty-four hours. But the hospital accountant, who is interested in determining appropriate hospital rates, must distinguish the variable costs of maintaining me in the hospital from the fixed costs of admitting, discharging, and billing me, because these latter costs are independent of the *length* of the period of confinement. So from his point of view I was confined to the hospital for two separate periods of twelve hours each.

If my imagination were not exhausted at this point, I could probably think of someone whose interests are such that the color of the pen in my pocket would be of such importance that he would not make what we earlier thought were the natural connections between individuals in our world and those in *p*.

Let me point out here that the results and the technical constructions of logicians who might be described as using the metaphysical method could also be described in terms of the present method. As conceived in accordance with the metaphysical position, the transworld identification of Hintikka appearing as a unicorn and Hintikka appearing as Timothy Leary was based on the previous isolation of Hintikka as common bare particular of the unicorn and Timothy Leary. This is the substance-before-accident point of view. But suppose instead that for some reason we wish to identify Timothy Leary and the unicorn solely in view of their extrinsic characteristics; possibly both exhibit a certain unique dreamy expression in which we are very interested. We might now conceive of the logician's representation of the two possible worlds by models in which a single entity, Professor Hintikka, appears as the unicorn in one model and as Timothy Leary in the other, as being simply a technical device to carry out the preconceived identification. You see we have reversed the whole procedure. This is the accident-before-substance point of view. First we decide how we want to connect individuals and then we treat those individuals that we want to connect as identical.

I rather like this last way of conceiving of models in connection with the transworld identification problem. The only remaining difficulty in representing our choice of essences in terms of the intrinsic characteristics of the elements of the universe of the model is that it lacks flexibility. It lacks flexibility in that it reduces the problem of transworld identification to a form of ordinary identity within the metalanguage, and so does not permit representation of essences which may merge in one world and divide in another. But once we adopt the relativistic method, such a restriction is plainly undesirable. In many cases, our interests in a person are solely in terms of his office. He is the butcher, or the baker, or the candlestick-maker. It may easily happen that the butcher and the baker are in fact one and the same person (possibly unbeknown to us). Or, though distinct in our world, they may be one in another.[9] In such cases I would say that two essences characterize a single individual in one world, but different individuals in another.

To move to cases where delineation of the essences is less clear-cut, imagine a world like ours through 1842 but in which the counterparts of the parents of William and Henry James have but a single son who is educated at (the counterpart of) Harvard and later accepts a chair in philosophy there, but takes frequent leaves, spent in England writing such novels as *The American, The Bostonians,* etc. His academic work consists of *The Will To Believe, Principles of Psychology* (2 vols.) etc. You fill in the details. If you doubt the possibility of such a combination of essences realized in a single person, just think of our own Bertrand Russell, who is clearly the counterpart of at least three distinct persons in some more plausible world.

There is a wider use for the intensional notions we have been considering than in application to what we would think of, properly speaking, as possible worlds. In considering the foundations of a logic of tenses, or a

9. This "they" is short for the phrase "the butcher and the baker"; it does not refer to the two gentlemen.

logic of token-reflexive words such as "I", "he", "now", and "here" we often come upon a situation in which we have a number of distinct *frames of reference,* which from an abstract logical standpoint function very much like possible worlds. Richard Montague has especially emphasized this idea by attempting to show how the logic of a wide variety of seemingly special theories can be unified within a single logical system which he calls *Pragmatics*.[10] A typical example is the case of temporal logic—a logic of change. Here the frames of reference, or possible worlds, are temporal slices of a world. Now what are the *things* of these possible worlds? Well, just as in the case of the elements of the universe of a model, there are two ways of looking at these things. From what we might call the *meta* point of view (metalanguage or metaphysical), we have some single individual appearing at different times in different roles: first as an infant, next as a child, etc. From this point of view, the infant of 1933 and the adolescent of 1948 are artificially constructed slices of a single person, slices which occur wholly within a single temporal stage. Looked at from the point of view of the temporal slices, i.e., the point of view of the possible world itself, we have as basic entities an infant in one time slice and an adolescent in another. From this point of view, we may undertake to construct the whole person in terms of some means for connecting an infant in one world with a child in another, with an adolescent in another, and so on. But whichever way we look at it, whether we start from the individual slices and construct persons like sandwiches, or start with persons and construct the person stages like slices of baloney, there are two kinds of entities involved: the entity specific to a frame of reference and the superentities which run across frames. If our logical system is viewed in this general way, it again seems undesirable to disallow the possibility of distinct superentities fusing in a single local entity at some particular frame of reference and dividing into two at another frame. Maybe I can express the kind of generality that I want to allow by saying that we should permit what appears as a single thing from one frame of reference to appear as distinct things from another frame. Such fusion and division through time is a feature of the ordinary behavior of corporations, iris, and the amoeba, not to mention pathological behavior in personalities and maple trees. Fusion and subsequent division through space is an ordinary feature of highways. Of course, we could insist that upon division the career of an amoeba ends and two new ones are born (or at least that the original

10. "Pragmatics" in Richard Montague, *Formal Philosophy,* ed. by Richmond Thomason (New Haven: Yale University Press, 1974).

amoeba is identified with one of the pair and one new one is born) and similarly for schizophrenia, corporate mergers, and the state and federal highway systems. But why not let the amoebaeologists, psychologists, economists, and traffic planners settle the question in their own way—in the way that best suits *their* interests.

Let me add here a note of caution to the overly enthusiastic transfer of these general notions back and forth between intensional logic proper (a theory of possible worlds) and, say, time logic (the theory of stages of a single world). I find on introspection that in most cases (though not all) it is the superentity that I think of as basic when considering temporal stages as the possible worlds (and similarly for spatial stages) and the slices, the entities specific to a stage, that I think of as somehow artificial. But when I think about different possible worlds proper (i.e., what might be but is not), the entities specific to a stage seem to be basic and naturally determined and the superentities (the transworld heir lines as I earlier called them) seem to me somehow artificial and determined only relative to certain interests. And I am not sure that further consideration of these intuitions would not lead to the discovery of a logical difference between the two kinds of frame of reference.

I would like to conclude by briefly outlining a formal system which embodies some of the ideas I've been talking about. I call the theory *Essentialism*[6] since it is a theory of the kind of transworld heir lines that I have identified with essences.

ESSENTIALISM

The Language

1. Logical Signs
    (i) Two styles of variables, V^e (the set of variables ranging over essences) and V^i (the set of variables ranging over individuals).
    (ii) $=$, $\forall$, $\exists$, $\rightarrow$, $-$, v, $\wedge$, $\longleftrightarrow$, (,).
    (iii) δ (for $\alpha \in V^e$, $\delta(\alpha)$ denotes the individual determined in the given world by the essence denoted by α).
    (iv) $\Box$ (a kind of logical necessity).

2. Nonlogical Signs
    (i) n-place predicates of individuals and n-place operation symbols applying to individuals.

    (ii) m-n-place propositional operators (these relate individuals and propositions).

    (iii) necessity operators.

3. Terms

    (i) The only terms whose values are essences are the variables in V^e.

    (ii) The *individual* terms (T^i) are given as follows:

        (a) if $x \in V^i$, then $x \in T^i$,

        (b) if $\alpha \in V^e$, then $\delta\,(\alpha) \in T^i$,

        (c) if $t_1, \ldots, t_n$ are in T^i and η is an n-place operator symbols, then $\eta(t_1, \ldots, t_n) \in T^i$.

4. Formulas

    (i) If $\alpha, \beta \in V^e$, $\alpha = \beta$ is a formula,

    (ii) If $t_1, t_2 \in T^i$, $t_1 = t_2$ is a formula.

    (iii) If $t_1, \ldots, t_n \in T^i$ and π is an n-place predicate, then $\pi(t_1, \ldots, t_n)$ is a formula.

    (iv) If ϕ, ψ are formulas, $-\phi$, $(\phi \wedge \psi)$, $(\phi v \psi)$, $(\phi \rightarrow \psi)$, and $(\phi \longleftrightarrow \psi)$ are formulas,

    (v) If ϕ is a formula and $v \in (V^i \cup V^e)$, then $\forall v\phi$, $\forall v\phi$ are formulas.

    (vi) If $t_1, \ldots, t_m \in T^i$, $\phi_1, \ldots, \phi_n$ are formulas, and $\P$ is an m-n-place propositional operator, then $(t_1, \ldots, t_m \;\P\; \phi_1, \ldots, \phi_n)$ is a formula.

For grammatical purposes, $\Box$ is a necessity operator, and all necessity operators are 0-1-place propositional operators.

Model Structures, Models, and Assignments

$\mathscr{A}$ is a model structure iff there are W, U, X, I, P, R, E such that $\mathscr{A} = \langle W, U, X, I, P, R, E \rangle$ and

    1. W is a nonempty set (the set of possible worlds w)

    2. for $w \in W$, U_w is a nonempty set (the set of individuals existing and otherwise, of w)

    3. for $w \in W$, $X_w \in U_w$ (the set of existing individuals of w, X_w may be empty)

    4. I is a function which assigns an appropriate intension to each predicate and operation symbol (e.g., if π is a n-place predicate, $n \rangle o$, then $I(\pi)\,(w)$ is

a set of n-tuples of individuals drawn from U_w. Note the treatment of O-place predicates in 5 below.

5. P is a function which assigns an appropriate intension to each m-n-place propositional operator (other than the necessity operators). Thus, if $\P$ is a m-n-place propositional operator $P(\P)$ is a function whose domain is W, and for $w\epsilon W$, $P(\P)\,(w)$ is a set of m-n-tuples $\langle i_1, \ldots, i_m, P_1, \ldots, P_n \rangle$ where $i_1, \ldots, i_m \epsilon U_w$ and $P_1, \ldots, P_n$ are propositions (a proposition, the sense of an O-place predicate, is here thought of as a subset of W, rather than a characteristic function).

6. R is a function which assigns an appropriate intension to each necessity operator (other than $\square$). Here the extension of a necessity operator is thought of in the way popularized by Kripke, as the set of possible worlds accessible from the given worlds. Thus if $\mathbb{N}$ is a necessity operator and $w\epsilon W$, the extension of $\mathbb{N}$ in w is a subset of W. Hence $R(\mathbb{N})$ is a function whose domain is W and for $w\epsilon W$, $R(\mathbb{N})\,(w) \subseteq W$. (An equivalent formulation is to let $R(\mathbb{N})\subseteq(W \times W)$).

7. E is included in the set of all individual concepts of $\mathcal{A}$. An individual concept of $\mathcal{A}$ is a function which assigns to each $w\epsilon W$, an element of U_w. (E is, intuitively, the set of essences of W).

If $\mathcal{A}$ is as above and $w\epsilon W$, then $\langle w\mathcal{A}\rangle$ is a model.

If $f\epsilon E^{Ve}$, then f is an $\mathcal{A}$-assignment to essence variables.

If $g\epsilon U_w^{vi}$, then g is a w-assignment to individual variables.

If f and g are as above, $(f\cup g)$ is a $\langle w\mathcal{A}\rangle$-assignment. (Every $\langle w\mathcal{A}\rangle$ assignment can be uniquely decomposed into the components f and g).

If h is an assignment and v is a variable in its domain $h_b^v = (h\sim\{\langle v,h(v)\rangle\})\cup\{\langle v,b\rangle\}$.

Value and Satisfaction

Let $\mathcal{A}$ be as above, $w\epsilon W$, and $h\ (=(f\cup g))$ be a $\langle w\mathcal{A}\rangle$ assignment.

The value (extension, denotation) of a term in a model is given as follows: (We treat $\mathcal{A}$ as fixed and write "h-val$_w$" for "h-val$\langle_w \mathcal{A}\rangle$"

1. if $v \epsilon(V^i\cup V^e)$, h-val$_w(v) = h(v)$
2. if $\alpha \epsilon v^e$, h-val$_w(\delta(\alpha)) = h(\alpha)\,(w)$
3. if $t_1, \ldots, t_n\epsilon T^i$, and η is a n-place operation symbol, h-val$_w$ $(\eta(t_1, \ldots, t_m)) = I(\eta)\,(w)\,(h$-val$_w(t_1), \ldots, h$-val$_w(t_n))$.

Satisfaction is given as follows: (Again "$\langle w\mathcal{A}\rangle$" is written as "$w$")

1. if α, $\beta \in V^e$, h sat$_w$ ($\alpha = \beta$) iff $h(\alpha) = h(\beta)$
2. if t_1, $t_2 \in T^i$, h sat$_w$($t_1 = t_2$) iff h-val$_w(t_1) = h$-val$_w(t_2)$
3. if $t_1, \ldots, t_n \in T^i$ and π is an n-place predicate h sat$_w$ ($\pi(t_1, \ldots, t_n)$) iff $\langle h$-val$_w(t_1), \ldots, h$-val$_w(t_n) \rangle \in I(\pi)$ (w)
4. if ϕ, ψ are formulas, h sat$_w(\phi \wedge \psi)$ iff h sat$_w \phi$ and h sat$_w \phi$.
5. Similarly for other sentential connectives
6. if ϕ is a formula, and $v \in V^i$ [$v \in V^e$] h sat$_w$ ($\forall v \, \phi$) iff for all $b \in X_w$ [for all $b \in \exists$] h_b^v sat $_w \phi$.
7. Similarly for existential quantifier.

Auxiliary notion: Given an assignment f of values to V^e, the proposition expressed by a formula Φ, is the one which consists of just those worlds w' in which Φ is true. Since we intend to connect individuals across worlds *only* by way of essences, *individual* variables free in Φ are treated as if bound by a universal quantifier ranging over all of $U_{w'}$ (note that the quantifier in our language allows the individual variables to range only over $X_{w'}$).

Let $f \in \exists^{V^e}$, Φ a formula, $w' \in W$, then $w' \in f$-prop(ϕ) iff for all $g \in U_w \cdot^{vi}$ ($f \cup g$) sat$_{w'}$.

8. If $t_1, \ldots, t_m \in T^i$, $\phi_1, \ldots, \phi_n$ are formulas, and $\P$ is an m-n-place propositional operator, h sat$_w(t_1 \ldots t_m \; \P \; \phi_1 \ldots \phi_n)$ iff h-val$^w(t_1), \ldots, h$-val$_w(t_m)$, f-prop $\phi_1, \ldots f$-prop $(\phi_m)) \in P(\P)$ (w) [recall $h = (f \cup g)$].
9. if $\mathbb{N}$ is a necessity operator and Φ is a formula h sat$_w$ ($\mathbb{N} \, \phi$) iff $R(\mathbb{N})$ (w) c f-propr(ϕ)
10. if ϕ is a formula, h sat$_w(\Box \phi)$ iff f-prop$(\phi) = W$

If ϕ is a formula, and $\langle w \mathscr{A} \rangle$ is a model, ϕ is *true* in $\langle w \mathscr{A} \rangle$ iff for all $\langle w \mathscr{A} \rangle$-assignments h, h sat$_w \phi$

If ϕ is a formula, ϕ is *valid* iff for every model $\langle w \mathscr{A} \rangle$, ϕ is true in $\langle w \mathscr{A} \rangle$.

Axiomatizability

The valid formulas are axiomatizable by means of a finite set of axiom schemes and rules.[11]

---

11. I have here made a deletion. In the original version I claimed that if it were required that E consist of *all* individual concepts of $\mathscr{A}$, the valid formulas would not be axiomatizable. It now seems, in view of recent results by Saul Kripke and independently by Hans Kamp, that this was in error.

If quantifiable variables ranging over all propositions were added, the valid formulas would not be axiomatizable.

Representation of Other Theories

Many known intensional logics, in particular modal logics, are interpretable in Essentialism or one of its extensions obtained by adding some special axioms for one of the necessity operators plus some special axioms about essences.

At least four different interesting propositional functions (in Russell's sense) expressed by "x is bald" can be explicitly represented in Essentialism.

The four propositional functions may be loosely expressed as follows: to the individual x, assign the proposition which includes all those possible worlds in which

(1) every counterpart of x which exists is bald,
(2) some counterpart of x exists and is bald,
(3) every counterpart of x exists and is bald,
(4) some counterpart of x is bald if it exists.

Let ¶ stand for the O-1 place propositional operator "It was asserted that." Then corresponding to the four propositional functions, we have four translations of "It was asserted that x is bald" (with free "x").

(5) $\forall \alpha(\delta(\alpha) = x \rightarrow \P[\forall y(\delta(\alpha) = y) \rightarrow y$ is bald)]),
(6) $\exists \alpha(\delta(\alpha) = x \wedge \P[\exists y(\delta(\alpha) = y) \wedge y$ is bald)]),
(7) $\forall \alpha(\delta(\alpha) = x \rightarrow \P[\exists y(\delta(\alpha) = y) \wedge y$ is bald)]),
(8) $\exists \alpha(\delta(\alpha) = x \wedge \P[\forall y(\delta(\alpha) = y) \rightarrow y$ is bald)]).

Among special axioms on essences the following are of particular interest:

(9) $\forall x \exists \alpha(\delta(\alpha) = x)$,
(10) $\forall \alpha \forall \beta(\exists x(\delta(\alpha) = x \wedge \delta(\beta) = x) \rightarrow \alpha = \beta)$,
      [Note that $[\alpha = \beta \longleftrightarrow \Box (\delta(\alpha) = \delta(\beta))]$ is already an axiom.
(11) $\forall \alpha(\exists x(\delta(\alpha) = x) \rightarrow \Box \exists x(\delta(\alpha) = x))$.

(9) says that everything which exists has at least one essence. (10) says that essences of existing things do not fuse and divide, or equivalently that

everything which exists has at most one essence. (11) says that every counterpart of an existing thing exists. Taken together (9)–(11) say that the "same" things exist in all possible worlds. (9) and (10) taken together say that each existing thing has exactly one counterpart (in each world) which may or may not exist. Note that in the presence of (9) and (10), (5) and (8) become equivalent as do (6) and (7) and that if (11) is added (5) and (6) become equivalent, thus reducing the four propositional functions to one.

If it is desired to treat some or all individual constants t as proper names expressing essences, this can be done by adding axioms of the form:

(12) $\exists \alpha \Box \, (\delta(\alpha) = t)$.

In addition to the four translations (5)–(8), iterated intensional operators provide another dimension of translation in which alternatives are available. Using the method of (5), we may translate "It was asserted that it was asserted that x is bald" in either of the following ways:

(13) $\forall \alpha(\delta(\alpha) = x \rightarrow \P \; \P[\exists y(\delta(\alpha) = y) \rightarrow \delta(\alpha)$ is bald])

(14) $\forall \beta(\delta(\beta) = x \rightarrow \P[\exists z(\delta(\beta) = z) \rightarrow \forall \alpha(\delta(\alpha) = \delta(\beta) \rightarrow$
$\P[\exists y(\delta(\alpha) = y) \rightarrow \delta(\alpha)$ is bald])]).

The first might be thought of as obtaining by applying a compound intensional operation ($\P \; \P$) to a proposition, whereas the second results from iterative application of a single operator. The distinction is connected with an argument by Church in footnote 22 of "A Formulation of the Logic of Sense and Denotation" in *Structure, Method, and Meaning: Essays in Honor of Henry M. Sheffer,* ed. by Pául Henle, H. M. Kallen, and S. K. Langer (New York: Liberal Arts Press, 1951).

A formal system of slightly greater flexibility can be obtained by allowing the class of essences to vary from one possible world to another.

5

Counterpart Theory
and Quantified Modal Logic

DAVID LEWIS
Princeton University

*I. Counterpart Theory**

We can conduct formalized discourse about most topics perfectly well by
means of our all-purpose extensional logic, provided with predicates and a
domain of quantification suited to the subject matter at hand. That is what
we do when our topic is numbers, or sets, or wholes and parts, or strings
of symbols. That is not what we do when our topic is modality: what
might be and what must be, essence and accident. Then we introduce
modal operators to create a special-purpose, nonextensional logic. Why
this departure from our custom? Is it a historical accident, or was it forced
on us somehow by the very nature of the topic of modality?

It was not forced on us. We have an alternative. Instead of formalizing
our modal discourse by means of modal operators, we could follow our
usual practice. We could stick to our standard logic (quantification theory
with identity and without ineliminable singular terms) and provide it with
predicates and a domain of quantification suited to the topic of modality.
That done, certain expressions are available which take the place of modal
operators. The new predicates required, together with postulates on them,
constitute the system I call *Counterpart Theory*.

The primitive predicates of counterpart theory are these four:

Originally published in the *Journal of Philosophy,* 65 (1968), 113–126; reprinted here with
permission of the author and the *Journal of Philosophy.*

*I am indebted to David Kaplan, whose criticisms have resulted in many important im-
provements. A. N. Prior has informed me that my theory resembles a treatment of *de re*
modality communicated to him by P. T. Geach in 1964.

Wx   (x is a possible world)
Ixy   (x is in possible world y)
Ax   (x is actual)
Cxy   (x is a counterpart of y).

The domain of quantification is to contain every possible world and every-thing in every world. The primitives are to be understood according to their English readings and the following postulates:

P1: $\forall x \forall y(Ixy \supset Wy)$
     (Nothing is in anything except a world)
P2: $\forall x \forall y \forall z(Ixy \, \& \, Ixz \, . \supset y = x)$
     (Nothing is in two worlds)
P3: $\forall x \forall y(Cxy \supset \exists z Ixz)$
     (Whatever is a counterpart is in a world)
P4: $\forall x \forall y(Cxy \supset \exists z Iyz)$
     (Whatever has a counterpart is in a world)
P5: $\forall x \forall y \forall z(Ixy \, \& \, Izy \, \& \, Cxz \, . \supset x = z)$
     (Nothing is a counterpart of anything else in its world)
P6: $\forall x \forall y(Ixy \supset Cxx)$
     (Anything in a world is a counterpart of itself)
P7: $\exists x(Wx \, \& \, \forall y(Iyx \equiv Ay))$
     (Some world contains all and only actual things)
P8: $\exists x Ax$
     (Something is actual).

The world mentioned in P7 is unique, by P2 and P8. Let us abbreviate its description:

$$@ =_{df} \imath x \forall y(Iyx \equiv Ay) \quad \text{(the actual world)}.$$

Unactualized possibles, things in worlds other than the actual world, have often been deemed "entia non grata",[1] largely because it is not clear when they are or are not identical. But identity literally understood is no problem for us. Within any one world, things of every category are indi-viduated just as they are in the actual world; things in different worlds are *never* identical, by P2. The counterpart relation is our substitute for identity between things in different worlds.[2] Where some would say that you are in

1. W. V. O. Quine, *Word and Object* (Cambridge, Mass.: MIT Press, 1960), p. 245.

2. Yet with this substitute in use, it would not matter if some things *were* identical with their counterparts after all! P2 serves only to rule out avoidable problems of individuation.

several worlds, in which you have somewhat different properties and somewhat different things happen to you, I prefer to say that you are in the actual world and no other, but you have counterparts in several other worlds. Your counterparts resemble you closely in content and context in important respects. They resemble you more closely than do the other things in their worlds. But they are not really you. For each of them is in his own world, and only you are here in the actual world. Indeed we might say, speaking casually, that your counterparts are you in other worlds, that they and you are the same; but this sameness is no more a literal identity than the sameness between you today and you tomorrow. It would be better to say that your counterparts are men you *would have been,* had the world been otherwise.[3]

The counterpart relation is a relation of similarity. So it is problematic in the way all relations of similarity are: it is the resultant of similarities and dissimilarities in a multitude of respects, weighted by the importances of the various respects[4] and by the degrees of the similarities.[5]

Rudolf Carnap,[6] Stig Kanger,[7] Jaakko Hintikka,[8] Saul Kripke,[9] Richard Montague,[10] and others have proposed interpretations of quantified modal logic on which one thing is allowed to be in several worlds. A reader of this persuasion might suspect that he and I differ only verbally: that what I call a thing in a world is just what he would call a (thing, world) pair, and that what he calls the same thing in several worlds is just what I would call a class of mutual counterparts. But beware. Our difference is not just verbal, for I enjoy a generality he cannot match. The counterpart relation will not, in general, be an equivalence relation. So it will not hold just between

3. This way of describing counterparts is due to L. Sprague de Camp, ''The Wheels of If,'' in *Unknown Fantasy Fiction,* October 1940.

4. As discussed in Michael A. Slote, ''The Theory of Important Criteria,'' *Journal of Philosophy,* 63 (1966), 211–224.

5. The counterpart relation is very like the relation of intersubjective correspondence discussed in Rudolf Carnap, *Der Logische Aufbau der Welt* (Berlin-Schlactensee: Weltkreis-Verlag, 1928), sec. 146.

6. ''Modalities and Quantification,'' *Journal of Symbolic Logic,* 11 (1946), 33–64.

7. *Provability in Logic* (Stockholm: Almqvist and Wiksell, 1957).

8. ''Modality as Referential Multiplicity,'' *Ajatus,* 20 (1957), 49–63.

9. ''A Completeness Theorem in Modal Logic,'' *Journal of Symbolic Logic,* 24 (1959), 1–14; ''Semantical Considerations on Modal Logic,'' *Acta Philosophica Fennica,* 16 (1963), 83–94.

10. ''Logical Necessity, Physical Necessity, Ethics, and Quantifiers,'' *Inquiry,* 3 (1960), 259–269.

those of his (thing, world) pairs with the same first term, no matter how he may choose to identify things between worlds.

It would not have been plausible to postulate that the counterpart relation was transitive. Suppose x_1 in world w_1 resembles you closely in many respects, far more closely than anything else in w_1 does. And suppose x_2 in world w_2 resembles x_1 closely, far more closely than anything else in w_2 does. So x_2 is a counterpart of your counterpart x_1. Yet x_2 might not resemble you very closely, and something else in w_2 might resemble you more closely. If so, x_2 is not your counterpart.

It would not have been plausible to postulate that the counterpart relation was symmetric. Suppose x_3 in world w_3 is a sort of blend of you and your brother; x_3 resembles both of you closely, far more closely than anything else in w_3 resembles either one of you. So x_3 is your counterpart. But suppose also that the resemblance between x_3 and your brother is far closer than that between x_3 and you. If so, you are not a counterpart of x_3.

It would not have been plausible to postulate that nothing in any world had more than one counterpart in any other world. Suppose x_{4a} and x_{4b} in world w_4 are twins; both resemble you closely; both resemble you far more closely than anything else in w_4 does; both resemble you equally. If so, both are your counterparts.

It would not have been plausible to postulate that no two things in any world had a common counterpart in any other world. Suppose you resemble both the twins x_{4a} and x_{4b} far more closely than anything else in the actual world does. If so, you are a counterpart of both.

It would not have been plausible to postulate that, for any two worlds, anything in one was a counterpart of something in the other. Suppose there is something x_5 in world w_5—say, Batman—which does not much resemble anything actual. If so, x_5 is not a counterpart of anything in the actual world.

It would not have been plausible to postulate that, for any two worlds, anything in one had some counterpart in the other. Suppose whatever thing x_6 in world w_6 it is that resembles you more closely than anything else in w_6 is nevertheless quite unlike you; nothing in w_6 resembles you at all closely. If so, you have no counterpart in w_6.

II. Translation

Counterpart theory and quantified modal logic seem to have the same subject matter; seem to provide two rival ways of formalizing our modal discourse. In that case they should be intertranslatable; indeed they are. Hence I need not give directions for formalizing modal discourse directly by means of counterpart theory; I can assume the reader is accustomed to formalizing modal discourse by means of modal operators, so I need only give directions for translating sentences of quantified modal logic into sentences of counterpart theory.

Counterpart theory has at least three advantages over quantified modal logic as a vehicle for formalized discourse about modality. (1) Counterpart theory is a theory, not a special-purpose intensional logic. (2) Whereas the obscurity of quantified modal logic has proved intractable, that of counterpart theory is at least divided, if not conquered. We can trace it to its two independent sources. There is our uncertainty about analyticity, and, hence, about whether certain descriptions describe possible worlds; and there is our uncertainty about the relative importance of different respects of similarity and dissimilarity, and, hence, about which things are counterparts of which. (3) If the translation scheme I am about to propose is correct, every sentence of quantified modal logic has the same meaning as a sentence of counterpart theory, its translation; but not every sentence of counterpart theory is, or is equivalent to, the translation of any sentence of quantified modal logic. Therefore, starting with a fixed stock of predicates other than those of counterpart theory, we can say more by adding counterpart theory than we can by adding modal operators.

Now let us examine my proposed translation scheme.[11] We begin with some important special cases, leading up to a general definition.

First consider a closed (0-place) sentence with a single, initial modal operator: $\Box\phi$ or $\Diamond\phi$. It is given the familiar translation: $\forall\beta(W\beta\supset\phi^\beta)$ (ϕ holds in any possible world β) or $\exists\beta(W\beta\ \&\ \phi^\beta)$ (ϕ holds in some possible world β). To form the sentence ϕ^β (ϕ holds in world β) from the given sentence ϕ, we need only restrict the range of each quantifier in ϕ to the domain of things in the world denoted by β; that is, we replace $\forall\alpha$ by $\forall\alpha(I\alpha\beta\supset\ \cdots\ )$ and $\exists\alpha$ by $\exists\alpha(I\alpha\beta\ \&\ \cdots\ )$ throughout ϕ.

Next consider a 1-place open sentence with a single, initial modal oper-

---

11. NOTATION: Sentences are mentioned by means of the Greek letters 'ϕ,' 'ψ,' . . . ; variables by means of 'α,' 'β,' 'γ,' 'δ,' . . . . If ϕ is any n-place sentence and $\alpha_1 \ldots \alpha_n$ are any n different variables, then $\phi\alpha_1\cdots\alpha_n$ is the sentence obtained by substituting α_1 uniformly for the alphabetically first free variable in ϕ, α_2 for the second, and so on. Variables introduced in translation are to be chosen in some systematic way that prevents confusion of bound variables. Symbolic expressions are used autonymously.

ator: $\Box\phi\alpha$ or $\Diamond\phi\alpha$. It is given the translation $\forall\beta\forall\gamma(W\beta\ \&\ I\gamma\beta\ \&\ C\gamma\alpha\ .\ \supset \phi^\beta\gamma)$ (ϕ holds of every counterpart γ of α in any world β) or $\exists\beta\exists\gamma(W\beta\ \& I\gamma\beta\ \&\ C\gamma\alpha\ \&\ \phi^\beta\gamma)$ (ϕ holds of some counterpart γ of α in some world β). Likewise for an open sentence with any number of places.

If the modal operator is not initial, we translate the subsentence it governs. And if there are quantifiers that do not lie within the scope of any modal operator, we must restrict their range to the domain of things in the actual world; for that is their range in quantified modal logic, whereas an unrestricted quantifier in counterpart theory would range at least over all the worlds and everything in any of them. A sentence of quantified modal logic that contains *no* modal operator—a nonmodal sentence in a modal context—is therefore translated simply by restricting its quantifiers to things in the actual world.

Finally, consider a sentence in which there are modal operators within the scopes of other modal operators. Then we must work inward; to obtain ϕ^β from ϕ we must not only restrict quantifiers in ϕ but also translate any subsentences of ϕ with initial modal operators.

The general translation scheme can best be presented as a direct definition of the translation of a sentence ϕ of quantified modal logic:

T1: The translation of ϕ is $\phi^{@}$ (ϕ holds in the actual world); that is, in primitive notation, $\exists\beta(\forall\alpha(I\alpha\beta \equiv A\alpha)\ \&\ \phi^\beta)$

followed by a recursive definition of ϕ^β (ϕ holds in world β)

T2a: ϕ^β is ϕ, if ϕ is atomic

T2b: $(\sim\phi)^\beta$ is $\sim\phi^\beta$

T2c: $(\phi\ \&\ \psi)^\beta$ is $\phi^\beta\ \&\ \psi^\beta$

T2d: $(\phi\ v\ \psi)^\beta$ is $\phi^\beta\ v\ \psi^\beta$

T2e: $(\phi\supset\psi)^\beta$ is $\phi^\beta\ \supset\ \psi^\beta$

T2f: $(\phi\ \equiv\ \psi)^\beta$ is $\phi^\beta\ \equiv\ \psi^\beta$

T2g: $(\forall\alpha\phi)^\beta$ is $\forall\alpha(I\alpha\beta\ \supset\ \phi^\beta)$

T2h: $(\exists\alpha\phi)^\beta$ is $\exists\alpha(I\alpha\beta\ \&\ \phi^\beta)$

T2i: $(\Box\phi\alpha_1\ldots\ \alpha_n)^\beta$ is $\forall\beta_1\forall\gamma_1\ \ldots\ \forall\gamma_n$
$(W\beta_1\ \&\ I\gamma_1\beta_1\ \&\ C\gamma_1\alpha_1\ \&\cdots\&\ I\gamma_n\beta_1\ \&\ C\gamma_n\alpha_n\ .\ \supset\ \phi^{\beta_1}\gamma_1$
$\ldots\ \gamma_n)$

T2j: $(\Diamond\phi\alpha_1\ldots\ \alpha_n)^\beta$ is $\exists\beta_1\exists\gamma_1\ \ldots\ \exists\gamma_n$
$(W\beta_1\ \&\ I\gamma_1\beta_1\ \&\ C\gamma_1\alpha_1\ \&\ \ldots\ \&\ I\gamma_n\beta_1\ \&\ C\gamma_n\alpha_n\ \&\ \phi^{\beta_1}\gamma_1\ldots\ \gamma_n)$.

Using these two definitions, we find, for example, that

$$\forall x F x$$
$$\Diamond \exists x F x$$
$$\Box F x$$
$$\forall x (F x \supset \Box F x)$$
$$\Box \Diamond F x$$

are translated, respectively, as

$\forall x (Ix@ \supset Fx)$
(Everything actual is an F)

$\exists y (Wy$ & $\exists x (Ixy$ & $Fx))$
(Some possible world contains an F)

$\forall y_1 \forall x_1 (Wy_1$ & $Ix_1 y_1$ & $Cx_1 x . \supset Fx_1)$
(Every counterpart of x, in any world, is an F)

$\forall x (Ix@ \supset . Fx \supset \forall y_1 \forall x_1 (Wy_1$ & $Ix_1 y_1$ & $Cx_1 x . \supset Fx_1))$
(If anything is a counterpart of an actual F, then it is an F)

$\forall y_1 \forall x_1 (Wy_1$ & $Ix_1 y_1$ & $Cx_1 x . \supset \exists y_2 \exists x_2 (Wy_2$ & $Ix_2 y_2$ & $Cx_2 x_1$ & $Fx_2))$
(Every counterpart of x has a counterpart which is an F).

The reverse translation, from sentences of counterpart theory to sentences of quantified modal logic, can be done by finite search whenever it can be done at all. For if a modal sentence ψ is the translation of a sentence ϕ of counterpart theory, then ψ must be shorter than ϕ and ψ must contain no predicates or variables not in ϕ. But not every sentence of counterpart theory is the translation of a modal sentence, or even an equivalent of the translation of a modal sentence. For instance, our postulates P1–P7 are not.

It may disturb us that the translation of $\forall x \Box \exists y (x = y)$ (everything actual necessarily exists) comes out true even if something actual lacks a counterpart in some world. To avoid this, we might be tempted to adopt the alternative translation scheme, brought to my attention by David Kaplan, in which T2i and T2j are replaced by

T2i': $(\Box \phi \alpha_1 \ldots \alpha_n)^\beta$ is $\forall \beta_1 (W\beta_1 \supset \exists \gamma_1 \ldots \exists \gamma_n (I\gamma_1 \beta_1$ & $C\gamma_1 \alpha_1$ & $\ldots$ & $I\gamma_n \beta_1$ & $C\gamma_n \alpha_n$ & $\phi^{\beta_1} \gamma_1 \ldots \gamma_n))$

T2j': $(\Diamond \phi \alpha_1 \ldots \alpha_n)^\beta$ is $\exists \beta_1 (W\beta_1$ & $\forall \gamma_1 \ldots \forall \gamma_n (I\gamma_1 \beta_1$ & $C\gamma_1 \alpha_1$ & $\ldots$ & $I\gamma_n \beta_1$ & $C\gamma_n \alpha_n . \supset \phi^{\beta_1} \gamma_1 \ldots \gamma_n))$

with heterogeneous rather than homogeneous quantifiers. Out of the frying pan, into the fire: with T2j′, $\exists x \diamond (x \neq x)$ (something actual is possibly non-self-identical) comes out true unless everything actual has a counterpart in every world! We might compromise by taking T2i′ and T2j, but at the price of sacrificing the ordinary duality of necessity and possibility.[12] So I chose to take T2i and T2j.

III. Essentialism

Quine has often warned us that by quantifying past modal operators we commit ourselves to the view that "an object, of itself and by whatever name or none, must be seen as having some of its traits necessarily and others contingently, despite the fact that the latter traits follow just as analytically from some ways of specifying the object as the former traits do from other ways of specifying it."[13] This so-called "Aristotelian essentialism"—the doctrine of essences not relative to specifications— "should be every bit as congenial to [the champion of quantified modal logic] as quantified modal logic itself."[14]

Agreed. Essentialism is congenial. We do have a way of saying that an attribute is an essential attribute of an object—essential regardless of how the object happens to have been specified and regardless of whether the attribute follows analytically from any or all specifications of the object.

Consider the attribute expressed by a 1-place sentence ϕ and the object denoted by a singular term[15] ζ. To say that this attribute is an essential attribute of this object is to assert the translation of $\Box \phi \zeta$.

But we have not yet considered how to translate a modal sentence containing a singular term. For we know that any singular term ζ may be treated as a description $\iota \alpha (\psi \alpha)$ (although often only by letting ψ contain some artificial predicate made from a proper name); and we know that any description may be eliminated by Russell's contextual definition. Our translation scheme did not take account of singular terms because they need

12. If we also postulate that the counterpart relation is an equivalence relation, we get an interpretation like that of Føllesdal in "Referential Opacity in Modal Logic" (Ph.D. dissertation, Harvard University, 1961), sec. 20, and in "A Model-Theoretic Approach to Causal Logic," forthcoming in *Det Kongeliger Norske Videnskabers Selskabs Forhandlinger*.

13. "Reference and Modality," in *From a Logical Point of View*, 2d ed. (Cambridge, Mass.: Harvard University, 1961), p. 155.

14. "Reply to Professor Marcus," in *The Ways of Paradox and Other Essays* (New York: Random House, 1966), p. 182.

15. NOTATION: Terms are mentioned by means of the Greek letters 'ζ,' 'η,'. . . . The sentence $\phi \zeta$ is that obtained by substituting the term ζ uniformly into the 1-place sentence ϕ.

never occur in the primitive notation of quantified modal logic. We must always eliminate singular terms before translating; afterward, if we like, we can restore them.

There is just one hitch: before eliminating a description, we must assign it a scope. Different choices of scope will, in general, lead to nonequivalent translations. This is so even if the eliminated description denotes precisely one thing in the actual world and in every possible world.[16]

Taking ζ as a description $\imath\alpha(\psi\alpha)$ and assigning it narrow scope, our sentence $\Box\ \phi\zeta$ is interpreted as

$$\Box\ \exists\alpha(\forall\delta(\psi\delta \equiv \delta = \alpha)\ \&\ \phi\alpha).$$

Its translation under this interpretation is

$$\forall\beta(W\beta \supset \exists\alpha(I\alpha\beta\ \&\ \forall\delta(I\delta\beta \supset.\ \psi^\beta\delta \equiv \delta = \alpha)\ \&\ \phi^\beta\alpha))$$
(Any possible world β contains a unique α such that $\psi^\beta\alpha$; and for
     any such α, $\phi^\beta\alpha$).

This is an interpretation *de dicto*: the modal operator attaches to the already closed sentence $\phi\zeta$. It is referentially opaque: the translation of an ostensible use of Leibniz's Law

$$\Box\phi\zeta$$
$$\underline{\eta = \zeta}$$
$$\therefore \Box\ \phi\eta$$

or of an ostensible existential generalization.

$$\underline{\Box\phi\zeta}$$
$$\therefore \exists\alpha\Box\phi\alpha$$

is an invalid argument if the terms involved are taken as descriptions with narrow scope.

Taking ζ as a description with wide scope, $\Box\phi\zeta$ is interpreted as

$$\exists\alpha(\forall\delta(\psi\delta \equiv \delta = \alpha)\ \&\ \Box\phi\alpha)$$

---

16. I follow Arthur Smullyan's treatment of scope ambiguity in modal sentences, given in "Modality and Description," *Journal of Symbolic Logic,* 13 (1948), 31–37, as qualified by Wilson's objection, in *The Concept of Language* (Toronto: University Press, 1959), p. 43, that some ostensible uses of Leibniz's law on modal sentences are invalid under *any* choice of scope in the conclusion.

and translated as

$\exists \alpha (I\alpha@ \ \& \ \forall \delta (I\delta@ \supset . \ \psi^{@}\delta \equiv \delta = \alpha) \ \& \ \forall \beta \forall \gamma (W\beta \ \& \ I\gamma\beta \ \& \ C\gamma\alpha . \supset \phi^{\beta}\gamma))$

(The actual world contains a unique α such that $\psi^{@}\alpha$; and for any counterpart γ thereof, in any world β, $\phi^{\beta}\gamma$).

This is an interpretation *de re*: the modal operator attaches to the open sentence ϕ to form a new open modal sentence $\Box\phi$, and the attribute expressed by $\Box\phi$ is then predicated of the actual thing denoted by ζ. This interpretation is referentially transparent: the translation of an ostensible use of Leibniz's law or of an ostensible existential generalization is a valid argument if the terms involved are taken as descriptions with wide scope.

How are we to choose between the two interpretations of $\Box\phi\zeta$? Often we cannot, unless by fiat; there is a genuine ambiguity. But there are several conditions that tend to favor the wide-scope interpretation as the more natural: (1) whenever ζ is a description formed by turning a proper name into an artificial predicate; (2) whenever the description ζ has what Keith Donnellan calls its referential use;[17] (3) whenever we are prepared to accept

ζ is something α such that necessarily $\phi\alpha$

as one possible English reading of $\Box\phi\zeta$. (The force of the third condition is due to the fact that $\exists\alpha(\zeta = \alpha \ \& \ \Box\phi\alpha)$ is unambiguously equivalent to $\Box\phi\zeta$ with ζ given wide scope.[18])

The translations of $\Box\phi\zeta$ under its two interpretations are logically independent. Neither follows from the other just by itself. But with the aid of suitable auxiliary premises we can go in both directions. The inference from the narrow-scope translation to the wide-scope translation (exportation[19]) requires the further premise

$\exists\alpha(I\alpha@ \ \& \ \forall\beta\forall\gamma(I\gamma\beta \ \& \ C\gamma\alpha . \supset \forall\delta(I\delta\beta \supset . \ \psi^{\beta}\delta \equiv \delta = \gamma)))$

(There is something α in the actual world, any counterpart γ of which is the only thing δ in its world β such that $\psi^{\beta}\delta$)

---

17. "Reference and Definite Descriptions," *Philosophical Review*, 75 (1966), 281–304.

18. Cf. Hintikka, *Knowledge and Belief: An Introduction to the Logic of the Two Notions* (Ithaca, N.Y.: Cornell University Press, 1962), pp. 156–157.

19. I follow Quine's use of this term in "Quantifiers and Propositional Attitudes," in *The Ways of Paradox*, p. 188.

which is a simplified equivalent of the translation of $\exists\alpha\square(\zeta = \alpha)$ with ζ given narrow scope.[20] The inference from the wide-scope translation to the narrow-scope translation (importation) requires the same auxiliary premise, and another as well:

$\exists\alpha(I\alpha@ \;\&\; \forall\delta(I\delta@ \supset .\; \psi@\delta \equiv \delta = \alpha) \;\&\; \forall\beta(W\beta \supset \exists\gamma\,(I\gamma\beta \;\&\; C\gamma\alpha)))$

(The unique α in the actual world such that $\psi^{@}\alpha$, has at least one counterpart γ in any world β).

This second auxiliary premise is not equivalent to the translation of any modal sentence.[21]

In general, of course, there will be more than two ways to assign scopes. Consider $\square\diamond(\eta = \zeta)$. Each description may be given narrow, medium, or wide scope; so there are nine nonequivalent translations.

It is the wide-scope, *de re*, transparent translation of $\square\;\phi\zeta$ which says that the attribute expressed by ϕ is an essential attribute of the thing denoted by ζ. In short, an essential attribute of something is an attribute it shares with all of its counterparts. All your counterparts are probably human; if so, you are essentially human. All your counterparts are even more probably corporeal; if so, you are essentially corporeal.

An attribute that something shares with all its counterparts is an essential attribute of that thing, part of its essence. The whole of its essence is the intersection of its essential attributes, the attribute it shares with all and only its counterparts. (*The* attribute, because there is no need to distinguish attributes that are coextensive not only in the actual world but also in every possible world.) There may or may not be an open sentence that expresses the attribute that is the essence of something; to assert that the attribute expressed by ϕ is the essence of the thing denoted by ζ is to assert

$\exists\alpha(I\alpha@ \;\&\; \forall\delta(I\delta@ \supset .\; \psi^{@}\delta \equiv \delta = \alpha) \;\&\; \forall\beta\forall\gamma(I\gamma\beta \supset .\; C\gamma\alpha \equiv \phi^{\beta}\gamma))$

(The actual world contains a unique α such that $\psi^{@}\alpha$; and for anything γ in any world β, γ is a counterpart of α if and only if $\phi^{\beta}\gamma$).

This sentence is not equivalent to the translation of any modal sentence.

---

20. Cf. Hintikka, *op. cit.*, pp. 138–155.

21. But under any variant translation in which T2i is replaced by T2i′, it would be equivalent to the translation of $\square\;\exists\alpha(\zeta = \alpha)$ (ζ necessarily exists) with ζ given wide scope.

Essence and counterpart are interdefinable. We have just defined the essence of something as the attribute it shares with all and only its counterparts; a counterpart of something is anything having the attribute which is its essence. (This is not to say that that attribute is the *counterpart's* essence, or even an essential attribute of the counterpart.)

Perhaps there are certain attributes that can only be essential attributes of things, never accidents. Perhaps every human must be essentially human; more likely, perhaps everything corporeal must be essentially corporeal. The attribute expressed by ϕ is of this sort, incapable of being an accident, just in case it is closed under the counterpart relation; this is, just in case

$$\forall\alpha\forall\beta\forall\gamma\forall\beta_1(I\alpha\beta \ \& \ I\gamma\beta_1 \ \& \ C\gamma\alpha \ \& \ \phi^\beta\alpha. \supset \phi^\beta\gamma)$$

(For any counterpart γ in any world β_1 of anything α in any world β, if $\phi^\beta\alpha$ then $\phi^{\beta_1}\gamma$).

This is a simplified equivalent of the translation of

$$\Box\forall\alpha(\phi\alpha \supset \Box\phi\alpha).$$

We might wonder whether these attributes incapable of being accidents are what we call "natural kinds." But notice first that we must disregard the necessarily universal attribute, expressed, for instance, by the open sentence $\alpha = \alpha$, since it is an essential attribute of everything. And notice second that arbitrary unions of attributes incapable of being accidents are themselves attributes incapable of being accidents; so to exclude gerrymanders we must confine ourselves to *minimal* attributes incapable of being accidents. All of these may indeed be natural kinds; but these cannot be the only natural kinds, since some unions and all intersections of natural kinds are themselves natural kinds.

IV. Modal Principles

Translation into counterpart theory can settle disputed questions in quantified modal logic. We can test a suggested modal principle by seeing whether its translation is a theorem of counterpart theory; or, if not, whether the extra postulates that would make it a theorem are plausible. We shall consider eight principles and find only one that should be accepted.

$$\Box\phi \prec \Box \ \Box \ \phi \quad \text{(Becker's principle)}.$$

The translation is not a theorem unless ϕ is a closed sentence, but would have been a theorem in general under the rejected postulate that the counterpart relation was transitive.

$$\phi \prec \Box \Diamond \phi \quad \text{(Brouwer's principle)}.$$

The translation is not a theorem unless ϕ is a closed sentence, but would have been a theorem in general under the rejected postulate that the counterpart relation was symmetric.

$$\alpha_1 = \alpha_2 \prec \Box \alpha_1 = \alpha_2 \quad (\alpha_1 \text{ and } \alpha_2 \text{ not the same variable}).$$

The translation is not a theorem, but would have been under the rejected postulate that nothing in any world had more than one counterpart in any other world.

$$\alpha_1 \neq \alpha_2 \prec \Box \; \alpha_1 \neq \alpha_2 \quad (\alpha_1 \text{ and } \alpha_2 \text{ not the same variable}).$$

The translation is not a theorem, but would have been under the rejected postulate that no two things in any world had a common counterpart in any other world.

$$\forall \alpha \Box \phi \alpha \prec \Box \forall \alpha \phi \alpha \quad \text{(Barcan's principle)}.$$

The translation is not a theorem, but would have been under the rejected postulate that, for any two worlds, anything in one was a counterpart of something in the other.

$$\exists \alpha \Box \phi \alpha \prec \Box \exists \alpha \phi \alpha.$$

The translation is not a theorem, but would have been under the rejected postulate that, for any two worlds, anything in one had some counterpart in the other.

$$\Box \forall \alpha \phi \alpha \prec \forall \alpha \Box \phi \alpha \quad \text{(Converse of Barcan's principle)}.$$

The translation is a theorem.

$$\Box \exists \alpha \phi \alpha \prec \exists \alpha \Box \phi \alpha.$$

The translation is not a theorem, nor would it have been under any extra postulates with even the slightest plausibility.

V. Relative Modalities

Just as a sentence ϕ is necessary if it holds in all worlds, so ϕ is causally necessary if it holds in all worlds compatible with the laws of nature; obligatory for you if it holds in all worlds in which you act rightly; implicitly known, believed, hoped, asserted, or perceived by you if it holds in all worlds compatible with the content of your knowledge, beliefs, hopes, assertions, or perceptions. These, and many more, are *relative* modalities, expressible by quantifications over restricted ranges of worlds. We can write any dual pair of relative modalities as

$$\Box^i \delta_1 \ldots \delta_m$$
$$\Diamond^i \delta_1 \ldots \delta_m$$

where the index i indicates how the restriction of worlds is to be made and the m arguments $\delta_1, \ldots, \delta_m$, with $m \geq 0$, denote things to be considered in making the restriction (say, the person whose implicit knowledge we are talking about). To every dual pair of relative modalities there corresponds a characteristic relation

$R^i xyz_1 \ldots z_m$ (world x is i-related to world y and $z_1, \ldots, z_m$ therein)

governed by the postulate

P9: $\forall x \forall y \forall z_1 \ldots \forall z_m (R^i xyz_1 \ldots z_m \supset. \; Wx \; \& \; Wy \; \& \; Iz_1 y \; \& \; \ldots \; \& \; Iz_m y)$.

The characteristic relation gives the appropriate restriction: we are to consider only worlds i-related to whatever world we are in (and certain things in it). Necessity and possibility themselves are that pair of relative modalities whose characteristic relation is just the 2-place universal relation between worlds.[22]

We can easily extend our translation scheme to handle sentences containing miscellaneous modal operators. We will treat them just as we do

---

22. Cf. Jaakko Hintikka, "Quantifiers in Deontic Logic," *Societas Scientiarum Fennica, Commentationes Humanarum Litterarum*, 23 (1957); Kanger, *op. cit.;* Kripke, *op. cit.;* Montague, *op. cit.;* Arthur Prior, "Possible Worlds," *Philosophical Quarterly,* 12 (1962), 36–43; Hintikka, *Knowledge and Belief,* pp. 42–49; Dagfinn Føllesdal, "Quantification into Causal Contexts," in *Boston Studies in the Philosophy of Science,* II (New York: Humanities Press, 1965), pp. 263–274; Hintikka, "The Logic of Perception," presented at the 1967 Oberlin Colloquium in Philosophy.

necessity and possibility, except that quantifiers over worlds will range over only those worlds which bear the appropriate characteristic relation to some world and perhaps some things in it. The translation of ϕ remains $\phi^{@}$; we need only add two new clauses to the recursive definition of ϕ:

T2i*: $(\square^i \delta_1 \ldots \delta_m \phi \alpha_1 \ldots \alpha_n)^\beta$ is $\forall \beta_1 \forall \gamma_1 \ldots \forall \gamma_n$
$(R^i \beta_1 \beta \delta_1 \ldots \delta_m \ \& \ I\gamma_1\beta_1 \ \& \ C\gamma_1\alpha_1 \ \& \ \ldots \ \& \ I\gamma_n\beta_1 \ \&$
$C\gamma_n\alpha_n \ . \supset \ \phi^{\beta_1}\gamma_1 \ldots \gamma_n)$

T2j*: $(\Diamond^i \delta_1 \ldots \delta_m \phi \alpha_1 \ldots \alpha_n)^\beta$ is $\exists \beta_1 \exists \gamma_1 \ldots \exists \gamma_n$
$(R^i \beta_1 \beta \delta_1 \ldots \delta_m \ \& \ I\gamma_1\beta_1 \ \& \ C\gamma_1\alpha_1 \ \& \ \ldots \ \& \ I\gamma_n\beta_1 \ \& \ C\gamma_n\alpha_n$
$\& \ \phi^{\beta_1}\gamma_1 \ldots \gamma_n)$

(since necessity and possibility are relative modalities, we no longer need T2i and T2j). For example, our translation of

$\square^i \phi$
$\square^j \delta \psi \alpha$
$\square^i \square^j \delta \phi$

where ϕ is a 0-place sentence, ψ is a 1-place sentence, $\square$ is a 0-place relative modality, and $\square^j$ is a 1-place relative modality, are, respectively,

$\forall\beta(R^i\beta@ \supset \phi^\beta)$
(ϕ holds in any world i-related to the actual world)

$\forall\beta\forall\gamma(R^j\beta@\delta \ \& \ I\gamma\beta \ \& \ C\gamma\alpha \ . \supset \ \psi^\beta\alpha)$
(ψ holds of any counterpart γ of α in any world β j-related to the actual world and δ therein)

$\forall\beta_1\forall\gamma(R^i\beta@ \ \& \ I\gamma\beta_1 \ \& \ C\gamma\delta.\supset \forall\beta_2(R^j\beta_2\beta_1\gamma \supset \phi^{\beta_2}))$
(ϕ holds in any world β_2 such that, for some world β_1 that is i-related to the actual world and for some counterpart γ in β_1 of δ, β_2 is j-related to β_1 and γ).

The third example illustrates the fact that free variables occurring as arguments of relative modal operators may need to be handled by means of the counterpart relation.

Our previous discussion of singular terms as eliminable descriptions subject to ambiguity of scope carries over, with one change: in general, the auxiliary premise for exportation (and the first of two auxiliary premises for importation) must be the translation of $\square^i \delta_1 \ldots \delta_m(\zeta = \zeta)$ with one occurrence of ζ given wide scope and the other given narrow scope. The translation of $\exists\alpha\square^i\delta_1 \ldots \delta_m(\zeta = \alpha)$ will do only for those relative modalities, like necessity, for which $R^i @@ \delta_1 \ldots \delta_m$—and, hence, the translation of $\Box^i \delta_1 \ldots \delta_m \phi \supset \phi$—are theorems under the appropriate postulates on the i-relation. More generally, the argument

$$\frac{\Box^i \delta_1 \ldots \delta_m \phi \eta}{\Box^i \delta_1 \ldots \delta_m (\eta = \zeta)}$$
$$\therefore \Box^i \delta_1 \ldots \delta_m \phi \zeta$$

where ϕ is a 1-place sentence, has a valid translation if ζ is given wide scope and η is given narrow scope throughout.

Principles corresponding to those discussed in section IV can be formulated for any relative modality (or, in the case of Becker's and Brouwer's principles, for any mixture of relative modalities). The acceptability of such principles will depend, in general, not just on the logical properties of the counterpart relation and the i-relations involved, but on the logical relations *between* the counterpart relation and the i-relations. For example, consider a relative necessity without arguments, so that its characteristic i-relation will be 2-place. (Such an i-relation is often called an *accessibility* relation between worlds.) And consider Becker's principle for this relative necessity (but with ' $\prec$ ' still defined in terms of necessity itself): $\Box^i \phi \prec \Box^i \Box^i \phi$; that is, $\Box(\Box^i \phi \supset \Box^i \Box^i \phi)$. It is often said that Becker's principle holds just in case accessibility is transitive, which is correct if ϕ is a closed sentence. But for open ϕ, Becker's principle holds just in case

$$\forall x_1 \forall y_1 \forall x_2 \forall y_2 \forall x_3 \forall y_3 (Ix_1 y_1 \ \& \ Ix_2 y_2 \ \& \ Ix_3 y_3 \ \& \ Cx_2 x_1 \ \& \ Cx_3 x_2 \ \&$$
$$R^i y_2 y_1 \ \& \ R^i y_3 y_2 . \supset . \ Cx_3 x_1 \ \& \ R^i y_3 y_1)$$

even if neither accessibility nor the counterpart relation is transitive.

VI. Postscript*

The trouble is that this presumes that we have the very same Ripov active at several worlds: ours, where he bribes the judge and wins, and others, where he does not bribe the judge and does not win. What makes the

---

*[Editor's note: The Postscript is taken from David Lewis' *Counterfactuals* (Cambridge, Mass.: Harvard University Press, 1973), copright 1973 by David Lewis. The selection is meant as a supplement and partial correction to "Counterpart Theory and Quantified Modal Logic." In the previous paragraphs, Lewis has been developing a possible-worlds account of potentialities; his example is a man named Ripov, who "is the winner because he bribed the judge," and his concern is that a possible-worlds account of Ripov's potentialities to act otherwise entails that "we have the very same Ripov active at several worlds."]

inhabitant of another world, who does not bribe and does not win, identical with our Ripov? I suppose the answer must be *either* that his identity with our Ripov is an irreducible fact, not to be explained in terms of anything else, *or* that his identity with our Ripov is due to some sort of similarity to our Ripov—he is Ripov because he plays much the same role at the other world that our Ripov plays here. Neither answer pleases me. The first answer either posits transworld identities between things arbitrarily different in character, thereby denying what I take to be some of the facts about *de re* modality, or else it makes a mystery of those facts by denying us any way to explain why there are some sorts of transworld identities but not others. The second answer at least is not defeatist, but it runs into trouble because similarity relations lack the formal properties—transitivity, for instance—of identity.

The best thing to do, I think, is to escape the problems of transworld identity by insisting that there is nothing that inhabits more than one world. There are some abstract entities, for instance numbers or properties, that inhabit no particular world but exist alike from the standpoint of all worlds, just as they have no location in time and space but exist alike from the standpoint of all times and places. Things that do inhabit worlds—people, flames, buildings, puddles, concrete particulars generally—inhabit one world each, no more. Our Ripov is a man of our world, who does not reappear elsewhere. Other worlds may have Ripovs of their own, but none of these is our Ripov. Rather, they are counterparts of our Ripov. What comes from transworld resemblance is not transworld identity, but a substitute for transworld identity: the counterpart relation. What our Ripov cannot do in person at other worlds, not being present there to do it, he may do vicariously through his counterparts. He himself is not an honest man at any world—he is dishonest here, and nonexistent elsewhere—but he is vicariously honest through his honest counterparts.

In general: something has for *counterparts* at a given world those things existing there that resemble it closely enough in important respects of intrinsic quality and extrinsic relations, and that resemble it no less closely than do other things existing there. Ordinarily something will have one counterpart or none at a world, but ties in similarity may give it multiple counterparts. Two special cases: (1) anything is its own unique counterpart at its own world, and (2) the abstract entities that exist alike from the standpoint of all worlds, but inhabit none, are their own unique counterparts at all worlds.

I have proposed elsewhere that the counterpart relation ought to be used as a substitute for transworld identity in explaining *de re* modality.[23] The realm of essence and accident is the realm of the vicarious. What something *might* have done (or might have been) is what it does (or is) vicariously; and that is what its counterparts do (or are). What is essential to something is what it has in common with all its counterparts; what it nowhere vicariously lacks. Ripov's honest counterparts make him someone who might have been honest. His lack of inanimate counterparts makes him essentially animate. In terms of satisfaction of modal formulas: something satisfies $\Box \phi_x$ at a world i if and only if any counterpart of it at any world j accessible from i satisfies ϕ_x at j; something satisfies $\Diamond \phi_x$ at a world i if and only if it has some counterpart at some world j accessible from i that satisfies ϕ_x at j. Alternatively, we can say that something *vicariously satisfies* ϕ_x at a world i if and only if it has some counterpart at i that satisfies ϕ_x at i. (At one's own world, vicarious satisfaction coincides with satisfaction.) Then we can restate the conditions in terms of vicarious satisfaction. Something satisfies $\Box \phi_x$ at i if and only if there is no world accessible from i where it vicariously satisfies $\sim \phi_x$. Something satisfies $\Diamond \phi_x$ if and only if there is some world accessible from i where it vicariously satisfies ϕ_x.[24]

The method of counterparts seems to me to have many virtues as a theory of *de re* modality. (1) It has the same explanatory power as a theory of *de re* modality that employs transworld identity based on transworld resemblance. The facts about what things might have been and might have done are explained by our standards of similarity—that is, of the comparative importances of respects of comparison—plus facts about how things actually are. Modal facts are grounded in facts about actual character, not mysteriously independent. It is because of the way Ripov actually is that certain honest men at other worlds resemble him enough to be his counterparts, and inanimate things at other worlds do not. (2) However, we are rid of the worst burden of a theory of transworld identity based on transworld resemblance: the counterpart relation is not identity, so we need not try to

23. "Counterpart Theory and Quantified Modal Logic," *Journal of Philosophy*, 65 (1968), 113–126; Chapter 5 of this anthology; "Counterparts of Persons and Their Bodies," *Journal of Philosophy*, 68 (1971), 203–211.

24. An alternative definition of vicarious satisfaction would put the double negation in the satisfaction conditions for $\Diamond \phi_x$ instead of those for $\Box \phi_x$; but we would be stuck with it one place or other. The reason is that something with more or less than one counterpart at a world may vicariously satisfy both or neither of ϕ_x and $\sim \phi_x$, so vicariously satisfying $\sim \phi_x$ is not the same as not vicariously satisfying ϕ_x.

force it to have the logical properties of identity. (3) Therefore we have a desirable flexibility. For instance, we can say that something might have been twins because it has twin counterparts somewhere, without claiming that it is literally identical with two things not identical to one another. (4) Since the counterpart relation is based on similarity, the vagueness of similarity infects *de re* modality. And that is all to the good. It goes a long way toward explaining why questions of *de re* modality are as difficult as we have found them to be. (5) We can plead this same vagueness to explain away seeming discrepancies among our *de re* modal opinions. For instance, consider two inhabitants of a certain world that is exactly like ours in every detail until 1888, and thereafter diverges. One has exactly the ancestral origins of our Hitler; that is so in virtue of events within the region of perfect match that ended just before his birth. In that region, it is quite unequivocal what is the counterpart of what. The other has quite different ancestral origins, but as he grows up he gradually duplicates more and more of the infamous deeds of our Hitler until after 1930 his career matches our Hitler's career in every detail. Meanwhile the first lives an obscure and blameless life. Does this world prove that Hitler might have lived a blameless life? Or does it prove that he might have had different ancestral origins? I want to be able to say either—though perhaps not both in the same breath—depending on which respects of comparison are foremost in my mind; and the method of counterparts, with due allowance for vagueness, allows me to do so. (6) There are also cases where we need to mix different counterpart relations in a single sentence in order to make sense of it as a reasonable thing to think; for instance, sentences of *de re* contingent identity. We shall see other cases in connection with counterfactuals. I see no way to get the same effect by means of transworld identity alone, though one might get it by mixing in transworld identity along with the counterpart relations.

6

The World Is Everything
That Is the Case

M. J. CRESSWELL
Victoria University, Wellington

My principal aim in this paper is to show how a basically atomistic metaphysics can support a theory of meaning for languages which are rich enough to invite the hope that natural languages such as English can be translated into them.*

1. Syntax

The class of languages I shall have in mind will be what I shall call *name/sentence* languages. I shall in fact only deal in detail with a very restricted class of these which I shall call *zero-order name/sentence* languages or, for short, simply zero-order languages. Although a fully fledged formal definition of a zero-order language is not essential to the purpose of this paper it is a good thing to have up one's sleeve. Those not symbolically inclined may skip the formalism.

> 1.1 A zero-order language $\mathscr{L}$ is an ordered triple $\langle \Phi, F, S \rangle$ where $\Phi = \langle \Phi_0, \Phi_1, \ldots, \Phi_m \rangle$ and $F = \langle F_0, F_1, \ldots, F_k \rangle$ are finite sequences of pairwise disjoint (possibly empty) finite sets.
> Φ_0 is often referred to as N and the members of the sets in

Originally published in *Australasian Journal of Philosophy*, 50 (1972), 1–13; reprinted here with the permission of the author and the editor of *Australasian Journal of Philosophy*.
*The research involved in this paper was supported solely by my salary from the Victoria University of Wellington.

$\Phi \cup F$ are called the *symbols* of $\mathcal{L}$. S is the (unique) smallest set such that:

1.2 $F_0 \subset S$

1.3 If $x_1, \ldots, x_n \in N$ and $\phi \in \Phi_n$
then $\langle \phi, x_1, \ldots, x_n \rangle \in S$

1.4 If $\alpha_1, \ldots, \alpha_n \in S$ and $f \in F_n$
then $\langle f, \alpha_1, \ldots, \alpha_n \rangle \in S$

What all this means is that $\mathcal{L}$ consists of a number of symbols which combine according to various rules to form a set of sequences called sentences. The symbols are either names (the members of N), n-place predicates (the members of Φ_n), simple sentence symbols (the members of F_0), or n-place functors (the members of F_n). Predicates make sentences out of names; functors (frequently called 'connectives') make sentences out of sentences. S is the set of well-formed (grammatical) sentences of $\mathcal{L}$ and 1.2–1.4 are the rules which determine which sequences of symbols are to count as sentences.

The only restriction we have placed on Φ and F is that their members be finite. It is possible to think of a symbol as a class of marks or sounds (or perhaps as a type of which the marks or sounds are tokens). In such a case the sentences are represented by concatenations of marks (left to right in English) or temporally ordered sequences of sounds. A language which has a physical realization of this kind we shall call a *surface language*.

To illustrate the formation rules, suppose that N contains the words 'I' and 'Arabella' and that Φ_2 contains 'love'. Then (by 1.3) the sequence

$\langle love, I, Arabella \rangle$

will be a member of S, i.e., a sentence of $\mathcal{L}$. Suppose further that F_1 contains 'possibly'. Then (by 1.4) the sequence

$\langle Possibly, \langle love, I, Arabella \rangle \rangle$

is also a sentence of $\mathcal{L}$. Of course even if the sets of symbols contained all the English words of the appropriate kind we would still be quite a way from obtaining ordinary English. E.g. the formation rules would also allow:

$\langle Possibly, \langle love, Arabella, I \rangle \rangle$

and we would need what are called transformations to change 'love' into 'loves' 'I' into 'me' and to reverse the order of 'loves' and 'Arabella' and

so produce 'Possibly Arabella loves me'. The hope, however, as expressed
e.g. by David Lewis[1] is that with a precisely formulable set of such transformations a natural language like English could be based on a generalization of the kind of language I have described.

Let's look at a zero-order language more closely. Its symbols can each be
put into one of a number of what Kasimir Adjukiewicz called 'semantic
categories'.[2] These will either be basic categories or derived categories. The
basic categories of zero-order languages are names and sentences and the
derived categories are (obviously) the predicates and the functors because
they make sentences out of names or out of other sentences. Extra
categories could be got by allowing mixed arguments or by operating in
different ways on primitive or derived categories. E.g. we could have a
symbol, say the word 'that' which makes a complex name (often called a
noun phrase) out of a sentence. Thus

$\langle that, \langle love, I, Arabella \rangle \rangle$

would be a name and if Φ_2 contained, say, the word 'prefer' we would
have as sentences of $\mathscr{L}$ such sequences as

$\langle Prefer, I, \langle that, \langle love, I, Arabella \rangle \rangle \rangle$
$\langle Prefer, I, Arabella \rangle$
$\langle love, \langle that, \langle love, I, Arabella \rangle \rangle, Arabella \rangle$

and many others. In ordinary English some of these look a little odd: e.g.
the last would have to be transformed into something like

'That I love Arabella loves Arabella'.

This is one of those cases in which we don't know whether the semantical
oddness of a proposition's loving something infects the grammar of the
sentence. On the whole I prefer to say that it doesn't. At any rate its formal
counterpart is well formed.

Another kind of generalization of a zero-order language would be a

---

1. [11, p. 22]. Lewis' article is an excellent example of the kind of recent semantical work
in the philosophy of language which the early part of the present paper is referring to. He has
also a large and useful bibliography.

2. Adjukiewicz [1]. Bar Hillel [2, chapter 8] calls the rules for generating a language based
on a set of semantic categories a 'categorial grammar.' He proves that categorial grammars
are precisely equivalent to simple phrase structure grammars. That language might be trans-
formationally based on a simple phrase structure grammar would seem to be implied by
Chomsky in several places in [3], e.g. pp. 120, 139, and 141f. Cf. also [2, pp. 144f.].

language enriched by quantifiers. These would be words like 'everything', 'everyone', 'most', 'few', and so on. For absolute clarity we might then wish to add individual variables to our stock of names and so have sentences like

$$\langle Everyone\ (x),\ \langle love,\ x,\ Arabella \rangle \rangle.$$

Here in getting ordinary English the transformation would simply delete the x's; though cases involving multiple quantification require more elaborate treatment. Quantifiers can be thought of as making sentences out of predicates. I.e. making sentences out of things which make sentences out of names.

What I have just said is intended to indicate the ways in which the languages I do consider, viz, zero-order languages can be extended to more general kinds of name/sentence languages for it would be some kind of name/sentence language that I would like to think of as providing the deep structure sentences which could be transformed by the application of syntactical transformation rules into the ordinary sentences we know and love. Although authors seldom explicitly restrict their basic categories to names and sentences most applications of categorial languages need only these two.[3] It should be obvious that almost everything I say about zero-order languages will be capable of routine though tedious and complex generalization to all name/sentence languages. So if we can give an adequate metaphysical analysis of the semantics of zero-order languages then we should at least be on the road to giving an adequate metaphysical analysis of the semantics of a language actually used to talk about reality.

2. Semantics

Richard Montague [13, footnote 2] has said that one of the basic aims of semantics is a definition of truth. His model is Alfred Tarski's definition for the lower predicate calculus but made incomparably more powerful by

---

3. Adjukiewicz [1, pp. 209f.] following Lesniewski restricts himself to name/sentence languages 'for the sake of simplicity' though he seems to believe there are many other basic categories. Both Bar Hillel [2, chapter 5] and Geach [5] have only names and sentences as basic though Bar Hillel on p. 81 claims that for English more basic categories would be necessary. Lewis [11, p. 20] has the additional category of common noun but it's not obvious that this cannot be dispensed with.

The only plausible-looking alternative I have come across is Lewis' intriguing suggestion on pp. 49–52 of treating names as quantifiers and eliminating the category N altogether. Predicates (verb phrases) then become a basic category.

his use of the methods of semantical analysis derived from intensional logic. The semantic notion which writers like Richard Montague have taken as a primitive is that familiar from recent work in modal logic of a 'possible world' or perhaps better a 'conceivable or envisageable state of affairs'.[4] One of our present aims is to try to say what such a thing could be but we shall first show how it can be used in providing a universal semantics for zero-order languages.

The semantical analysis of a language is a process of assigning values to the symbols of the language in such a way that we can calculate values for the sentences. If we take the ordinary two-valued propositional calculus as an example the values of the sentences are the truth values. Indeed one might say that the name 'propositional calculus' is misleading since the values of the sentences are not propositions but simply either 'The True' or 'The False'. Or one might say that as far as the propositional calculus is concerned propositions (i.e., values of sentences) just *are* truth values and that there are therefore only two propositions. However truth-functional logic is only a small part of even zero-order language let alone name: sentence languages in general for it is implausible to claim that two sentences have the same meaning simply because they have the same truth value. What is perhaps more plausible is to say that two sentences have the same meaning if they have the same truth *conditions*. I.e., if every state of affairs which would make the first true would also make the second true and vice versa. The meaning of a sentence can then be thought of as the set of states of affairs or possible worlds in which it would be true. In this way, provided we have the notion of a possible world, we can define a proposition as a set of possible worlds and say that each sentence of our language is to be assigned a proposition, i.e., a set of possible worlds.[5] The sentence is to be regarded as true in a possible world if that possible world is in the set assigned to the sentence and false if it is not.

This takes care of one of the basic categories. The other basic category is the category of names. In logic we assume an initially specified set or domain of individuals or 'things' and let the names be assigned members of this domain.

Assignments for the derived categories now fall into place. Consider

---

4. An introductory account of the possible-world semantics for modal logic is given in chapter 4 of [7] with their intuitive interpretation discussed briefly on pp. 75–80.

5. The idea of defining a proposition as a set of possible worlds is implicit in a great deal of recent work but is rarely made explicit. An exception is Stalnaker's [17, p. 273] and Montague's [12, p. 163]. Perhaps the term 'proposition' to refer to the meaning of a sentence has been so suspect in the past that authors dislike using it.

e.g. the predicate 'loves'. Now whatever we may intuitively think of as the meaning of this predicate the job which the meaning has to do is simple. Viz., the meaning of 'loves' must enable us, given say the values of the names 'Bill' and 'Arabella' to work out the value of the sentence

$\langle$ *love, Bill, Arabella* $\rangle$.

The value of this sentence will be a set of worlds (the worlds in which Bill loves Arabella) and what the value of 'loves' must do is to specify who loves whom in which worlds. So just as in extensional logic we let the value of 'loves' be the set of all pairs $\langle x, y \rangle$ such that x loves y so in our present semantics we let 'loves' be assigned the set of all triples $\langle x, y, w \rangle$ such that x loves y in w [7, p. 146]. In other words the meaning of 'loves' is simply a rule which takes us from the values of its arguments to the value of the resulting sentence; for if we want to know whether a given world w is in the set assigned to the sentence

$\langle$ *love, Bill, Arabella* $\rangle$

we need merely see whether the triple consisting of the value assigned to the name 'Bill' (viz., Bill) and the value assigned to the name 'Arabella' (viz., Arabella) and the world w is in the set of triples assigned to the predicate 'loves'.

The evaluation of propositional functors is analogous. Suppose that we wish to know whether

$\langle$ *possibly,* $\langle$ *love, Bill, Arabella* $\rangle\rangle$

is true in a world w. We simply see whether the pair consisting of the set of worlds assigned to the embedded sentence $\langle$ *love, Bill, Arabella* $\rangle$, (i.e., the value of this sentence) together with the world w is in the set of pairs assigned to the propositional functor 'possibly'. And when we know for any given w whether the sentence is true or not in w we can use this to determine the set of worlds which should be assigned to the whole sentence $\langle$ *possibly,* $\langle$ *love, Bill, Arabella* $\rangle\rangle$ so that it can, in its turn, feature as the argument of another functor. By this means every one of the infinite number of sentences of a zero-order language has a truth value in every world which is determined by the assignments to the finite number of primitive symbols of the language.

We can if we like sum all this up formally by defining what we shall call a *Fregean Assignment* (cf. Montague [13, section 4]).

2.1 A Fregean assignment for a zero-order language $\mathscr{L}$ is an ordered triple $\langle W, D, V \rangle$ where W is a set of possible worlds and D a domain of individuals and V a function such that

2.2 If $p \in F_0$ then $V(p) \subseteq W$

2.3 If $x \in N$ then $V(x) \in D$

2.4 If $\phi \in \Phi_n$ then $V(\phi) \subseteq D^n \times W$

2.5 If $f \in F_n$ then $V(f) \subseteq (\mathscr{P}W)^n \times W$

2.6 If $\phi \in \Phi_n$ and $x_1, \ldots, x_n \in N$ then $V(\langle \phi, x_1, \ldots, x_n \rangle) = \{w \in W: \langle V(x_1), \ldots, V(x_n), w \rangle \in V(\phi)\}$

2.7 If $f \in F_n$ and $\alpha_1, \ldots, \alpha_n \in S$ then
$$V(\langle f, \alpha_1, \ldots, \alpha_n \rangle) = \{w \in W: \langle V(\alpha_1), \ldots, V(\alpha_n), w \rangle \in V(f)\}$$

If we single out one possible world as the 'real world' we can define a sentence to be true (without qualification) iff the real world is in the set of worlds assigned to that sentence. The semantical generality of our definition of an assignment may easily be shown by demonstrating that for any set T of sentences of $\mathscr{L}$ there is a Fregean assignment together with a designated real world such that any sentence α is true in the real world iff $\alpha \in T$. The proof of this consists in exhibiting sets of sentences of $\mathscr{L}$ as the possible worlds with T itself as the real world. Like most completeness proofs in logic its metaphysical import is a little suspect since it only shows that there is *some* structure which is a model for T and the structure it actually produces might be very unilluminating about the nature of possible worlds. It does however show that we really have got the maximum generality in our semantics.

3. Metaphysics

So far, despite any appearance of novelty, I have said little that is original and less that is metaphysical. So I turn now to the metaphysical collation I promised you at the beginning of the paper. I shall ask you to assume a set (which I shall refer to as B) of 'Basic Particular Situations'. These can be thought of as rather like the atomic facts of the logical atomists in that a basic particular situation is something which may or may not be present without affecting any other basic particular situation. The members of B play a role analogous to that of theoretical entities in physical theories and what sorts of things we take them to be will of course depend on a thoroughgoing analysis of the particular language we are interested in. However for the purposes of illustration, but I stress only for the purposes of illustration, I shall give one account of the kinds of things basic particular situations might be.

The illustration is really a very simple one. B is nothing more nor less than the set of all space-time points. Of course we need to say a little more to show why it might be plausible to have the set of all space-time points as our set of basic particular situations if only to prevent the suspicion of a pun on the word 'situation'. The plausibility comes when we think of B as the conceptual framework of a physical theory whose ultimate entities are conceived of as things whose properties can all be expressed in terms of the space-time points they occupy. To say that a space-time point is occupied is simply to say that a certain spatial point is filled at a certain time. In terms of this framework the complete state of the world is determined by a set of points of space-time viz., those points which are occupied. And a set of points of space-time is, in terms of this illustration, just a subset of B.

I've chosen the illustration because apart from its intuitive intelligibility it's a highly materialistic illustration. I am not myself concerned to argue for materialism; in fact I don't know whether I believe in it. But in view of the fact that I am developing semantics for languages which are manifestly nonextensional it is rather important to show that they are not incompatible with materialism. If, in my introduction of propositions, attributes, and the like I am to be accused of Platonism then I take comfort in the fact that it is the kind of Platonism which, provided he accepts classes, need not cause the most sensitive of materialists the least interruption to his dogmatic slumbers.

Definition: A possible world is a set of basic particular situations.

In terms of the illustration this means that the way things are is determined by a set of points of space-time. The real world of course is that set of space-time points which actually are occupied. But any other set could be occupied and so counts as a possible world.

A proposition is, as before, a set of possible worlds. Proceeding in this direction makes life a great deal easier than beginning with propositions, for we have been able to define possible worlds in terms of basic situations which can, if necessary, be given a materialistic interpretation. We shall refer to the set of all worlds (i.e., the set of all subsets of B) as W and to the set of all propositions (i.e., the set of all subsets of W) as P.

To develop a semantics based on B all that remains is to define our domain D of what we have called 'individuals'. Actually of course we want it to be rather bigger than that. We want it to be everything there is. In everyday speech what counts as a 'thing' is not at all clear, but we are interested not in what *is* regarded as a thing but in what can be so regarded and it might seem a little parochial of us to refuse accommodation in our metaphysical stable simply on the ground that there is no room in the inn of ordinary language. So we shall let D contain members of B, sets of members of B, sets of sets of members of B, relations between members of B, and so on, and in fact quite generally anything which can be made up out of B by the standard set-theoretical operations. This ought to be as large as we could want and provided standard set theory is consistent will not get us into trouble. Making D this large will of course mean that propositions and worlds are 'things' but this merely shows how widely we are using the word 'thing'.

A particularly important class of things is the class of what I shall call *basic individuals*. In this class might perhaps be physical objects, events, states, processes, and the like. A basic individual is a function from a world to a part of that world. Strictly since a subset of a world can itself be a world a basic individual σ is a function from possible worlds into possible worlds provided that for any world w, $\sigma(w)$ is a subset of w. $\sigma(w)$, i.e., the value of the function σ in the world w is called the *manifestation* of σ in w. In more standard terminology we could call it the *extension* of σ in w.

In terms of our illustrative model the manifestation of an individual σ in a world w would be a space-time portion of w. Say σ is the blackboard. Then where w is the real world $\sigma(w)$ is that subset of space-time which makes up the blackboard throughout its history. It would be implausible to identify the blackboard with its manifestation for we can ask, 'Would the blackboard have been better placed nearer the window?' and one cannot ask this of a space-time slice. Where two distinct individuals have the same manifestation in world w we shall say that they are contingently identical in w. Where the manifestation of σ in w is null (for the null set is a world, and indeed a subworld of any world) we shall say that σ does not exist in w.

(A word here about the fact that the manifestations of individuals are worlds. There is perhaps something marginally messy about this but on reflection it doesn't, I think, seem quite as unreasonable as all that. After all a manifestation of an individual, a bit of experience *might* have been the totality of experience, i.e., it *is* a possible total experience, i.e., a possible world.)

4. Contexts

So much for basic individuals. Let us return to the semantics for natural languages. Now if, as we have suggested earlier, the sentences of a natural language can be derived by syntactical transformations from the sentences of a name/sentence language then all the semantical features of the natural language will have to be incorporated into the base language.[6] One of the most striking ways in which natural languages have differed semantically from formal languages has been that the meaning of a sentence in a natural language depends to a large extent on the context in which the sentence is used. Recently attempts have been devised in which 'contexts of use' are taken as primitive coordinates along with possible worlds. Authors like Dana Scott [15, pp. 148–152] who wish to be noncommittal lump all these together and call them 'points of reference' or simply 'indices'. This neutrality is admirable when doing logic but would be the death of metaphysics. Writers who, like David Lewis [11], do try to give a bit more body to these notions talk about times, places, speakers, hearers, . . . etc. and then go through agonies of conscience in trying to decide whether they have taken account of enough.

It seems to me impossible to lay down in advance what sort of thing is going to count as a context of use.

> I have no pain, dear mother now,
> But Oh! I am so dry;
> Just fetch your Jim another quart
> To wet the other eye. [Anon.]

There is a sense in which we already know the meaning of this little poem but another sense in which we are very much in the dark.

> 'I have no pain, dear mother, now'.

To know the truth of this sentence (indeed to know the proposition which is being asserted) we have to know who the 'I' refers to and what time is 'now.' We need at least a user context and a time context.

> 'Just fetch your Jim another quart'.

Assuming that we are clear about who is addressed there's still the problem of the quart. Are we to suppose that the author is a renegade Pythagorean

---

6. This is one of the main themes of Katz and Postal [9] though of course they have a rather different conception of semantics from the one developed in this paper.

who has broken his vows and wants a quart measure to sit on? Probably not. One suspects that he is interested in obtaining a quantity of alcoholic beverage. But what sort? What we seem to need is a 'previous drinks' context.

The moral here seems to be that there is no way of specifying a finite list of contextual coordinates. Yet since contexts play such a crucial role in any theory of meaning for a natural language we shall, if we are to succeed in our metaphysical analysis, have to show how they can be built into our semantics for zero-order languages. In particular we want to show how contexts can be defined in terms of our set B of basic particular situations.

Definition: A context of use is a proposition.

Deceptively simple and therefore requiring some explanation. The sort of case I have in mind is the sentence

⟨ *love, I, you* ⟩

when used by Bill in addressing Arabella on the 21st March 1971. In this context the sentence means that Bill loves Arabella on the 21st March 1971. The context here is the proposition that the sentence ⟨ *love, I, you* ⟩ is being used by Bill when addressing Arabella on 21st March 1971. The meaning rule for 'I' could be stated as something like this:

$V(I)$ is that function δ from propositions into individuals such that if p is a proposition which states *inter alia* of a unique person that a sentence containing 'I' is being used by that person then $\delta(p)$ is that person.

$V(love)$ is that function δ from propositions into predicates such that if p states *inter alia* that a sentence containing 'love' is used at a time t, then $\delta(p)$ is the relation '———— loves ———— at t'.

$V(you)$ is that function δ from propositions into individuals such that if p states *inter alia* that a sentence containing 'you' is being addressed to a unique person then $\delta(p)$ is that person.

Note that these are illustrations only and many terms are left vague, e.g., the notion of 'using' a sentence. But enough ought to have been said to give some kind of content to the general definition. Contexts of this kind I shall call distributive, because they work by making the meaning of a complex sentence in a given context depend on the meaning of each simple part of it in that context. Not all propositions will be suitable as contexts. E.g. a proposition which does not specify the user of a sentence or which specifies more than one will not be a suitable context for evaluating a sentence with 'I' in it. This means that the functions referred to above which give the value of the term in a given context will have to be partial functions. The semantics we are about to present will therefore allow terms which, with respect to some propositions, are not assigned a value. If we follow Montague's terminology we shall call the value of a term in a given context its sense. Thus the Fregean Assignments we have talked about should be properly thought of as assigning senses rather than meanings. The distinction is not perhaps found in ordinary language but what it comes down to is this. The meaning of the sentence $\langle love, I, you \rangle$ is fixed for all speakers and hearers. For its meaning is the rule for getting from a proposition (context) which specifies a speaker, hearer, and time of utterance to the proposition that the speaker specified by the context loves the hearer specified by the context at the time specified by the context. The sense of the sentence however differs with the context and is the actual proposition asserted. E.g. if said by Bill to Arabella on 21st March 1971 the sense of $\langle love, I, you \rangle$ is the proposition that Bill loves Arabella on the 21st March 1971.[7]

With the set W of possible worlds defined as the set of all subsets of B and with the set P of propositions defined as the set of all subsets of W we can define a *meaning assignment* for a zero-order language $\mathscr{L}$ as follows:

4.1 $\langle B, V \rangle$ is a meaning assignment for $\mathscr{L}$ iff V is a function such that

4.2 If $p \in F_0$ then $V(p)$ is a partial function from P into P. Where $\alpha \in P$ we write the value of p by V at a as $V(p,a)$.

4.3 If $x \in N$ then $V(x)$ is a partial function from P into D. $V(x,a)$ is the value of x at a.

4.4 If $\phi \in \Phi_n$ then $V(\phi)$ is a partial function from P into subsets of $D^n \times W$. $V(\phi,a)$ is the value of ϕ at a.

4.5 If $f \in F_n$ then $V(f)$ is a partial function from P into subsets of $P^n \times W$. $V(f,a)$ is the value of f at a.

4.6 $V(\langle \phi, x_1, \ldots, x_n \rangle, a) = \{ w \in W : \langle V(x_1,a), \ldots, V(x_n,a), w \rangle \in V(\phi,a) \}$

7. The distinction between meaning and sense can be used to explain why a perfectly meaningful sentence like 'I feel no pain dear mother now' can fail, in a given context to have a sense. The conditions needed for it to have a sense could be called the *presuppositions* of the sentence. Our analysis of meaning would then come close to being a formalization of much of what Strawson says in [18].

$$\cdot 4.7 \ \ V(\langle f, \alpha_1, \ldots, \alpha_n \rangle, a) = \{w \ \epsilon \ W; \ \langle V(\alpha_1, a), \ldots, V(\alpha_n, a), w \rangle \ \epsilon \ V(f, a)\}$$

Instead of a sentence being assigned a set of worlds and an individual symbol a member of the domain of individuals a sentence is now assigned a partial function from propositions into propositions and an individual symbol a partial function from propositions into individuals. Predicates and functors are treated likewise and the evaluation rules for complex formulas (4.6 and 4.7) ensure that the value of a complex sentence in a given context can be calculated from the values of its parts in that context in the usual way.

We have defined contexts very generally and in fact it is easy to see that our definition will let in as languages some very funny things. E.g. consider the following rather Parmenidean language. It contains only one propositional symbol, the word ἔστι. Its semantic rule is simple:

> V(ἔστι) is that function δ from propositions into propositions such that if p is the proposition that ἔστι' is used by a person who intends it to mean that q then $\delta(p)$ is q.

This is a kind of radical Humpty Dumpty language, in which the word means whatever the user intends it to mean. The reason why it won't work for normal human beings is because there is very often no independent way of finding out what a person means than through what he says. One could imagine two omniscient beings who knew each other's minds communicating by uttering ἔστι from time to time, but they would not need a language any way. So radical Parmenidese as we might call it brings us to one of the limits of what we shall regard as a language. In general, natural languages will allow as contexts only propositions whose truth could reasonably be expected to be known by those involved in the communication.

5. Indeterminacy

Context dependence is one semantical feature of natural languages which we have had to incorporate into our formal languages. Another feature is what might loosely be called the vagueness or indeterminacy of natural languages. If a person says 'It's warm today' this clearly has a meaning. But can we say what, precisely, its meaning is? The first point to note is that it is context-dependent. Not only is a time reference needed for the 'today' but also some fact about the climate for that time of the year in that place. 65°F might be a warm day in London in winter but cool in Singapore in the hot season. But this cannot be the whole story, for even if we grant that it is Wellington in April a person might hesitate to say whether 65° is warm or not. Or one person may be quite sure that it is warm and another equally certain that it is not. It is not the lack of a context which is worrying, it is rather that the meaning of warm is not precise. And what this seems to mean is that 'warm' denotes a range of precise meanings. E.g. by 'warm' (for a given context) we might mean 'between 60 and 70°' or 'between 60 and 75°' or 'between 61 and 72°'. I.e., we have not one meaning assignment but a class of meaning assignments. The important thing about this class is that it should be adequate for communication, i.e., if a person is using 'warm' in one of these precise senses he can, for all practical purposes, communicate with someone who is using it in another, or if he is not clear in which sense he is using it, it will make no practical difference to him. We shall call such a class of meaning assignments a *communication class*. Note that this definition, involving as it does such notions as 'communication', 'practical purposes', 'practical difference' is deliberately vague. There would be no point in having a precise definition of vagueness.

If we think of a class K of meaning assignments there are three possibilities:

1. α is true in all members of K
2. α is true in some but not all members of K
3. α is true in no members of K.

And this is so whether we are thinking of truth with reference to a specified world or simply truth with respect to the real world. In case 1. we might say that α is $(K-)$ true and in case 3. that it is $(K-)$ false and in case 2. perhaps say that it is indeterminate. Note that this does not mean that α has no meaning. Every meaning assignment in K gives α a meaning. Indeterminacy is not to be confused with meaninglessness. In our example a temperature of 71° would make the sentence 'It is warm today' neither K−true nor K−false.

We can perhaps give an explanation along these lines to certain kinds of 'nonsensical' sentences, e.g.

'This toothpaste smells red'.

Now there is nothing about our use of the word 'smells' to prevent our saying that

'x smells ϕ', where ϕ is a colour word, means that x has the smell
normally associated with things of colour ϕ.

On the other hand there is nothing about our use of the word 'smells' which
requires this. The reason is simple. In the real world smells are not as a rule
associated with colours and so there would not arise any situations where it
would make any practical difference in which way we were using the word
'smells'. We have to imagine a world rather remote from the real world before the decision becomes a sensible one. The air of absurdity about 'This
toothpaste smells red' arises because with respect to the communication-
class of English, it is neither true nor false.[8]

The idea of worlds too 'remote' from the real world for us to need to take
into account in deciding what we mean by the words we use has another
application. There might be some worlds which are so remote and so
bizarre that we have no idea how to apply our ordinary talk to them. We
might decide to ignore these worlds as too absurd to worry about. This
would give us one way in which we could have a notion of logical equivalence between propositions which was less strict than identity. We might
say that two propositions are logically equivalent iff they have the same
truth-value in all worlds except in the absurd ones. Since the identity
criterion for propositions is clearly equivalence of truth value in all worlds
logical equivalence is a less strict notion than propositional identity, though
of course stricter than material equivalence which is no more than identity
of truth value in the real world.[9]

Note that what I have just been saying applies only to sentences and not
to propositions. E.g. every proposition has a unique truth value in every
world (since a world is either in a set of worlds or not) and so a fortiori
every proposition is either true or false, even though sentences, with respect to a communication class may be neither. Further, although we have
a clear notion of identity it does not follow, with respect to any given

8. In this way a communication class will determine a set of 'selection restrictions' of the
kind considered by Katz [8, pp. 154–186] and others. Its advantages over these latter approaches are first that it actually tries to explain why some sentences sound nonsensical and
second that it distinguishes quite clearly between sentences which are ungrammatical (i.e.
syntactically deviant) and those which are semantically deviant. The failure of other linguists
to stress the importance of this distinction is noted by Seuren in [16, pp. 13–25].

9. For an elaboration of this point v. [4] where the absurd worlds are called 'non-classical'.
The big problem about this solution is to give an adequate characterisation of just what it is
about a world which makes it count as 'absurd'. A rather different approach is taken by Lewis
in [11, pp. 31–40].

meaning assignment that any two sentences or names have the same sense in any context let alone the same meaning (which would imply the same sense in all contexts).

Again although there will be logically necessary propositions viz., those which contain all the nonabsurd worlds) yet for a given meaning assignment there may be no sentences which are assigned a necessary proposition in all contexts, i.e., no sentences which are analytic in all contexts. It would even be possible, though this seems highly unlikely, that there are no sentences analytic in any context. In our metaphysics analyticity of sentences is parasitic upon the logical truth of propositions and not vice versa. Thus we have no need to go into the relations between analyticity and synonomy for the purpose of understanding logical truth and we are unworried by the fact that languages may contain no pairs of perfectly synonomous expressions and no sentences which are analytic in all contexts.[10]

It should be clear from what I have said how to extend the semantic treatment I have sketched to any language whose basic categories are Sentences and Names. If we can get along with these as the only basic categories, and if the programme of basing natural languages on categorial languages proves methodologically viable, and I recognize these are very big ifs, then the kind of atomistic metaphysics I have proposed can after all serve as the logical basis of talk about reality.

REFERENCES

[1] KASMIR ADJUKIEWICZ, "Syntactic Connection," in *Polish Logic,* ed. by Storrs McCall (Oxford: Clarendon Press, 1967), pp. 207–231.
[2] YEHOSUA BAR HILLEL, *Language and Information* (Addison-Wesley, 1964).
[3] NOAM CHOMSKY, *Aspects of the Theory of Syntax* (Cambridge, Mass.: MIT Press, 1965).

10. Although this paper is not intended as a reply to Quine's views on language as stated in [14] and elsewhere nevertheless the programme I have described seems to meet much of his criticism. Perhaps the most important feature is the possibility of giving a set-theoretical analysis of possible worlds in terms of space-time points. Also it is known that the philosophical substance of Quine's objections to model logic turns on whether it makes sense to speak of the same individual existing in more than one possible world (v. e.g. [12, p. 166], [6] and [10]). I have attempted to give a definition of 'individual' which shows when and how this can be so. Third, the notion of a communication class may help to explain why we can never be sure that a given sentence is analytic or that a given translation is correct since the members of the class may not be precisely fixed.

[4] M. J. CRESSWELL, "Intensional Logic and Logical Truth," *Journal of Philosophical Logic* 1 (1972), 2-15.

[5] P. T. GEACH, "A Programme for Semantics," *Synthese,* 22 (1970), 3-17.

[6] K. J. J. HINTIKKA, "The Semantics of Model Notions and the Indeterminacy of Ontology," *Synthese* 21 (1970), 408-424.

[7] G. E. HUGHES AND M. J. CRESSWELL, *An Introduction to Modal Logic* (London: Methuen, 1968).

[8] JERROLD J. KATZ, *The Philosophy of Language* (New York: Harper and Row, 1966).

[9] JERROLD J. KATZ AND PAUL POSTAL, *An Integrated Theory of Linguistic Descriptions* (Cambridge, Mass.: MIT Press, 1964).

[10] DAVID LEWIS, "General Semantics," *Synthese,* 22 (1970), 18-67.

[11] DAVID LEWIS, "Counterpart Theory and Quantified Modal Logic," *Journal of Philosophy,* 65 (1968), 113-126; Chapter 5 of this anthology.

[12] RICHARD MONTAGUE, "On the Nature of Certain Philosophical Entities," *Monist,* 35 (1969), 159-194.

[13] RICHARD MONTAGUE, "Universal Grammar," *Theoria,* 36 (1970), 373-398.

[14] W. V. O. QUINE, *Word and Object* (Cambridge, Mass.: MIT Press, 1960).

[15] DANA SCOTT, "Advice on Modal Logic," in *Philosophical Problems in Logic,* ed. by Karel Lambert (Dordrecht: Reidel, 1970), pp. 143-173.

[16] P. A. M. SEUREN, *Operators and Nucleus* (Cambridge: Cambridge University Press, 1969).

[17] ROBERT STALNAKER, "Pragmatics," *Synthese,* 22 (1970), 272-289.

[18] P. F. STRAWSON, "On Referring," *Mind,* 59 (1950), 320-344.

7

Transworld Identity or Worldbound Individuals?

ALVIN PLANTINGA

Calvin College

I

The idea of *possible worlds* has seemed to promise understanding and insight into several venerable problems of modality—those of essence and accident, for example, necessary and contingent truth, modality *de dicto* and *de re,* and the nature of subjunctive conditionals. But just what is a possible world? Suppose we take it that a possible world is a *state of affairs* of some kind—one which either obtains, is real, is actual, or else *could have* obtained. But then how shall we understand "could have" here? Obviously no *definition* will be of much use: Here we must give examples, lay out the connections between the concept in question and other concepts, reply to objections, and hope for the best. Although I cannot do this in detail here,[1] I do wish to point out that the sense of possibility in question is wider than that of *causal* or *natural* possibility—so that *Agnew's swimming the Atlantic Ocean,* while it is perhaps causally or naturally impossible, is not impossible in the sense under discussion. On the other hand, this sense is narrower than that captured in first-order logic, so that many states of affairs are necessary, in the sense in question, although

Reprinted from *Logic and Ontology,* edited by Milton Munitz, © 1973 by New York University, with permission of New York University Press.

1. See my "De Re et De Dicto," *Noûs,* 3 (1969), 235–258, and "World and Essence," *Philosophical Review,* 74 (1970).

their corresponding propositions are not provable in first-order logic. Examples of such states of affairs would include those corresponding to truths of arithmetic and mathematics generally, as well as many more homely items such as *Nobody's being taller than himself, red's being a color,* (as well as a *thing's being colored if red*), *Agnew's not being a composite number,* and the like. Other and less homely candidates include *every person's being conscious at some time or other, every human person's having a body at some time during his career,* and *the existence of a being than which it's not possible that there be a greater.*

In the sense of necessity and possibility in question, furthermore, a pair of states of affairs S and S' may be so related that it is not possible that both obtain, in which case *S precludes S'*; and if it is impossible that S obtain and S' *not* obtain, then *S includes S'*. So, for example, *Agnew's having swum the Atlantic* includes *Agnew's having swum something or other* and precludes *Agnew's not being able to swim.* Still further, a state of affairs S may be such that for any state of affairs S', S either includes or precludes S', in which case S is *maximal.* Now we may say that a possible world is just a maximal possible state of affairs. Corresponding to each possible world W, furthermore, there is a unique class of propositions, C, of which a proposition P is a member just in case it is impossible that W be actual and P be false. Call this class *the book on W.* Like possible worlds, books too have a maximality property: each book contains, for any proposition P, either P or the negation of P. And the book on the actual world, obviously, is the set of true propositions.

Now it is plausible and natural to suppose that the same individual exists in various different states of affairs. There is, for example, the state of affairs consisting in *Paul R. Zwier's being a good tennis player*; this state of affairs is possible but does not in fact obtain. It is natural to suppose, however, that if it *had* obtained, Zwier would have existed and would have been a good tennis player. That is, it is natural to suppose that Zwier *exists in* this state of affairs. But, of course, if he exists in this state of affairs, then he exists in every possible world including it; that is, every possible world including *Zwier's being a good tennis player* is such that, had it been actual, Zwier would have existed. So Zwier exists in many possible worlds. I say it is natural to make this supposition; but many philosophers otherwise kindly disposed toward possible worlds are inclined toward its denial. Among them, there is, for example, Leibniz, whose credentials on this subject are certainly impeccable; Leibniz apparently held that each object exists in just one world.[2] The idealists, furthermore, in arguing for their doctrine of internal relations, were arguing in essence that an object exists in exactly one possible world—indeed, some of them may have thought that there is only one such world. More recently, the view that individuals are thus confined to one world—let's call it The Theory of Worldbound Individuals—has been at least entertained with considerable hospitality by David Kaplan.[3] Roderick Chisholm, furthermore, finds difficulty and perplexity in the claim that the same object exists in more than one possible world.[4] Still further, The Theory of Worldbound Individuals is an explicit postulate of David Lewis' Counterpart Theory.[5] In what follows I shall explore this issue. Now perhaps the most important and widely heralded argument for the Theory of Worldbound Individuals (hereafter 'TWI') is the celebrated *Problem of Transworld Identification,* said to arise on the supposition that the same object exists in more than one world. Accordingly I will concentrate on these two topics: TWI and the problem of Transworld Identity.

Why, then, should we suppose that an individual is confined to just one world—that you and I, for example, exist in this world and this world only? According to G. E. Moore, the idealists, in arguing for their view that all relations are internal, were really arguing that all relational properties are essential to the things that have them. The argument they gave, however, if it is sound, establishes that *all* properties—not just relational properties—are thus essential to their owners. If this is correct, however, then for no object x is there a possible state of affairs in which x lacks a property that in fact it has; so x exists only in the actual world, the world that does in fact obtain.

Now an argument for a conclusion as sweeping as this must pack quite a punch. What did the idealists come up with? A confusion, says Moore. What the idealists asserted is

2. As has been argued by Benson Mates, "Leibniz on Possible Worlds," *Logic, Methodology, and Philosophy of Science,* 3d ed. (Amsterdam: Van Rootsclaar and Staal, 1968).

3. "Transworld Heir Lines," read at an APA Symposium, Chicago, 1967; Chapter 4 of this anthology.

4. "Identity through Possible Worlds: Some Questions," *Noûs,* 1 (1967), 1; Chapter 3 of this anthology.

5. "Counterpart Theory and Quantified Modal Logic," *Journal of Philosophy,* 65 (1968), 113; Chapter 5 of this anthology.

(1) If P be a relational property and A a term to which it does in fact belong, then, no matter what P and A may be, it may always be truly asserted of them, that any term which had *not* possessed P would necessarily have been other than or numerically different from A . . . .[6]

Perhaps we may put this more perspicuously as

(1') If x has P, then for any object y, if there is a world in which y lacks P, then y is distinct from x

which clearly entails the desired conclusion. What they suggested as a reason for accepting (1), however is

(2) If A has P and x does not, it *does* follow that x is other than A.[7]

If we restate (2) as the claim that

(2') For any object x and y, if x has P and y does not, then x is distinct from y

holds in every world, we see that (2) is just the thesis that the Indiscernibility of Identicals is necessarily true. This thesis seems accurate enough, but no reason at all for (1) or (1'). As Moore, says, (1) and (2) are easily conflated, particularly when they are put in the idealists' typically opaque and turgid prose; and the idealists seized the opportunity to conflate them.

Initially, then, this argument is unpromising. It has a near relative, however, that we may conceivably find in Leibniz and that often surfaces in contemporary discussion. Leibniz writes Arnauld as follows:

Besides, if, in the life of any person and even in the whole universe anything went differently from what it has, nothing could prevent us from saying that it was another person or another possible universe which God had chosen. It would then be indeed another individual.[8]

6. "External and Internal Relations," *Philosophical Studies* (London: Routledge and Kegan Paul, 1922), p. 287.

7. Ibid., p. 289.

8. Letter from Leibniz to Arnauld, July 14, 1686. Leibniz makes very nearly the same statement in a letter to Count von Hessen-Rheinfels, May 1686 (p. 111), *Discourse on Metaphysics* (La Salle, Ill.: Open Court, 1962), pp. 127–128. Published in the *Discourse* as well.

This is on its face a dark saying. What Leibniz says here and elsewhere, however, may suggest the following. Suppose Socrates exists in some world W distinct from the actual world (which for purposes of easy reference I shall name "Charley"). Taking the term 'property' in a broad sense, we shall be obliged to concede that there must be some property that Socrates has in Charley but lacks in W. (At the very least, if we let 'π' name the book on Charley, then one property Socrates has in Charley but lacks in W is that of being such that every member of π is true.) So let us suppose that there is some property—snubnosedness, let us say—that Socrates has in Charley but lacks in W. That is, the Socrates of Charley, Socrates-in-Charley, has snubnosedness, while the Socrates of W does not. But surely this is inconsistent with the Indiscernibility of Identicals, a principle than which none sounder can be conceived. For according to this principle, if Socrates-in-Charley has snubnosedness but Socrates-in-W does not, then Socrates-in-Charley is distinct from Socrates-in-W. We must conclude, therefore, that Socrates does not exist both in Charley and in W. There may be some person in W that much resembles our Socrates, Socrates-in-Charley; that person is nonetheless distinct from him. And of course this argument can be generalized to show that nothing exists in more than one world.

Such an argument, however, is less than impeccable. We are asked to infer

(3) Socrates-in-Charley is snubnosed and Socrates-in-W is not

from

(4) Socrates is snubnosed in Charley but not in W.

We need not quarrel with this request; but the Indiscernibility of Identicals in no way licenses the inference that Socrates-in-Charley and Socrates-in-W are distinct. For, contrary, perhaps, to appearances, there is no property that (3) predicates of Socrates-in-Charley and withholds from Socrates-in-W. According to (3) [so taken that it follows from (4)], Socrates-in-Charley (that is, Socrates) has the property of being snubnosed, all right, but *in Charley*. Socrates-in-W, however, lacks that property *in W*. But this latter, of course, means only that Socrates-in-W has the property of being such that, if W had obtained, he would not have been snubnosed. And, of course, this property—the property an object x has iff x would not have been snubnosed, had W obtained—is not the complement of snubnosedness. Indeed, this property is not even incompatible with snubnosedness; Socrates himself is snubnosed, but would not have been had W been actual. So the Indiscernibility of Identicals does not apply here; there is no property P which (3) asserts that Socrates-in-Charley has but Socrates-in-W lacks. To suppose that Socrates has P in the actual world but lacks it in W is to suppose only that Socrates does in fact have P but would not have had it, had W been actual. The Indiscernibility of Identicals casts not even a hint of suspicion upon this supposition. This objection, therefore, is a snare and a delusion.

A more popular and more promising argument for TWI is the dreaded *Problem of Transworld Identity* said to confront anyone who rashly supposes the same object to exist in more than one world. Here the claim is that there are deep conceptual difficulties in *identifying* the same object from world to world—difficulties that threaten the very idea of Transworld Identity with incoherence. These difficulties, furthermore, presumably do not arise on TWI.[9]

But what, exactly, *is* the problem of Transworld Identity? What difficulties does it present for the notion that the same object exists in various possible worlds? Just how does this problem go? Although published statements of it are scarce,[10] the problem may perhaps be put as follows. Let us suppose again that Socrates exists in some world W distinct from this one—a world in which let us say, he did not fight in the battle of Marathon. In W, of course, he may also lack other properties he has in this world—perhaps in W he eschewed philosophy, corrupted no youth, and thus escaped the wrath of the Athenians. Perhaps in W he lived in Corinth, was six feet tall, and remained a bachelor all his life. But then we must ask ourselves how we could possibly *identify* Socrates in that world. How could we *pick him out?* How could we *locate* him there? How could we possibly tell which of the many things contained in W is *Socrates?* If we try to employ the properties we use to identify him in *this* world, our efforts may well end in dismal failure—perhaps in that world it is Xenophon or maybe even Thrasymachus that is Plato's mentor and exhibits the splendidly single-minded passion for truth and justice that characterizes Socrates in this. But if we cannot identify him in W, so the argument continues, then we really do not understand the assertion that he exists

9. So David Lewis: "P_2 [the postulate according to which nothing exists in more than one world] serves only to rule out avoidable problems of individuation," found in Chapter 5 of this anthology.

10. But see R. Chisholm, "Identity through Possible Worlds: Some Questions," pp. 1–8; Chapter 3 of this anthology.

there. If we cannot even identify him, we would not know whom we were talking about, in saying that Socrates exists in that world or has this or that property therein. In order to make sense of such talk, we must have a *criterion* or *principle* that enables us to identify Socrates from world to world. This criterion must include some property that Socrates has in each world in which he exists—and if it is sufficient to enable us to *pick him out* in a given world, distinguish him from other things, it must be a property he alone has in these worlds. Further, if the property (or properties) in question is to enable us to pick him out, it must in some broad sense be "empirically manifest"—it must resemble such properties as having such-and-such a name, address, Social Security number, height, weight, and general appearance in that we can tell by broadly empirical means whether a given object has or lacks it. How, otherwise, could we use it to *pick out* or *identify* him? So, if it is intelligible to suppose that Socrates exists in more than one world, there must be some empirically manifest property that he and he alone has in each of the worlds in which he exists. Now obviously we do not know of any such property, or even that there is such a property. Indeed, it is hard to see how there *could* be such a property. But then the very idea of Transworld Identity is not really intelligible—in which case we must suppose that no object exists in more than one world.

The first thing to note about the objection outlined above is that it seems to arise out of a certain *picture* or *image*. We imagine ourselves somehow peering into another world; we ask ourselves whether Socrates exists in it. We observe the behavior and characteristics of its denizens and then wonder which of these, if any, is Socrates. Of course, we realize that he might look quite different in *W*, if he exists there at all. He might also live at a different place, have different friends and different fingerprints, if, indeed, he has fingers. But how then can we tell which one he *is?* And does it so much as make sense to say that he exists in that world, if there is no way in principle of identifying him, of telling which thing there *is* Socrates?

Now perhaps this picture is useful in certain respects; in the present context, however, it breeds nothing but confusion. For it is this picture that slyly insinuates that the proposition *Socrates exists in other possible worlds* is intelligible to us only if we know of some empirically manifest property that he and he alone has in each world in which he exists. But suppose we consider an analogous temporal situation. In Herbert Spiegelberg's book *The Phenomenological Movement* there are pictures of Franz Brentano at ages twenty and seventy respectively. The youthful Brentano looks much like Apollo; the elderly Brentano resembles nothing so much as Jerome Hines in his portrayal of the dying Czar in *Boris Godounov*. Most of us will concede that the same object exists at several different times; but do we know of some empirically manifest property *P* such that a thing is Brentano at a given time *t* if and only if it has *P*? Surely not; and this casts no shadow whatever on the intelligibility of the claim that Brentano existed at many different times.

Still, isn't the argument made above available here? No doubt there was a time, some fifty years ago, when Spiro Agnew was a precocious baby. But if I understand that assertion, must I not be able to *pick him out, locate* him, at that time? If I cannot identify him, if I cannot tell which of the things that existed at that time was Agnew, then (so goes the argument) I cannot make sense of the claim that he existed at that time. And I could identify him, at *t*, only if I know of some empirically manifest property that he and he alone has at *t*.

But here the argument is manifestly confused. To suppose that Agnew was a precocious baby at *t* it is not necessary that I be able to pick his picture out of a gallery of babies at *t*. Of course I must know *who he is* to understand this assertion; and perhaps to know that I must know of some property that he and he alone has. Indeed, we might go so far as to concede that this property must be 'empirically manifest' in some sense. But surely it is asking too much to require that I know of such a property that he and he only has *at every time at which he exists*. Of course I must be able to answer the question "Which of the things existing at *t* is Agnew?" But the answer is trivial; it's that man sitting right over there—the Vice President of the United States.

If this is correct, however, why suppose otherwise in the Transworld case? I understand the proposition that there is a possible world in which Socrates did not teach Plato. Now let *W* be any such world. Why suppose that a condition of my understanding this is my knowing something about what he would have looked like or where he would have lived, had *W* been actual? To understand this proposition I must know who Socrates is. Perhaps this involves my knowing of some property that is empirically manifest (whatever exactly that comes to) and unique to Socrates. But what earthly (or otherwise) reason is there for supposing that I must know of some empirically manifest property he has *in that world W?* The picture suggests that I must be able to look into *W* and sift through its inhabitants until I run across one I recognize as Socrates—otherwise I cannot identify him, and hence I do not know whom I am talking about. But here the picture is not doing right by us. For, taken literally, of course, this notion makes no sense. All I know about this world W is that Socrates would not have taught Plato had W obtained. I do not know anything about which other persons would have existed, or—except for his essential properties—which other properties Socrates has in that world. How could I know more, since all I have been told about W is that it is one of the many worlds in which Socrates exists but does not teach Plato?

Accordingly, the claim that I must be able somehow to identify Socrates in W—pick him out—is either trivial or based on a confusion. Of course, I must know which of the persons existing in W—the persons who would have existed, had W been actual—I am talking about. But the answer, obviously, and trivially, is Socrates. To be able thus to answer, however, I need know nothing further about what Socrates would have been like had W been actual.

But let us imagine the objector regrouping. "If Socrates exists in several worlds," he says, "then even if there need be no *empirically manifest* property he and he alone has in each of them, there must at any rate be some property or other that he and only he has in each world in which he exists. Let us say that such a property is an essence of Socrates. Such an essence meets two conditions: (1) Socrates has it in every world he graces, and (2) nothing distinct from him has it in any world. (By contrast, a property need meet only the first condition to be *essential* to Socrates.) Now a property P entails a property Q if there is no world in which there exists an object that has P but lacks Q. So any essence of Socrates entails each of his essential properties—each property that Socrates has in every world in which he exists. Furthermore, if E is an essence of Socrates, then the class C of his essential properties—the properties he has in each world in which he exists—will obviously entail E in the sense that there is no world in which something exemplifies all of these properties but does not exemplify E. (What makes this particularly obvious is that any essence of Socrates is essential to him and hence is a member of C.) An essence of Socrates, therefore, is, in this sense, equivalent to the class of his essential properties; and Socrates exists in more than one possible world only if he has at least one essence in the explained sense. But at best it is far from clear which (if any) of Socrates' properties are essential to him and even less clear that he has an essence. Nor does there seem to be any way of determining whether he has such a property or, if he does, which properties are entailed by it. So is not the suggestion that he has an essence both gratuitous and problematic? We can and should avoid this whole problem by accepting TWI.'' Thus far the objector.

What can be said by way of reply? First, that if we follow this counsel, we gain all the advantages of theft over honest toil, as Russell says in another connection. The question is whether Socrates has an essence and whether objects do or do not exist in more than one world—not whether we would be saved some work or perplexity if we said they did not. But more fundamentally, TWI does not avoid the question which of Socrates' properties are essential to him. Obviously it gives an answer to that question, and an unsatisfactory one at that; for it says that *all* of his properties are essential to him and that any property he alone has—that of being married to Xantippe, for example—is one of his essences.

These caveats entered, however (and I shall return below to the second), let us consider the objector's main complaint. Is it really so difficult, on The Theory of Transworld Identity, to determine whether Socrates has an essence? In fact, in the actual world, Socrates has the property of being snubnosed. But now consider a world W in which he is not snubnosed. Had W obtained, Socrates would not have been snubnosed; we may say, therefore, that Socrates is nonsnubnosed-in-W. In general, where P is a property and W a world, to say that x has P-in-W is simply to say that x would have had P if W had been actual. So Socrates has the property of *being nonsnubnosed-in-W*; that is, he has this property in Charley, the actual world. In W, on the other hand, Socrates has the property of *being-snubnosed-in-Charley*. Indeed, in *any* world in which Socrates exists, he has the property of being snubnosed-in-Charley.[11] This property, therefore, is essential to him. And of course we can generalize the claim: Where P is any property Socrates has, the property of having-P-in-Charley is essential to him. But now consider some property P that Socrates has in fact and that he alone has—*being married to Xantippe,* perhaps, or *being born at such and such a place and time,* or *being A. E. Taylor's favorite philosopher.* The property *having-P-in-Charley* will, of course, be essential to Socrates. Furthermore, each thing distinct from Socrates has its complement essentially, for everything distinct from Socrates has the complement $\bar{P}$ of P; hence each such thing has $\bar{P}$-*in-Charley,* and has it essentially, that is, in every world in which it exists. But then everything distinct from Socrates

---

11. If, as I do, we make the S_5-like supposition that if a given state of affairs (or proposition) S is possible, then S is possible in every world. See ''World and Essence,'' p. 475.

has the complement of *having-P-in-Charley* and has that property essentially. So there is no possible world in which some object distinct from Socrates has the property of having *P*-in-Charley. Not only, then, is this property essential to him; it is also one of his essences. And obviously we can find as many essences of Socrates as you like. Take any property *P* and world *W* such that Socrates alone has *P* in *W*; the property of having *P* in *W* is an essence of Socrates.[12]

Now you may think the very idea of a property like *being snubnosed in Charley* is muddled, perverse, ungainly, or in some other way deserving of abuse and contempt. But where, exactly (or even approximately), is the muddle? We must not let this terminology mislead us into thinking that if there is such a property, then Charley must be a geographical unit or place—like Wyoming, for example—so that this property would be like *being mugged in New Jersey*. Socrates elected to remain in Athens and drink the hemlock, instead of fleeing to Thebes. He had the opportunity to take the latter course, however, and it was certainly possible that he do so. So there are possible worlds in which Socrates flees to Thebes and does not drink the hemlock. Now let *W* be any such world. Certainly it is true of Socrates that if *W* had been actual, he would have fled to Thebes; but that is all that is meant by saying that Socrates has the property of fleeing-to-Thebes-in-*W*. It is certainly not easy to see that this property is mysterious, underhanded, inelegant, or that it merits much by way of scorn and obloquy.

The objector, therefore, is right in claiming that if Socrates exists in several worlds, he must have an essence. His objection to the latter idea, however, is not impressive. Is there really something problematic or untoward in the idea of Transworld Identity? Is there really a problem of Transworld Identification? If there is, I am at a loss to see what it might be.

Of course there are legitimate problems in the neighborhood—problems that often are exposed when the subject ostensibly under discussion is Transworld Identity. For we might ask such questions as these: Is there a world *W* and an object *x* existing in *W* such that *x* is identical with Socrates, and *x*, let us say, was born in 1500 B.C. or was an eighteenth-century Irish washerwoman? These questions advertise themselves as questions about Transworld Identity; in fact they are questions concerning which of Socrates' properties are essential to him. Could he have had the

---

12. For more discussion of his essences (and for discussion of more of his essences) see "World and Essence," pp. 487ff.

property of being disembodied-at-some-time-or-other? Or the property of having-an-alligator-body-at-some-time-or-other? These are legitimate questions to which there are no easy answers. (Socrates himself suggests that everyone actually has the former property, while some of his more snappish acquaintances may have the latter.) These are real questions; but they need not shake our confidence that some of Socrates' properties are ones he could have lacked, so that Charley is not the only possible world in which he exists. The fact that we are not confident about their answers means only that Socrates has *some* properties such that we cannot easily tell whether or not they are essential to him; it does not so much as suggest that *all* his properties are thus inscrutable. And further, of course, the Theory of Worldbound Individuals, as so far explained, does not avoid these questions; it simply answers them by fiat in insisting that each of Socrates' properties is essential to him.

II

The arguments for the Theory of Worldbound Individuals, then, are based upon error and confusion. But are there positive reasons for rejecting it? I think there are. The basic thrust of the theory is the contention that no object exists in more than one possible world; this implies the outrageous view that—taking property in the broadest possible sense—no object could have lacked any property that in fact it has. Had the world been different in even the tiniest, most Socrates-irrelevant fashion, Socrates would not have existed. Suppose God created n electrons. The theory in question entails the absolute impossibility of His having created both Socrates and $n + 1$ electrons. It thereby fails to distinguish the relation in which he stands to inconsistent attributes—being both married and unmarried, for example— from his relation to such attributes as *fleeing to Thebes*. It is as impossible, according to this theory, that Socrates should have had the latter as the former. Consider furthermore, a proposition like

(5) Socrates is foolish

a proposition which predicates of Socrates some property he lacks. Now presumably (5) is true, in a given possible world, only if Socrates exists in that world and has the property of being foolish therein. But on TWI, there is no such world, and (5) accordingly, is necessarily false, as will be any proposition predicating of Socrates a property he does not in fact have. In the same vein, consider any proposition P that is false but contingent.

Since *Socrates exists* is true only in Charley, where *P* is false, there is no world in which *P* and *Socrates exists* are both true. The latter, therefore, entails the denial of the former. Accordingly, *Socrates exists* entails every true proposition. And all of this is entirely too extravagant to be believed. If we know anything at all about modality, we know that some of Socrates' properties are accidental, that *Socrates is foolish* is not necessarily false, and that *Socrates exists* does not entail every true proposition.

But here we must consider an exciting new wrinkle to this old theory. Embracing the Theory of Worldbound Individuals, David Lewis adds to it the suggestion that a worldbound individual typically has *counterparts* in other possible worlds:

> The counterpart relation is our substitute for identity between things in different worlds. Where some would say that you are in several worlds, in which you have somewhat different properties and somewhat different things happen to you, I prefer to say that you are in the actual world and no other, but you have counterparts in several other worlds. Your counterparts resemble you closely in content and context in important respects. They resemble you more closely than do the other things in their worlds. But they are not really you. For each of them is in his own world, and only you are here in the actual world. Indeed we might say, speaking casually, that your counterparts are you in other worlds, that they and you are the same; but this sameness is no more a literal identity than the sameness between you today and you tomorrow. It would be better to say that your counterparts are men you *would have been,* had the world been otherwise.[13]

Fortified with Counterpart Theory, TWI is no longer obliged to hold that each of Socrates' properties is essential to him; instead, a property is essential to him if and only if each of his counterparts (among whom is Socrates himself) has it. Accordingly, while indeed there is no world in which Socrates, *our* Socrates—the object that in our world is Socrates—lacks the property of being snubnosed, there are no doubt worlds contain-

13. "Counterpart Theory," pp. 114–115; found in Chapter 5 of this anthology. I said David Lewis embraces TWI; but this is not entirely accurate. Speaking of the Counterpart Relation, he says, "Yet with this substitute in use, it would not matter if some things *were* identical with some of their counterparts after all! P_2 [the postulate according to which objects are worldbound] serves only to rule out avoidable problems of individuation." One may offer and study means of formalizing modal discourse for a variety or reasons, and TWI is not really essential to Lewis' program. What I shall be quarreling with in ensuing pages is not that program, but the view which takes TWI as the sober, metaphysical truth of the matter.

ing *counterparts* of Socrates—counterparts which are not snubnosed. So the property of being snubnosed is not essential to him.

And let us now return to

(5) Socrates is foolish.

TWI seems to imply, paradoxically enough, that this statement is necessarily false. Can Counterpart Theory be of help here? Indeed it can, for, no doubt, Socrates has foolish counterparts in other worlds; and this is sufficient, according to TWI fortified with Counterpart Theory, for the contingency of (5). This proposition is contingently false if there is another world in which it is true; but its truth in a given world does not require the existence, in that world, of what is denoted by 'Socrates' in this. Like 'the first man to climb Mt. Rainier,' 'Socrates,' according to the present view, denotes different persons in different worlds. Or, as we may also put it, in different worlds different things have the property of being Socrates—just as, in different worlds, different things have the property of being the first man to climb Rainier.

Socrateity, then, or the property of being Socrates, is not the property of being identical with the person who in Charley, the actual world, is Socrates; it is not the property of being that person. It is, instead, a property that could have been had by someone else; roughly, it is the property that is unique to Socrates and his counterparts. You may think it difficult to see just what property that is; and indeed that *is* difficult. In the present context, however, what is important to see is that Socrateity is had by different objects in different worlds. Indeed, on Counterpart Theory an object may have more than one property in a given world; so no doubt there are worlds in which several distinct things exemplify Socrateity. And the point is that (5) is true, in a world W, just in case W contains an object that is both Socratic and foolish—that is, just in case Socrates has a foolish counterpart and Socrateity a foolish instance in W. So what (5) says is or is equivalent to

(6) Something exemplifies both Socrateity and foolishness.

And, of course, this proposition will be true in some but not all worlds.

But what about

(7) Socrates exists?

If nothing exists in more than one world, then presumably Socrates does not, in which case on TWI (fortified with Counterpart Theory though it be), (7) still seems to be true in just one world and still seems paradoxically to entail every true proposition. But here perhaps appearances are deceiving. Counterpart Theory affords the means of denying that (7) is true in only one world. For this proposition, we may say, is true in any world where Socrateity has an instance; since there are many such, there are many worlds in which it is true; hence there are many worlds in which both (7) and some false propositions are true. So the former does not entail every true proposition. But if (7) is true in many worlds, how does the central claim of TWI—that nothing exists in more than one—fit in? If Socrates, along with everything else) exists in only one world, that is, if

(8) Socrates exists in more than one world

is false, how can (7) be true in more than one world?

But perhaps the partisan of TWI can go so far as to deny that his theory commits him to the falsity of (8). Perhaps he can construe it as the entirely accurate claim that *Socrates exists* is true in more than one world. But how, then, does (8) comport with the central claim of TWI? According to the latter, nothing has the property of existing in more than one world. How, then, can TWI sensibly hold that (8) is true? As follows, perhaps. Suppose the predicate "exists in more than one world" expresses a property that, according to TWI, no object has. Then (8), if true, must not, of course, be seen as predicating that property of Socrates—if it did, it would be false. Perhaps it *looks* as if it predicates that property of Socrates; in fact, however, it does not. What it does instead is to predicate *truth in more than one world of Socrates exists*. There is an instructive parallel between (8) so construed and

(9) The number of planets is possibly greater than nine.

Read *de dicto*, (9) quite properly predicates possibility of

(10) The number of planets is greater than nine.

It is plausible to add, furthermore, *that* the words "is possibly greater than nine" express a property—the property a thing has just in case it is possibly greater than nine. Every number greater than nine enjoys this property; that is to say, each number greater than nine is *possibly* greater than nine. The number of planets, however, being nine, does not have the property in question. (9), therefore, can be read as a true *de dicto* assertion; but, thus read, it does not predicate of the object named by "the number of planets" the property expressed by "is possibly greater than seven."

Similarly, then, for (8); the words "exists in more than one world" express a property that (if TWI is true) nothing has; the proposition in question, however, does not predicate that property of anything and hence need not (at any rate on that account) be false. Furthermore the argument from

(11) Nothing exists in more than one world

to the falsehood of (8) is to be rejected. We may compare this argument with another:

(12) Every number greater than seven is necessarily greater than seven.

(13) The number of planets is greater than seven.

Hence

(14) The number of planets is necessarily greater than seven.

If we construe (14) as the *de dicto* claim that

(15) The number of planets is greater than seven

is necessarily true, then it obviously fails to follow from (12) and (13). (12) says that every number meeting a certain condition has a certain property—that of being necessarily greater than seven. According to (13), the number of planets meets that condition. (14), however, is not the consequent *de re* assertion that the number of planets has that property; it is instead the false (and inconsequent) *de dicto* assertion that (15) is necessarily true. But now the same can be said for (8). This is not the *de re* assertion that some specific object has the property that (11) says nothing has. *That* assertion, indeed, is precluded by (11) and thus is false on TWI. Instead, we must look upon (8) as the *de dicto* allegation that *Socrates exists* is true in more than one world—an allegation quite consistent with (11). What we have here, then, as in the inference of (14) from (12) and (13), is another *de re*–*de dicto* ambiguity.

So the partisan of TWI need not hold that Socrates has all his properties essentially, or that *Socrates exists* entails every true proposition. Indeed, he can go so far as to join the upholder of Transworld Identity in affirming the truth of sentence (8). You may think this course on his part less ingenuous than ingenious; and so, perhaps it is. Indeed, as we shall see, a certain disingenuousness is perhaps a salient feature of TWI. But so far the addition of Counterpart Theory seems to provide TWI with a solution for difficulties it could not otherwise cope with.

Despite its fortification with Counterpart Theory, however, the Theory of Worldbound Individuals is open to a pair of decisive objections. Perhaps we can approach the first of these as follows. Consider the following eccentric proposition:

(16) Everyone is at least as tall as he is.

It is plausible to consider that this proposition predicates a certain property of each person—a property that is universally shared. It predicates of Lew Alcindor, for example, the property of being at least as tall as he himself is, a property that in no way distinguishes him from anyone else. But the proposition also predicates of each person a property he need not share with others. For what it also says of Lew Alcindor is that he has the property of being at least as tall as Lew Alcindor—a property he shares with nearly no one. The same things hold for

(17) Everything is identical with itself.

This proposition predicates of each object the property of being self-identical—a property it shares with everything else. But it also says of any given object x that it has the property of being identical with x—a property unique to x. Socrates, for example, has the property of being essentially identical with Socrates, as well as that of being essentially self-identical. It is natural to say that these two properties *coincide* on Socrates in the sense that it is impossible that he have one but not the other.

But in TWI (henceforth understood to include Counterpart Theory) these two properties come apart. For while Socrates, of course, has no counterparts that lack self-identity, he does have counterparts that lack identity-with-Socrates. He alone of all of his counterparts, in fact, has the property of being identical with Socrates—the property, that is, of being identical with the object that in fact instantiates Socrateity. It is true, no doubt, that each of Socrates' counterparts has Socrateity, so that a counterpart (Socrates$_w$, say) of Socrates in a world W has the property of being identical with the thing that *in W* is Socrates or has Socrateity. But, of course, Socrates$_w$ is *distinct from* Socrates—the person who *in fact* is Socrates.

Accordingly, some of Socrates' counterparts have the property of being distinct from Socrates. This means that (according to Counterpart Theory) the two properties predicated of Socrates by (17) do not coincide on Socrates. Indeed he has the property of being essentially self-identical, but he does not have the property of being essentially identical with Socrates. And this is the first of the two objections I promised. According to Counterpart Theory, the property of being identical with myself, unlike the property of self-identity, is not essential to me. Hence I could have been someone else. And this, I take it, is genuinely paradoxical. I could have been different in many ways, no doubt; but it makes no sense to suppose that I could have been someone else—someone, who, had he existed, would have been distinct from me. And yet Counterpart Theory, thus explained, implies not merely that I *could* have been distinct from myself, but that I *would* have been distinct from myself had things gone differently in even the most miniscule detail.

We can approach the same matter a bit differently. According to Counterpart Theory,

(18) I could have been taller than I am

is no doubt true. For what (18) requires is that there be a world in which I have a counterpart whose height exceed the height I actually enjoy. But then similarly

(19) I could have been a different person from the one I am

will be true just in case there is a world in which I have a counterpart who is a different person from the one I actually am. And of course the Counterpart Theorist will hold that I do have such counterparts; so he must hold that (19) is true. Indeed, he must put up with something even worse; Counterpart Theory implies, not merely that I *could* have been a different person from the one I am, but that I *would* have been a different person, had things gone differently in even the most miniscule detail. More exactly, what Counterpart Theory implies is the truth of

(20) If S, then either I would not have existed or I would have been a different person from the one I am

where 'S' is replaced by any false sentence. For such an instance of (20) will be true if every world in which S holds is one in which I lack a counterpart or have one that is a different person from the one I am. And, of course, if S is false, then every world in which it holds *is* one in which I either lack a counterpart or have one who is a different person from the one I am. If a leaf deep in the mountain fastness of the North Cascades had fallen in October 31, 1876, the day before it actually fell, then (according to Counterpart Theory) I should have been either nonexistent or else a different person from the one I am. And surely this is false.

According to TWI-Counterpart Theory, therefore, I have self-identity essentially but identity with myself accidentally. Although I could not have had self-diversity, I could have been diverse from myself, I could have been someone else. But there is a related and perhaps more important objection. The characteristic feature of TWI is that each of us (and every-thing else) would not so much as have existed had things been different in even the most insignificant fashion. This is itself not at all easy to believe. Asked to think of possible but non-actual states of affairs, we come up with such items as *Paul's being a good tennis player;* we suppose that there is a possible state of affairs such that, had it obtained, Paul himself—the very person we know and love so well—would have existed and had some property that, lamentably enough, he lacks. Perhaps this point becomes even more poignant if we take it personally. According to TWI, I would not have existed had things been in even the slightest way different. Had I had an extra cornflake for breakfast, I should not now exist. A narrow escape if there ever was one! The very idea fills one with existential Angst; the merest misstep has dramatic consequences indeed.

But of course the Angst is misplaced. For, according to TWI, there is no world in which I have that extra cornflake; it is not logically or metaphysi-cally possible that I should have done so. And this holds whether or not TWI is fortified with Counterpart Theory; the latter's promise to relieve the former of this embarrassing consequence is not fulfilled. I am now con-fronted with what seems to me to be a choice; I can load my pipe with Dunhill's Standard Mixture or with Balkan Sobranie, both being available and congenial. I believe that it is possible for me to do either of these things and that which I do is up to me. According to TWI, however, one of these events will take place and the other has not so much as a ghost of a chance. For one of these takes place in the actual world and the other occurs in no possible world whatever. If I shall, in fact, smoke Sobranie, then smoking Dunhill is as far out of the question as smoking the number 7. No doubt the partisan of TWI will protest that it is possible for me to take an action A if there is a world in which I have a counterpart who takes that action. But is not this just to redefine, change, the meaning of the locution 'it is possible for me'? Of what relevance to my being able to take an action A is the fact, if it is a fact, that there is a possible state of affairs such that, had it obtained, someone very like but distinct from me would have taken A? Surely this gives me no reason at all for supposing it possible that I take this action. Of course we can give a new sense to the terms involved; but to do so is just to change the subject.

The difficulty with TWI in its original Leibnizian forms, I said, was that it implied that each object has each of its properties essentially; and the original attractiveness of Counterpart Theory was its promise to overcome that difficulty. This promise, I think, is illusory. Of course we can define the location 'has P essentially' in the way suggested by Counterpart Theory; and then we will be in verbal agreement with the truth that objects have some of their properties accidentally. But the agreement, I suggest, is *only* verbal. For according to TWI, if in fact I have a property P, then there is no possible world in which I lack it. It is not possible that I should have lacked it. Of course there may be a state of affairs S such that had it obtained, there would have existed someone similar to me that would have lacked P; but how is this even relevant to the question where I could have lacked P—whether it is possible that I should not have had P? This seems no more to the point than the possibility that there be someone with my *name* who lacks P. And hence I do not think Counterpart Theory succeeds in overcoming the main objection to TWI; that difficulty remains.

By way of summary and conclusion, then: our initial insight into these matters is that objects have only some of their properties essentially; and an object x has a property P contingently only if there is a possible state of affairs S such that x would not have had P had S obtained. This joint affirmation obviously implies that the same object exists in more than one possible world—an idea that some find difficult or incoherent. The objections to this idea, however, do not withstand careful scrutiny. To reject it, furthermore, is to hold that an object exists in exactly one possible world, and this alternative entails—with or without the fortification of Counterpart Theory—that each object has each of its properties essentially.

8

The Ontology of the Possible

NICHOLAS RESCHER

University of Pittsburgh

I. Preliminaries

The sphere of the possible covers a wide range. There are as yet unrealized possibilities that await us in the future. And there are the possible albeit unrealized doings of actual things such as my possible attendance at the film I failed to see last night. There are those things which are "possible for all I know," many of which will be as real as anything can be. But some states of affairs and some things are *merely* possible. They are not going to come to be realized in the future. Further inquiry is not going to have them turn out to be real. They are not simply alternative permutations of the actual. They are wholly unreal—*merely* possible in the most strictly hypothetical sense. These possible things and states of affairs—we may call them *hard-core possibilities*—are paradigmatic of what I have in mind here in speaking of "the possible." These hard-core, totally unactualized possibilities will be central to the ensuing discussion.

The conception of "nonentities," or "unactualized possibles," or "negative things," or "unreal particulars," or "nonexistent individuals" is among the most ancient and persistent notions in the history of philosophy. In surveying this area of conceptual historiography it is my aim to show the idea of nonexistent individuals to be historically respectable in its antecedents, as well as to have substantial philosophical interest.

The fountainhead of subsequent discussions of nonexistent individuals is

Reprinted from *Logic and Ontology*, edited by Milton Munitz, © 1973 by New York University, with permission of New York University Press.

to be found in the dialogues of Plato. In the *Sophist*[1] Plato espoused the Parmenidean view that all meaningful discourse (*logos*) must be *about a being* of some kind. Since winged horses and other nonexistent things can obviously be talked of meaningfully,[2] a rigid adherence to this doctrine would suggest for them a mode of being that is intermediate between the actually existent and the utterly nonexistent which could not even be talked about or thought of. Plato did not hesitate to draw this consequence, and his view of these matters is the precursor of all later treatments of the problem. We shall not, however, pursue these historical byways further on this occasion, referring the interested reader to other discussions.[3]

II. The Ontological Status of Possibilities

Putting aside historical observations, we turn now to the systematic issues. The central question of this paper can be posed in very old-fashioned terminology: What is the ontological status of nonexistent possibilities?

Possibilistic claims have their principal point where the contrast between the actually real and the hypothetically possible prevails, and where the domain of what is or what does happen is to be augmented by that of what can be or what might happen. Now the items of this second, hypothetical sphere clearly cannot just "objectively be" the case. It is my central thesis that by the very nature of hypothetical possibilities they cannot exist as such, but must be thought of: They must be hypothesized, or imagined, or assumed, or something of this sort. For, unlike real acts, hypothetical ones, by their very nature, lack, *ex hypothesi,* that objective foundation in the

1. See especially 236 E ff. "It is also plain, that in speaking of something (*ti*) we speak of being (*ontos*), for to speak of an abstract something naked and isolated from all being is impossible" (ibid., 237 D, tr. Jowett). Cf. also the discussion in the *Theaetetus,* 189 A.

2. However, positive statements about nonexistents will presumably be false according to the correspondence theory of truth of *Sophist,* 261 E-263 B, since reality cannot provide the corresponding circumstances. Cf. Francis Cornford, *Plato's Theory of Knowledge* (London: Routledge & Kegan Paul, 1936), p. 313. Compare however, J. Xenakis' article "Plato on Statement and Truth-Value," *Mind,* 66 (1957), 165-172, where it is argued that for Plato, claims about nonexistents do not represent proper statements at all, and so do not have a truth value. However, see also the reply by J. M. E. Moravcsik, "Mr. Xenakis on Truth and Meaning," ibid., 67 (1958), 533-537.

3. Nicholas Rescher, "The Concept of Nonexistent Possibles," *Essays in Philosophical Analysis* (Pittsburgh: University of Pittsburgh Press, 1969).

existential order which alone could render them independent of conceiving minds.

This critical point that the realm of the hypothetical is mind-dependent must be argued in detail. Just what can be said regarding the existential status of that which is possible but not actual? In considering this, let us begin by asking the question: What sorts of items are at issue with the locution ''X is possible but not actual''? We can best answer this question by referring to the two traditional modes of modality, modality *de dicto* and modality *de re*. When we say that X is possible (but unactualized) then X is to be taken either (1) as a certain proposition (it is possible that-the-cat-is-on-the-mat) or (2) as a certain state of affairs (the cat's being on the mat is possible). But in dealing with the *ontology* of the possible, only this second category of possible states of affairs or things could conceivably concern us. For then we are certainly *not* concerned with the question of whether *propositions* exist as such: Our interest is in the existential status of *what is asserted by them*. Thus the *ontological* issues that concern us here are those posed by modality on the *de re* side; the question is not one of the existential status of the *proposition* ''that the cat is on the mat'' (*qua* proposition), but rather one of the existential status of the state of affairs that this proposition claims to obtain.

But just exactly what can the existential status of a possible-but-unrealized state of affairs be? Clearly—*ex hypothesi*—the state of affairs or things at issue does not exist as such: Only *actual* things or states of affairs can unqualifiedly be said to exist, not those that are possible but unrealized. By definition, only the *actual* will ever exist in the world, never the unactualized possible. For the world does not have two existential compartments, one including the actual and another that includes the unactual. Of course, unactualized possibilities can be conceived, entertained, hypothesized, assumed, and so on. That is to say, they can, in a way, exist—or ''subsist'' if one prefers—not, of course, unqualifiedly in themselves, but in a *relativized* manner, as the objects of certain intellectual processes. But it goes without saying that if their ontological footing is to rest on this basis, then they are clearly mind-dependent.

In the cases of actual existence we have a dualism. There is

    (1) The actually existing thing or state of affairs (for example, with
         ''that dogs have tails'' we have the tailed dogs)

and

    (2) The thought or entertainment of this thing or state of affairs.

But with nonexistent possibilities (such as, that dogs have horns) the ontological situation becomes monistic since item (1) is altogether lacking. And this difference is crucial. For, in the dualistic cases of actual existence, (1) would remain even if (2) were done away with. But with nonexistent possibles there are (*ex hypothesi*) no items of category (1) to remain, and so category (2) is determinative. Exactly this is the basis of the ontological mind-dependence of nonexistent possibles.

I insisted above that, in dealing with the *ontology* of the possible, our concern is not with modality *de dicto* (or rather *de cogitatione*) but with modality *de re*; not with the (very actual) *thought-of-the-possibility* but with *the possibility itself*, the (utterly nonexistent) state of affairs that is thought of. We must distinguish clearly between these two items:

(i) the thought of the (nonexistent) possibility (*der Gedanke des Nichtseiendes*)

(ii) the (nonexistent) possibility thought of (*das nichtseiende Gedachte*)

When this distinction is duly observed, the "ontological" aspect of the matter becomes quite clear:

(A) The ontological status per se of item (ii), the possibility at issue, is simply zero: *ex hypothesi* the item in question does not exist at all.

(B) Clearly item (i), the thought of the possibility, exists unproblematically in the manner of thoughts in general. And while its object, item (ii), does not "exist" in reality, it does "exist" (or "subsist" or what have you) *as the object* of the thought.

(C) And then it is perfectly clear that *this* mode "being"—not as a reality but solely as an object of thought—is mind-dependent.

One point of caution is immediately necessary. We are not saying that to be a possible (but unactualized) state of affairs requires that this state must *actually* be conceived (or entertained, hypothesized, and so on)—so as in fact to stand in relation to some *specific* mind. Rather, what we are saying is that possible, albeit unrealized, states of affairs or things obtain an ontological footing, that is, they can be said to "exist" in some appropriately qualified way only insofar as it lies within the generic province of minds to conceive (or to entertain, hypothesize, and so on) them. Thus the ontological footing of unactualized possible states of affairs involves the mind in this generic sense that the very concept at issue is viable only with

reference to concepts the analysis of which demands reference to the working of minds.

The case for the mind-dependency of hypothetical possibilities is obviously not based on any sort of empirical considerations as to the workings
of minds, but is purely a matter of a priori conceptual analysis. Possibilities
are mind-dependent because the essential purport of the very conception of
possibility is mind-involving. There simply can be no unrealized possibilities lying about in the real and "objective" world: unreal possibilities
can only be imagined, supposed, and so on. They cannot be located but
only *assumed* to be located; they cannot be handled, seen, heard, but only
supposed to be handled, seen, heard. Of course, it is not a *property* of the
imaginary dollar bill that it is not to be seen anywhere. Kant is quite right
about this; the imaginary dollar bill is not to be imagined as an *invisible*
dollar bill (then it would not be a dollar bill at all) but as one that is
real—and so visible, and capable of being handled, among other things.
But although invisibility is *ex hypothesi* not a descriptive *property* that
characterizes an imaginary dollar, it is all the same a regulative *fact* about
it. It is not by way of their internal and constitutive properties but by way of
the external and regulative facts about them that hypothetical possibilities
are mind-involving. (And these are not just contingent facts about them,
but necessary ones that serve to make the items at issue what they are.)

The argument that hypothetical possibilities depend on the mind thus
proceeds as follows:

(1) The natural world of mind-independent reality comprises only the
     actual. This world does not contain a region where nonexistent or
     unactualized possibilities somehow "exist." Unactualized hypothet-
     ical possibilities *ex hypothesi* do not exist in the world of objective
     reality at all.

(2) Nor do unactualized possibilities exist in some mind-accessible
     Platonic realm of mind-independent reality existing wholly outside
     the natural world order.

(3) The very foundation for the distinction between something actual
     and something merely hypothetically possible is thus lacking in a
     "mindless" world. Unactualized hypothetical possibilities lack an
     independent ontological footing in the sphere of objective reality:
     They can be said to "exist" only insofar as they are *conceived*, or
     thought of, or *hypothesized*, and the like. For such a possibility to be

(*esse*) is therefore to be conceived (*concipi*).[4] In consequence, possibility is mind-dependent.

The procedure described above outlines the general strategy for arguing in denial of the thesis that possibilities exist in some self-subsisting realm that is "independent of the mind." Inorganic nature—subrational nature generally—encompasses only the actual: The domain of the possible is the creation of intelligent organisms, and is a realm accessible to them alone. A "robust realism of physical objects" is all very well, but it just will not plausibly extend into the area of the hypothetical. We can plausibly argue that it would be foolish (or philosophically perverse) to deny the thesis: "This (real) stone I am looking at would exist even if nobody ever saw it." But we cannot reason by analogy to support the thesis: "This nonexistent but possible stone I am thinking of would be there even if nobody could imagine it." The existential objectivity and autonomy of the real world does not underwrite that of the sphere of hypothetical possibility. This sphere is mind-dependent, and so consequently are all those intellectual resources of whatever kind they be—that are hinged upon it.

I do not want to wander off into Bishop Berkeley's forest. For the present we are not concerned with the general idealist position that substance—real and unreal unlike—will in general require minds. We are prepared to recognize and admit the crucial distinction between the attribution of a property to an object by someone (which obviously requires a mind), and the *possession* of the property by the object (which is or may be presumed to be an "objective," mind-independent fact). But hypothetical possibilities are *inherently* mind-related: The hypothetical cannot just "objectively be" the case, but must be hypothesized, or imagined, or assumed, or whatever. Unlike real facts, merely hypothetical ones lack, *ex hypothesi*, that objective foundation in the existential order which alone could render them independent of minds.

The following line of objection is more or less inevitable: "To make possibility *in toto* mind-dependent is surely fallacious. Take physical possibility, for example. This acorn has the potentiality to develop into an oak. How can the possible development of a tree in such cases possibly be

4. To say this is not to drop the usual distinction between a thought and its object. If I imagine this orange to be an apple, I imagine it *as an apple* and not as an *imaginary* apple. But this does not gainsay the fact that the apple at issue *is* an imaginary apple that "exists only in my imagination."

mind-dependent?'' We reply: Regardless of the status of the acorn as being independent of the existence of the mind, and whatever the acorn *in fact* does, the strictly *modal* aspect of what it may or may not do is not and cannot be an aspect of objective reality. (The potentiality of function and teleology is invariably based upon *lawfulness* and this—as we shall argue below—represents an inherently mind-dependent conception.) The possibility of developmental processes involves the mind in just this respect that possibility (or indeed all modality outside the actual) requires the existence of minds.

On such a view, then, mere or strictly hypothetical possibilities are mind-made. Does it follow from this position that if there were no men—or rather no rational minds—there would be no unreal possibilities? Are we driven to a possibility-idealism as the logical terminus of the line of thought we have been tracing out? These questions must, I believe, be answered affirmatively. If the conceptual resources that come into being with rational minds and their capabilities were abolished, the realm of supposition and counterfact would be abolished too, and with it the domain of unrealized, albeit possible, things would also have to vanish.

But to put the matter in this way is somewhat misleading. Our present preoccupation is not with a point of conjectural natural history, but is strictly *conceptual* in character. The conceptual unraveling of the idea of ''hypothetical possibilities'' demands deployment of mind-related conceptions. Thus the dependence at issue is conceptual and not causal. We are certainly not saying that the world (the extramental world) somehow becomes different with the introduction of minds.

The objection that ''Surely it was possible before there were any minds in the universe that there should be minds; hence possibilities antedate minds and accordingly cannot be mind-dependent'' thus misses its target if aimed at our position. The whole issue of historico-causal dependencies is quite beside the point, and even to talk of a mental *creation* of possibility is to set up something of a straw man. Doubtless there were colors (in the sense of phenomenal colors) in the universe before there were sight-endowed beings. But this in no way saves phenomenal color from being *conceptually* sight-referring. In fine, it is a *conceptual* dependency upon mind-referring notions rather than any *causal* dependency upon the functionings of minds that is at issue in our discussion.

It is crucial that our concern is not with assertions regarding or ideas about possibilities—which are obviously and trivially mind-involving—but the possibilities themselves. We recognize and admit—indeed regard as crucial—the distinction between the *attribution* of a property to an object by someone (which evidently requires a mind), and the *possession* of the property by the object (which is or may be supposed to be an "objective" fact that does not require any reference to mind). But unrealized possibilities are insuperably mind-related: the hypothetically possible cannot just "objectively be" the case; it must be hypothesized, or imagined, or assumed, and so on. Unlike real facts, hypothetical ones lack, *ex hypothesi,* that objective foundation in the existential order which alone could render them independent of minds.

Of course, in a trivial sense, everything that is discussed—real or unreal—bears *some* relationship to a mind. Unquestionably, no matter what truth *we* may think of, *somebody* thinks of; but what people think of is not the crux. Being thought of is not essential to the truthfulness of a truth. This whole way of approaching the matter—with reference to what "is thought" to be the case—loses sight of our specifically focal issue of unrealized possibilities. I have no desire to question the distinction between a fact, say, that the cat is on the mat (which could continue unchanged in a world devoid of intelligence), and the thought or statement of a fact (which could not). My point is that the *condition* of possibility, unlike the *condition* of factuality, involves something (namely, a reference to the hypothetical) that would be infeasible in the face of a postulated absence of minds. Unrealized possibility is not something that we can meaningfully postulate objectively of a mindless world, that is, a world from which all mind-involving conceptions have been abstracted. For if the hypothetical element (which is clearly accessible only in a world endowed with minds) were *aufgehoben* (annihilated), possible things and states of affairs would be *aufgehoben* as well. Of course, *we* can think of an "alternative possible world" that is unpopulated, and so denuded of minds, but yet endowed with unrealized possibilities—so long as we do not postulate a genuinely mindless universe and abandon reference—however implicit—to the sphere of mind. But if we rigorously put aside minds and their capabilities, eliminating any and all reference to the mental, then the hypothetical element is lost, and unrealized possibility is lost with it.

We have no desire to be pushed to the extreme of saying that the "being" of nonexistent "possible beings" lies in their being actually *conceived;* rather, we take it to reside in their being *conceivable.* The "being" of an unactualized item does not inhere in its relation to this or that specific mind, but to its conceivability by mind-in-general, in terms of the linguistic resources that are a common capability of intelligence as we know it. This independence of any specific mind establishes the *objectivity* of nonexistent possibilities despite their mind-dependence. Just as an actual thing or state of affairs remains as such when not known, so an unactualized item is not affected if not conceived by any actual person. But this independence of specific minds does not render unactualized possibles independent of mind as such. Their mind-dependence is not *particularistic* (like that of a headache) but *generic*: a dependence on the capability of minds as such. (And, of course, generic mind-dependence is mind-dependence all the same.)

But are we not involved in a circle of some kind in saying that possibility resides in conceivability, something which in turn requires reference to the possible—to what *can be conceived?* Is not the qualification of possibility in terms of possibilities a nonproductive circumambulation? Not really. What we are saying is that the "reality" of certain possible states of affairs and things (that is, nonexistent possibilities) resides in the reality of possibility-involving *processes* [the *construction* of verbal descriptions, and the *hypothesizing* (assuming, postulating) of their existence]. We are saying that, when the-possibility-of-the-thing is its only "reality," this "reality" inheres in a possibilistic intellectual process. Here actuality is indeed prior to possibility—the actuality of one category of things, namely, minds with their characteristic modes of functioning, underwrites the *construction* of the totality of nonexistent possibles that can be contemplated.

Nonexistent possibilities thus have an amphibious ontological basis: They root in the capability of *minds* to perform certain operations—to describe and to hypothesize (assume, conjecture, suppose)—operations to which the use of *language* is essential, so that both thought processes and language enter the picture. The dependency of unrealized possibilities on language gives them the *objective* ontological foothold they undoubtedly possess. "The possibility existed alright only nobody thought of it at the time" is a perfectly viable locution, the import of which we might gloss as follows: "The means for its description exist and the possibility *could* therefore have been formulated, though in fact no one had then hypothesized it." And the statement, "There are possibilities no one will ever conceive of" is also perfectly viable and can be glossed along just the same lines. Actuality is prior to possibility (as Aristotle was wont to insist), but we must amend this by the thesis that the possibility of a thing (that is, entity possibility) is posterior to the possibility of a process (that is, conceptual possibility). *It is the actuality of minds capable of deploying by way of hypotheses and assumptions the descriptive mechanisms of language that provides the ontological basis of nonexistent possibilities.* For such possibilities "exist" insofar as they can be stated or described in the context of their being supposed, assumed, posited, or the like.

From this standpoint several conclusions emerge: (1) *Substantive* possibility (the possibility of states of affairs and things) is conceptually consequent upon *functional* possibility (the possibility of process). (2) The processes at issue here are those intellectual processes through which the descriptions of nonexistent things are constructed and the existence of such things hypothesized. (3) Intellectual possibilities are fundamental; the basic category of possible things are possible descriptions and thus are terms that are in large measure linguistic in nature. Thus on our view the possibility-for-being is secondary to and consequent upon the possibility-for-description (construed rather broadly to include imaging and imagining). And finally (4) whatever "being" or "quasireality" nonexistent possibilities have is thus consequent upon the actuality of minds and their modes of functioning.

The last point deserves special emphasis. It is important to distinguish between *existential* possibility, the possibility-of-item (that is, the of states of affairs or things), which, at the "hard-core" level underwrites the conception of such nonexistent possible items as the Cheshire cat and *functional* possibility, the possibility-of-process, perhaps better designated as *contingent potentiality,* such as the possibility of an apple tree to bear certain fruit or of a speaker to utter certain words. Our point is that even a "mere possibility" of the existential type always can, and in the final analysis, *must* have a grounding in the range of functional possibility—and indeed of functional possibility relating to mental functions. In affording the mechanisms of conceivability minds come to be functionally operative and to render the whole range of possibility in general mind-involving.

What we are saying is the "mere" possibility of the existential type is based upon and derivative from a real functional potentiality of mental processes. It is in this sense that all possibility in general involves some reference to the mental—namely, because the *functional possibility* of mental processes is basic to and fundamental for the realm of possibility in general.

One very basic line of objection must be considered. Someone might protest as follows:

> "I grant," says the objector, "that it makes sense to speak of possible nonexistent states of affairs, such as its being (merely) possible that a cat be on the mat. But such a *propositional* possibility posed

by a that clause, surely does not give rise to possible *things,* and so does not justify us in speaking of *a* or *the* (nonexistent) cat on the mat. To speak of possible things or entities is to reify, quite illegitimately, the strictly propositional possibility that a thing of that sort exists. But this substantizing move from a possible-that situation to the setting up of a *possible-thing* is wholly improper."

I wholly endorse this objection in all regards, except that it claims to being an objection. Nothing we have said gainsays its complaint as to the queerness and dispensability of a realm of possible *entities.* Throughout our discussion of ontology we have been careful to use such locutions as "possibilities," "possible state of affairs or things," or "possible item." The ontology of possibilities that has concerned us does not have a specifically thing-directed orientation in any sense that requires *entities.* The existence-claims with which we are concerned are posed by locutions of the propositional variety typified by:

that-there-be-a-cat-on-the-mat.

It does *not* require us to postulate some queer entity, a possibilistic cat, that is somehow present upon the mat. The mode of being or existence at issue in the thesis

It is (merely) possible that there be (exist) a cat on the mat

is the target of our discussion, and not the being or existence of that queer entity, the *ex hypothesi* nonexistent cat that is mysteriously placed upon the mat.[5]

III. The Linguistic Foundations of
   Possibility

Among contemporary logicians W. V. O. Quine especially has been concerned to attack the very idea of possible but nonexistent objects. Quine has assaulted this conception not only with weighty argument but also with

5. This section elaborates and develops some points made almost in passing in the section "Lawfulness as Mind-Dependent" in my book *Scientific Explanation* (New York: Free Press, 1970), pp. 113–121.

clever invective. In his influential paper "On What There Is," he has made great fun of possible nonexistent entites:

> Take, for instance, the possible fat man in that doorway; and, again, the possible bald man in that doorway. Are they the same possible men, or two possible men? How do we decide? How many possible men are there in that doorway? Are there more possible thin ones than fat ones? How many of them are alike? Or would their being alike make them one? Are no *two* possible things alike? Is this the same as saying that it is impossible for two things to be alike? Or, finally, is the concept of identity simply inapplicable to unactualized possibles? But what sense can be found in talking of entities which cannot meaningfully be said to be identical with themselves and distinct from one another?[6]

Quine is seeking for a principle of individuation (*principium individuationis*) for nonexistent, yet possible, items. But—his inclination to the contrary notwithstanding—this problem does not in fact pose any insuperable obstacles. Presumably a nonexistent possible is to be identified by means of a *defining description*. And on this, the classical approach to the matter, the problems so amusingly posed by Quine encounter no decisive theoretical difficulties. How many possible objects are there? Clearly as many as can be described distinctly—presumably an *infinite* number. When are two possible objects identical? When their defining descriptions are "logically identical," that is, equivalent. The doctrine of possible objects entails no major logical anomalies. With nonexistents everything save existence alone (and its implications) remains precisely the same as it does with objects that "really" exist, subject to one exception only: Existents can be differentiated by purely ostensive processes—pointing or other means of placement within "this actual world"—whereas possibilities cannot be so indicated; they must be differentiated by purely descriptive means, that is, by indicating property differences.

The theory of nonexistent possibles in the sense of *merely possible things* is actually, as I see it, a somewhat misleading derivation from the

---

6. "On What There Is," *Review of Metaphysics*, 2 (1948), 21–38; reprinted in Leonard Linsky, ed., *Semantics and the Philosophy of Language* (Urbana: University of Illinois Press, 1952), pp. 189–206. See pp. 23–24 (pp. 191–192 of the Linsky reprint). A cognate denial of nonexistent individuals and of the "reality" of unrealized possibilities is found in J. M. E. McTaggart, *The Nature of Existence*, I (Cambridge: Cambridge University Press, 1921), Bk. I, chap. 2.

conception of *unactualized states of affairs,* which is itself supervenient upon certain actualities. Thus the actual state of affairs:

(1) that there is no cat on the mat

automatically gives rise (under appropriate conditions) to the following unactualized states of affairs

(2) that there should be a cat on the mat.

And it is because of the states of (2) as a "mere possibility" that we can appropriately speak of an unactualized possible entity such as

(3) the possible cat on the mat

and in turn such more detailed (description-laden) variants as

(4) the possible Siamese tomcat on the mat.

In the manner of this example, nonexistent particular things are in general parasitic upon unactualized states of affairs.

To say (as I have done) that the doctrine of nonexistent possibles poses no insuperable theoretical difficulties is not to deny that their introduction into our conceptual framework may complicate the logical situation somewhat. Here one consideration comes to mind primarily—one connected with their mode of individuation—namely their *descriptive incompleteness.*

With respect to any existent (that is, any actual existent) x it will have to be the case that the principle

(P) For any property ϕ: If "ϕx" is false, then "$[\sim\phi]x$" is true

obtains. This principle holds whenever x is an actually existent object. Moreover, it holds whenever x is a possible object described completely through its Leibnizian "*complete* individuation notion." Unlike the more realistic situation we envisage, *Leibnizian* possibilia are defined through their complete individual notions in such a way that for any such individual and any predicate ϕ, either "ϕx" is true or "$[\sim\phi]x$" is true. Now the thesis (P) will not hold for nonexistent possibles that are individuated—on the approach adopted here—through an identifying characterization that is descriptively incomplete. Thus to individuate a nonexistent particular is to provide a description of it, but this description will, in general, have the feature of logical incompleteness.[7] This inherent incompleteness of (non-Leibnizian) possibilia serves to set them apart from paradigm (extant) things.

The essential role here of descriptive mechanisms indicates the indispensable part played in this connection by language. However closely the descriptive machinery of our language—its stock of adjectives, verbs, and adverbs—may be tied to reality, the link to reality is broken when we move from universals to particulars and from their features to the things themselves. Once we have enough descriptive machinery to describe real things (such as this pen, which is pointed, blue, 6 inches long, and so on) we are ipso facto in a position to describe nonexistents (a pen in other respects like this one but 10 inches long). It is in principle impossible to design a language in which the descriptive mechanisms suffice for discourse about real things alone, without affording the means for introducing nonexistents into discussion. The mechanisms of reference to nonexistents are an inherent linguistic feature. Any language adequate to a discussion of the real cannot but burst the bounds of reality.

Our view of the "ontology" of the matter can now be put into brief compass. Unrealized possibilities do not exist as such. What exist are minds and their capabilities, and consequently languages and their rules. Unrealized possibilities are *generated* by minds, and so they can be said to "exist" only in a secondary and dependent sense, as actual or potential objects of thought. Such possibilities are the products of an *intellectual construction*. The ontological status of the possible is thus fundamentally mind-dependent, the domain of the possible being a mental construct.[8]

7. Actually the description might be formulated more effectively on a three-valued basis. From this standpoint, given an individual x and a predicate ϕ three situations can obtain:

ϕx: ϕ holds of x ("4 is even")

$[\sim\phi]x$: non-ϕ (the primitive negation predicate of ϕ) holds of x ("4 is nonprime")

ϕ is inapplicable to x: the predicate ϕ is in principle inapplicable to x, that is, it fails to apply for categorial reasons because x is the kind of thing with respect to which the predicate ϕ as well as its negation predicate $[\sim\phi]$ are "just not in the running" (4 is neither green nor non-green).

If this trichotomy were adopted, then an ordinary (existing) thing—as well as a Leibnizian possibility—would invariably determine the given predicate within the framework of one of the three groups. But a nonexistent possible can now fail to fit anywhere, exactly as with the initially simplified dichotomy it could fail to fit either way.

8. In this discussion we have taken a distinctly verbal (that is, description-centered) view of unrealized possibilities. I have neglected, for example, the prospect of unreal things or states

IV. Historical Retrospect

Basically four positions have been taken in the history of philosophy with respect to the ontology of hard-core possibilities.

Position	This Position Attributes the Reality of Nonexistent Individuals to	Exponent
Nominalism	language	Russell, Quine
Conceptualism	the mind	Stoics, Descartes, Kant, Brentano
Conceptualistic Realism	the mind of God	Some Scholastics, Leibniz
Realism	a realm of possibility existing independently of human language and thought	Some Arabic Mu'tazilites, MacColl, Meinong

Let us consider these positions with a contemporary perspective. Regarded from this point of view, realism is not an attractive position. Present-day philosophers have a (well-advised) aversion toward postulating a Platonic realm of being that is distinct from the worlds of nature and of thought. Nor would Conceptualistic Realism nowadays be viewed as a viable position, for contemporary philosophers are unwilling to follow in the path of their predecessors (both before and after Descartes, Leibniz, and Berkeley) and obtain by theft—that is, by falling back upon theological considerations—what they believe ought to be the fruits of honest philosophical toil. Moreover, a rigorous Conceptualism, with reference to nonexistent possibilities, would not, I think, be regarded as an appealing position. For such a view must hold, regarding nonexistent possibilities, that *To be is to be conceived*—their *esse* is *concipi*. But the notion of *unthought-of possibilities* is certainly too viable to be so easily dismissed. (Note that while "it is possible though not conceived," is a perfectly viable conclusion, "it is possible though not conceivable" is not viable, at any rate, not in the *quasilogical,* rather than *psychological,* sense of "conceivability" that is relevant in my present discussion.[9] For our concern

---

of affairs as presented quasivisually (for example in hallucination). This is no serious deficiency because in such cases of *illusion* (rather than hypothesis) the mind-dependency aspect of the matter is all the more clear and noncontroversial.

9. On the issue of psychologism that arises here cf. Chapter 7 of Rescher, *Essays in Philosophical Analysis*, pp. 171-180.

here is not with what people will in fact conceive of but with what is conceivable in principle.) And nonexistent possibilities would seem to have a solidity and objectivity of status that we hesitate to subject to the vagaries of what is and is not in fact thought of. I have preferred to move in the direction of going from "to be *conceived*" to "to be *conceivable*"— construing this in a broad sense that includes imaging and imagining. And once this approach has been purged of its psychologistic connotations, we have moved near to the nominalistic realm of what can be described and discussed, assumed and stated. Just here, in the sphere of linguo-centric considerations, we reach the ground which is, in any rate, most congenial to contemporary philosophers. The fashionably "modern" view that the ultimate foundation for nonexistent individuals is linguistic comes close to returning in a full circle to the language-oriented conceptualism expounded in classical antiquity by the Stoics in the context of their theory of *lekta* ("meanings"). The problem of nonexistent possibles once more illustrates the fundamental continuities of *philosophia perennis*.[10]

Postscript

Throughout, I have been dealing with *hard-core* possibilities that are altogether unreal. The paradigm of our "mere" possibilities relates to items that do not exist at all, with nonexistent possibilities rather than the merely unrealized possibilities that involve some assumed change in the actual (such as moving my birthday ahead by a day or two). We have taken this line because hypothetical changes in actual things do not pose ontological issues of equal seriousness. But the thrust of my present discussion, namely that the mind-dependency of the merely possible, would be quite unaffected if I broadened my focus. My key point that "mere possibility" is dependent on the mind holds not just for the utterly unreal, but applies equally throughout the whole realm of supposition and counterfact—to "what would happen if." The "ontological" problems are less pressing here but the infusion of mind-dependency is just as pressing. Hypotheses regarding the unrealized circumstances regarding real things are just as hypothetical as those relating to altogether nonexistent states of affairs and things.

10. Some of the materials of this paper—and particularly of this section—have been drawn from Chapter 4, "The Concept of Nonexistent Possibles," in my *Essays in Philosophical Analysis*, pp. 73-110.

9

Possible Worlds

DAVID LEWIS

Princeton University

I believe that there are possible worlds other than the one we happen to inhabit. If an argument is wanted, it is this. It is uncontroversially true that things might be otherwise than they are. I believe, and so do you, that things could have been different in countless ways. But what does this mean? Ordinary language permits the paraphrase: there are many ways things could have been besides the way they actually are. On the face of it, this sentence is an existential quantification. It says that there exist many entities of a certain description, to wit 'ways things could have been'. I believe that things could have been different in countless ways; I believe permissible paraphrases of what I believe; taking the paraphrase at its face value, I therefore believe in the existence of entities that might be called 'ways things could have been'. I prefer to call them 'possible worlds'.

I do not make it an inviolable principle to take seeming existential quantifications in ordinary language at their face value. But I do recognize a presumption in favor of taking sentences at their face value, unless (1) taking them at face value is known to lead to trouble, and (2) taking them some other way is known not to. In this case, neither condition is met. I do not know any successful argument that my realism about possible worlds leads to trouble, unless you beg the question by saying that it already *is*

From *Counterfactuals* (Cambridge, Mass.: Harvard University Press, 1973), pp. 84–91, Copyright 1973 by David Lewis; reprinted here with the permission of the author.

trouble. (I shall shortly consider some unsuccessful arguments.) All the alternatives I know, on the other hand, do lead to trouble.

If our modal idioms are not quantifiers over possible worlds, then what else are they? (1) We might take them as unanalyzed primitives; this is not an alternative theory at all, but an abstinence from theorizing. (2) We might take them as metalinguistic predicates analyzable in terms of consistency: *'Possibly* ϕ*'* means that ϕ is a consistent sentence. But what is consistency? If a consistent sentence is one that could be true, or one that is not necessarily false, then the theory is circular; of course, one can be more artful than I have been in hiding the circularity. If a consistent sentence is one whose denial is not a theorem of some specified deductive system, then the theory is incorrect rather than circular: no falsehood of arithmetic is possibly true, but for any deductive system you care to specify either there are falsehoods among its theorems or there is some falsehood of arithmetic whose denial is not among its theorems. If a consistent sentence is one that comes out true under some assignment of extensions to the nonlogical vocabulary, then the theory is incorrect: some assignments of extensions are impossible, for instance one that assigns overlapping extensions to the English terms 'pig' and 'sheep'. If a consistent sentence is one that comes out true under some possible assignment of extensions, then the theory is again circular. (3) We might take them as quantifiers over so-called 'possible worlds' that are really some sort of respectable linguistic entities: say, maximal consistent sets of sentences of some language. (Or maximal consistent sets of atomic sentences, that is *state descriptions;* or maximal consistent sets of atomic sentences in the language as enriched by the addition of names for all the things there are, that is, *diagrammed models.*) We might call these things 'possible worlds', but hasten to reassure anyone who was worried that secretly we were talking about something else that he likes better. But again the theory would be either circular or incorrect, according as we explain consistency in modal terms or in deductive (or purely model-theoretic) terms.

I emphatically do not identify possible worlds in any way with respectable linguistic entities; I take them to be respectable entities in their own right. When I profess realism about possible worlds, I mean to be taken literally. Possible worlds are what they are, and not some other thing. If asked what sort of thing they are, I cannot give the kind of reply my questioner probably expects: that is, a proposal to reduce possible worlds to something else.

I can only ask him to admit that he knows what sort of thing our actual world is, and then explain that other worlds are more things of *that* sort, differing not in kind but only in what goes on at them. Our actual world is only one world among others. We call it alone actual not becaue it differs in kind from all the rest but because it is the world we inhabit. The inhabitants of other worlds may truly call their own worlds actual, if they mean by 'actual' what we do; for the meaning we give to 'actual' is such that it refers at any world *i* to that world *i* itself. 'Actual' is indexical, like 'I' or 'here', or 'now': it depends for its reference on the circumstances of utterance, to wit the world where the utterance is located.[1]

My indexical theory of actuality exactly mirrors a less controversial doctrine about time. Our present time is only one time among others. We call it alone present not because it differs in kind from all the rest, but because it is the time we inhabit. The inhabitants of other times may truly call their own times 'present', if they mean by 'present' what we do; for the meaning we give to 'present' is such that it is indexical, and refers at any time *t* to that time *t* itself.

I have already said that it would gain us nothing to identify possible worlds with sets of sentences (or the like), since we would need the notion of possibility otherwise understood to specify correctly which sets of sentences were to be identified with worlds. Not only would it gain nothing: given that the actual world does not differ in kind from the rest, it would lead to the conclusion that our actual world is a set of sentences. Since I cannot believe that I and all my surroundings are a set of sentences (though I have no argument that they are not), I cannot believe that other worlds are sets of sentences either.

What arguments can be given against realism about possible worlds? I have met with few arguments—incredulous stares are more common. But I shall try to answer those that I have heard.

It is said that realism about possible worlds is false because only our own world, and its contents, actually exist. But of course unactualized possible worlds and their unactualized inhabitants do not *actually* exist. To actually exist is to exist and to be located here at our actual world—at this world that we inhabit. Other worlds than ours are not our world, or inhabitants thereof. It does not follow that realism about possible worlds is false. Realism about unactualized possibles is exactly the thesis that there are more things than actually exist. Either the argument tacitly assumes what it

1. For more on this theme, see my ''Anselm and Actuality,'' *Noûs,* 4 (1970), 175-188.

purports to prove, that realism about possibles is false, or it proceeds by equivocation. Our idioms of existential quantification may be used to range over everything without exception, or they may be tacitly restricted in various ways. In particular, they may be restricted to our own world and things in it. Taking them as thus restricted, we can truly say that there exist nothing but our own world and its inhabitants; by removing the restriction we pass illegitimately from the truth to the conclusion that realism about possibles is false. It would be convenient if there were one idiom of quantification, say *'there are . . .'*, that was firmly reserved for unrestricted use and another, say *'there actually exist . . .'*, that was firmly reserved for the restricted use. Unofrtunately, even these two idioms of quantification can be used either way; and thus one can pass indecisively from equivocating on one to equivocating on another. All the same, there are the two uses (unless realism about possibles is false, as has yet to be shown) and we need only keep track of them to see that the argument is fallacious.

Realism about possible worlds might be thought implausible on grounds of parsimony, though this could not be a decisive argument against it. Distinguish two kinds of parsimony, however: qualitative and quantitative. A doctrine is qualitatively parsimonious if it keeps down the number of fundamentally different *kinds* of entity: if it posits sets alone rather than sets and unreduced numbers, or particles alone rather than particles and fields, or bodies alone or spirits alone rather than both bodies and spirits. A doctrine is quantitatively parsimonious if it keeps down the number of instances of the kinds it posits; if it posits 10^{29} electrons rather than 10^{37}, or spirits only for people rather than spirits for all animals. I subscribe to the general view that qualitative parsimony is good in a philosophical or empirical hypothesis; but I recognize no presumption whatever in favor of quantitative parsimony. My realism about possible worlds is merely quantitatively, not qualitatively, unparsimonious. You believe in our actual world already. I ask you to believe in more things of that kind, not in things of some new kind.

Quine has complained that unactualized possibles are disorderly elements, well-nigh incorrigibly involved in mysteries of individuation.[2] That well may be true of any unactualized possibles who lead double lives, lounging in the doorways of two worlds at once. But I do not believe in any of those. The unactualized possibles, I do believe in, confined each to his

---

2. W. V. O. Quine, "On What There Is," in *From a Logical Point of View* (Cambridge, Mass.; Harvard University Press, 1953), p. 4.

own world and united only by ties of resemblance to their counterparts elsewhere do not pose any special problems of individuation. At least, they pose only such problems of individuation as might arise within a single world.

Perhaps some who dislike the use of possible worlds in philosophical analysis are bothered not because they think they have reason to doubt the existence of other worlds, but only because they wish to be told more about these supposed entities before they know what to think. How many are there? In what respects do they vary, and what is common to them all? Do they obey a nontrivial law of identity of indiscernibles? Here I am at a disadvantage compared to someone who pretends as a figure of speech to believe in possible worlds, but really does not. If worlds were creatures of my imagination, I could imagine them to be any way I liked, and I could tell you all you wish to hear simply by carrying on my imaginative creation. But as I believe that there really are other worlds, I am entitled to confess that there is much about them that I do not know, and that I do not know how to find out.

One comes to philosophy already endowed with a stock of opinions. It is not the business of philosophy either to undermine or to justify these preexisting opinions, to any great extent, but only to try to discover ways of expanding them into an orderly system. A metaphysician's analysis of mind is an attempt at systematizing our opinions about mind. It succeeds to the extent that (1) it is systematic, and (2) it respects those of our pre-philosophical opinions to which we are firmly attached. Insofar as it does both better than any alternative we have thought of, we give it credence. There is some give-and-take, but not too much: some of us sometimes change our minds on some points of common opinion, if they conflict irremediably with a doctrine that commands our belief by its systematic beauty and its agreement with more important common opinions.

So it is throughout metaphysics; and so it is with my doctrine of realism about possible worlds. Among my common opinions that philosophy must respect (if it is to deserve credence) are not only my naive belief in tables and chairs, but also my naive belief that these tables and chairs might have been otherwise arranged. Realism about possible worlds is an attempt, the only successful attempt I know of, to systematize these preexisting modal opinions. To the extent that I am modally opinionated, independently of my philosophizing, I can distinguish between alternative versions of realism about possible worlds that conform to my opinions and versions that do not. Because I believe my opinions, I believe that the true version is one of the former. For instance, I believe that there are worlds where physics is different from the physics of our world, but none where logic and arithmetic are different from the logic and arithmetic of our world. This is nothing but the systematic expression of my naive, prephilosophical opinion that physics could be different, but not logic or arithmetic. I do not know of any noncircular argument that I could give in favor of that opinion; but so long as that *is* my firm opinion nevertheless, I must make a place for it when I do metaphysics. I have no more use for a philosophical doctrine that denies my firm, unjustified modal opinions than I have for one that denies my firm, unjustified belief in chairs and tables.

Unfortunately, though, I am not opinionated enough. There are too many versions of realism about worlds that would serve equally well to systematize my modal opinions. I do not know which to believe; unless I become more opinionated, or find unsuspected connections between my opinions I may never have any way to choose. But why should I think that I ought to be able to make up my mind on every question about possible worlds, when it seems clear that I may have no way whatever of finding out the answers to other questions about noncontingent matters—for instance, about the infinite cardinals?

Quine has suggested one way to seek fixation of belief about possible worlds by proposing that worlds might be put into correspondence with certain mathematical structures representing the distribution of matter in space and time.[3] Suppose, for simplicity, that we are concerned with worlds where space-time is Euclidean and four-dimensional, and where there is only one kind of matter and no fields. (Quine calls these *Democritean* worlds.) We can represent any such world by a mapping from all quadruples $\langle x, y, z, t \rangle$ of real numbers to the numbers 0 and 1. We are to think of the quadruples as coordinates, in some coordinate system, of space-time points; and we are to think of the quadruples mapped onto 0 as coordinates of points unoccupied by matter, and of quadruples mapped onto 1 as coordinates of points occupied by matter. Thus the entire mapping represents a possible distribution of uniform matter over Euclidean space-time. Since there are many different coordinate systems—differing in the location of the $\langle 0, 0, 0, 0 \rangle$ point, the length of the units of spatial and of temporal distance, and the directions of the spatial axes—there are many different mappings (differing by a transformation of coordinates) that we

3. W. V. O. Quine, "Proportional Objects," in *Ontological Relativity and Other Essays* (New York: Columbia University Press, 1969), pp. 147–155.

regard as representing the same distribution of matter. To overcome this dependence of the mapping on an arbitrary choice of coordinates, we take not the mappings themselves, but equivalence classes of mappings under transformations of coordinates. We get a perfectly well-defined, well-understood set of mathematical entities, exactly one for every different possible distribution of matter.

Of course, this is a simplified example. The construction must be generalized in several ways to cover possibilities so far overlooked. Space-time might be non-Euclidean; there might be scalar, vector, or tensor fields independent of the distribution of matter; there might be more than one kind of matter, or more or less density of matter, even in the small. We would have to go on generalizing as long as we could think of possibilities not yet taken into account. But generalizing Quine's simplified example is easy mathematical work. We can hope that soon we will reach the end of the generalizations required and permitted by our opinions about what is possible, and then we will have a well-defined set of mathematical entities of a familiar and well-understood sort, corresponding one-to-one in a specified way with the possible worlds.

I do not, of course, claim that these complicated mathematical entities *are* the possible worlds. I cannot believe (though I do not know why not) that our own world is a purely mathematical entity. Since I do not believe that other worlds are different in kinds from ours, I do not believe that they are either. What is interesting is not the reduction of worlds to mathematical entities, but rather the claim that the possible worlds stand in a certain one-to-one correspondence with certain mathematical entities. Call these *ersatz possible worlds.* Any credible correspondence claim would give us an excellent grip on the real possible worlds by their ersatz handles. It would answer most of our questions about what the possible worlds are like.[4]

We already have a good grip, in this way, on at least *some* of the

---

4. Even the indefinite correspondence claim that *some* generalization of Quine's simplified example is right is enough to answer one important question about the possible worlds. How many are there? Answer: at least $\beth_2$, the infinite cardinal of the set of all subsets of the real numbers. It can easily be shown that this is the number of ersatz worlds in Quine's original construction. Indeed, it is the number of ersatz worlds at any level of generality that seems to me clearly called for. Here is another reason why possible worlds are not sets of sentences of a language. If we take 'language' at all literally, so that sentences are finite strings over a finite alphabet, there are not enough sets of sentences to go around. There are at most $\beth_1$, the infinite cardinal of the set of all real numbers.

possible worlds: those that correspond to mathematical ersatz worlds constructed at the highest level of generality that our modal opinions clearly require and permit. It is only because there may be higher levels of generality that we have failed to think of, and because our modal opinions are indecisive about whether there really are possibilities corresponding to some of the levels of generality we have thought of (what about letting the number of spatial dimensions vary? what about letting there be entities that are temporally but not spatially located? what about letting the distinction between space and time be local rather than global, like the distinction between up and down?), that we fail to have a good grip on all the worlds.

The mathematical construction of ersatz worlds may seem to depend too much on our current knowledge of physics. We know that we must generalize enough to include non-Euclidean worlds, for instance, just because the physicists have found reason to believe that we live in one. But physics is contingent. If we look to physics to tell us what is possible, will we get all possible worlds? Or only the physically possible worlds, according to current physics?

More, at least, than the latter. We will certainly construct ersatz worlds that disobey currently accepted physical laws; for instance, ersatz worlds where mass-energy is not conserved. Still, we cannot be sure of getting all possible worlds, since we cannot be sure that we have constructed our ersatz worlds at a high enough level of generality. If we knew only the physics of 1871, we would fail to cover some of the possibilities that we recognize today. Perhaps we fail today to cover possibilities that will be recognized in 2071. Our modal opinions do change, and physicists do a lot to change them. But this is *not* to say that we can argue from the contingent results of empirical investigation to conclusions about what possibilities there are. It is only to say that when we find it hard to locate our actual world among the possibilities that we recognize, we may reasonably be stimulated to reconsider our modal opinions. We may try to think of credible possibilities hitherto overlooked, and we may consider whether we are still as sure as we were about those of our modal opinions that have turned out to be restrictive. It is this reconsideration of modal opinions that may influence our construction of ersatz worlds, not the results of empirical investigation itself. We are concerned not with physics proper, but with the preliminary metaphysics done by physicists.

10

Theories of Actuality

ROBERT MERRIHEW ADAMS

University of California, Los Angeles

I

The problem which I wish to discuss can be introduced by the following presumptuous exercise in imagination. Let us imagine ourselves in the position of Leibniz's God. In His infinite understanding, He has a perfect knowledge of infinitely many possible worlds, each of them completely determinate (presumably in infinite detail). One of them is the single world on which He has conferred actuality: the actual world. But what is it that He has conferred on that world in actualizing it? What does that world have by virtue of being actual that the other possible worlds do not have? In what does the actuality of the actual world consist?

My purpose here is to consider critically the principal solutions which have been suggested for this problem, and to try to find the best one. Most of the theories to be discussed are at least suggested by things that Leibniz says. (This is not an issue on which he held consistently to one settled view.)

I shall not begin by assuming any one theory about what a possible world is or what it is for there to be a plurality of possible worlds, because we shall see that a disagreement on this issue underlies some of the diversity of theories of actuality. I shall normally assume, however, that there is a plurality of completely determinate possible worlds. In saying that the possible worlds which we discuss are completely determinate, I mean to

Reprinted with permission of the author and of the editor of *Noûs,* 8 (1974), 211-231.

imply at least the following two claims. (1) For every possible world, w, and every pair of contradictory propositions, one member of the pair is true in w and the other member is false in w. (2) Each possible world, if temporally ordered at all, is a complete world history and not a momentary stage of one. The actual world, therefore, includes what has actually existed or happened and what will actually exist or happen, as well as what now exists or happens; and they all count as actual.

In accepting the presupposition that there is a plurality of completely determinate possible worlds, I am already ruling out one theory of actuality. According to Charles Hartshorne, the actuality of the actual world consists precisely in its complete determinateness, and there are, strictly speaking, no other possible worlds but only other possible kinds of world. The admission "that a possible world is as definite and complex as the corresponding actual one . . . reduces the distinction between possible and actual to nullity. Value is in definiteness, and definiteness is 'the soul of actuality.' Were possibility equally definite it would be redundant to actualize it" ([4], pp. 189f.).

Another important preliminary point is the following. Problems of actuality have been discussed by philosophers very largely in terms of existence. I believe there has been a tendency to confuse two distinct issues here. If (and only if) a thing exists in the actual world, it is an *actual thing*. But the question, what it is for a thing to be actual (given that an actual thing is one that exists in the actual world) can be divided into two questions: (1) What is it for a possible world to be the actual world? (2) What is it for a thing to exist in a given possible world (whether or not it is the actual world)? I will call the first of these the *problem of actuality* and the second the *problem of existence*. It is the problem of actuality, and not the problem of existence, which I am trying to solve in this paper, though what is said here may have some implications for the problem of existence.

II

Let us begin with a couple of simple but clearly unsatisfactory theories of actuality which are strongly suggested by some fragments of Leibniz. The first of them may be called the *divine choice theory of actuality*.

> [E]ven if it is certain that what is more perfect will exist, still, the less perfect is none the less possible. Propositions of fact involve existence. But the

notion of existence is such, that the existent is the sort of state of the universe which GOD chooses [*literally,* which pleases GOD]. But GOD freely chooses what is more perfect. Thus finally a free action is involved. ([5], p. 405.)[1]

The theory suggested here is that for a possible world to be the actual world is for it to be the world that God chooses. (Perhaps it will be suggested that what is offered in this passage is not a theory of actuality but a theory of existence, according to which, for a thing to exist in any possible world is for it to be chosen by God *in that world.* But, I think, that is not what Leibniz intended. For according to Leibniz, what God freely chooses the more perfect of, as He is said to choose here, is complete possible worlds, and not components thereof.)

It is evidently also a part of the theory that God (who exists necessarily, according to Leibniz) chooses freely and could have chosen another possible world instead of the one he has chosen. I doubt that Leibniz or anybody else has held the alternative version of the divine choice theory, according to which the actual world is the only one God could have chosen. In any case, such a necessitarian form of the theory would be liable to objections very similar to some which I shall raise, below, against the optimistic theory of actuality.

The historic, nonnecessitarian version also faces difficulties, however. For if there is a plurality of possible divine world-choices, the actual world must be distinguished from the other possible worlds as the object of God's *actual* choice. But if that is what the divine choice theory of actuality says, it does not solve the problem of actuality. At best it merely pushes back, from worlds to divine choices, the question, in what actuality consists. (Leibniz seems to have thought of this problem; see [7], p. 388.)

One way in which Leibniz did think that God's actual choice is different from all His other possible choices is that God's actual choice is the choice of the best of all possible worlds. But this brings us, in effect, to another theory of actuality. The *optimistic theory of actuality* is the theory that the actuality of the actual world consists in its being the best of all possible worlds. It is clearly suggested by Leibniz, when he says that "in fact nothing else is explicable in existence, except the entering into the most perfect series of things" ([5], p. 9).

The optimistic theory treats actuality as a value property; and that may seem somewhat strange. Perhaps, indeed, the theory is not as optimistic as

---

1. I am responsible for all the translations from Leibniz in this paper.

it seems. What is so wonderful about the tidings that the best of all possible worlds is actual, if its actuality just as its being best?

It may be suggested that the wonderful thing about the actual world's being the best is that the actual world is after all *our* world. But that may be doubted. Unfortunately, the optimistic theory leaves us without a reason for believing that *we* are in the actual world. Maybe our world is indeed the best of all possible worlds. And if it is, God is doubtless in a position to know it. But we are not in a position to know it. Unlike God, we cannot survey all possible worlds as wholes in order to see whether ours is the best. Perhaps it will be replied that the goodness of God guarantees that our world is the best possible. But it is difficult to see any reason why the goodness of God would imply the bestness of our world, unless it is first assumed that our world is the *actual* world in some sense other than that of being the best world—that is, in some sense other than the only sense allowed by the optimistic theory of actuality.[2] If we adopt the optimistic theory of actuality, we do not have any reason that I can discern for believing that we are in the actual world. And in this way, I think, the theory fails one of the most basic tests for adequacy of a theory of actuality. We do know that we are actual. Surely a satisfactory theory of actuality must not render unintelligible our possession of this knowledge.

III

According to the *indexical theory of actuality,* "the actual world", "actual", and "actually" are indexical expressions. An indexical expression is one whose meaning is given by the way in which its reference varies systematically with variation of relevant features of the context of use. The relevant feature of the context of use in this case is which possible world the use takes place in. On any occasion of its use in any possible world *w,* "the actual world" refers to that world *w,* if it is used on that occasion in the sense in which the indexicalist thinks we use it. On this view, "the actual world" means only "*this* world", "the world *we* are in", or "the world in which *this* act of linguistic utterance occurs". And "actual" means only "occurring in *this* world". According to the indexical theory of actuality, the actuality of the actual world consists in its being *this* world—that is, the world in which *this act of linguistic utterance occurs.*

---

2. I do not believe that the goodness of God implies the bestness of the actual world in any case, but that is a different issue. See Adams [1].

The indexical theory is suggested by some things said in a fragment by Leibniz ([5], pp. 271f.),[3] although I do not know that Leibniz ever really held the theory. The theory has found a contemporary sponsor, however; it has recently been defended by David Lewis, in [8].

The indexical theory does not have the difficulty that the optimistic theory of actuality has in accounting for our knowledge of our own actuality. The argument that Lewis has given for the indexical theory is based on this fact:

> The strongest evidence for the indexical analysis of actuality is that it ex-
> plains why skepticism about our own actuality is absurd. How do we know
> that we are not the unactualized possible inhabitants of some unactualized
> possible world? . . . The indexical analysis of actuality explains how we
> know it: in the same way I know that I am me, that *this* time is the present, or
> that I am here. All such sentences as "This is the actual world," "I am
> actual," "I actually exist," and the like are true on any possible occasion of
> utterance in any possible world. That is why skepticism about our own
> actuality is absurd. ([8], p. 186)

I shall argue in sections IV and VI, however, that the indexical theory is not the only theory by which the certainty of our own actuality can be explained. And the indexical theory is liable to important objections which render it unacceptable, in my opinion. I will discuss two of these objections here.

(i) The first and most fundamental is this. According to the indexical theory, actuality is a property which the actual world possesses, not absolutely, but only in relation to us, its inhabitants. Absolutely considered, the actual as such does not have a different status from the possible as such. Lewis's purpose in introducing the indexical theory in [8] depends on this point.

This indexicalist doctrine seems very implausible to me. It is greatly at variance with our normal way of thinking about actuality, which I am very reluctant to give up. We normally believe that actuality as such is, absolutely considered, a special metaphysical status—that the actual is, absolutely considered, more real than the merely possible. We do not think that

---

3. Leibniz says here that what "the adjective 'existent' always means" is that "this series of things is posited." Part of what he is saying is quite trite and leaves many theories of actuality open to him: an actual (existent) F is an F that is found (exists or occurs) in the actual world. What concerns us here is the way in which Leibniz identifies, or refers to, the actual world. He refers to it indexically, as "*this* series of things."

the difference in respect of actuality between Henry Kissinger and the Wizard of Oz is just a difference in their relations to us.

Our normal belief in the absoluteness of actuality is reflected in our value judgments too. We may be moved by the joys and sorrows of a character known to be fictitious; but we do not really believe it is bad that evils occur in a nonactual possible world, or good that joys occur in a non-actual possible world, though of course it would be bad and good, respectively, for them to be actual. I think that our very strong disapproval of the deliberate actualizing of evils similarly reflects a belief in the absolutely, and not just relatively, special status of the actual as such. Indeed, if we ask, "What is wrong with actualizing evils, since they will occur in some other possible world anyway if they don't occur in this one?", I doubt that the indexical theory can provide an answer which will be completely satisfying ethically.

(ii) Another grave objection to the indexical theory has to do with problems about the identity of persons and events in different possible worlds. I believe that it leads to the conclusion that the indexical theory does not provide a correct analysis of actuality concepts which we normally use in making predictions.

The cases in which we are most interested in individual identity in different possible worlds are cases in which there is a question of alternative possible continuations of the history of an individual whose identity has already been established by its past history. We normally suppose that at many junctures in my past it would have been at least logically possible for *me* (the very same person that I am) to have done something that I did not in fact do or to have omitted an act that I did. We also normally suppose that there are many future acts which it is at least logically possible for *me* either to perform or to fail to perform. These suppositions may be rather important to us; they seem to be involved in many of our attitudes and beliefs about moral rights and wrongs and responsibilities. And it seems plausible to express them by saying that *I*, identically the same person, exist in many different possible worlds—in worlds in which I do things that I have refrained, or will refrain, from doing—as well as in the actual world.

This suggests that the following would be a very plausible sufficient condition for the identity of individuals in different possible worlds:

(C) If (1) individual *a* exists in possible world *w* at time *t*, and individual *a'* exists in possible world *w'* at time *t'*; and (2) the

whole history of w' up to and including t' (and no other time
in w') is precisely the same, qualitatively, as the whole history
of w up to and including t (and no other time in w); and (3) the
whole previous history and present state of a' (and of no other
individual in w') at t' is precisely the same, qualitatively, as
the whole previous history and present state of a (and of no
other individual in w) at t; then a is numerically identical with
a'.

Several explanatory remarks about this condition are in order. It is intended
to express such intuitions as, for example, that nothing which could possibly have happened after the time when I was born could have made it not to
be the case that I (the very same individual I in fact am) had been born and
existed. When it is said that the history and state of a and of a' at t and t'
are qualitatively the same, it is implied that there is a sameness of relation
to qualitatively the same previous events but not necessarily to the same
future events. The uniqueness condition is attached to the times in clause
(2) in order to exclude the possibly problematic satisfaction of condition
(C) by individuals in possible worlds which have been, throughout an
infinite past prior to the crucial time, Nietzschean perpetually repeating
worlds. The uniqueness condition is attached to the individuals in clause
(3) in order to avoid any implication that different individuals in one
possible world might be identical with the same individuals in another
possible world, which would give rise to questions about the transitivity of
identity. I believe that condition (C) is sufficiently guarded that it gives rise
to no problems about the transitivity or symmetry of identity such as David
Lewis has suggested are apt to arise from acceptance of the strict identity of
individuals in different possible worlds ([10], pp. 115f.).

I propose condition (C) as a *sufficient* condition of individual identity in
different possible worlds. Whether it ought to be taken as a necessary as
well as sufficient condition, or how it might be modified to yield a necessary and sufficient condition, I will not discuss here. I would not claim that
condition (C), even as only a sufficient condition, agrees precisely with all
our intuitions about counterfactual identity; but I suspect that it comes as
close to such agreement as is possible without excessive sacrifice of generality.

It also seems very plausible to extend (C) to provide a sufficient condition for identity of *events* in different possible worlds. If I invest some
money in the stock market, for instance, we would normally suppose that it

is logically possible for that event to be followed by my making a profit and logically possible for that very same event to be followed by my taking a loss instead. This view of the matter can be expressed by (C_e), which is the result of substituting "event" for "individual", "has occurred" for "exists", and "the whole history of . . . up to and including . . ." for "the whole previous history and present state of . . . at . . ." in (C). This brings us to our problem about prediction.

I now perform the inscription-act of stating in writing, "Actually, men will land on Mars by A.D. 2100."[4] Let us call that statement (S_1). I also perform the inscription-act of stating in writing, "Actually, it is not the case that men will land on Mars by A.D. 2100." Let us call that statement (S_2). It is now time T, after I have made both of these statements. It is plausible to suppose that there are logically possible worlds in which men will have landed on Mars by A.D. 2100 and logically possible worlds in which men will not have landed on Mars by A.D. 2100. It is also plausible to suppose that some worlds of both types have histories precisely the same as the history of the actual world up to and including time T. If we accept (C_e), then we can reasonably assume that some worlds of both types include the events which are my acts of making statements (S_1) and (S_2).

But now let us ask, "Is (S_1) true? Is (S_2) true?". The answers depend on the interpretation of "actually". If "actually" in (S_1) and (S_2) means "in *the* possible world in which this act of linguistic utterance occurs", then neither (S_1) nor (S_2) is true. For my acts of making them occur in many possible worlds, and therefore the uniqueness of reference which is implied or presupposed by the definite description fails to obtain. On the other hand, if "actually" means "in *some* possible world in which this act of linguistic utterance occurs", then (S_1) and (S_2) are both true. Both of these interpretations make a mockery of prediction.

An alternative indexicalist view would be that "actually" in (S_1) and (S_2) means "in this possible world", where "this possible world" ambiguously designates all the possible worlds in which my acts of making (S_1) and (S_2) occur—including, for example, w_m, in which men land on Mars by A.D. 2100, and w_n, in which men do not land on Mars by A.D. 2100. But on this interpretation, (S_1) is ambiguous as between the truth that in w_m men will land on Mars by A.D. 2100 and the falsehood that in w_n men will land on Mars by A.D. 2100. And (S_2) is similarly ambiguous as among many truths and many falsehoods. This renders all such predictions

4. Cf. Lewis's example in [8], p. 186.

pointless. For whatever prediction we make will be ambiguous as among many truths and many falsehoods.

It remains for the indexicalist to claim that "actually" in (S_1) and (S_2) means "in this possible world" and that in every world, w, in which my acts of making (S_1) and (S_2) occur, that world, w, and no other, is *un*ambiguously designated by "this possible world". Thus, while my act of making (S_1) occurs in both w_m and w_n, (S_1) is unambiguously true in w_m and unambiguously false in w_n. I have qualms about the plausibility of this claim that by one and the same utterance of "this possible world" I unambiguously designate many different possible worlds. But even if we accept this indexicalist account of the meaning of "actually" and "this possible world", it deprives prediction of its normal point. If the account is right, I can know in advance that if I make (S_1), it will be true in some worlds in which my act of making it occurs and false in others; and I can know in advance that (S_2) will be true in the worlds in which (S_1) is false and false in those in which (S_1) is true. But there is none of these worlds which is distinguished for me, at the time I make the statement, in such a way that I have a reason to want to assert what will be true in it rather than what will be true in another of the worlds. For I, and all of my acts and states at that time, occur in exactly the same way in all of them.

I do not see any more satisfactory way in which an indexicalist who accepted (C_e) could deal with this problem. But I believe it is clear that David Lewis will want to deal with it by rejecting (C_e) and holding that each possible event occurs in only one possible world. He certainly rejects (C). He holds that each possible individual exists or occurs in only one possible world. He does recognize, and works out a formal logical treatment of, a relation of "counterpart" which an individual in one world can bear to a sufficiently similar individual (or to more than one) in another world (as well as to itself, but to nothing else, in its own world). But he denies that any individual in any possible world is strictly identical with any individual in another possible world (Lewis [10]). The reasons that Lewis has given for rejecting transworld identity in favor of counterpart theory are not specifically indexicalist reasons. I do not find them convincing reasons; but this is not the place for a full discussion of them.[5] It should be clear from what I have already said, however, that Lewis's indexical

---

5. Lewis seems to be much influenced by the view that transworld identity is apt to give rise to problems about the transitivity and symmetry of identity. I have already suggested that there are ways of avoiding such problems without rejecting transworld identity.

theory of actuality gives him powerful additional incentives to reject strict identity of individuals, and especially events, in different possible worlds.

So long as we are willing to speak of possible worlds at all, we cannot very well deny Lewis the right to speak of his world-specific individuals and world-specific events. If we start with transworld individuals which exist in several possible worlds, we can, as Lewis points out, construct world-specific individuals as ordered pairs, of which the first member is a transworld individual and the second member is a possible world ([10], p. 115). But neither can we be denied the right to speak of transworld individuals and events. For even if we start with Lewisian world-specific individuals and events, we can construct the transworld ones.[6] We might begin, for instance, by saying that a transworld individual is a set of world-specific individuals, every member of which satisfies condition (C)[7] with respect to every other member. And similarly for events.

Both transworld and world-specific individual concepts and event concepts are possible, then. But which kind do we normally use? The transworld ones, I believe. We think of individuals as having alternative futures which are possible for them as the very same individuals, and we think of events as having alternative successors by which they, the very same events, could possibly be succeeded. I never use the indexical expressions "I" and "this" to pick out one world-specific individual or event from among others which belong to the same transworld individual or event.

It therefore seems to me very implausible to suppose that when we predict that a certain event will actually occur, the chief thing that we are doing is ascribing to that event a certain relation to ourselves and our speech-acts as *world-specific* individuals and events. But that is what the indexical theorist must say is the chief thing we are doing. Otherwise I do not see how he can make sense of prediction at all.

IV

The theory that actuality is a simple, unanalyzable property of the actual world, by which it is distinguished from the other possible worlds, and that the concept of actuality therefore does not stand in need of analysis may be

---

6. I owe this point to John Perry.

7. Here, I am, for convenience, treating (C) as a necessary as well as sufficient condition of transworld identity. If a more adequate necessary and sufficient condition is developed, it can be substituted here.

called the *simple property theory of actuality*. It can be found in Descartes, and I suspect its pedigree could be traced even farther back than that. Descartes claimed that the notion of existence (in the sense of actuality, I think) is one of those "notions of the simplest possible kind" which it would be confusing to try to explain by definitions (*Principles*, I, 10, in [2], I, 222). Leibniz says similar things about existence (again, I think, in the sense of actuality). "Existence therefore is a noncomposite, or un-analyzable (*irresolubilis*) notion" ([6], I, 271). "*Existent* cannot be de-fined . . . in such a way, that is, that some clearer notion might be shown to us" ([7], p. 325).

Unlike the indexical theory, the simple property theory of actuality presents actuality as a property which the actual world possesses abso-lutely, rather than only in relation to its own inhabitants. For if there is no need to analyze actuality at all, there is no need to analyze it as an indexical property.

The certainty of our knowledge of our own actuality can also be ac-counted for on the simple property theory, as it cannot on the optimistic theory. For it can be maintained that actuality is a simple property which is possessed, not only by the actual world as a whole, but by every thing that exists in the actual world, and that we are as immediately acquainted with our own actuality as we are with our own thoughts, feelings, and sensa-tions. It would be plausible, on this account of the matter, to suppose that acquaintance with our own actuality plays an important part in our acquisi-tion of the concept of actuality, providing us with a paradigm of actuality, so that it would be reasonable to say, "If I am not actual, I do not know what actuality is."

Although it has these advantages over the indexical and optimistic theories, the simple property theory of actuality, like the divine choice theory and for very similar reasons, fails to provide a complete solution to the problem of actuality. For presumably the nonactual possible worlds could have been actual and are possibly actual. Each possible world is actual in some possible world—namely, in itself. How, then, does the actual world differ from the other possible worlds in relation to the primi-tive property of actuality? It has the property actually, of course, and not just possibly. To have a property *actually* is presumably to have it in the actual world. So the actual world has the property of actuality in the actual world. But that tells us only that the actual world is actual *in itself*. And every possible world is actual *in itself*. So how is the actual world different from the other possible worlds? What is the difference between the actually actual and the possibly actual? Thus, the problem of distinguishing between the actual and the merely possible rearises with respect to the very property of actuality by which it was supposed to be solved.

The problem could be solved by a simple property theory only if we were prepared to deny that the nonactual possible worlds are possibly actual. But that denial entails that there is no such thing as contingent actuality. We would have to conclude that the actual world, in all its infinite detail, is the only possible world that could have been actual. And we would be left to wonder in what sense the other possible worlds are possible, since they could not have been actual.

V

The problem which presents the simple property theorist with these unattractive alternatives can be generalized in an interesting way. The possible worlds are completely determinate; and therefore, for all possible worlds, w and w', and every interpretation of the notion of actuality, the proposition that w is actual is either true or false in w'. We seem to have two options.

(i) We can say that for every possible world, w, the proposition that w is actual is true in w and false in every other possible world. This preserves the intuition that each possible world could have been actual, and is actual in itself. But it has the consequence that the property of actuality is world-relative. Each world is actual, but only in itself. On these assumptions, it is difficult to see what difference there could be between being *the* actual world and being possibly actual, like all the other possible worlds, as we discovered in discussing the divine choice and simple property theories of actuality. If any possible world is to be distinguished as *the* actual world, it must be distinguished relative to some standpoint within the system of possible worlds. The obvious standpoint to choose is that of the person who is doing the distinguishing. The indexical theory of actuality makes that choice, frankly accepting the relativity of actuality.

(ii) Alternatively, we can say that there is a world, w, such that the proposition that w is actual is true in every possible world. w is actual *in* every possible world, and no other world is actual in any possible world. Thus, w is, absolutely, *the* actual world. But then there is no contingent actuality. No other world than w could have been actual. The optimistic theory of actuality fits this alternative. For presumably the answer to the question which possible world is the best (if there is a best) does not vary from one world to another. We have also seen that the simple property theory, which has some advantage over the optimistic theory, can be adapted to this alternative.

On the assumptions we have been making thus far, we seem to be compelled to give up either the absoluteness or the contingency of the actual world's actuality. Both alternatives seem unacceptable to me. In order to escape from this dilemma, however, we must modify our assumptions.

One way of doing this would be by abandoning or modifying the assumption that the possible worlds are completely determinate, by saying that actuality is a property (perhaps a simple property) which possible worlds possess or lack absolutely and not *in* any possible world. For any possible world, *w*, we would hold that the proposition that *w* is actual is true or false, but we would deny that it is true or false *in w* or *in* any other possible world. We would thus not be treating actuality as a world-relative property. Neither would we have to say that the world which is actual is necessarily actual, for we would not have to say that it is actual *in* every possible world. On the other hand, I believe that the intuitive attractiveness of the notion of possible worlds is diminished by any qualification of the assumption that they are completely determinate. It would also be diminished if we were unable to apply to some cases of possibility the idea that what is possible is what is the case in some possible world. We are faced with that inability if, in following the approach now before us, we claim (as we want to) that worlds which are not actual could possibly have been actual. For that claim could not be regarded as equivalent to the claim (which would be ruled out) that each of those worlds is actual *in* some possible world.

I prefer, therefore, a different approach, which I call an *actualist* theory of actuality, as opposed to the theories discussed in sections II–IV above, which I call *possibilist*. They begin with the whole system of possible worlds and see the actual world first of all as a possible world, a member of that system. I propose to begin, instead, with the actual world, to treat talk about the system of possible worlds as a way of talking about a proper part of the actual world, and thus to gain, so to speak, a standpoint outside the system of possible worlds from which judgments of actuality which are not world-relative may be made. *Actualism*, with respect to possible worlds, is the view that if there are any true statements in which there are said to be nonactual possible worlds, they must be reducible to statements in which the only things there are said to be are things which there are in the actual world and which are not identical with nonactual possibles.[8] The actualist will not agree that there are nonactual possible worlds, if the notion of possible worlds is to be regarded as primitive. *Possibilism*, with respect to possible worlds, is the view that there are nonactual possible worlds and that the notion of a possible world is not to be analyzed in terms of actual things. The difference between actualism and possibilism may be seen in some cases as a difference in order of analysis, but it is not a trivial difference. As we shall see, it may involve the difference between an absolute and a world-relative concept of truth.

Some philosophers who would agree with me in rejecting the possibilist theories of actuality may be inclined to say that the way to avoid such theories and their implausibilities is simply to deny that there are any merely possible worlds. *Hard actualism* is the position expressed by this denial. The hard actualist can still use what he regards as the fiction of a plurality of possible worlds as a heuristic device in thinking about theories and problems in modality; but the possible worlds will not figure in any theory which he asserts at the conclusion of his deliberations. According to *soft actualism*, on the other hand, there are nonactual possible worlds, but they are logically constructed out of the furniture of the actual world; truths in which they are said to exist are reducible in the way demanded by actualism. It might seem that the difference between hard and soft actualism is merely verbal, but in fact it can be quite substantial. For the soft actualist is committed, as the hard actualist is not, to ascribe to the actual world furniture which is rich enough for the logical construction of a plurality of completely determinate possible worlds. This is a large commitment, as will appear. I find it an attractive commitment, because it maintains our ability to assert the intuitively very plausible thesis that possibility is holistic rather than atomistic, in the sense that what is possible is possible only as part of a possible completely determinate world. I therefore prefer soft actualism to hard and will sketch a soft actualist theory of actuality.

8. The word "actualism" has already been used by Donald Williams, in [13]. His actualism is a form of what I would call actualism, since it rejects possible worlds as primitive entities. But I would also recognize as forms of actualism theories which are considerably less restrictive in their ontologies than his. His excludes forces, for example, and appears to exclude intensions.

VI

More than one type of soft actualist analysis of the notion of a possible world may be possible. For example, the reduction of statements about possible worlds to statements ascribing dispositional properties to actual objects, which is suggested by Nelson Goodman ([3], pp. 49-57), might be seen as a soft actualist analysis. But the analysis which I have in mind is a reduction of talk about possible worlds to talk about sets of propositions.

Let us say that a *world-story* is a maximal consistent set of propositions. That is, it is a set which has as its members one member of every pair of mutually contradictory propositions, and which is such that it is possible that all of its members be true together. The notion of a possible world can be given a contextual analysis in terms of world-stories. Of the following statement forms, for example, (1), (3), and (5) are to be analyzed as equivalent to (2), (4), and (6), respectively.

(1) There is a possible world in which *p*.
(2) The proposition that (*p*) is a member of some world-story.[9]
(3) In every possible world, *q*.
(4) The proposition that (*q*) is a member of every world-story.
(5) Let *w* be a possible world in which *r*. In *w, t*.
(6) Let *s* be a world-story of which the proposition that (*r*) is a member. The proposition that (*t*) is a member of *s*.

A similar contextual analysis can now be given to the notion of actuality. "In the actual world, *p*" is to be analyzed as "The proposition that (*p*) is true." In accordance with this analysis, we can say that the actual world differs from the other possible worlds in that all the members of its world-story (the set of all the propositions that are true in it) are true, whereas the stories of all the other possible worlds have false propositions among their members. This soft-actualist analysis may therefore be called the *true-story theory of actuality*.

It is free of the chief disadvantages of the possibilist theories that we have considered. It presents the actuality of the actual world as a distinction which it possesses absolutely and not just in relation to itself. And it does so without implying that the actual world is one which is actual in every possible world and therefore necessarily rather than contingently actual.

---

9. I use parentheses to indicate the scope of the oblique-context-forming expression "that" in cases where I fear that some confusion might otherwise arise.

Unlike the optimistic theory of actuality, moreover, the true-story theory does not make it impossible to understand how we can know that we are actual. To begin with, we must simply assume that we recognize the truth of some very ordinary propositions about ourselves. Suppose, for example, that I feel a pain. In that case, I know that it is true that I feel a pain. Knowing that, and accepting the true-story theory of actuality, I can infer that I feel a pain in the actual world. In a similar way, I can know that I have many other experiences in the actual world. Hence, I can infer that I exist in the actual world—though this last inference takes us beyond the theory of actuality to a theory of existence.

If someone asks how I know that I'm not just feeling a pain in some possible (but nonactual) world, the answer is that feeling a pain in the actual world and just feeling a pain in some possible world are very different things, and it will not be easy to mistake one for the other if we understand the difference between them. For me to feel a pain in some possible world is just for a proposition, to the effect that I feel a pain, to be a member of a certain kind of set of propositions (namely, of some world-story).[10] But for me to feel a pain in the actual world is for me to feel a pain. And if I understand, even nearly as well as I think I understand, what it is to feel a pain, then when I feel a pain, I normally know that I feel one.

Anticipating certain objections to my theory, I will conclude by discussing two ways in which the order of analysis which is followed in the true-story theory differs from the order that is apt to be preferred by possibilists.

(i) We must distinguish between the notion of truth and the world-relative notion of truth *in* a possible world. In the true-story theory of actuality, the notion of truth is presupposed, if not as primitive,[11] at least as prior to the notion of actuality, since the latter is analyzed in terms of the former. This order of analysis is a central feature of the theory and is very natural for a soft actualist. Because he regards the merely possible worlds as constructed rather than primitive entities, the problem of distinguishing

10. In saying that a proposition, to the effect that *I* feel a pain, is included in some world-story, we may commit ourselves to a modality *de re* which some may find objectionable, although it is not objectionable to me. But in any case exactly the same commitment to a modality *de re* is involved in the claim that *I* feel a pain *in some possible world*.

11. As Russell once took it to be (in [12], pp. 523f.). It was surely a notion of absolute, rather than world-relative, truth which he believed to be unanalyzable. Indeed, I do not think there have been many philosophers who have thought that the notion of truth must be based on a prior notion of truth *in* a possible world.

the actual world from other possible worlds does not arise for him except at a conceptual level much less fundamental than that to which the notion of truth belongs.

Some possibilists may wish to take the crucial concepts in a different order, treating the notions of truth *in* a possible world and actuality as prior to the notion of truth and defining truth as truth *in* the *actual* world. (David Lewis seems to be following a strategy somewhat similar to this in [9], pp. 173f.) From the possibilist point of view, truth in a possible world may be thought of as a relation between a proposition or sentence and an object (the possible world) whose ontological status is quite independent of the ontological status of the sentence or proposition, and truth may be thought of as just a special case of that relation, distinguished from other cases only by the actuality of the world involved in it. The true-story theorist, however, regards a merely possible world as logically constructed out of the set of propositions that are true in it, and he sees the truth of a proposition *in* a possible world as basically a matter of relations of consistency among propositions, rather than of correspondence with an independent object. From such a point of view, it is much less natural to try to understand the notion of truth as just a special case of the notion of truth *in* a possible world.

It is to be expected that possibilists will find the notion of absolute truth as difficult to understand as the notion of absolute actuality. It will be difficult for them to see how *any* property possession can be absolute rather than world-relative; if anything, x, has any property, f, it must have it relative to some possible world, *in* which x has f. We have already noted this difficulty for the case in which x is a possible world and f is actuality. Similar considerations apply to the case in which x is a proposition and f is truth.

But in the true-story theory, both absolute and world-relative property ascriptions can be made, and neither crowds out the other. This is because having f, and having f in a possible world in which p, are *not* thought of as essentially the same sort of thing, differing only with respect to something like a location. The true-story theorist can say that x has f absolutely, meaning just that x has f. He can also say that x has f in a possible world in which p, meaning just that the proposition that (x has f) is a member of some world-story of which the proposition that (p) is also a member. And this applies in the case in which x is a proposition and f is truth.

(ii) The possibilist's order of analysis is apt to differ from that of the true-story theory in yet another respect. If the possibilist countenances the notion of a proposition at all, he very likely cherishes the project of analyzing it in terms of possible worlds—perhaps as the notion of a function from possible worlds to truth values (as in Montague [11], p. 163). There is a not unfamiliar trade-off here, between nonactual possibles and intensions (such as propositions); given either, we may be able to construct the other or to do the work that was supposed to be done by talking about the other.

Is it better, then, to begin with possible worlds and construct propositions out of them, or to begin with propositions and construct possible worlds out of them? If possibilism and the true-story theory are the alternatives we are weighing, this is a crucial question. And I am not in a position to say that *all* the advantages lie on the side of beginning with propositions rather than possible worlds. For there are problems about the notion of a proposition; it is the weakest point in the true-story theory. What is a proposition? If we are to have an ontology of propositions rich enough for the construction of completely determinate possible worlds, we must not suppose that propositions are linguistic signs or utterances, nor that they are all expressible in any one language, nor even that there are only a countable infinity of them. We might take the notion of a proposition as primitive and suppose that propositions are self-subsistent objects; but we need not do so. We might try to construct them logically out of some other feature of the (actual) world. Leibniz, for example, held (in [6], V, 429, VI, 226f., 229; in Sections 43–44 of his "Monadology"; and elsewhere) that the ontological status ("reality") of essences, necessary truths, and possibles depends on their being actually thought by God. This is an actualist strand in Leibniz's philosophy which contrasts strikingly with the possibilist tendencies of his thought. And if we were to say that propositions are reducible to thoughts in the mind of God, that would be consistent with the true-story theory of actuality. But the development of an adequate answer to the question, what a proposition is, must be left here as an unfinished task for the true-story theorist.

Notoriously, the development of a satisfactory logic theory of propositions (or of intensions generally) is also beset by formal problems and threats of paradox. One such threat particularly concerns the true-story theory of actuality. The theory seems to imply that there are *consistent* sets composed of one member of *every* pair of mutually contradictory propositions. Furthermore, it follows from the theory, with the assumption that every possible world is actual *in* itself, that every world-story, s, has among its members the proposition that all the members of s are true. Here we are teetering on the brink of paradox. Only on the brink, because we have not formulated definitions and axioms of the theory precisely enough to determine that paradoxes can be derived in it. But if we replaced "proposition" by "sentence" throughout these apparent consequences of the true-story theory, understanding "consistent" as a semantical predicate, the resulting claims about sentences would be incompatible with the stratification into object- and metalanguages which is commonly used as a means to avoid semantical paradoxes. This may give rise to a suspicion that the true-story theory could not be precisely formulated without engendering some analogue of the semantical paradoxes. This suspicion can be laid to rest only by a satisfactory precise formulation, which I am not in a position to give here. I have some hope that such a formulation can be found. Perhaps it would involve a modification of the notion of world-stories, restricting membership in them to certain types of propositions. There is some plausibility to the suggestion that a maximal consistent set of *nonsemantical* propositions would be sufficient for the construction of a completely determinate possible world. If our world-story includes the proposition that there exist giraffes, we do not need to add the proposition that it is *true* that there exist giraffes. We could say that the latter proposition is true in the constructed possible world by virtue of being implied by a proposition which is a member of the world-story, even if it is not itself a member. It is much less easy, however, to see how we should handle the putative proposition that (someone believes that some propositions are true). Perhaps it can safely be a member of a world-story; perhaps it does not need to be . I do not know whether a satisfactory solution is possible along these lines. The attempt to formulate a solution should probably be part of a more comprehensive development of a logical theory of propositions.[12]

These unresolved problems must certainly be counted, at least for the time being, as disadvantages of the true story theory of actuality. The theory also has two important advantages, however. The first advantage is that it embodies the soft actualist view that there are in some sense many completely determinate possible worlds but that they are logically constructed out of features of the actual world. I think that actualism in general, and soft actualism in particular, have great intuitive appeal. The second advantage is that as I hope I have shown, if the difficulties about the theory of propositions can be resolved, that the true-story theory provides a

---

12. I am indebted to Tyler Burge for pointing out to me this problem about the true-story theory, and for much helpful discussion of it.

very satisfying solution of the problem of actuality—more satisfying, I think, than any of the possibilist solutions.[13]

REFERENCES

[1] ROBERT M. ADAMS, "Must God Create the Best?" *Philosophical Review*, 81 (1972), 317–332.

[2] RENÉ DESCARTES, *The Philosophical Works of Descartes*, trans. by E. S. Haldane and G. R. T. Ross (New York: Dover, 1955).

[3] NELSON GOODMAN, *Fact, Fiction, and Forecast*, 2d ed. (Indianapolis: Bobbs-Merrill, 1965).

[4] CHARLES HARTSHORNE, *Anselm's Discovery* (LaSalle, Ill.: Open Court, 1965).

[5] G. W. LEIBNIZ, *Opuscules et Fragments inedits de Leibniz*, ed. by L. Couturat (Paris, 1903).

[6] G. W. LEIBNIZ, *Die philosophischen Schriften von Gottfried Wilhelm Leibniz*, ed. by C. I. Gerhardt (Berlin, 1875–1890).

[7] G. W. LEIBNIZ, *Textes inedits*, ed. by G. Grua (Paris: Presses Universitaires de France, 1948).

[8] DAVID K. LEWIS, "Anselm and Actuality," *Noûs*, 4 (1970), 175–188.

[9] DAVID K. LEWIS, *Convention* (Cambridge, Mass.: Harvard University Press, 1969).

[10] DAVID K. LEWIS, "Counterpart Theory and Quantified Modal Logic," *Journal of Philosophy*, 65 (1968), 113–126; Chapter 5 of this anthology.

[11] RICHARD MONTAGUE, "On the Nature of Certain Philosophical Entities," *The Monist*, 53 (1969), 159–194.

[12] BERTRAND RUSSELL, "Meinong's Theory of Complexes and Assumptions," *Mind*, 13 (1904), 204–219, 336–354, 509–524.

[13] DONALD WILLIAMS, "Mind as a Matter of Fact," *Review of Metaphysics*, 13 (1959–1960), 203–225.

13. Drafts of this paper have been presented to philosophical colloquia at the University of Michigan, MIT, and UCLA. I am indebted to many for helpful discussion and criticism. I must mention particularly Marilyn McCord Adams, John Gates Bennett, Tyler Burge, David Kaplan, David Lewis, John Perry, and referees for *Noûs*.

11

How to Russell a Frege-Church

DAVID KAPLAN

University of California, Los Angeles

The philosophies of language of Frege and Russell are the two great competing classical theories, and any exact comparison of them requires attention to their intensional logics, which represent the pure theoretical (in the
sense of theoretical vs. observational) superstructures—or perhaps one
should say deep structures—of their theories. My earlier work on the logic
of demonstratives, which argued against what I take to be tenets of Frege's
philosophy of language, had led me to a greater appreciation of Russell's
views. I wanted to determine what essential features of Frege's doctrine
could not be accommodated within a Russellian approach. This attempt led
to a surprising result.

I

I began by noting that, for a variety of puzzles, including Frege's puzzle
about the meaning of identity statements and the three puzzles explicitly
discussed by Russell in "On Denoting," one can directly compare the
solutions of Frege and Russell and assess the theoretical apparatus each
brings into play. (When I refer to Russell's logical doctrines, I have in
mind the doctrines of "On Denoting" and the first edition of *Principia
Mathematica*. Russell held several other doctrines throughout his career,
and, of course, the doctrine of *Principia* was not his alone. In attributing

Originally published in the *Journal of Philosophy*, 72 (1975), 716–729; copyright 1975 by
David Kaplan. Reprinted here with the permission of the author.

doctrines to Frege, I take account not only of his own writings but of those of his great modern exponent and proponent, Alonzo Church.) Despite some superficial resemblance—both held something like a disguised definite-description theory of proper names (*most* proper names, for Russell; *all* proper names, and even demonstratives like 'I', for Frege)—the theories are quite different. Frege employs his doctrines of sense and denotation, indirect denotation, and senseful but denotationless expressions. As Church points out, the hierarchy of intensions—senses of expressions denoting individuals, senses of expressions denoting such senses, senses of expressions denoting *such* senses, etc.—seems to be inevitable in such a theory; if not directly from the analysis of iterated operators whose operands have indirect denotation, then by repeating the analysis of contingent identity sentences for entities of higher intensional types. For example, by constructing an identity sentence using descriptions such as 'the sense of Russell's favorite name for Frege' we show the need for senses of expressions denoting senses of expressions denoting individuals.

Russell seems entirely to avoid both the sense/denotation doctrine and the attendant ontological hierarchy by means of his theory of contextually defined incomplete symbols and the consequent doctrine of scope. According to this theory certain expressions, notably definite descriptions, have no meaning in isolation, although each sentence containing such an expression does have a meaning. When the underlying logical form of these sentences, which may be quite different from their apparent grammatical form, is made explicit, the contextually defined expressions completely disappear. Russell's well-known analysis of sentences containing definite descriptions has as an immediate consequence the doctrine that molecular sentences containing definite descriptions are syntactically ambiguous as regards the scope of the definite description.

Thus we see two quite different arrays of conceptual tools, and even distinct ontologies. For Russell, there are individuals, propositions, and, for each n, n-place functions to propositions (such functions are usually called *propositional functions*). For Frege, there are individuals, truth values, for each kind of entity, a second kind capable of being a sense of a name of something of the first kind, and, for each n, n-place functions to entities of *any* given kind. For Frege, sentences are names of truth values. If we take the senses of sentences to be propositions, it would appear that Russell's intensional ontology is a part—and a small part—of Frege's intensional ontology.

We would expect Frege's larger intensional ontology to have some direct utility in the analysis of language, and it appears that we have found such if we turn to the analyses offered by Frege and Russell of certain so-called "intensional" verbs. There is a general form of invalid but seemingly correct inference which involves interchanging two definite descriptions with a common denotation within the scope of such a verb. The seeming correctness of such an inference is due to the fact that it appears to be an instance of Leibniz's law. Frege blocks such inferences by means of his doctrine of indirect denotation, according to which the two descriptions *in this context* do not have a common denotation. Thus, the premise of Leibniz's law fails (or, if thought of as asserting the identity of the ordinary denotations, is irrelevant). Russell blocks the inference by eliminating the description within the sentential complement of the intensional verb. With the descriptions gone, Leibniz's law is inapplicable and there remains no other source of plausibility for the inference. If the descriptions were eliminated from the whole sentence, rather than just the sentential complement, the inference would be valid (though still not directly by Leibniz's law). This suggests that Russell's solution will fail for intensional verbs that do not take sentential complements, for example, 'seeks'. In "Schliemann sought the site of Troy" there is no *secondary* scope elimination that Russell can use to mimic Frege's analysis. Given, then, that the site of Troy is the site of Burbank, Russell seems unable to block the inference to a false conclusion. But Frege's solution is unaffected. Here we seem to see the value of Frege's additional entities (in the case in question, the senses of names of places).

There is also an important—though less often noted—difference between Frege and Russell regarding the structure of intensional entities. According to Russell, an individual may be an immediate element of a proposition. In fact, certain *atomic propositions* consist of just individuals and attributes (or relations); whereas, for Frege, the immediate elements of a proposition must themselves be intensional entities of one sort or another. There is a direct link between this difference in the two theories and the problem of interpreting quantification across intensional verbs (the kind of quantification that arises when a description which appears to stand within the scope of an intensional verb is regarded as taking the whole sentence as its scope and is eliminated from that context). In our modern-day possible-worlds semantics for intensional languages, the problem of identifying individuals across worlds is yet another manifestation of this same theoretical difference. As I will try to show, this is the crucial difference between Frege and Russell.

II

Most of the above-mentioned features of the intensional doctrines of Frege and Russell—their competing theories of definite descriptions, Frege's larger intensional ontology, and their competing views on the structure of propositions—are well-known. What is less well known, or, more accurately, was surprising to me, is the interdependence of these features. I have obtained a result which tends to show that, given Russell's theory of the structure of intensional entities, we can represent all of Frege's ontology within that part of it which constitutes Russell's ontology. Furthermore, the representation is such that the Fregean analysis of sentences containing descriptions within the scope of an intensional verb translates into an approximation to the natural Russellian analysis.

There are several difficulties, both historical and systematic, in my arguments for the above results. From a historical point of view, one problem is that Frege himself gave no formalization of his intensional logic, and Church's recent attempts to do so are not entirely satisfactory for my purposes. Thus I have constructed my own formalization.

A second problem in the historical realm arises from the fact that I give a purely semantical (i.e., model-theoretic) argument for the representation of Frege's ontology within Russell's. This in itself would not be objectionable except for the fact that I have used a possible-worlds form of semantics. This form of semantical theory takes the notions of a possible world and a possible individual in a world as basic, and then uses logical constructions to represent such intensional entities as propositions, individual concepts, properties, etc. But the notions of the structure of intensional entities which underlay Frege's and Russell's proposals were quite different. For Russell, for example, the only basic intensional notion seems to be that of an attribute (or relation in intension). Propositions and propositional functions (which are distinct from attributes) are constructed from these and individuals. Possible worlds might then be represented by maximally consistent sets of propositions, but there is a hitch to the smooth translation between modern possible-worlds semantics and Russellian semantics. Insofar as I have been able to formulate a model-theoretic semantics based on Russell's ideas, what has resulted is a *ramified* theory, which has no absolutely maximal sets of propositions but only maximal sets of propositions of a fixed order.

Another way in which I do not perfectly represent Russell's theory is this. In presenting the Frege-Church ontology I follow Church in using the Schönfinkel reduction of n-place functions, for $n > 1$, to higher-order 1-place functions. Thus the Russellian subontology to which I reduce the full Frege-Church ontology contains functions whose values are not propositions. These are non-Russellian kinds of entities. This is not a serious defect because it is easy to represent a 1-place function by a 2-place propositional function.

I do not merely reduce the Frege-Church ontology to a Russellian ontology; I also provide an effective set of rules for translating any sentence of the Frege-Church language into one of the Russellian fragment. This translation preserves meaning in the sense of intension. Thus, whatever can be said using the full resources of the ontology can be said with reference only to entities of the Russellian sub-ontology. These sentences, whose ontology is Russellian, are not yet in the language of Russell. They may contain definite descriptions, whereas it is a tenet of Russell's theory that all expressions, and especially definite descriptions, whose denotation is dependent on contingent circumstances must be eliminated. Furthermore, these sentences denote truth values, whereas the sentences in Russell's language denote (or *signify*, to use his term) propositions. However, if we take the natural Fregean symbolization of a sentence of English, form a name of the sense of this sentence (rules are given for transforming an arbitrary expression into a name of its sense), and then apply my translation to this name, the result will be an expression whose ontology is Russellian and which is equivalent to the natural Russellian symbolization of the original sentence of English.

Of course, if the Fregean and Russellian symbolizations produce sentences of differing truth values—as is sometimes claimed for English sentences involving improper definite descriptions—there is no hope for an intension preserving translation which will carry the one into the other. However, from my perspective, the essential difference between Frege's and Russell's treatments of definite descriptions does not lie in these truth-value disparities at all, but rather in how they regard these parts of speech. Thus we could modify the Russellian analysis of sentences containing improper descriptions to make it conform always *in truth value* with Frege's analysis. Or we could modify Frege's analysis of sentences containing improper definite descriptions to make it conform always *in truth value* with Russell's analysis. In neither case would we affect the essential difference between the theories. I have taken the former course and followed Frege-Carnap in regarding 'the' as containing implicit reference to a chosen object. The resulting deviation from Russell, which appears only in the case of an improper description, is only a slight embarrassment. The alternative of adjusting the Fregean theory to conform with Russell's intuitions regarding truth value would have been more complicated, because I use the chosen objects anyway in the course of the ontological reduction.

III

The Frege-Church Ontology—"Churcho" for short—consists of entities of the following nonoverlapping types: individuals (type ι); truth values (type o); for any types α, β, functions from entities of type β to entities of type α (type $(\alpha\beta)$); and for any type α, concepts of things of type α (type α_1). It is this last iterative principle that produces the hierarchy of intensions.

We can represent the ontology in the now familiar possible-worlds way as follows. Let W be a nonempty set—thought to represent the set of possible worlds—and let I be a function which assigns to each $w \epsilon W$ a nonempty set—thought to represent the individuals of the possible world represented by w. [To carry through the reduction in detail, we require also a chosen $I^*(w)$ from each of the sets $I(w)$.] For a given $w \epsilon W$ and a given type α, *the universe of the type α at w* is represented in the standard way using Carnap's idea that a concept whose type is β_1 (which would be a concept of an entity whose type is β) can be represented by a function which assigns to each possible-world representative w, an element of the universe of the type β at w.

The Language of the Frege-Church ontology—"El Churcho" for short—contains variables of every type, along with logical constants for: the truth-functional conditional, universal quantification, definite descriptions, the lambda operator, the relation *is a concept of,* and the operation of *composition.* Both Churcho and El Churcho are closely modeled on the systems of Church's "A Formulation of the Logic of Sense and Denotation"[1] and "Outline of a Revised Formalization of the Logic of Sense and Denotation."[2] The difference is that Church identifies the type $(\alpha\beta)_1$ with

---

1. In Paul Henle, H. M. Kallen, and S. K. Langer, eds., *Structure, Method, and Meaning: Essays in Honor of Henry M. Sheffer* (New York: Liberal Arts Press, 1951).
2. *Noûs,* 7 (1973), 24–33 (part I); 8 (1973), 135–156 (part II).

the type $(\alpha_1\beta_1)$. Since I do not, I require the additional notion of *composi-tion* in order to combine a concept of a function with a concept of one of its arguments in order to produce a concept of the function value. Correspond-ing to each constant of any type α, we require a second of type α_1 to denote the sense of the first, and a third of type α_{1_1} to denote the sense of the second, and so on. Given any closed well-formed expression A, we can effectively find a well-formed expression $\overline{A}$ which denotes the sense of A.

Our possible-worlds representation of Churcho can be converted into a model for El Churcho by adding a function i which assigns to each constant of type α an *intension* drawn from the universe of α_1. (Since for types of the form α_1, the universes at w and at w' do not differ, we may ignore the relativization to a possible world.) If we let w represent the actual world, a model takes the form $\langle w, W, I, i \rangle$.

IV

When we construct a model of something, we must distinguish those features of the model which represent features of that which we model, from those features which are intrinsic to the model and play no repre-sentational role. The latter are *artifacts of the model*. For example, if we use string to make a model of a polygon, the shape of the model represents a feature of the polygon, and the size of the model may or may not repre-sent a feature of the polygon, but the thickness and three-dimensionality of the string is certainly an artifact of the model.

Given any possible-worlds representation of Churcho, constructed from a particular set W and a particular function I, and given any distinct elements w and w' of W, some definite relation, either of overlap or disjointness, will hold between $I(w)$ and $I(w')$. To put it another way, there is no intrinsic problem—within the model—of *identifying* members of $I(w)$ with members of $I(w')$; we need no *criteria* to make precise the question whether a given member of $I(w)$ is also a member of $I(w')$. Thus, the overlaps (or disjointness) between such pairs as $I(w)$ and $I(w')$ is a definite feature of our model. Is it an *artifact of the model* of a *feature of the metaphysical reality* being modeled?

Suppose that we adhere to a metaphysics of possible worlds and possible individuals. Then we probably believe that for each possible world there is a definite number of possible individuals that exist in it. Thus the cardinal-ity of the sets $I(w)$ is not an artifact. But there seems to be some disagree-ment as to whether we can meaningfully ask whether a possible individual that exists in one possible world also exists in another without taking into account the attributes and behavior of the individuals that exist in the one world and making a comparison with the attributes and behavior of the individuals that exist in the other world. The doctrine that holds that it does make sense to ask—without reference to common attributes and behavior—whether *this* is the same individual in another possible world, that individuals can be extended in logical space (i.e., through possible worlds) in much the way we commonly regard them as being extended in physical space and time, and that a common "thisness" may underlie extreme dissimilarity or distinct thisnesses may underlie great resemblance, I call *Haecceitism*. (I prefer the pronunciation Hex'-ee-i-tis-m.) It would be more exact to speak of Haecceitism *with respect to* a given kind of entity, but for present purposes we may assume that only individuals are in question and that our individuals are themselves some well-defined kind of entity, perhaps animals.

The opposite view, *Anti-Haecceitism,* holds that for entities of distinct possible worlds there is no notion of transworld being. They may, of course, be linked by a common concept and distinguished by another concept—as Eisenhower and Nixon are linked across two moments of time by the concept *the president of the United States* and distinguished, at the same pair of moments, by the concept *the most respected member of his party*—but there are, in general, many concepts linking any such pair and many distinguishing them. Each, in his own setting, may be clothed in attributes which cause them to *resemble* one another closely. But there is no metaphysical reality of sameness or difference which underlies the clothes. Our interests may cause us to *identify* individuals of distinct worlds, but we are then creating something—a transworld continuant—of a kind different from anything given by the metaphysics. Although the Anti-Haecceitist may seem to assert that no possible individual exists in more than one possible world, that view is properly reserved for the Haecceitist who holds to an unusually rigid brand of metaphysical determinism.

Haecceitism holds that we can meaningfully speak of a thing itself—without reference either explicit, implicit, vague, or precise to individuating concepts (other than being *this* thing), defining qualities, essential attributes, or any other of the paraphernalia that enable us to distinguish one thing from another. It may be that each thing has essential attributes with which it is vested at all times and in each possible world in which it exists. But that is an issue posterior to whether things have transworld being.

If I may reuse the analogy between possible worlds and moments of time, the Haecceitist regrets that we can come to know whether *this* is Anastasia only by a painstaking study and comparison of present attributes with past ones. The Anti-Haecceitist believes there is nothing more to know.

Probably, most of us are Haecceitists with respect to most things through time, but the very inaccessibility of other possible worlds seems to have produced a goodly number of Anti-Haecceitists with respect to transworld identifications. Even when their quantified modal logics look Haecceitistic, their pre-systematic remarks may explain the so-called identities as a manner of speaking.

The supposition that we adhere to a metaphysics of possible worlds and possible individuals is not inevitable. After all, our primary goal was to model the ontology of the Frege-Church intensional hierarchy. We may, as I believe Church does, regard such remarks as "think of W as representing the set of possible worlds" as of heuristic value but as reflecting no metaphysical commitment. Possible worlds and possible individuals, insofar as it is metaphysically sound to speak of them at all, may be thought of as constructs from such *given* entities of the ontology as propositions, attributes, individual concepts, and the like. This view—that the ontology of Churcho reflects the basic metaphysical commitments—seems more consonant with the outlook of Frege, Russell, and, of course, Church.

I believe that the issue of Haecceitism reappears, within this metaphysical framework, as the question whether an individual itself—as opposed to an individual-under-a-concept—can be an immediate constituent of a proposition. Let us adopt the terminology *singular proposition* for those (purported) propositions which contain individuals as immediate constituents, and *general proposition* for the others. The sentences "All men are mortal" and "The finest man, whosoever he may be, is mortal" are generally conceded to express general propositions. "I am mortal" and "This is blue" are thought by some to express singular propositions.

Why is the acceptance of singular propositions simply another version of Haecceitism? For two reasons: first, if propositions, attributes, etc. are represented in the usual way by functions on possible worlds, then in representing a singular proposition that contains an individual x we would want to assign truth to those possible worlds in which x has whatever property is attributed to him. But this presupposes that, for each world, it is a determinate question which, if any, of its individuals is x. If we are only asked to represent general propositions, we can confine our attention, in each possible world, to considerations *internal* to the life of the world, and the *external* question, "But is it *x*?" need never arise. The second reason is that if possible worlds are represented as sets of propositions and we permit such singular propositions as that expressed by "I exist" (a true— perhaps even analytic—but contingent proposition), then we have, by way of the individuals that are immediate constituents of such propositions, a metaphysically sound way of identifying certain individuals of one possible world with those of another. On the other hand, if we limit ourselves to general propositions, any such transworld identifications would require a special and independent justification. (There are complexities here which I will not now attempt to elucidate.) Thus we see that, whichever outlook we take as basic, the acceptance of singular propositions is linked to the acceptance of transworld identities.

The question of Haecceitism is important to the philosophy of language. I have counted myself a Haecceitist since I saw the issue starkly during my study of the logic of demonstratives. (I have held the position since that time, but it was only recently that Robert Adams suggested the epithet.) If one believes, as I do, that whatever attributes are capitalized upon for the demonstration, demonstratives are devices of pure reference, then one seems committed to accepting something like singular propositions in one's semantics. If one regards the usual form of quantification into modal and other intensional contexts—modality *de re*—as legitimate (without special explanations), then again one seems committed to some form of Haecceitism.

As is well known, there are those who reject the meaningfulness of such forms of speech or suggest other analyses. Frege, for example, seems to reject singular propositions and to believe that all names, even such demonstratives as 'I', are to be analyzed as disguised definite descriptions. Frege is an Anti-Haecceitist. Church, I believe, follows Frege in this aspect of his philosophy.

There can be little doubt that Russell was a Haecceitist. The metaphysics of *Principia Mathematica* (and earlier of *Principles of Mathematics*) gives us atomic propositions with individuals as constituents. Thus "Dion walks" expresses a proposition that contains Dion himself as a constituent (and the attribute *walks* as a component). I believe that, if Russell were willing to adopt the possible-worlds terminology, he would say that such a proposition is represented by that function which assigns truth to a possible world in which the constituent has the attribute and falsehood to one in which he lacks it. I am not sure what he would say about a possible world in which Dion does not exist. Probably he would choose falsehood, not because of his analysis of definite descriptions or disguised definite descriptions—Dion is a genuine constituent of this proposition—but just because his instincts seemed to go that way. (There is, to my knowledge, almost no relevant evidence because Russell did not take modal logic seriously. The situation is further confused by the fact that he regarded 'Dion exists', with 'Dion' a genuine name, as meaningless.[3])

Some may not think of Russell as a Haecceitist because they confuse his epistemology with his metaphysics. We *know* (and thus express) very few such singular propositions, according to Russell. The proposition *we* express when we utter "Socrates was wise" does not have Socrates as a constituent. But there *is* such a proposition. We can't know it or even, I suppose, entertain or apprehend it, because we are not acquainted with Socrates. Russell's theory of proper names which are disguised definite descriptions is motivated by epistemological considerations. Although he seems, thus, to explain away singular propositions, in fact they are still required by his metaphysics to construct the general propositions that we do express. I don't fully agree with Russell's epistemology, but the important point is that Haecceitism goes quite smoothly at the metaphysical level, but raises many difficulties at the epistemological level.

Here we are concerned with metaphysics. My aim is to apply Russell's methods in intensional logic—which depend on his Haecceitism—to the Frege-Church hierarchy, hoping to show that Haecceitism is all that stands between Frege-Church and Russell.

Before going on, I wish to call attention to the fact that some may have adopted an Anti-Haecceitist position as a form of *Actualism*. (Again, I am indebted to Robert Adams for the terminology.) We have spoken of possible worlds other than the actual one and possible individuals other than the actual ones. Many, myself included, find such talk ultimately unsatisfactory (though a useful stopgap). They are pleased to say, "It is possible that there is an individual such that so and so" but recoil at "There is a possible individual such that so and so." To be concrete, I can assert that it is possible that there be an individual who is not among the actual individuals (for there might be more individuals than there, in fact, are), without committing myself to the existence of a possible individual who is not actual. It may be feared that Haecceitism must be a two-way street. If it

---

3. This point was brought to my attention by Joseph Lambert.

opens the door to let actual individuals into other possible worlds, how can it help but allow what were merely possible individuals from slipping into the actual world? It can. Haecceitism vs. Anti-Haecceitism is a distinct and independent dimension from Actualism vs. Possibilism. All four combinations are consistent. One might claim that Possibilism and Anti-Haecceitism is represented by David Lewis, Possibilism and Haecceitism by Richard Montague, Actualism and Anti-Haecceitism by Church, and Actualism and Haecceitism by myself. I think that Saul Kripke also shares the last position, though he has not spoken explicitly on Acutalism vs. Possibilism in print. At any rate, the treatment of quantification in "Semantical Considerations on Modal Logic"[4] is Actualistic, whether by fancy or determination I do not know. (Note that the remark about 'Sherlock Holmes' denoting a possible individual is withdrawn in the Addenda to "Naming and Necessity."[5]) An Actualist can accept the existence of propositions which are only possibly true. He cannot accept the existence of those possible propositions which, independent of truth value, depend on what is not actual, for example, the additional singular propositions which would exist if there were additional individuals.

V

The Haecceitist will regard overlaps between $I(w)$ and $I(w')$ as representing features of the metaphysical reality; the Anti-Haecceitist will regard them as artifacts of the model.

How can we represent the Anti-Haecceitist's position in our model theory? As was remarked above, not by requiring that $I(w)$ and $I(w')$ be disjoint for $w \neq w'$, since this would equally well represent the metaphysical thesis that no individual exists in more than one possible world, and both this thesis and its negation should count as meaningless according to the Anti-Haecceitist. Those who regard such overlaps as artifacts of the model must "factor out" this feature by defining a notion of *isomorphism* between models which preserves structure except for such overlaps. This is easily done.

4. *Acta Philosophica Fennica,* 16 (1963), 83–94; reprinted in Leonard Linsky, ed., *Reference and Modality* (New York: Oxford University Press, Oxford: Clarendon Press, 1971).
5. In Donald Davidson and Gilbert Harman, eds., *Semantics of Natural Language* (Dordrecht: Reidel, 1972), pp. 764–765.

Church's position seems to be that models that are isomorphic in this sense represent (i.e., model) the same reality. Thus, he has carefully adopted a form of language for which isomorphic models preserve the truth value of all sentences. (A stronger result holds: given any well-formed expression A of any type and two isomorphic models, the denotation of A in the one model is the image under the isomorphism of the denotation of A in the other model.) Any form of language that violated this would contain elements which, from this viewpoint, were metaphysically meaningless, since the notation would contain sentences whose truth value was determined not by features of reality but by the artificial stipulations required to fix a particular model. Such sentences would permit us to discern the indiscernible!

VI

Returning now to my hypothesis that Frege-Church + Haecceitism = Russell, I will explain the leading idea. For Church, an attribute—the meaning of a predicate—combines with an individual concept to yield a proposition. This suggests that an attribute can be represented as a function from individual concepts to propositions. (This is the one feature of "A Formulation of the Logic of Sense and Denotation," which I have abandoned in El Churcho.) For Russell, an attribute combines with an individual to yield a (singular) proposition (here the Haecceitism comes into play). This suggests that an attribute can be represented as a function from individuals to propositions, that is, as the simplest kind of propositional function. Suppose the attribute has uniqueness built into it, so that it can be attributable to no more than one individual per world. Let us, for the moment, think of propositions as sets of possible worlds rather than as characteristic functions of such sets. Then the propositional function F, which represents an attribute with uniqueness built in, never assigns compatible propositions (i.e., those containing a common possible world) to distinct individuals. Thus, for a given world w there is at most one individual x such that $w \epsilon F(x)$. The propositional function F is now barely distinguishable from an individual concept. By a slight variation on Russell's scheme for representing attributes—adding uniqueness—we see how to represent an individual concept as a function from individuals to propositions. (A final caveat: the propositional function must, of course, have all possible individuals in its domain. This can be achieved either by assuming a fixed domain of individuals common to all possible worlds or by taking the values of the individual variables to be all possible individuals and adding a predicate to distinguish the actual. It also seems possible to treat the case of overlapping domains without quantifying over possible individuals, but new ideas are required and the result is less simple.)

An individual concept c will be represented by that propositional function F which assigns to a possible individual x exactly that set of worlds w such that $c(w) = x$. *This idea generalizes.* Concepts of entities of type α_1 can be represented by functions from (possible) entities of type α to propositions.

The role of Haecceitism in this reduction is apparent. In models that are isomorphic (in the Anti-Haecceitist's sense), corresponding individual concepts will not necessarily be reduced to corresponding propositional functions. The particular propositional function to which an individual concept is reduced depends on the transworld identities.

The result of applying this reduction to entities of successively higher intensional types is that we can ultimately represent all of the entities of Churcho within the sub-ontology whose types are just ι, o, o_1, and $(\alpha\beta)$ for any types α and β which are already included. In this development, the only basic intensional entities that remain are the propositions.

VII

Two final points are worthy of note. First, the concept that is the Fregean sense of a definite description like 'the site of Troy' is reduced to the propositional function F such that if x is any individual, $F(x)$ is the proposition: *that x is a unique site of Troy.* (Of course, for the Anti-Haecceitist, there is no such proposition; the place in the that-clause occupied by the variable must be filled by a sense-bearing name, and the place in the singular proposition occupied by x must be filled by an individual concept.) This is in accord with Russell's views about definite descriptions and provides us with his solution to the earlier-mentioned problem regarding such intensional verbs as 'seeks', which do not take a sentential complement. *Seeks* becomes a relation between an individual and an attribute (I do not here distinguish between attributes and the corresponding propositional functions), for example, between Schliemann and the attribute of *being a unique site of Troy.* Frege's analysis seems superior only so long as we focus on "Schliemann sought the site of Troy" in which 'seek' takes a singular term as direct object, and ignore "Schliemann sought a wealthy benefactor." Russell would regard the second form, in which 'seeks' takes an indefinite noun phrase as complement, as showing the *deep* structure for 'seeks', and analyzes the first on that model.

Finally, I note that the basic technique for reducing the hierarchy of intensions to propositional functions is quite general. It is not limited to the kind of intensions generated by the possible-worlds methodology, wherein two expressions have the same intension if they are logically equivalent. If we find Haecceitism acceptable—and most writers seem to do so—this raises the prospect that in attempting to construct new intensional logics (for example, logics with a more fine-grained principle of individuation for intensions) we can concentrate our efforts on the much simpler Russellian form.[6]

6. The work reported above is an outgrowth of and was inspired by the seminar "Recent Developments in the Logic of Sense and Denotation" given in fall 1973 by Professor Alonzo Church. It has benefited from the comments and suggestions of several persons. The deficiencies of the present report are due, in part, to the severe time constraints under which it was prepared. Its merits are due, in part, to the "instant criticism" of Robert Adams, Tyler Burge, Montgomery Furth, Donald Kalish, and Joseph Lambert. Both the thought and the writing were supported by the National Science Foundation.

12

Possible Worlds

ROBERT C. STALNAKER

Cornell University

According to Leibniz, the universe—the actual world—is one of an infinite number of possible worlds existing in the mind of God.* God created the universe by actualizing one of these possible worlds—the best one. It is a striking image, this picture of an infinite swarm of total universes, each by its natural inclination for existence striving for a position that can be occupied by only one, with God, in his infinite wisdom and benevolence, settling the competition by selecting the most worthy candidate. But in these enlightened times, we find it difficult to take this metaphysical myth any more seriously than the other less abstract creation stories told by our primitive ancestors. Even the more recent expurgated versions of the story, leaving out God and the notoriously chauvinistic thesis that our world is better than all the rest, are generally regarded, at best, as fanciful metaphors for a more sober reality. J. L. Mackie, for example, writes "... talk of possible worlds ... cries out for further analysis. There *are* no possible worlds except the actual one; so what are we up to when we talk about them?" ([3], p. 90). Lawrence Powers puts the point more bluntly: "The whole idea of possible worlds (perhaps laid out in space like raisins in a pudding) seems ludicrous" ([4]).

These expressions of skepticism and calls for further analysis are of course not directed at Leibniz but at recent uses of parts of his metaphysical

Reprinted with permission of the author and of the editor of *Noûs*, 10 (1976), 65–75.
*I am indebted to the John Simon Guggenheim Memorial Foundation for support during the time when this paper was written.

myth to motivate and give content to formal semantics for modal logics. In both formal and philosophical discussions of modality, the concept of a possible world has shown itself to have considerable heuristic power. But, critics have argued, a heuristic device should not be confused with an explanation. If analyses of modal concepts (or of the concept of a proposition) in terms of possible worlds are to be more than heuristic aids in mapping the relationships among the formulas of a modal logic, the concept of a possible world itself must be explained and justified.

Although it is commonly taken to be an obvious truth that there really are no such things as possible worlds—that the myth, whether illuminating or misleading, explanatory or obfuscating, is nevertheless a myth—this common opinion can be challenged. That is, one might respond to the possible worlds skeptic not by explaining the metaphor but by taking the story to be the literal truth. David Lewis responds in this way, and he cites common opinion and ordinary language on his side:

> I believe that there are possible worlds other than the one we happen to inhabit. If an argument is wanted, it is this. It is uncontroversially true that things might be otherwise than they are. I believe, and so do you, that things could have been different in countless ways. But what does this mean? Ordinary language permits the paraphrase: there are many ways things could have been besides the way they actually are. On the face of it, this sentence is an existential quantification. It says that there exist many entities of a certain description, to wit, 'ways things could have been'. I believe that things could have been different in countless ways; I believe permissible paraphrases of what I believe; taking the paraphrase at its face value, I therefore believe in the existence of entities that might be called 'ways things could have been'. I prefer to call them 'possible worlds'. ([2], p. 84)

Lewis does not intend this as a knockdown argument. It is only a presumption that the sentences of ordinary language be taken at face value, and the presumption can be defeated if the naive reading of the sentences leads to problems which can be avoided by an alternative analysis. The aim of the argument is to shift the burden to the skeptic who, if he is to defeat the argument, must point to the problems which commitment to possible worlds creates, and the alternative analysis which avoids those problems. Lewis does not think the skeptic can do either.

The rhetorical force of Lewis's argument is in the suggestion that possible worlds are really not such alien entities as the metaphysical flavor of this name seems to imply. The argument suggests not that ordinary language and our common beliefs commit us to a weighty metaphysical theory, but rather that what appears to be a weighty metaphysical theory is really just some ordinary beliefs by another name. Believing in possible worlds is like speaking prose. We have been doing it all our lives.

But for this to be convincing, the shift from "ways things might have been" to "possible worlds" must be an innocent terminological substitution, and I do not believe that, as Lewis develops the concept of a possible world, it is. To argue this point I will state four theses about possible worlds, all defended by Lewis. Together they constitute a doctrine which I will call extreme realism about possible worlds. It is this doctrine against which the skeptic is reacting, and against which, I shall argue, he is justified in reacting. I believe the doctrine is false, but I also believe that one need not accept or reject the theses as a package. The main burden of my argument will be to show the independence of the more plausible parts of the package, and so to defend the coherence of a more moderate form of realism about possible worlds—one that might be justified by our common modal opinions and defended as a foundation for a theory about the activities of rational agents.

Here are Lewis's four theses: (1) *Possible worlds exist.* Other possible worlds are just as real as the actual world. They may not *actually* exist, since to actually exist is to exist in the actual world, but they do, nevertheless, exist. (2) *Other possible worlds are things of the same sort as the actual world—"I and all my surroundings"* ([2], p. 86). They differ "not in kind but only in what goes on at them. Our actual world is only one world among others. We call it alone actual not because it differs in kind from all the rest but because it is the world we inhabit" ([2], p. 85). (3) *The indexical analysis of the adjective 'actual' is the correct analysis.* "The inhabitants of other worlds may truly call their own worlds actual, if they mean by 'actual' what we do; for the meaning we give to 'actual' is such that it refers at any world i to that world i itself. 'Actual' is indexical, like 'I' or 'here' or 'now': it depends for its reference on the circumstances of utterance, to wit the world where the utterance is located" ([2], pp. 85–86). (4) *Possible worlds cannot be reduced to something more basic.* "Possible worlds are what they are, and not some other thing." It would be a mistake to identify them with some allegedly more respectable entity, for example a set of sentences of some language. Possible worlds are "respectable entities in their own right" ([2], p. 85).

The first thesis, by itself, is compatible with Lewis's soothing claim that believing in possible worlds is doing no more than believing that things might have been different in various ways. What is claimed to exist are things which ordinary language calls "ways things might have been", things that truth is defined relative to, things that our modal idioms may be understood as quantifiers over. But the first thesis says nothing about the nature of the entities that play these roles. It is the second thesis which gives realism about possible worlds its metaphysical bite, since it implies that possible worlds are not shadowy ways things could be, but concrete particulars, or at least entities which are made up of concrete particulars and events. The actual world is "I and my surroundings". Other possible worlds are more things like that. Even a philosopher who had no qualms about abstract objects like numbers, properties, states, and kinds might balk at this proliferation of fullblooded universes which seem less real to us than our own only because we have never been there.

The argument Lewis gives for thesis one, identifying possible worlds with ways things might have been, seems even to be incompatible with his explanation of possible worlds as more things of the same kind as I and all my surroundings. If possible worlds are ways things might have been, then the actual world ought to be *the way things are* rather than *I and all my surroundings. The way things are* is a property or a state of the world, not the world itself. The statement that the world is the way it is is true in a sense, but not when read as an identity statement (Compare: "the way the world is is the world"). This is important, since if properties can exist uninstantiated, then *the way the world is* could exist even if a world that is that way did not. One could accept thesis one—that there really are many ways that things could have been—while denying that there exists anything else that is like the actual world.

Does the force of thesis two rest, then, on a simple equivocation between "the actual world", in the sense that is roughly captured in the paraphrase "I and all my surroundings", and the sense in which it is equivalent to "the way things are"? In part, I think, but it also has a deeper motivation. One might argue from thesis three—the indexical analysis of actuality—to the conclusion that the essential difference between our world and the others is that we are here, and not there.

Thesis three seems to imply that the actuality of the actual world—the attribute in virtue of which it is actual—is a world-relative attribute. It is an attribute which our world has relative to itself, but which all the other worlds have relative to themselves too; so the *concept* of actuality does not distinguish, from an absolute standpoint, the actual world from the others. But if there is no absolute property of actuality, does this not mean that, looking at things from an objective point of view, merely possible people and their surroundings are just as real as we and ours?

The mistake in this reasoning, I think, is in the assumption that the absolute standpoint is a neutral one, distinct from the view from within any possible world. The problem is avoided when one recognizes that the standpoint of the actual world *is* the absolute standpoint, and that it is part of the concept of actuality that this should be so. We can grant that fictional characters are as right, from their point of view, to affirm their fullblooded reality as we are to affirm ours. But their point of view is fictional, and so what is right from it makes no difference as far as reality is concerned.

My point is that the *semantical* thesis that the indexical analysis of "actual" is correct can be separated from the metaphysical thesis that the actuality of the actual world is nothing more than a relation between it and things existing in it. Just as one could accept the indexical analysis of personal pronouns and be a solipsist, and accept the indexical analysis of tenses and believe that the past exists only as memory and the future only as anticipation, one can accept the indexical analysis of actuality while excluding from one's ontology any universes that *are* the way things might have been.

In fact, I want to argue, one must exclude those analogues of our universe from one's ontology. The thesis that the actual world alone is real is superficially analogous to solipsism—the thesis that I alone am real, but solipsism has content, and can be coherently denied, because it says something substantive about what alone is real. In effect, solipsism says that the actual world is a person, or a mind. But the thesis that the actual world alone is real has content only if "the actual world" means something other than the totality of everything there is, and I do not believe that it does. The thesis that there is no room in reality for other things than the actual world is not, like solipsism, based on a restrictive theory of what there is room for in reality, but rather on the metaphysically neutral belief that "the actual world" is just another name for reality.

So the moderate realism whose coherence I am trying to defend accepts theses one and three, and rejects thesis two. What about thesis four? If we identify possible worlds with ways things might have been, can we still hold that they are "respectable entities in their own right", irreducible to anything more fundamental? Robert Adams has argued that to avoid extreme realism we must find an eliminative reduction of possible worlds. "If there are any true statements in which there are said to be nonactual possible worlds," he argues, "they must be reducible to statements in

which the only things there are said to be are things which there are in the
actual world and which are not identical with nonactual possibles'' ([1], p.
224). Unless the reminder that by ''possible world'' we mean nothing more
than ''way things might have been'' counts as such a reduction, I do not
see why this should be necessary. Why cannot *ways things might have
been* be elements of the actual world, as they are?

Two problems need to be separated: the first is the general worry that the
notion of a possible world is a very obscure notion. How can explanations
in terms of possible worlds help us to understand anything unless we are
told what possible worlds are, and told in terms which are independent of
the notions which possible worlds are intended to explain? The second
problem is the specific problem that believing in possible worlds and in the
indexical analysis of actuality seems to commit one to extreme realism,
which (many believe) is obviously false. Now to point to the difference
between a way our world might have been and a world which *is* the way
our world might have been, and to make clear that the possible worlds
whose existence the theory is committed to are the former kind of thing and
not the latter, is to do nothing to solve the first problem; in fact it makes it
more acute since it uses a modal operator to say what a possible world is.
But this simple distinction does, I think, dissolve the second problem
which was the motivation for Adams's demand for an analysis.

Not only is an eliminative reduction of possible worlds not necessary to
solve the second problem, it also may not be sufficient to solve the first. I
shall argue that the particular reduction that Adams proposes—a reduction
of possible worlds to propositions—by itself says nothing that answers the
critic who finds the concept of a possible world obscure. His reduction says
no more, and in fact says less, about propositions and possible worlds than
the reverse analysis that I would defend—the analysis of propositions in
terms of possible worlds.

Adams's analysis is this: ''Let us say that a *world-story* is a maximal
consistent set of propositions. That is, it is a set which has as its members
one member of every pair of mutually contradictory propositions, and
which is such that it is possible that all of its members be true together. The
notion of a possible world can be given a contextual analysis in terms of
world-stories'' ([1], p. 225). For a proposition to be true in some or all
possible worlds is for it to be a member of some or all world-stories. Other
statements that seem to be about possible worlds are to be replaced in a
similar way by statements about world-stories.

There are three undefined notions used in Adams's reduction of possible worlds: *proposition, possibility,* and *contradictory.* What are propositions? Adams leaves this question open for further discussion; he suggests that it might be answered in various ways. Little is said about them except that they are to be thought of as language independent abstract objects, presumably the potential objects of speech acts and propositional attitudes.

What is possibility? The notion used in the definition of world-story is a property of *sets* of propositions. Intuitively, a set of propositions is possible if all its members can be true together. This notion cannot, of course, be defined in terms of possible worlds, or world-stories, without circularity, but it should be a consequence of the theory that a set of propositions is possible if and only if its members are simultaneously true in some possible world (are all members of some world-story). Presumably, an explicit formulation of the world-story theory would contain postulates sufficient to ensure this.

What is a contradictory? This relation between propositions might be defined in terms of possibility as follows: A and B are contradictories if and only if $\{A, B\}$ is not possible, and for every possible set of propositions Γ either $\Gamma \cup \{A\}$ or $\Gamma \cup \{B\}$ is possible. The theory tacitly assumes that every proposition has a contradictory; in an explicit formulation, this would be an additional postulate.

These definitions and postulates yield a minimal world-story theory. It is minimal in that it imposes no structure on the basic elements of the theory except what is required to justify what Adams calls the "intuitively very plausible thesis that possibility is holistic rather than atomistic, in the sense that what is possible is possible only as part of a possible completely determinate world" ([1], p. 225). But the theory justifies this thesis only by postulating it.

It will be useful to compare this reduction of possible worlds to propositions with the competing reduction of propositions to possible worlds. What is at stake in choosing which of these two notions to define in terms of the other? Adams refers to the "not unfamiliar trade-off... between nonactual possibles and intensions (such as propositions); given either, we may be able to construct the other or to do the work that was supposed to be done by talking about the other" ([1], p. 228). But the two proposals are not equivalent. Part of what distinguishes them is an elusive question of conceptual priority, but there are also more substantive differences, both in the structure imposed on propositions and possible worlds and in the questions left to be answered by further developments of the respective theories.

If we set aside questions of conceptual priority—of which concepts and principles should be primitive and which defined or derived—what is the difference between the two analyses? The world-story theory is weaker, leaving open questions which are settled by the possible-worlds analysis of propositions. The following two theses are consequences of the possible-worlds analysis, but not of the world-story theory; the first concerns identity conditions; the second is a closure condition:

(I) Necessarily equivalent propositions are identical.
(C) For every set of propositions, there is a proposition which, necessarily, is true if and only if every member of the set is true.

Are these consequences of the possible worlds analysis welcome or not? I believe that thesis (I) can be defended independently of the possible-worlds analysis of propositions, but that is a long story for another occasion. The thesis does have some notoriously problematic consequences, but I believe, first, that it is implied by a widely held and plausible assumption about the nature of propositional attitudes—the assumption that attitudes like belief and desire are dispositions of agents displayed in their rational behavior—and second, that the apparently paradoxical consequences of the thesis can be explained away. But for now let me just point out that the possible-worlds analysis has this substantive consequence, and leave the part of my argument which depends on it conditional on the assumption that this consequence is welcome. The thesis is not implied by the minimal world-story theory, but it is compatible with it, so the world-story theorist who agrees with me about thesis (I) can add it to his theory as an additional postulate.

Thesis (C) seems reasonable on almost any theory of propositions and propositional attitudes. Whatever propositions are, if there are propositions at all then there are sets of them, and for any set of propositions, it is something determinately true or false that all the members of the set are true. If one is willing to talk of propositions at all, one will surely conclude that that something is a proposition. It may not be possible to express all such propositions since it may not be possible, in any actual language, to refer to all such sets; it may not be humanly possible to believe or disbelieve some such propositions, since it may not be humanly possible to grasp them. But if this is so, it is surely a contingent human limitation which should not restrict the range of potential objects of propositional attitudes. So I will assume that the world-story theorist will want to add thesis (C) to his theory.

If (I) and (C) are added as postulates to the minimal world-story theory, then it becomes equivalent to the possible-worlds analysis with respect to the structure it imposes on the set of propositions, and on the relation between propositions and possible worlds. The sole difference that remains between the two theories is that one takes as primitive what the other defines. And even this difference will be eliminated if we make one more change in response to a question about the further development of the world-story theory.

The next question for the world-story theorist is this: can he say more about his fundamental concept, the concept of a proposition? In particular, are there some *basic* propositions out of which all the rest can be constructed? The usual way to answer this question is to model basic propositions on the atomic sentences of a first order language; propositions are constructed out of individuals and primitive properties and relations in the same way that sentences are constructed out of names and predicates. But this strategy requires building further structure into the theory. There is another way to answer the question which needs no further assumption. We can deduce from what has already been built into the world-story theory that there is a set of propositions of which all propositions are truth-functions: this is the set of strongest contingent propositions—those propositions which are members of just one world-story. It is thus a harmless change, a matter of giving the theory a more economical formulation, to take these to be the basic propositions. (This change does not foreclose a further reduction of what are here called basic propositions. Any alternative reduction could be expressed as a further reduction; this is why the move is harmless.) We can then define propositions generally as sets of basic propositions (or, for a neater formulation, call the basic elements *propositional elements* and let their unit sets be the basic propositions). A nonbasic proposition will be true just in case one of its members is true. This reduction has the added advantage that it allows us to define the previously primitive property of possibility, and to derive all of the postulates. With these primitive notions and assumptions eliminated, the world-story theory looks as good as the theory that takes possible worlds as primitive and defines propositions. This is, of course, because it is exactly the same theory.

I have gone through this exercise of changing the world-story theory into the possible-worlds analysis of propositions in order to make the following point: first, the minimal world-story theory with which I began is indeed a minimal theory of propositions, a theory that assumes nothing about them except that they have truth values and are related to each other by the standard propositional relations (entailment, compatibility, and so forth). But second, every step in the metamorphosis of this minimal theory into the possible-worlds analysis is motivated by independently plausible assumptions about propositions or by theory-neutral considerations of economy of formulation. If this is right, then the possible-worlds analysis is not just one theory which makes the assumptions about propositions that I have made. More than this, it is the whole content of that analysis to impose the minimal structure on propositions which is appropriate to a theory which understands propositions in this way. Anyone who believes that there are objects of propositional attitudes, and who accepts the assumptions about the formal properties of the set of these objects, must accept that there are things which have all the properties that the possible-worlds theory attributes to all possible worlds, and that propositions can be reduced to these things.

Is the form of realism about possible worlds that I want to defend really realism? It is in the sense that it claims that the concept of a possible world is a basic concept in a true account of the way we represent the world in our propositional acts and attitudes. A full defense of this kind of realism would require a development and defense of such an account. All I have tried to do here is show that there is a coherent thesis about possible worlds which rejects extreme realism, but which takes possible worlds seriously as irreducible entities, a thesis that treats possible worlds as more than a convenient myth or a notational shortcut, but less than universes that resemble our own.

REFERENCES

[1] ROBERT M. ADAMS, "Theories of Actuality," *Noûs*, 8 (1974), 211-231; Chapter 10 of this anthology.

[2] DAVID LEWIS, *Counterfactuals* (Cambridge, Mass.: Harvard University Press, 1973); the relevant passages are reprinted as Chapter 9 of this anthology.

[3] J. L. MACKIE, *Truth, Probability, and Paradox* (Oxford: Clarendon Press, 1973).

[4] LAWRENCE POWERS, "Comments on Stalnaker's 'Propositions,' " in *Issues in the Philosophy of Language*, ed. A. F. MacKay and D. D. Merrill (New Haven: Yale University Press, 1976), 93-103.

13

Modal Realism: The Poisoned Pawn

FABRIZIO MONDADORI

University of Pennsylvania

ADAM MORTON

University of Ottawa

Geller came closer to actual qualification than Ljubojevic ever did. Very few could have expected that the so-far undefeated Portisch would suffer his first and only defeat just in the last round against Polugaevsky, thus allowing the uncertainty of a further competition in which either he, Polugaevsky or Geller would be eliminated from the candidates. Later, in Portoroz, if Geller had only whispered to Portisch the word "draw!" a few seconds before his flag fell while a pawn up and unaware of the approaching time control, Geller and not Polugaevsky would have been among the candidates.

—S. Gligoric, "The Unlucky Ones,"
Chess Life and Review, 29 (1974), 17.

A Prejudice in Favor of the Actual

Ljubojevic might have won the Petropolis Interzonal, for the quality of his play in previous tournaments, his inventiveness, and his ability systematically to surprise his opponents were sure signs of an extraordinarily talented chess player. Up to the time at which he was leading the Interzonal he had played very strongly, he had scored brilliant victories, and all he needed to go on and win was simply to play less inventively and more quietly.

The conclusion of the argument, that Ljubojevic might have won the

Originally published in the *Philosophical Review,* 85 (1976), 3–20; reprinted here with the permission of the authors and the editors of the *Philosophical Review.*

tournament, is modal; it concerns what might have happened. But the argument concerns the world as it actually is, its chess players, tournaments, and games. We think that all reasoning about modality is about actual objects, facts, and processes. "Ljubojevic might have won the Petropolis Interzonal" gives just as definite and objective a report about actual individuals and situations as "Mecking won the Petropolis Interzonal" does. We think that this is true of most modal assertions: "a might ϕ," "a would ϕ," "a could ϕ," "a would ϕ if . . . ," "a might ϕ if . . . ," the dispositional "-ble" ("-ible," "-able"), and so on. When such statements are true, understood in the ordinary nonepistemic way, they are true by virtue of actual facts about actual individuals; their truth is not determined by human convention or human knowledge, nor by facts about any exotic metaphysical apparatus.

As David Lewis has written, "Modal facts are grounded in facts about actual character, not mysteriously independent."[1] And as Hilary Putnam has written, "Introducing the modal connectives . . . is not introducing new kinds of objects, but rather extending the kinds of things we can say about ordinary objects and sorts of objects."[2] We will develop the ideas expressed in these two quotations. Our project is metaphysical rather than linguistic. What interests us about modality is the difficulty of reconciling the truth of modal statements with the common-sense view of the world as composed of individuals, possessing properties and connected by relations, interacting in various causal processes. If this is the way the world is, what makes it true, for example, that *if* Geller had whispered the word "Draw!" to Portisch a few seconds before his flag fell, *then* Geller would have been among the candidates? What is the constitution of this kind of fact? Our primary aim is to answer this question. Our main claim is that one can answer it, one can give a naturalistic analysis of modality, without giving extensional, or otherwise nonmodal, paraphrases of modal idioms. While this is what the reader is likely to find most interesting about what we say, it makes it difficult to see the relations between our analyses and well-known theories in the field, which do mostly seem to be trying to describe what modality is about by finding other ways of saying what modal idioms

    1. *Counterfactuals* (Cambridge, Mass.: Harvard University Press, 1973), p. 40. But Lewis has developed a model of the metaphysics we dislike. He claims that "insofar as we understand modal reasoning at all, we understand it as disguised reasoning about possible beings," "Anselm and Actuality," *Noûs,* 4 (1970), 175.
    2. "Mathematics without Foundations," *Journal of Philosophy,* 64 (1967), 21. See also Arthur Prior, "The Notion of the Present," *Studium Generale,* 23 (1970), 245–248.

say. The difficulties are real; it is not at all clear what the relations are, and while we will refer to other people's views we will not describe ours in terms of them.

Just as it is the ordinary physical world that interests us, our concern is with the ordinary modal idioms that we have used and mentioned above rather than with the philosopher's and logician's domesticated "it is possible (necessary) that . . ." We mistrust these expressions, that modal logic is intended to capture and clarify. And we are not sure that modal logic *has* at all captured and clarified them in a philosophically interesting way. We suspect that the intuitions that guide one's reactions and allegiances to modal logic are at best a confused and indiscriminate composite deriving in large part from one's intuitions about the larger and more ordinary list. No doubt it is in principle possible to discover which of one's prejudices about "It is possible that . . . ," "It is necessary that . . . ," or "Necessarily" actually come from one's use of these idioms, which from one's knowledge of philosophy, and which from one's use of "might," "must," "has to," and others, but we would rather not try. We shall concentrate instead on the sturdier laboring class of idioms that we have listed above.[3] First, however, we make a few remarks on the notions of objectivity and realism.

Objectivity and Realism

Modality might have the appearance of objectivity if it were concerned with objects which though independent of human conception were specific to modality itself, objects about which all one knew was that they were the objects of modal discourse. After all, mathematics is objective, and is "about" its own unnatural objects.

There is a very general temptation here. One wants to argue that a category of belief or discourse is objective, and so one posits a kind of object, facts about which are to be the required objective correlate of truths of the category in question. This is the realist's gambit. He offers one a pawn, the objectivity of the subject matter; he hopes to gain something strategic, the admission of objects peculiar to that subject matter. We think that the realist's strategy is faulty: one can accept the pawn without being

---

3. Two qualifications. First, the semantics of modal logics may well do more to help us understand modality than the logics themselves. And second, the investigations of the counterfactual conditional now in vogue are considerably more to our point than the classical investigations of the box and the diamond.

forced into the trap. The pawn is not poisoned. But we do not want to seem to deny the general virtues of realism. We believe that most of our discourse is indeed true or false by virtue of being about real objects. But if one wants to understand how this objectivity is achieved, one must understand the objects that are referred to. One must have independent reasons for believing them to exist and independent characterizations of their natures.

In the philosophy of mathematics acceptance of the realist's gambit results in mathematical realism, sometimes called Platonism, the view that there is a domain of specifically mathematical objects such as numbers and sets, by reference to which mathematical statements acquire their truth values. In the philosophy of modality it results in what we shall call *modal realism*, the doctrine that there are specifically modal objects: possible worlds, counterparts of actual objects, positions in logical space, or what have you, which are the specific subject matter of modal discourse, by reference to which modal sentences are true or false. It has been most clearly and bravely defended by David Lewis in his Counterpart Theory and his indexical analysis of actuality.[4] It seems to underly a number of attempts to understand modality by use of "possible-worlds" semantics.

The general problems of objectivity and realism have been most explicitly discussed not in the philosophy of modality but in the philosophy of mathematics. By referring to it we can explain our intentions with respect to modality most easily. It is worth noting that on several attractive accounts of mathematics the problems of objectivity and realism in mathematics are a special case of the corresponding problems in modality, for according to these views mathematical assertions can be seen as covertly modal.[5]

G. Kreisel once remarked that the problem is not whether or not there are mathematical objects, but whether or not mathematical statements are objective.[6] In a similar vein, Hilary Putnam has claimed that "The issue of the 'existence' of 'mathematical entities' must be separated from the question of the objectivity of mathematical statements."[7] Objectivity is fairly

4. "Counterpart Theory and Quantified Modal Logic," *Journal of Philosophy*, 65 (1968), 113–126; Chapter 5 of this anthology; "Anselm and Actuality," *op. cit.*, esp. pp. 184–188.

5. See Putnam, *op. cit.*, and Terence Parsons, "Ontology and Mathematics," *Philosophical Review*, 80 (1971), 151–176.

6. See the Introduction to Paul Benacerraf and Hilary Putnam, eds., *Philosophy of Mathematics* (Englewood Cliffs, N.J.: Prentice-Hall 1964), p. 9, n. 5.

7. "Foundations of Set Theory," in R. Klibansky, ed., *Contemporary Philosophy—La Philosophie Contemporaire* (Florence, 1968), p. 284.

easy to formulate for mathematical statements because of the presence of the notion of proof. To say that mathematics is objective is to say that all statements expressed in the vocabulary of mathematics are either true or false, independently of whether we can *prove* them. This does not entail—not obviously, anyway—what we have called mathematical realism: the view that there is a domain of specifically mathematical objects such as numbers and sets, by reference to which mathematical statements acquire their truth values.

Mathematical realism is, however, the only way of arguing for the objectivity of mathematics that has been formulated coherently. This is one of the reasons it is at all plausible. The other main reason it may seem plausible is almost the opposite: the truth of mathematical realism is sometimes taken to consist just in that of mathematical objectivity. The claim that mathematical objects exist simply amounts—according to this view— to the claim that mathematics is objective. Michael Dummett, for instance, seems to argue this.[8] Now surely there is something right about such a view, for very likely the almost universal recognition that mathematics is objective lies behind the almost universal recognition that it is in some sense harmless to admit that there are numbers and sets.

If one could explain why mathematics is objective without appealing to mathematical realism, then mathematical realism would become practically harmless. For we could then take the existence of mathematical entities to consist just in the objectivity of mathematics (and in particular in the objectivity of certain quantified mathematical truths). And in fact much work in the foundations of mathematics can be seen as just this: as attempts to understand the objectivity of mathematics without appealing to specifically mathematical objects. This work can coexist with more Platonistic accounts of mathematics, for it attempts to understand what it is that makes the Platonistic accounts work.

Our project is to understand why modal realism works, just as much foundational work in mathematics tries to understand why mathematical realism works. To the extent that we succeed we will have shown that it is possible to be a realist with respect to modal truth without being a modal realist. The feeling among modalists tends to be that possible worlds, and the like, are harmless if properly understood; we would like to agree, and so hope to find a proper understanding.

We will operate with a rough characterization of the objectivity of modal

8. See, e.g., *Frege: Philosophy of Language* (New York: Harper & Row, 1973), pp. 464 ff., 506 ff.

assertions, which we will sharpen later. A modal assertion is objectively true if its truth does not depend on what people believe or agree. For example, a modal sentence whose subject is a referring proper name (for example, "Ljubojevic might have won the Petropolis Interzonal") is objective if its truth or falsity depends just on whether the object named is as it is said to be, independently of our beliefs or conventions.[9] To put it differently, such a sentence is objective if there is a property such that the sentence is true if and only if the object has it.

Dispositions

One function of modal operators such as "might," "must," and "can" is to operate on predicates of individuals to make other predicates of individuals. From "breaks" we can make "can break," "might break," "would break if... ," "breakable," and so on. Let us begin by discussing what seems to be the very simplest case, that of dispositional suffixes. "Dissolves" applies to things that actually do dissolve when immersed (for a minute in lukewarm water, say), "soluble" to things that would dissolve if immersed. "Dissolves" is true of things that possess a certain straightforward property, that of being immersed in water and of turning from a tangible solid to a visually inseparable component of the liquid. "Soluble" is true of things which possess a rather more recondite property, of which only physical chemists can give a very explicit characterization. The presence of this property accounts for the truth, and objectivity, of "*a* is soluble"; it is true whenever *a* has the property.

It does not follow that solubility just is this microstructural property. What to identify solubility with is a dismayingly subtle question, depending in part on how one chooses to individuate properties. The limitations of individuating them by the meanings of predicates denoting them have been pointed out by several recent writers.[10] One can individuate properties in terms of their definability in terms of the basic properties of physical theory.[11] Or one can individuate properties by their role in the workings of the world, their function in the production of phenomena. On the first of

9. Except of course modal assertions *about* beliefs or conventions. These are objective if their truth value does not depend on beliefs or conventions about beliefs or conventions.

10. See Jaegwon Kim, "On the Psycho-Physical Identity Theory," *American Philosophical Quarterly*, 3 (1966), 227–235.

11. See Putnam, "On Properties" in Nicholas Rescher, ed., *Essays in Honor of C. G. Hempel* (Dordrecht: Reidel, 1969), pp. 267–268.

these, solubility may be the microstructural property that accounts for things dissolving. On some versions of the second it will not be, for had the world been somewhat different, a different microstructural property would have been involved in dissolvings, but solubility would still be solubility.[12] We might therefore take solubility to be the property of having whatever microstructural characteristics are responsible for things dissolving, when they do.

The issue is evidently very tricky. But it does not really matter for our purposes which way it is settled. For in any case "soluble" applies to an object if it has a definite physical property—namely, that property which is responsible for things of the kind dissolving, if they are immersed.[13] As a theory or analysis of dispositions this is little more than common sense, but it is all that is needed to see why one's natural inclination to take ascriptions of dispositions as objectively true and false is right, and why nothing at all exotic is involved. In miniature, this has the essential features of the analyses we will suggest for other modal idioms. A dispositional predicate is true of an object by virtue of the physical properties it possesses; the relevant properties can rarely be described without using modal words (*"responsible* for things of that kind dissolving, *if* they are immersed"); the analysis can therefore be used not to eliminate modality but to see what in the world makes it work.

Modal idioms are not all as guileless as dispositions. Our treatment of dispositions cannot be directly extended to other modal idioms—for instance, "might have." To see why, suppose we were to try to adapt a suggestion of Nelson Goodman's[14] and construe "Ljubojevic might have won the Petropolis Interzonal" as "Ljubojevic is Petropolis Interzonal winnable." We would be unable to analyze the latter along the lines indicated in the previous paragraph. We cannot say, for instance, that Ljubojevic is Petropolis Interzonal winnable in virtue of possessing some

12. If fully spelled out this would be a complicated argument, but it is like others in the literature. See, e.g., Saul Kripke on the necessity of true identities, in "Naming and Necessity" in Donald Davidson and Gilbert Harman, eds., *Semantics of Natural Language* (Dordrecht, and Boston: Reidel, 1972). Note, however, that Kripke argues that since various identities are true they are necessary, while the argument here is that since an identity is not necessary it is not true.

13. Quine says something like this in "Natural Kinds," in W. V. O. Quine, *Ontological Relativity and Other Essays* (New York: Columbia University Press, 1969), pp. 130 ff. He seems to require, however, that, in order for a disposition to be intelligible, we know how to describe the property in question. We see no reason for this.

14. In *Fact, Fiction, and Forecast,* 2d ed. (Indianapolis: Bobbs-Merrill, 1965), pp. 53 ff.

property that is responsible for players' winning tournaments, for there is no such property. Neither can we say that Ljubojevic is Petropolis Interzonal winnable in virtue of sharing with some other tournament winner— say, Bronstein or Larsen—whatever property he owes his success to. For even if Ljubojevic were to possess this property it would not follow that he would win the tournament. Indeed it may well be that if Ljubojevic had acquired the relevant characteristics of Bronstein or Larsen it would have been *impossible* for him to have won.

So we cannot treat all modal idioms as dispositions. Still, just as it is clear that "*a* is ϕ-ible" is true or false by virtue of physical facts, it is plausible that, for example, "Ljubojevic might have won the Petropolis Interzonal" is true by virtue of physical facts. (We include psychological facts among physical facts; think of this as a terminological aberration, if need be.) For the reasons that Ljubojevic might have won are, as we said in the first paragraph of this paper, physical ones. We try to work this out in the next section.

Might

If at some time *t* during the Petropolis Interzonal "Ljubojevic might win the Interzonal" or "Ljubojevic should (be able to) win the Interzonal" or "Ljubojevic can yet win the Interzonal" or "Ljubojevic has all it takes in order to win the Interzonal" were true, then "Ljubojevic might have won the Petropolis Interzonal" is true now, by virtue of the same facts.[15] And the objectivity of the former predications may be argued for as follows.

Before the tournament the facts were symmetrical between Ljubojevic's winning and his losing. If he had won, it would have been essentially by virtue of a chain of events and facts which began with certain events and facts leading up to the twelfth round of the tournament; these would have been perfectly objective, and responsible for his victory. And although he did not win, that which was true of him up to the twelfth round of the tournament, which would have been the basis for his victory if he had won, *was* in fact true of him. It provides the actual objective reasons for the assertion that he might have won.

In short, if Ljubojevic might have won, then there was a time at which

15. Michael Dummett makes a similar observation, *op. cit.*, p. 131. Dummett says that "It may truly be said of President Nixon, . . . that he might never have been a politician, because there was a time in his life at which it would have been true to say that he might never become a politician."

"he might (should, can yet, has all it takes to) win" was true, and the facts that made this true then make it true now that he might have won. The truth at t of "a might ϕ" entails the truth at t' of "a might have ϕ'd," where t' is any time later than the time at which a's ϕ'ing does or does not occur.[16]

This is so because possibilities pass. The past is a linear array of actualized possibilities, and the future is a branching maze of things that may or may not happen.[17] Possibilities that have yet to pass are expressed by "might" idioms ("might," "can yet," "should be able to") and "might have" is made true by "might" and the passing of time. What makes "might" true? There usually is not much doubt about the general category of the relevant facts. In the Ljubojevic example they presumably consist in Ljubojevic's great chess talent, the quality of his play up to a certain point during the tournament, the quality of his opponents' play up to that point, and the history of the tournament up to that point.

There is no shortage of objective physical facts to account for the truth of "might" sentences. The difficult thing is to be sure *which* facts are responsible, which are the facts that are necessary for the relevant possibility to be. To identify these facts one has to know what in the physical workings of the world brings about events of the kind in question. More precisely, in order to know what facts are responsible for the truth at t of "a might have ϕ'd" one has to know the properties which a possessed at some earlier time t, which, if he had gone on to ϕ, would have been the major part of the reason for his ϕ'ing. Rough as this is, it seems true, and gives us a way of circumscribing and picking out the actual facts, conditions, and so on, about an object which determine what might have been true of it.[18]

It is important to realize, and important for us to admit, that to know which physical facts are relevant to the truth of "a might have ϕ'd" one

16. So "might have" is not exactly a past (perfect) tense of "might." The past truth of "might" does not entail the truth of "might have" until the time at which the event in question happens or does not. It is not true today, November 12, 1974, that Karpov might have taken the championship away from Fischer, although it was true yesterday that Karpov might take it from Fischer (next year). Tenses like "might have" are a sort of future in the past, just as the future perfect tense is a past in the future. For such a "perfect future" construction is indexed *twice* to the past: first, to the time at which the corresponding "might" statement is true and, second, to a time which is *future* with respect to the first time.

17. This is a familiar idea from the semantics of tense logics. It is also implicit in Aristotle's attitude to time; for a recent discussion of this see Dorothea Frede, *"Omne quod est quando est necesse est esse,"* Archiv für Geschichte der Philosophie, 54 (1972), 153–167.

18. In this connection see pp. 313 and 314 of Saul Kripke's "Naming and Necessity," already cited.

usually has to have knowledge about these facts that one can express only in modal terms. To know that someone was in a position to win a tournament one might have to know that various generalizations hold—for example, that imaginative players get out of tight spots more often than unimaginative players—and moreover one may have to know that this generalization is a law of nature, or at any rate of chess nature, for one may have to know that it would have held even if the player had got himself into a particular tight spot. But the generalization itself, as a fact relevant to the modal truth, describes a simple physical fact, that imaginative players get out of tight spots more often than unimaginative players.

Although it is not in general possible to say a priori what makes a "might have" statement true, there are exceptions. There are cases in which we can completely specify the required facts. "The game might have been won" is a case in point, for its truth depends just on the existence of a winning strategy (at some time or other during the game). A borderline case is provided by the following passage: "Petrosian is not a player who likes vague sacrifices, but Tal—as Black! [Tal was in fact White]—might have considered here 11.   ... KN-Q4...."[19] Here the truth of "Tal—as Black!—might have considered 11.   ... KN-Q4..." seems to depend almost exclusively on the fact that Tal is a player who likes vague sacrifices.

General "might have" statements such as "There might have been no winner of the tournament" or "All winners might have been Russian" are certainly not true by virtue of any *particular* player's characteristics at any point in the tournament. Nor do they seem to depend just on properties of the players who satisfy their predicates—for instance, the actual winners of the tournament. In fact, however, the same is true (up to a point at least) of singular "might have" statements, for what made it true (at some time t) that Ljubojevic might win was not just his state at t but also the state of his opponents and of the tournament generally. Facts not only about Ljubojevic's strength and inventiveness, but also about the constitution of his immediate environment at t and the history of the tournament up to t were such that they would have been a major part of what would have been responsible for his victory if he had won. Similarly, if there might have been no winner of the tournament, then there was a time at which the tournament itself, the players and the psychological atmosphere, was so constituted as to make it possible that there be no winner.

19. P. Keres, "Battle of Chess Styles," *Chess Life and Review,* 29 (1974), 249.

The syntactical contrast between singular "might" or "might have" statements and general ones is thus not very important. In either case the references to actual objects have to be taken as establishing a reference to an actual causal process involving those objects, which is such that it might have eventuated in the result indicated.

Instructive cases are provided by such statements as "Eric Ambler might not have existed," "L'empire des lumières II' might not have been painted," "*Tristram Shandy* might not have been written," and so on. Their truth cannot be accounted for in terms of any particular object's properties at any time during its history. But they too refer to actual causal processes—namely, those which resulted in Eric Ambler's coming into existence, in "L'empire des lumières II," 's being painted, and in *Tristram Shandy*'s being written.

To say that Eric Ambler might not have existed (or that "L'empire des lumières II" might not have been painted, or that *Tristram Shandy* might not have been written) is to say that the processes in question might not have resulted in Eric Ambler's coming into existence (in "L'empire des lumières II" 's being painted, in *Tristram Shandy*'s being written). And the analysis of this is essentially the same as that of any other "might have" statement: at some time in the past the facts about that process at that time were symmetrical between the process's resulting or not resulting in Eric Ambler's coming into existence, in "L'empire des lumières II" 's being painted, and so on. These facts could form a large part of the explanation of either. The truth or falsity of a "might" (or, *mutatis mutandis*, a "might have") sentence depends on the existence or nonexistence of certain states and causal processes. In most cases these clearly exist or do not, independently of what people believe or agree. Our analysis thus goes some way toward characterizing and establishing the objectivity of these idioms.

Counterfactuals

We consider only counterfactuals of the form "if *e* had occurred then *f* would have occurred," where *e* and *f* are descriptions of events. Counterfactuals are more complex than "might" idioms, just as "might" idioms are more complicated than dispositions. "If *e* then *f*" is not the same as "*e* cannot (may not) occur without *f*." This is evident from the quotation which introduces the paper. If Geller had whispered "Draw" to Portisch at the right moment, and Portisch had accepted the offer, Geller would have been among the candidates. But the reason for this is not that Geller could not have whispered "Draw" to Portisch and not have been among the candidates. For the counterfactual may be true even if there might have been circumstances—for example, Ljubojevic's playing better than he did (from the twelfth round on in the Petropolis Interzonal)—under which Geller might have whispered "Draw" to Portisch and not have been among the candidates. The reason that this possibility is consistent with the truth of the counterfactual is just that, as the quotation puts it, Geller came closer to actual qualification than Ljubojevic ever did: it is more possible that Geller whisper "Draw" to Portisch and subsequently be among the candidates than that Geller whisper "Draw" to Portisch and Ljubojevic have played so well (from the twelfth round on in the Petropolis Interzonal) that he rather than Geller was among the candidates. That is, the truth of this counterfactual requires that at the relevant point in time it be more possible that Geller whisper "Draw" to Portisch and subsequently be among the candidates than that he whisper "Draw" to Portisch and subsequently *not* be among the candidates.[20] This entails neither that Geller might nor that he might not have whispered "Draw" to Portisch without becoming one of the candidates.

There are, however, resemblances between "might" and the counterfactual. In each case it is essential that there be a point in time—we call it the *nodal time*—at which things have not yet been decided. For "*f* might occur" the nodal time is that at which *f* has not yet occurred or failed to occur and there are facts which would largely explain its occurrence if it did occur. For "if *e* occurred *f* would occur" the nodal time is that at which neither *e* nor *f* has occurred or failed to, and certain facts could explain the occurrence of both *e* and *f*. But beneath the similarity there is a difference. In the case of "might" we may find actual facts at the nodal time which would be largely responsible for *f*'s occurrence, were it to occur. But in the case of the counterfactual the facts that would be responsible for *f*'s occurrence—in particular those involved in *e*'s occurrence— may not in fact ever become actual. Beneath this difference there is a similarity. In both cases if *f* were to occur it would be explicable in terms of the occurrence of a physical process that begins with actual events and ends with *f*. In the "might" case what is required is just that the actual

20. This is a formulation of the basic idea of Robert Stalnaker's "A Theory of Conditionals," in *Studies in Logical Theory*, ed. by Nicholas Rescher (Oxford: Blackwell, 1968), pp. 98–112; see also David Lewis, *Counterfactuals* (Cambridge, Mass.: Harvard University Press, 1973), esp. pp. 52–56.

facts are such as to permit such a process; the counterfactual requires somewhat more.

What has to be taken into account is the fact that if the counterfactual is true, then any physical process beginning with actual facts at the nodal time and leading to e and f would be more possible, make fewer demands on the way the world actually is, than one that leads to e but not to f. We must say something like the following: the actual facts at the nodal time would have made up a larger part of any explanation of f, had e occurred and f ensued, than they would have of any explanation of f's failing to occur, had e occurred and f not ensued.[21]

In particular cases we can fill out this vague formula in accordance with our understanding of how things work. Thus Geller's offering Portisch a draw at the appropriate moment and subsequently being among the candidates is a process that could have been accounted for in terms of the situation of the play-off match at that moment, current F.I.D.E. regulations, and the fact that Geller needed only half a point in order to qualify for the candidates' tournament, while to explain Geller's offering Portisch a draw and not subsequently being among the candidates one would have had to place greater reliance on events that might have occurred but did not occur.

Therefore the crucial fact for the truth of "If e had occurred then f would have occurred," and "e and not f" involves a greater departure from actuality[22] than "e and f" does is itself a fact about actuality. It follows that counterfactuals can be said both to describe unrealized possibilities (as expressed by, for example, "x whispers 'Draw' to Portisch and subsequently x is among the candidates") *and* to be true, not by virtue of those possibilities, but by virtue of the way things actually are in the world.

Modal Properties

We have argued for the objectivity of modal idioms. The content of this claim has turned out to be that modal statements have truth values which

---

21. It would be hard to translate this back into possible-worlds terms, such as those of Stalnaker and Lewis. Our comparison of two potential explanations depends on reference to the nodal time, and it would be hard to translate this into a comparison of two possible worlds whose time axes are not very intimately correlated. For this reason what we say here seems not to run afoul of Jonathan Bennett's examples in §8 of his "Counterfactuals and Possible Worlds," *Canadian Journal of Philosophy*, 4 (1974), 381–402.

22. The notion of departure from actuality is due to David Lewis. See his "Causation," *Journal of Philosophy*, 70 (1973), 560.

depend on the presence or absence of physical properties and conditions of actual objects, independently of our knowledge or conventions. But these conditions and properties have a curious feature. What is responsible for the fact that one person might win a chess tournament can be very different from what is responsible for another person's being able to win. Ljubojevic might have won because of his sparkling imagination, while Portisch might have won because of his prudence and meticulousness. Yet if we say of each person that he might have won we are in a clear sense saying the same thing of each of them, and thus, in a somewhat less clear sense, ascribing the same property to each of them.

We propose to express this by saying that "might have won the Petropolis Interzonal" expresses a *modal property*—being a possible winner of the Petropolis Interzonal—related, in ways we discuss below, to the physical properties of the people to whom it applies.[23] Modal properties suffer in even more acute form the sensitivity to differences in criteria of property individuation that complicated our account of dispositions. *Sometimes* a disposition to exhibit ϕ is based on one microstructure as things actually are and another in a counterfactual situation. Moreover, *sometimes* two objects (two actual objects) are disposed to ϕ as a result of their possession of quite different microstructures. "Might ϕ" is sensitive in both these ways. *Usually* its applicability is accounted for by different microstructures and other physical properties in counterfactual situations, and *usually* different (actual) objects fall under "might ϕ" for quite different reasons. (Recall Ljubojevic and Portisch.)

We should therefore not describe the causal grounds for possession by, for example, Ljubojevic of the modal property *possibly having won the Petropolis Interzonal* as "that by virtue of which the Petropolis Interzonal might have been won" but as, say, "that by virtue of which *Ljubojevic* might have won the Petropolis Interzonal" (or, stylistic considerations aside, "that by virtue of which *Ljubojevic* has *possibly having won the Petropolis Interzonal*").

___

23. Using the notation of Robert Stalnaker and Richmond Thomason in "Modality and Reference," *Noûs*, 2 (1968), 359-372, we could express "*a* might have ϕ'd" by means of "$\hat{x} \Diamond \phi(x)$ (a)." The only trouble with this notation is that it does not allow us to distinguish between such properties as *possibly ϕ'ing* and such properties as *possibly having ϕ'd*. Notice, further, that Thomason and Stalnaker provide an analysis of modal properties in possible-worlds terms, whereas on our view they ought to be understood in terms of actual conditions and properties. The philosophically clearest treatment of modal predicates as having extensions, thus permitting there to be modal properties, is found in Kripke's "Naming and Necessity," already cited.

If we are right, whenever one makes a modal predication one is referring directly to a modal property and indirectly to whatever accounts for its possession. The semantical analysis of what one is doing is somewhat like that of what happens when one first introduces a nonmodal predicate. For just as, to quote Kripke, "the reference of 'yellowness' is fixed by the description 'that (manifest) property of objects which causes them, under normal circumstance, to be seen as yellow (i.e., to be sensed by certain visual impressions),'"[24] so too we can say that the reference of a modal predicate—say, "might P" (in application to a given object a)—is "fixed" by some such description as "that property (or set of properties), possession of which by a causes it to be able to P."

Notice that, strictly speaking, this is not a case of fixing of reference in exactly Kripke's sense, for one of Kripke's requirements for reference-fixing is that, if "a" fixes the reference of "b", then "a" and "b" have the *same* reference. In the case we have just described, however, this condition is not satisfied, for "might ϕ" in "a might ϕ" does not refer unambiguously. It may be taken to refer either to that set of properties possession of which by a enables it to ϕ (and here we have a genuine case of reference-fixing), or to the modal property itself by virtue of which different objects have "might P" (and here Kripke's condition for reference-fixing is not satisfied).

Are modal properties physical? It all depends on what one means by "physical." Quite often there may be a potential characterization, in terms of the basic predicates of physics, of what is predicated in a particular modal predication of a particular individual. (We say "potential" because it may be too long for anybody to bother stating it, and require too much physical knowledge for anyone to get it exactly right.) But even when this can be done one has not characterized the modal property in physical terms, for other objects may possess it on the basis of quite different physical facts. There is rarely a set of conditions in the language of physics such that *all* the objects possessing a modal property do so as a result of satisfying all the conditions.

Yet modal properties are, for all that, possessed by physical objects, as a matter of objective independent fact. They are part of the physical workings of the world, but we cannot always describe them in terms of our basic vocabulary for describing these workings.

We think that the contrast between modal and nonmodal properties is not an ontological one. That is, it consists *just* in the fact that we have to use

24. Kripke, *op. cit.*

modal words to pick out modal properties.[25] If we had chosen other terms
to do physics with, then we might be treating mass, for example, as a
dispositional property (perhaps as a disposition to accelerate in accordance
with Newton's second law when affected by a force.) It would require
something like a miracle for this not to be so; for the contrast to originate in
the world rather than in language, language would somehow have to em-
body the knowledge of which properties are really, independently, involved in the working of nature and which are merely modal or dispositional. We see no reason for believing this.

Paraphrase

At this point it would be natural to suspect that we have left out something
important. For while we have indicated in very general terms the (kinds of)
facts that make a "might" statement true (and hence account for possession of a given modal property by a given object), we have not, it would
seem, provided a general explanation of the meaning of "-able" or
"might" or "would-if." For what we have said does not provide a noncircular paraphrase of modal idioms in terms of the objective conditions,
properties, and so forth on which we put such emphasis. Our specifications
of modal properties are themselves expressed in modal terms, and a complete specification of the relevant nonmodal properties is simply impossible.

Now we think that the demand for a paraphrase of this sort is unreasonable. It is unobtainable and unnecessary. It is unobtainable on anyone's
account. If one uses the sort of account we are trying to construct one finds
that, for reasons we have already discussed, one cannot describe in nonmodal terms the properties which account for different objects' satisfying
the same modal predicate. And if one constructs a more orthodox, modal
realist account one finds that one cannot give any clear sense to the technical terms of one's theory—for example, "possible world" and "accessible
from," except by explaining them in terms of possibility and necessity.

25. Technically speaking (in the language of *Principia Mathematica*), modal properties are
second-order properties of type one. That is, they are properties of individuals whose characterization involves a reference to first-order (nonmodal) properties of individuals. (Notice that
the same may be said of, e.g., solubility, at least given our account in "Dispositions,"
above.) But it is important to remember what Russell never appreciated, that the distinction of
predicates into orders is relative to a language. See also Stalnaker and Thomason, *op. cit.*, pp.
370–371.

One says, "One world is accessible from another when what is true in the one is possible in the other." It is unnecessary because, if our analysis is correct, modal assertions have perfectly clear truth conditions which can be described without the help of a paraphrase.

The feeling that paraphrase is necessary may come from a subtle confusion. It is natural to suppose that the real facts about the world are given by the physical data about the location, motions, and so on of the objects in it. These can be described in nonmodal terms; one might therefore suppose that anything that cannot be so described is somehow ungrounded in the real facts. But we have already seen the mistake in this. Each particular modal predication—for example, each "a might ϕ"—is indeed grounded in nonmodal fact, but the grounding is tied to the particular a and ϕ. We may not be able to find a specification general enough to apply when a is different, let alone when ϕ is different. To say in one breath what properties make an operator like "might" apply one would have to do both.

The Gambit Refuted

It may not be clear that our account gives a genuine escape from modal realism. For instead of a weird universe of possible worlds it presents a weird universe of modal properties. But we think that this is wrong, for three reasons.

First, on our account modal properties are not in their nature different from any other properties. If one ignores human language and human knowledge there is no distinction between modal and nonmodal properties; our inability to know the reasons why everything happens and our inability to express in common terms the reasons why different individuals have the same property make us unable to pick out certain aspects of the world without using modal idioms. But this reflects upon us rather than on the world.

Second, the objectivity of modal predications does not on our view depend on the existence of modal properties. For each particular modal predication is true and objective by virtue of the presence of certain properties, facts, or processes. The modal properties were a luxury that we introduced in order to have something which stands to a modal predicate as a nonmodal property does to a nonmodal predicate. But they do not have any ultimate explanatory power; it is not they but the physical facts that underly the particular true predications, that are the ultimate parameters of modal, as of nonmodal, truth.

Third, a theory like ours is not simply a rewriting of the usual modal semantics in terms of explanatory relations between actual facts and processes. For we have had to take account of features of ordinary modal idioms, particularly their reference to particular moments in time, that are ignored in the usual semantics. It is a substantive question which strategy will give the best theory of the ordinary concept of modality. Realistic modal semantics has its formal elegance to commend it. Theorists like ours have a systematic untidiness which may fit that of our unformalized modal discourse. The respect that our account pays to the relation between tenses and modality (see footnotes 16 and 21), and the stress it puts on the actual temporal origin of objects and events, are evidence that this may be the case.

One can accept the realist's gambit. For one can take the pawn, one can agree that modality is objective, without being forced into the realist's trap. Our analysis is clearly not complete; there is clearly a lot more to say about the ways in which modal sentences come to be true or false. But we think that we have provided enough evidence to make it plausible that one can be a realist about modal truth, and hold it to be objective, without being a *modal* realist.[26]

26. David Lewis, Margaret Wilson, the referee for the *Philosophical Review*, and especially Michael Slote have given us valuable comments on earlier drafts. Lewis persists in believing that our views are consistent with his.

14

Actualism and Possible Worlds

ALVIN PLANTINGA
Calvin College

The idea of possible worlds has both promised and, I believe, delivered understanding and insight in a wide range of topics. Pre-eminent here, I think, is the topic of broadly logical possibility, both *de dicto* and *de re*. But there are others: the nature of propositions, properties, and sets; the function of proper names and definite descriptions; the nature of counterfactuals; time and temporal relations; causal determinism; in philosophical theology, the ontological argument, theological determinism, and the problem of evil (see [7], chapters IV–X). In one respect, however, the idea of possible worlds may seem to have contributed less to clarity than to confusion; for if we take this idea seriously, we may find ourselves committed to the dubious notion that there are or could have been things that do not exist. Let me explain.

I. The Canonical Conception of
Possible Worlds

The last quarter century has seen a series of increasingly impressive and successful attempts to provide a semantical understanding for modal logic and for interesting modal fragments of natural language (see, for example [4]; [5], p. 169; and [6]). These efforts suggest the following conception of

Originally published in *Theoria,* 42 (1976), 139–160; reprinted here with the permission of the author and the editor of *Theoria.*

possible worlds: call it 'the Canonical Conception'. Possible worlds themselves are typically 'taken as primitive', as the saying goes: but by way of informal explanation it may be said that a possible world is a *way things could have been*—a *total* way. Among these ways things could have been there is one—call it 'α'—that has the distinction of being actual; this is the way things actually are. α is the one possible world that obtains or is actual; the rest are merely possible. Associated with each possible world W, furthermore, is a set of individuals or objects: the *domain* of W, which we may call '$\psi(W)$'. The members of $\psi(W)$ are the objects that *exist in* W; and of course different objects may exist in different worlds. As Saul Kripke put it in [4], p. 65,

> Intuitively, $\psi(W)$ is the set of all individuals existing in W. Notice, of course, that $\psi(W)$ need not be the same set for different arguments W, just as, intuitively, in worlds other than the real one, some actually existing individuals may be absent, while new individuals . . . may appear.[1]

Each possible world W, then, has its domain $\psi(W)$; but there is also the union—call it U—of the domains of all the worlds. This set contains the objects that exist in α, the actual world, together with those, if any, that do not exist in α but do exist in other possible worlds.

On the Canonical Conception, furthermore, *propositions* are thought of as set-theoretical entities—sets of possible worlds, perhaps, or functions from sets of worlds to truth and falsehood. If we think of propositions as sets of worlds, then a proposition is true in a given world W if W is a member of it. *Necessary* propositions are then the propositions true in every world; possible propositions are true in at least one world; impossible propositions are not true in any. Still further, the members of U are thought of as *having properties* and *standing in relations* in possible worlds. Properties and relations, like propositions, are set-theoretic entities: functions, perhaps, from possible worlds to sets of n-tuples of members of U. If, for simplicity, we ignore relations and stick with properties, we may ignore the n-tuples and say that a property is a function from worlds to sets of members of U. A property P, then, has an *extension* at a given world W: the set

---

1. For the sake of definiteness I substantially follow the semantics developed in this piece. The essentials of the canonical conception, however, are to be found not just here but in very many recent efforts to provide a semantics for modal logic or modal portions of natural language.

of objects that is the value of P for that world W. An object has a property P in a world W if it is in the extension of P for W; and of course an object may have different properties in different worlds. In the actual world, W. V. O. Quine is a distinguished philosopher; but in some other world he lacks that property and is instead, let us say, a distinguished politician. Modal properties of objects may now be explained as much like modal properties of propositions: an object x has a property P *accidentally* or *contingently* if it has P, but does not have P in every possible world; thus the property of being a philosopher is accidental to Quine. X has P *essentially* or *necessarily,* on the other hand, if x has P in every possible world. While *being a philosopher* is accidental to Quine, *being a person,* perhaps, is essential to him; perhaps there is no possible world in which he does not have that property.

Quantification with respect to a given possible world, furthermore, is over the domain of that world; such a proposition as

(1) $(\exists x)$ x is a purple cow

is true in a given world W only if $\psi(W)$, the domain of W, contains an object that has, in W, the property of being a purple cow. To put it a bit differently, (1) is true, in a world W, only if there is a member of U that is contained in the extension of *being a purple cow* for W and is also contained in $\psi(W)$; the fact, if it is a fact, that some member of U not contained in $\psi(W)$ has the property of being a purple cow in W is irrelevant. And now we can see how such propositions as

(2) $\Diamond(\exists x)$ x is a purple cow

and

(3) $(\exists x)$ $\Diamond$ x is a purple cow

are to be understood. (2) is true if there is a possible world in which (1) is true; it is therefore true if there is a member of U that is also a member of $\psi(W)$ for some world W in which it has the property of being a purple cow. (3), on the other hand, is true if and only if $\psi(\alpha)$, the domain of α, the actual world, contains an object that in some world W has the property of being a purple cow. (2), therefore, would be true and (3) false if no member of $\psi(\alpha)$ is a purple cow in any world, but some member of U exists in a world in which it is a purple cow; (3) would be true and (2) false if some member of $\psi(\alpha)$ is a purple cow in some world, but no member of U is a purple cow in any world in which it exists.

Now here we should pause to celebrate the sheer ingenuity of this scheme. Life is short, however; let us note simply that the Canonical Conception is indeed ingenious and that it has certainly contributed to our understanding of matters modal. In one regard, however, I think it yields confusion rather than clarity; for it suggests that there are things that do not exist. How, exactly, does the question of nonexistent objects rear its ugly head? Of course the Canonical Scheme does not as such tell us that there are some objects that do not exist; for perhaps $\psi(\alpha)$, the domain of the actual world coincides with U. That is, the Canonical Conception does not rule out the idea that among the possible worlds there are some in which exists everything that exists in any world; and for all the scheme tells us, α may be just such a world. There is, however, a very plausible proposition whose conjunction with the Canonical Conception entails that $\psi(\alpha) \neq U$. It is certainly plausible to suppose that there could have been an object distinct from each object that does in fact exist; i.e.,

> (4) Possibly, there is an object distinct from each object that exists in α.

If (4) is true, then (on the Canonical Scheme) there is a possible world W in which there exists an object distinct from each of the things that exists in α. $\psi(W)$, therefore, contains an object that is not a member of $\psi(\alpha)$; hence the same can be said for U. Accordingly, U contains an object that does not exist in α; this object, then, does not exist in the actual world and hence does not exist. We are committed to the view that there are some things that don't exist, therefore, if we accept the Canonical Conception and consider that there could have been a thing distinct from each thing that does in fact exist.

And even if we reject (4), we shall still be committed, on the canonical scheme, to the idea that there *could have been* some nonexistent objects. For surely there are possible worlds in which you and I do not exist. These worlds are impoverished, no doubt, but not on that account impossible. There is, therefore, a possible world W in which you and I do not exist; but then $\psi(W) \neq U$. So if W had been actual, U, the set of possible objects, would have had some members that do not exist; there would have been some nonexistent objects. You and I, in fact, would have been just such objects. The canonical conception of possible worlds, therefore, is committed to the idea that there are or could have been nonexistent objects.

II. The Actualist Conception of Possible Worlds

I said that the canonical conception of possible worlds produces confusion with respect to the notion of nonexistent objects. I said this because I believe there neither are nor could have been things that do not exist; the very idea of a nonexistent object is a confusion, or at best a notion, like that of a square circle, whose exemplification is impossible. In the present context, however, this remark may beg some interesting questions. Let us say instead that the canonical conception of possible worlds exacts a substantial ontological toll. If the insight and understanding it undeniably provides can be achieved only at this price, then we have a reason for swallowing hard, and paying it—or perhaps a reason for rejecting the whole idea of possible worlds. What I shall argue, however, is that we can have the insight without paying the price. (Perhaps you will think that this procedure has, in the famous phrase, all the advantages of theft over honest toil; if so, I hope you are mistaken.) Suppose we follow Robert Adams ([1], p. 211) in using the name 'Actualism' to designate the view that there neither are nor could be any nonexistent objects. Possible worlds have sometimes been stigmatized as "illegitimate totalities of undefined objects"; from an actualist point of view this stigmatisation has real point. But suppose we try to remove the stigmata; our project is to remain actualists while appropriating what the possible worlds scheme has to offer. I shall try to develop an actualist conception of possible worlds under the following five headings:

(1) worlds and books;
(2) properties;
(3) essences and the α-transform;
(4) domains and propositions;
and
(5) essences and truth conditions.

1. Worlds and Books.   We begin with the notion of *states of affairs*. It is obvious, I think, that there are such things as states of affairs: for example, *Quine's being a distinguished philosopher*. Other examples are *Quine's being a distinguished politician*, *9's being a prime number*, and the state of affairs consisting in all men's being mortal. Some states of affairs— *Quine's being a philosopher* and *7 + 5's being 12* for example—obtain or are actual. *Quine's being a politician*, however, is a state of affairs that is

not actual and does not obtain. Of course it isn't my claim that this state of affairs *does not exist,* or that there simply is no such state of affairs; indeed there is such a state of affairs and it exists just as serenely as your most solidly actual state of affairs. But it does not obtain; it isn't actual. It *could have been* actual, however, and had things been appropriately different, it *would* have been actual; it is a *possible* state of affairs. *9's being prime,* on the other hand, is an impossible state of affairs that neither does nor could have obtained.

Now a possible world is a possible state of affairs. But not just any possible state of affairs is a possible world; to achieve this distinction, a state of affairs must be *complete* or *maximal.* We may explain this as follows. Let us say that a state of affairs S *includes* a state of affairs S* if it is not possible that S obtain and S* fail to obtain; and let us say that S *precludes* S* if it is not possible that both obtain. A maximal state of affairs, then, is one that for every state of affairs S, either includes or precludes S. And a possible world is a state of affairs that is both possible and maximal. As on the Canonical Conception, just one of these possible worlds—α—has the distinction of being such that every state of affairs it includes is actual; so α is the actual world. Each of the others *could have been* actual but in fact is not. A possible world, therefore, is a state of affairs, and is hence an abstract object. So α, the actual world, is an abstract object. It has no center of mass; it is neither a concrete object nor a mereological sum of concrete objects; indeed α, like *Ford's being ingenious,* has no spatial parts at all. Note also that we begin with the notions of possibility and actuality for states of affairs. Given this explanation of possible worlds, we couldn't sensibly go on to explain possibility as inclusion in some possible world, or actuality as inclusion in the actual world; the explanation must go the other way around.

It is also obvious, I believe, that there are such things as *propositions*— the things that are true or false, believed, asserted, denied, entertained, and the like. That there are such things is, I believe, undeniable; but questions may arise as to their nature. We might ask, for example, whether propositions are sentences, or utterances of sentences, or equivalence classes of sentences, or things of quite another sort. We might also ask whether they are *states of affairs:* are there really *two* sorts of things, propositions and states of affairs, or only one? I am inclined to the former view on the ground that propositions have a property—truth or falsehood—not had by states of affairs. But in any event there are propositions and there are states of affairs; and what I say will be true, I hope, even if propositions just are states of affairs.

We may concur with the Canonical Conception in holding that propositions are true or false *in* possible worlds. A proposition p is true in a state of affairs S if it is not possible that S be actual and p be false; thus

(5) Quine is a philosopher

is true in the state of affairs *Quine's being a distinguished philosopher*. A proposition p is true in a world W, then, if it is impossible that W obtain and p be false; and the propositions true-in-α, evidently, are just the true propositions. Here, of course, it is *truth* that is the basic notion. Truth is not to be explained in terms of truth-in-the-actual-world or truth-in-α; the explanation goes the other way around. Truth-in-α, for example, is to be defined in terms of truth plus modal notions. The set of propositions true in a given world W is the *book* on W. Books, like worlds, have a maximality property: for any proposition p and book B, either B contains p or B contains $\bar{p}$, the denial of p. The book on α, the actual world, is the set of true propositions. It is clear that some propositions are true in exactly one world;

(6) α is actual,

for example, is true in α and α alone. If we wish, therefore, we can take a book to be, not a set of propositions, but a proposition true in just one world.

2. Properties.   On the canonical conception, objects have properties in worlds. As actualists we may endorse this sentiment: an object x has a property P in a world W if and only if x is such that W includes its having P. We *are* obliged, however, to reject the Canonical Conception of properties. On that conception, a property is a set-theoretical entity of some sort; perhaps a function from worlds to sets of individuals. This conception suffers from two deficiencies. In the first place, it entails that there are no distinct but necessarily coextensive properties—i.e., no distinct properties P and P^* such that there is no world W in which some object has P but not P^*. But surely there are. The property of being the square of 3 is necessarily coextensive with the property of being $\int_0^3 x^2 dx$; but surely these are not the very same properties. If the ontological argument is correct, the property of knowing that God does not exist is necessarily coextensive with that

of being a square circle; but surely these are not the *same* property, even if that argument is correct.

The second deficiency is more important from the actualist point of view. Clearly enough the property of being a philosopher, for example, would have existed even if one of the things that *is* a philosopher—Quine, let's say—had not. But now consider the Canonical Conception: on this view, *being a philosopher* is a function from possible worlds to sets of individuals; it is a set of ordered pairs whose first members are worlds and whose second members are sets of individuals. And this is in conflict with the truth just mentioned. For if Quine had not existed, neither would any set that contains him. Quine's singleton, for example, could not have existed if Quine had not. For from the actualist point of view, if Quine had not existed, there would have been no such thing as Quine at all, in which case there would have been nothing for Quine's singleton to contain; so if Quine had not existed, Quine's singleton, had it existed, would have been empty. But surely the set whose only member is Quine could not have existed but been empty; in those worlds where Quine does not exist, neither does his singleton. And of course the same holds for sets that contain Quine together with other objects. The set S of philosophers, for example—the set whose members are all the philosophers there are—would not have existed if Quine had not. Of course, if Quine had not existed, there would have been a set containing all the philosophers and nothing else; but S, the set that does in *fact* contain just the philosophers, would not have existed.

And here we come upon a crucial difference between sets and properties. No distinct sets have the same members; and no set could have lacked any member it has or had any it lacks. But a pair of distinct properties—*being cordate* and *being renate*, for example, or *being Plato's teacher* and *being the shortest Greek philosopher*—can have the same extension; and a property such as *being snubnosed* could have been exemplified by something that does not in fact exemplify it. We might put the difference this way: all sets but not all properties have their extensions essentially. If this is so, however, the actualist must not follow the canonical scheme in taking properties to be functions from worlds to sets of individuals. If no set containing Quine exists in any world where Quine does not, the same must be said for any set whose transitive closure contains him. So properties cannot be functions from worlds to sets of individuals; for if they were, then if Quine had not existed, neither would any of his properties; which is absurd.

As actualists, then, we must reject the canonical conception of properties; a property is not a function or indeed any set whose transitive closure contains contingent objects. We must agree with the canonical conception, however, in holding that properties are the sorts of things exemplified by objects, and exemplified by objects in possible worlds. An object x has a property P in a world W if x is such that W includes x's *having P*. Quine, for example, has the property of being a distinguished philosopher; since that is so he has that property in α, the actual world. No doubt he has it in many other worlds as well. Abstract objects as well as concrete objects have properties in worlds. The number 9 has the property of numbering the planets in α; but in some other worlds 9 lacks that property, having its complement instead. The proposition

(7) Quine is a distinguished philosopher

has the property *truth* in the actual world; in some other worlds it is false. A property P is *essential* to an object x if x has P in every world in which x exists; x has P *accidentally,* on the other hand, if it has P, but does not have it essentially. Thus Quine has the property of being a philosopher accidentally; but no doubt the property of being a person is essential to him. (7) has *truth* accidentally; but

(8) All distinguished philosophers are philosophers

has truth essentially. Indeed, a necessary proposition is just a proposition that has truth essentially; we may therefore see modality *de dicto* as a special case of modality *de re*. Some properties—truth, for example—are essential to some of the things that have them, but accidental to others. Some, like *self-identity,* are essential to all objects, and indeed *necessarily* essential to all objects; that is, the proposition

(9) Everything has self-identity essentially

is necessarily true. Others are essential to those objects that have them, but are had by only some objects; *being a member,* for example, or *being a person.*

Among the properties essential to all objects is *existence.* Some philosophers have argued that existence is not a property; these arguments, however, even when they are coherent, seem to show at most that existence is a special kind of property. And indeed it is special; like self-identity, existence is essential to each object, and necessarily so. For clearly enough, every object has existence in each world in which it exists. That is not to say, however, that every object is a *necessary being*. A necessary being is one that exists in every possible world; and only some objects—numbers, properties, pure sets, propositions, states of affairs, God—have this distinction. Many philosophers have thought there couldn't be a necessary being, that in no possible world is there a being that exists in every possible world. But from the present point of view this is a whopping error; surely there are as many necessary as contingent beings.

Among the necessary beings, furthermore, are states of affairs and hence possible worlds themselves. Now an object x exists in a world W if and only if it is not possible that W be actual and x fail to exist. It follows that every possible world exists in every possible world and hence in itself; α, for example, exists in α. This notion has engendered a certain amount of resistance, but not, so far as I can see, for anything like cogent reasons. A possible world W is a state of affairs; since it is not possible that W fail to exist, it is not possible that W be actual and W fail to exist. But that is just what it means to say that W exists in W. That α exists in α is thus, so far as I can see, totally unproblematic.

3. Essences and the α-transform.   Among the properties essential to an object, there is one (or some) of particular significance; these are its *essences*, or individual natures, or, to use Scotus' word, its hæcceities. I'll use 'essence'; it's easier. Scotus did not discover essences; they were recognized by Boethius, who put the matter thus:

> For were it permitted to fabricate a name, I would call that certain quality, singular and incommunicable to any other subsistent, by its fabricated name, so that the form of what is proposed would become clearer. For let the incommunicable property of Plato be called 'Platonity'. For we can call this quality 'Platonity' by a fabricated word, in the way in which we call the quality of man 'humanity'. Therefore, this Platonity is one man's alone, and this not just anyone's, but Plato's. For 'Plato' points out a one and definite substance, and property, that cannot come together in another.[2]

So far as I know, this is the earliest explicit recognition of individual essences; accordingly we might let "Boethianism" name the view that there are such things. On the Boethian conception, an essence of Plato is a property he has essentially; it is, furthermore, "incommunicable to any other" in that there is no possible world in which there exists something

2. In *Librium de interpretatione editio secunda*, PL 64, 462d–464c. Quoted in [2], pp. 135–136.

distinct from him that has it. It is, we might say, essential to him and essentially unique to him. One such property, says Boethius, is the property of being Plato, or the property of being identical with Plato. Some people have displayed a certain reluctance to recognise such properties as this, but for reasons that are at best obscure. In any event it is trivially easy to state the conditions under which an object has Platonity; an object has it, clearly enough, if and only if that object is Plato.

But this is not the only essence of Plato. To see the others we must note that Plato has *world-indexed* properties. For any property P and world W, there is the world-indexed property P-in-W; and an object x exemplifies P-in-W if x is such that W includes x's having P. We have already encountered one world-indexed property: truth-in-α. Truth-in-α characterizes all the propositions that are in fact true. Furthermore it characterizes them in every possible world; there are worlds in which

(7) Quine is a distinguished philosopher

lacks truth, but none in which it lacks truth-in-α. (7) could have been false; but even if it *had* been, α would have included the truth of (7), so that (7) would have been true-in-α. Truth-in-α is *noncontingent*; every object has it, or its complement, essentially. But the same goes for every world-indexed property; if P is a world-indexed property, then no object has P, or its complement, accidentally.

Where P is a property, let's say that the world-indexed property P-in-α (call it 'P_x') is the α-transform of P; and if P is a predicate expressing property P, its α-transform $\mathscr{P}_\alpha$ expresses P_α. And now consider any property Q that Quine alone has: *being the author of* Word and object, for example, or *being born at P, T*, where P is the place and T the time at which he was born. Q is accidental to Quine; but its α-transform Q_α is essential to him. Indeed, Q_α is one of Quine's essences. To be an essence of Quine, we recall, a property E must be essential to him and such that there is no possible world in which there exists an object distinct from him that has E. Since Q_α is world-indexed, it satisfies the first condition. But it also satisfies the second. To see this, we must observe first that the property of being identical with Quine is essential to anything that has it: i.e.,

(10) Necessarily, anything identical with Quine has *being identical with Quine* essentially.

But then it follows that anything that has the complement of *identity-with-Quine*—that is, *diversity from Quine*—has that property essentially:

(11) Necessarily, anything diverse from Quine has diversity from Quine essentially.

We must also observe that

(12) Necessarily, an essence of an object x entails each property essential to x,

where a property P entails a property Q if it is not possible that P be exemplified by an object that lacks Q. And now suppose there is a world W in which there exists an object x that is distinct from Quine but has Q_α Then there must be an essence E that is exemplified in W and entails (11) and (12), both *being distinct from Quine and* Q_α. Since E entails Q_α, E is exemplified in α—and exemplified by some object that is distinct from Quine and has Q. But by hypothesis there is nothing in α that is distinct from Quine and has Q; accordingly, $Q\alpha$ is an essence of Quine.

For any property P unique to Quine, therefore, $P\alpha$, its α-transform, is one of his essences. So for any definite description (ιx) Fx that denotes Quine, there is a description (ιx) $F_\alpha x$ that *essentially* denotes him—singles him out by expressing one of his essences. Here we see an explanation of a phenomenon noted by Keith Donnellan [3]. A sentence containing a description, he says, can sometimes be used to express a proposition equivalent to that expressed by the result of supplanting the description by a proper name of what it denotes. Thus the sentence

(13) the author of *Word and Object* is ingenious

can be used to express a proposition equivalent to

(14) Quine is ingenious.

The proposition expressed by (13) is true in a world W where not Quine but someone else—Gerald R. Ford, let's say—writes *Word and Object* if and only if it is *Quine* who is ingenious in W; Ford's ingenuity or lack thereof in W is irrelevant. We may see this phenomenon as an implicit application of the α-transform to 'the author of *Word and Object*', what (13) thus expresses can be put more explicitly as

(15) the (author of *Word and Object*)$_\alpha$ is ingenious,

a proposition true in the very same worlds as (14).

Now what Donnellan noted is that sentences containing *descriptions* display this phenomenon. For any predicate $\mathscr{P}$, however, there is its α-transform $\mathscr{P}_\alpha$. We should therefore expect to find Donnellan's phenomenon displayed in other contexts as well—by universal sentences for example. These expectations are not disappointed. Rising to address the Alpine Club, I say

(16) every member of the Alpine Club is a splendid climber!

Here, but for an untoward bit of prolixity, I might as well have gone through the membership roll, uttering a long conjunctive sentence of the form

(17) N_1 is a splendid climber & N_2 is a splendid climber & ... & N_n is a splendid climber

where for each member of the Club there is a conjunct attaching 'is a splendid climber' to his name. If $M_1 \ldots M_n$ are the members of the Club, the proposition expressed by (16) is true, in a given world W, only if each of $M_1 \ldots M_n$ is a splendid climber in W; the fact, if it is a fact, that in W the Club contains some nonclimbers, or some unsplendid ones, is irrelevant. But then (16) can be put more explicitly as

(18) every (member of the Alpine Club)$_\alpha$ is a splendid climber.

We may state the point a bit differently. Suppose 'S' is a name of the set of members of the Alpine Club; then (16), (17), and (18) express a proposition equivalent to

(19) every member of S is a splendid climber.

If we use (16) without implicitly applying the α-transform, of course, what we assert is not equivalent to (19); for what we then assert is true in a world W only if *in* W the Alpine Club contains none but splendid climbers.[3]

4. Domains and Propositions.   But now back to our main concern. As actualists we reject the canonical conception of properties while agreeing that objects have properties in worlds and that some of their properties are essential to them; and among the properties essential to an object we have noted, in particular, its essences. But what about domains? On the Canonical Conception, each possible world has its domain: the set of objects that exist in it. Here I have two *caveats*. First, what are domains *for*? For

---

3. The α-transform can also help us fathom the behavior of proper names; in particular it can help us bridge the gap between a broadly Fregean view and the anti-Fregean claims of Donnellan, Kaplan, Kripke, and others. See [8].

quantifiers to range over, naturally enough. But now we must be careful. On the usual domain-and-variables account, quantification is understood as follows. Consider a universally quantified sentence such as

(20) All spotted dogs are friendly

or

(20) (x) (if x is a spotted dog, then x is friendly).

Here the quantifier is said to range over a set D of objects; and what (20) says is true if and only if every spotted dog in D is also friendly. But this seems fair enough; why must we be careful? Because it suggests that (20) expresses a proposition equivalent if not identical to

(21) every member of D is friendly, if a spotted dog

where D is the domain of the quantifier in (20). And this suggestion is clearly false. For consider a possible world where D and its members exist, the latter being, if spotted dogs, then friendly, but where there are other spotted dogs—dogs not in D—of a nasty and churlish disposition. What (21) expresses is true in that world; what (20) expresses, however, is flatly false therein. (20) and (21) are materially but not logically equivalent— both true or both false, but not true in the same worlds. We may say, if we wish, that in a sentence of the form '$(x)Fx$' the quantifier has a domain D; but propositions expressed by such a sentence will not in general be equivalent to the claim that every member of D has F.

And now for the second, and, in the present context, more relevant caveat. On the canonical scheme, each world W has a domain: the set of objects that exist in W. And though it is seldom stated, it is always taken for granted that a possible world W with domain $\psi(W)$ has *essentially* the property of having $\psi(W)$ as its domain. Having $\psi(\alpha)$ as domain is essential to α; had another world β been actual, other individuals might have existed, but $\psi(\alpha)$ would have been the domain of α. From an actualist point of view, however, this pair of claims, i.e.,

(22) for any world W there is a set $\psi(W)$ that contains just those objects that exist in W,

and

(23) if D is the domain of W, then W has essentially the property of having D as its domain

leads to trouble. For a set, as we have already seen, can exist only in those worlds where all of its members exist. Hence $\psi(\alpha)$ would not have existed if any of its members had not. $\psi(\alpha)$, therefore, would not have existed had Socrates, let's say, failed to exist. But if, as (23) affirms, α has essentially the property of being such that $\psi(\alpha)$ is its domain, then α can exist only if $\psi(\alpha)$ does. Hence if Socrates had not existed, the same would have held for $\psi(\alpha)$ and α itself. If we accept both (22) and (23), we are burdened with the alarming consequence that possible worlds are not necessary beings; even the most insignificant pebble on the beach has the distinction of being such that if it had failed to exist, there would have been no such thing as α (or any other world whose domain includes that pebble) at all.

This difficulty induces another with respect to the Canonical Conception of propositions as set theoretical entities—sets of possible worlds, let's say. That conception must be rejected in any event; for it entails that there are no distinct but logically equivalent propositions. But clearly this is false.

(24) All bachelors are unmarried

and

(25) $\int_0^3 x^2 dx > 7$

are equivalent. There are those, however, who believe the first without believing or even grasping the second. The first, therefore, has a property not had by the second and is, accordingly, distinct from it. But the principal difficulty with the Canonical Conception is due to the deplorable fragility of sets and domains—their deplorable liability to nonexistence in the worlds where some of their members do not exist. For consider any true proposition p; on the Canonical Conception p will be a set of worlds containing α. But now suppose some object—the Taj Mahal, let's say—had not existed; then neither would $\psi(\alpha)$, α, or p. So if the Taj Mahal had not existed, the same would have held for the truths that $7 + 5 = 12$ and that Socrates was wise; and this is absurd. On the Canonical Conception, only necessarily false propositions together with such items as

(26) there are no contingent beings

turn out to be necessary beings. This is a distinction, surely, that they do not deserve.

How, then, shall we as actualists think of the domains of possible worlds? We may, if we wish, concur with the Canonical Conception that for each world W there is indeed the set $\psi(W)$ that contains just those objects that exist in W. On the actualist view, however, domains lose much of their significance; and they also display some anomalous properties. First of all, domains, as we have seen, are typically contingent beings. If Socrates had not existed, no set that includes him would have, so that $\psi(\alpha)$ would not have existed. Possible worlds, however, are necessary beings; hence worlds do not in general have their domains essentially. If Socrates had not existed, there would have been a set distinct from $\psi(\alpha)$ that would have been the domain of α; and if *no* contingent beings had existed, the domain of α would have contained only necessary beings. Secondly, the domain of any possible world W, from the actualist perspective, is a subset of $\psi(\alpha)$. Since there are no objects distinct from those that exist in α, $\psi(W)$ cannot contain an object distinct from each that exists in α. Of course the actualist will happily concede that there *could have been* an object distinct from any that exists in α. Hence there is a possible world W in which there exists an object distinct from any that actually exists. The actualist must hold, therefore, that $\psi(W)$ is a subset of $\psi(\alpha)$—despite the fact that W includes the existence of an object that does not exist in α. How can this be managed? How can the actualist understand

(27) There could have been an object distinct from each object that actually exists

if he holds that $\psi(W)$, for any W, is a subset of $\psi(\alpha)$?

5. Essences and Truth Conditions.   Easily enough; he must appeal to essences. Socrates is a contingent being; his essence, however, is not. Properties, like propositions and possible worlds, are necessary beings. If Socrates had not existed, his essence would have been unexemplified, but not nonexistent. In worlds where Socrates exists, Socrateity is his essence; *exemplifying Socrateity* is essential to him. Socrateity, however, does not have essentially the property of being exemplified by Socrates; it is not exemplified by him in worlds where he does not exist. In those worlds, of course, it is not exemplified at all; so *being exemplified by Socrates if at all* is essential to Socrateity, while *being exemplified by Socrates* is accidental to it.

Associated with each possible world W, furthermore, is the set $\psi_E(W)$, the set of essences exemplified in W. $\psi_E(W)$ is the *essential* domain of W;

and U_E, the union of $\psi_E(W)$ for all worlds W is the set of essences. Essential domains have virtues where domains have vices. Properties exist in every world; so, therefore, do sets of them; and hence essential domains are necessary beings. Furthermore, if $\psi_E(W)$ is the essential domain of a world W, then W has essentially the property of having $\psi_E(W)$ as its essential domain. And just as properties of other sorts are sometimes un-exemplified, so there may be unexemplified essences. If Socrates had not existed, then Socrateity would have been an unexemplified essence. Very likely there are in fact some unexemplified essences; probably there is a world W whose essential domain $\psi_E(W)$ contains an essence that is not in fact exemplified. U_E, therefore, no doubt contains some unexemplified essences.

We are now prepared to deal with (27). Before we do so, however, let us see how some simpler types of propositions are to be understood from the actualist perspective. Consider first

(1) $(\exists x)$ x is a purple cow.

(1) is true if and only if some member of U_E is coexemplified with the property of being a purple cow; and (1) is true in a world W if $\psi_E(W)$ contains an essence that is coexemplified with that property in W.

(2) Possibly $(\exists x)$ x is a purple cow

is true if there is a world in which (1) is true—if, that is, there is an essence that in some world is coexemplified with *being a purple cow*. (2) is therefore noncontingent—either necessarily true or necessarily false.

(3) $(\exists x)$ possibly x is a purple cow,

on the other hand, is true if some member of U_E is coexemplified with the property of possibly being a purple cow. So (3) is true if some exemplified essence is coexemplified in some possible world with the property *being a purple cow*. More generally, (3) is true in a possible world W if some member of $\psi_E(W)$ is coexemplified in some world W^* with *being a purple cow*. (3) entails (2); but if, as seems likely, it is possible that there be purple cows but also possible that there be no things that could have been purple cows, then (2) does not entail (3).

When we turn to singular propositions, it is evident that one like

(28) Ford is ingenuous

is true in a world W if and only if an essence of Ford is coexemplified with ingenuousness in W.

But what about

(29) Ford is not ingenuous?

The sentence (29) is in fact ambiguous, expressing two quite different propositions. On the one hand it expresses a proposition predicating a lack of ingenuousness of Ford, a proposition true in just those worlds where an essence of Ford is coexemplified with lack of ingenuousness. This proposition could be put more explicitly as

(29*) Ford is disingenuous;

i.e., Ford has the complement of ingenuousness. But (29) also expresses the denial of (28):

(29**) it is not the case that Ford is ingenuous.

(28) is clearly false in worlds where Ford does not exist; (29**), therefore, is true in those worlds. Indeed, a crucial difference between (29*) and (29**) is that the former but not the latter entails that Ford exists; (29**), unlike (29*), is true in worlds where Ford does not exist.

We may see the distinction between (29*) and (29**) as a *de re–de dicto* difference. (29*) predicates a property of Ford: disingenuousness. (29**), on the other hand, predicates falsehood of (28) but nothing of Ford. (29*) is true in those worlds where an essence of Ford is coexemplified with disingenuousness. Since there neither are nor could have been nonexistent objects, there neither are nor could have been nonexistent exemplifications of disingenuousness. (29*), therefore, entails that Ford exists. (29**), however, does not. It is true where (28) is false, and true in those worlds in which Ford neither exists nor has any properties.

We may see the ambivalence of the sentence (29) as due to scope ambiguity. In (29**) the sign for negation applies to a sentence and contains the name 'Ford' within its scope. In (29*), however, the sign for negation applies, not to a sentence, but to a predicate, yielding another predicate; and 'Ford' is not within its scope. Where 'Ford' has widest scope, as in (29*), the resulting sentence expresses a proposition that predicates a property of Ford and entails his existence; where the name has less than widest scope the proposition expressed may fail to predicate a property of Ford and may be true in worlds where he does not exist. This interplay between *de re–de dicto* distinctions and scope ambiguity is to be seen elsewhere. A sentence like

(30) If Socrates is wise, someone is wise

is ambiguous in the same way as (29). It can be read as predicating a property of Socrates: the property of being such that if he is wise, then someone is. What it expresses, so read, is put more explicitly as

(30*) Socrates is such that if he is wise, then someone is wise,

a proposition true in just those worlds where Socrates exists. But (30) can also express a proposition that predicates a relation of the propositions *Socrates is wise* and *someone is wise*. Since these propositions stand in that relation in every possible world, this proposition is necessarily true. Unlike (30*), therefore, it is true in worlds where Socrates does not exist. Similarly for

(31) If anything is identical with Socrates, then something is a person.

If we give 'Socrates' widest scope in (31), then what it expresses is a contingent proposition that predicates a property of Socrates and is true only in those worlds where he exists. If we give it narrow scope, however, (31) expresses a necessary proposition—provided, of course, that *being a person* is essential to Socrates.

What about singular existential propositions?

(32) Ford exists

is true in just those worlds where an essence of Ford is coexemplified with existence—the worlds where Ford exists.

(33) Ford does not exist,

however, is ambiguous in the very same way as (29); it may express either

(33*) Ford has nonexistence (the complement of existence)

or

(33**) it is not the case that Ford exists.

(33**) is the negation of (32) and is true in just those worlds where (32) is false. (33*), however, is true in just those worlds where an essence of Ford is coexemplified with nonexistence. As actualists we insist that there neither are nor could have been things that don't exist; accordingly there is no world in which an essence is coexemplified with nonexistence; so (33*) is a necessary falsehood.

We may now return to

> (27) there could have been an object distinct from each object that ' actually exists.

On the Canonical Conception, (27) is true only if there is a member x of U such that x does not exist in fact but does exist in some possible world distinct from α; (27), therefore, is true, on that conception, if and only if there are some things that don't exist but could have. On the actualist conception, however, there are no things that don't exist. How then shall we understand (27)? Easily enough; (27) is true if and only if there is a world where

> (34) there is an object that does not exist in α

is true. But (34) is true in a world W if and only if there is an essence that is exemplified in W but not in α. (27) is true, therefore, if and only if there is at least one essence that is exemplified in some world but not exemplified in fact—if and only if, that is, there is an unexemplified essence. Hence (27) is very likely true. As actualists, therefore, we may state the matter thus:

> (35) although there could have been some things that don't *in fact* exist, there are no things that don't exist but could have.

These, then, are the essentials of the actualist conception of possible worlds. It has the virtues but not the vices of the Canonical Conception; we may thus achieve the insights provided by the idea of possible worlds without supposing that there are or could have been things that don't exist.[4]

4. In "An Actualist Semantics for Modal Logic," Thomas Jager has developed and axiomatized a semantics for quantified modal logic that presupposes neither that things have properties in worlds in which they don't exist, nor that there are or could have been objects that do not exist. In the intended applied semantics, the domain of a model is taken to be a set of essences; and a proposition expressed by a sentence of the form $(\exists x)Fx$ is true in a world if and only if some essence is coexemplified, in that world, with the property expressed by F. Copies may be obtained from Professor Thomas Jager, Department of Mathematics, Calvin College, Grand Rapids, MI 49506, U.S.A.

REFERENCES

[1] ROBERT ADAMS, "Theories of Actuality," *Noûs,* 8 (1974), 211–231; Chapter 10 of this anthology.

[2] HECTOR-NERI CASTAÑEDA, "Individuation and Non-Identity: A New Look," *American Philosophical Quarterly,* 12 (1975), 131–140.

[3] KEITH DONNELLAN, "Speaking of Nothing," *Philosophical Review,* 83 (1974), 3–31.

[4] SAUL KRIPKE, "Semantical Considerations on Modal Logic," *Acta Philosophica Fennica,* 16 (1963), 83–94.

[5] DAVID LEWIS, "General Semantics," in *Semantics of Natural Language,* ed. by Gilbert Harman and Donald Davidson (Dordrecht: Reidel, 1972), pp. 169–218.

[6] RICHARD MONTAGUE, *Formal Philosophy,* ed. by Richmond Thomason (New Haven: Yale University Press, 1974).

[7] ALVIN PLANTINGA, *The Nature of Necessity* (Oxford: Clarendon Press, 1974).

[8] ALVIN PLANTINGA, "The Boethian Compromise," *American Philosophical Quarterly,* 15 (1978), 129–138.

15

The Trouble with Possible Worlds

WILLIAM LYCAN

Ohio State University

In what sense or senses, if any, should we admit that "there are" possible but nonexistent beings or possible but nonactual worlds? Sources of motivation for some such admission are powerful and various. By positing nonexistent individuals, it seems, we may understand true negative existentials and accommodate the intentionality of certain mental entities. By positing nonactual worlds or states of affairs, we may achieve our familiar but still remarkable reduction of the alethic modalities to quantifiers,[1] formulate Tarski-style semantics for propositional attitudes and hosts of other troublesome constructions, display the otherwise mysterious connec-

---

This paper appears here for the first time.

1. The idea that when worlds are introduced as the values of variables, the apparently distinctive inferential properties of the alethic modalities fall right out of the familiar inferential properties of the quantifiers, and the concomitant identification of necessity with truth in all possible worlds, are now so commonplace that we easily forget how stunning the idea is. It is almost universally credited to Leibniz, but I know of nowhere that it appears in Leibniz's standard texts—despite casual allusions to the doctrine, and even some (specious) page references, by a number of commentators. The most suggestive passage I have been able to find is this one: "Hinc jam discimus alias esse propositiones quae pertinet ad Essentias, alias vero quae ad Existentias rerum; Essentiales nimirum sunt quae ex resolutione Terminorum possunt demonstrari; quae scilicet sunt necessariae, sive virtualiter contradictorium. Et hae sunt aeternae veritatis, nec tantum obtinebunt, dum stabit Mundus, sed etiam obtinuissent, si DEUS alia ratione Mundum creasset" (Couturat, *Opuscules,* PHIL., IV, 3, a, 1, p. 18). I am indebted to Michael Hooker and Robert Sleigh for the reference.

tion between Fregean senses and linguistic meaning,[2] illuminate the pragmatics of counterfactuals and other conditionals, and provide a rigorous format for the theoretical study of decision making.[3] Even ordinary ways of speaking encourage us to reify nonexistent possibles at every turn.

And yet many philosophers are uneasy about yielding to this encouragement; and many, despite all the foregoing, openly scorn the idea of a thing or world that has the property of being nonactual. What is striking is that for years now the dispute between the friends and the foes of mere possibilia has consisted largely of intuitive ventings, dogged repetition of slogans, mutual accusations of perverse or willful misunderstanding, bad jokes, and simple abuse. Only very recently have several philosophers tried thoughtfully and painstakingly to get to the bottom of the problem. I shall here correct some common misunderstandings of the issue, set it up in what I think is the neatest and most illuminating way, distinguish some fundamentally different approaches to the vindication of nonexistent possibles, attack several prominent recent instances of these approaches, survey further prospects, and point in the direction that seems to me most promising.

I. Meinong vs. the Forces of Decency

As I understand him, Alexius Meinong took it to be intuitively obvious or self-evident that there are nonexistent possibles and even nonexistent impossibles.[4] We refer to such things by means of names and descriptions; and they are the objects of thought, after all. Serious researchers doing science and philosophy concern themselves primarily with what is really true, of course; this is as it should be, but unfortunately it produces in them

2. See David Lewis, "General Semantics," and Robert Stalnaker, "Pragmatics," in Donald Davidson and Gilbert Harman, eds., *Semantics of Natural Language* (Dordrecht: Reidel, 1973), pp. 169–218 and 380–397, for clear and well-motivated explications of this connection.

3. Cf. Jaakko Hintikka, "The Semantics of Modal Notions and the Indeterminacy of Ontology," in Davidson and Harman, eds., *Semantics of Natural Language,* n. 6.

4. He does not declare himself on the exact felt ground of his firm belief in possibilia. I believe that the intuitive irresistibility that his Objects had for him is best explained by ascribing the appropriate *semantical* views to him. The irresistibility in turn of a naive semantics for superficial singular terms is due to there having previously been no competing semantical theories such as Russell's to weigh against the naive account. (This is not to say that he would have gone on to accept Russell's account if he had thought of it.)

a bias toward the actual and a blindness toward the other sectors of our ontology.

Russell, and Quine a few decades later, expressed distaste for this way of looking at things.[5] Russell faulted Meinong's "sense of reality" and accused him of "doing a disservice to thought." Quine called Meinong's ("Wyman's") universe "overpopulated," "unlovely," "rank," a "slum," and "a breeding ground for disorderly elements." Russell and Quine thus found mere possibilia repugnant and wondered how Meinong could stomach them.

Meinong would not have been impressed by these gestures of distaste. He would simply have repeated his observation that philosophers who find nonexistent possibles aesthetically offensive have unhealthily (if understandably) restricted their diets to the actual.

> Without doubt, metaphysics has to do with everything that exists. However, the totality of what exists, including what has existed and what will exist, is infinitely small in comparison with the totality of the Objects of knowledge. This fact easily goes unnoticed, probably because the lively interest in reality which is part of our nature tends to favour that exaggeration which finds the non-real a mere nothing—or, more precisely, which finds the non-real to be something for which science has no application at all or at least no application of any worth.[6]

Besides, Meinong would remind his critics, the ordinary person speaks quite familiarly and often of possible things that do not exist; this is as natural as breathing and as palatable as beer. Russell and Quine have mongered the mystery, not he, and the cause of their doing so is their forgetting how such talk proceeds when the nature of the actual in particular is not what is specifically at issue.

A bit more can be said, however, about why Quine and Russell find mere possibilia so uncongenial. For one thing, notice that when in "A Theory of Objects" Meinong does try to spell out a vocabulary for talking about nonexistent possibles and impossibles, his discussion takes on a theoretical and moderately technical tone. Certainly an explanatory system is being envisioned and limned, though Meinong himself (I believe) re-

5. Bertrand Russell, "Descriptions," in *Logic and Knowledge*, ed. by R. C. Marsh (London: Routledge & Kegan Paul, 1956), and W. V. O. Quine, "On What There Is," in *From a Logical Point of View* (Cambridge, Mass.: Harvard University Press, 1953).

6. Alexius Meinong, "The Theory of Objects," in *Realism and the Background of Phenomenology*, ed. by Roderick Chisholm (Glencoe, Ill.: The Free Press, 1960), p. 79.

garded his work on Objects as purely descriptive;[7] and if Meinong's ontology is an explanatory system, it is the sort of thing that must be justified on grounds of elegance and coherence as well as by its explanatory power. Moreover, as soon as Meinong does begin to talk a bit more technically, his apparatus raises questions whose answers are not obvious and which call for ad hoc ramifications on his part. For example: (1) Quine notoriously demands identity and individuation-conditions for mere possibilia. When have we one possible man and when have we two? When have we 8,003,746? (2) Meinong seems to assume that any (well-formed) superficial singular term refers either to an existent or to a nonexistent being, and he certainly believes that any nonexistent being has any property expressed by the matrix of any description used to refer to it.[8] This prompted Russell at one point[9] to ask whether *the existent round square* exists. Similarly, we might ask whether *the Object that has no Sosein* has a *Sosein,* and so on. (3) The same assumption requires that the city that is five miles north of Columbus and five miles south of Cleveland is five miles north of Columbus and five miles south of Cleveland. Does this not in turn entail that Columbus is ten miles south of Cleveland and so falsify Meinong's theory? (4) Meinong's Objects are indeterminate or *incomplete* in a well-known way: given virtually any nonexistent possible *O* there will be any number of properties *P* such that it is not a fact that *O* has *P* and not a fact that *O* lacks *P*. Now, how can there be, or even "be," a man who is tall but whose height does not fall into any specific range? (5) Meinong characteristically refers to his Objects by using *definite* descriptions, such as "the golden mountain." But on Meinong's own view there are many golden mountains, such as the one which has a beebleberry bush on top, the one which has no beebleberry bush on top, the one on which the Marines stage practice assaults, and the one on top of which Descartes wrote his *Meditations.* How can our phrase, "*the* golden mountain," then succeed in uniquely denoting a single Meinongian Object?

7. David Lewis, probably the most notorious current defender of a strong form of Meinongianism, begins his discussion of possible worlds (in *Counterfactuals* [Cambridge, Mass.: Harvard University Press, 1973], sec. 4.1) with a brief paean to the hominess and familiarity of nonactual worlds. I shall argue below that his "natural as breathing" talk, like Meinong's, thinly masks a formidable theoretical apparatus which must be evaluated on theoretical grounds.

8. Meinong relies entirely on this principle in displaying the independence of *Sosein* from *Sein*: the round square, he says, must at least be round and be square.

9. "Critical Notice of Meinong (ed.), *Untersuchungen zur Gegenstandstheorie und Psychologie,*" *Mind,* 14 (1905).

A partisan of possibilia can set about to answer questions like these easily enough. Any elaborate way of herding possible men etc. into full-fledged worlds will settle question (1) determinately (e.g., David Lewis'); Saul Kripke's or Nicholas Rescher's stipulative methods would work just as well. In answer to (2) we might impose a type theory on Meinong's ontology that would rule out such troublesome "descriptions" as ill-formed.[10] Richard Routley responds to (3) by proposing a restriction on the assumption that generates the problem.[11] (4) may be handled by locating Objects within worlds, or by explicating their nature in such a way as to make their "incompleteness" familiar (as Hector-Neri Castañeda does). (5) leaves us any number of feasible alternatives. So Meinong need not be at all impressed by the fact that Quine and Russell can raise some trick questions for him. And there is some tendency in the recent literature to believe that Quine's objection to possibilia, at least, is based entirely on these trick questions. Any friend of possibilia who thinks this and who has answers to the questions will of course conclude that Quine need have no further quarrel with nonexistents. But such a person would miss the thrust of Quine's opposition entirely, as I shall now explain. The position I shall now ascribe to Quine never appears explicitly in his writings, but it falls trivially out of well-known views of his.

II. The Theoretical Status of Nonexistents

We have conceded that questions such as (1)–(5) are readily answerable by the theorist. That is exactly the point: that a theorist is needed to answer them. Meinong's view has generated the questions without any help from Russell or Quine, and any answers to them will necessarily involve elab-oration of a theoretical apparatus. Any such apparatus, along with the proclaimed nature of the possibila it posits, will have to be justified on theoretical grounds and submit to evaluation of the sort to which any philosophical theory is subject.

One concern that we have about theories is that of parsimony. Most philosophers subscribe to Occam's principle or something like it; at least, few philosophers posit entities that they admit to be totally gratuitous for

10. In fact, Richard Routley and Valerie Routley remind us in "Rehabilitating Meinong's Theory of Objects" (*Revue Internationale de Philosophie* [1973], fasc. 2–3) that Meinong did go on to impose a type theory of this sort.

11. Richard Routley proposes a solution to this problem in an unpublished paper.

purposes of philosophical explanation. Now, consider Meinong's ontology. Quine accuses it of bloated unloveliness. But the problem here is even worse than Quine explicitly observes: If Meinong's ontology is bloated, it is bloated to the bursting point. In fact, it is bloated well *past* the bursting point; Meinong believes not only in all the things there could possibly be, but also in all the things there could not be. And the point is not just that Meinong has swallowed some indigestible entities. The problem is that it is now hard to retain any use for Occam's Razor at all. A Meinongian has *already* posited everything that could, or even could not, be; how, then, can any subsequent brandishing of the Razor be to the point? How can the Meinongian explain the continuing usefulness (some would say the indispensability) of parsimony principles in philosophy and in science?

We know how Meinong would respond: he would accuse us again of aiming our tunnel vision only at the actual. Everyone agrees that we must not posit entities *as existing* if they are not needed for purposes of explanation; Occam's Razor certainly applies to existents. But, Meinong would point out, his remaining Objects are *non*existents, and so they are unscathed by Occam's Razor or Occam's Stomach Pump or whatever.[12]

The suggestion is that we should posit possibilia, but not posit them as existing. Quine's reaction is classic:

> Wyman, by the way, is one of those philosophers who have united in ruining the good old word 'exist.' Despite his espousal of unactualized possibles, he limits the word 'existence' to actuality—thus preserving an illusion of ontological agreement between himself and us who repudiate the rest of his bloated universe. . . . Wyman, in an ill-conceived effort to appear agreeable, genially grants us the nonexistence of Pegasus, and then, contrary to what *we* meant by nonexistence of Pegasus, insists that Pegasus *is*. Existence is one thing, he says, and subsistence is another. The only way I know of coping with this obfuscation of issues is to give Wyman the word 'exist'. I'll try not to use it again; I still have 'is'. So much for lexicography; let's get back to Wyman's ontology. ("On What There Is," p. 3)

The important point here is not that Quine does not care which verbs we use to mark ontological distinctions. Meinong does not care which terms might be used to mark his ontological distinctions either; all he insists is

---

12. What is to prevent our positing any crackpot kind of abstract entity we like and immunizing ourselves against criticism by adding that the entity is nonactual? For that matter, what is to prevent our positing lavish supplies of *physical* things such as unexplored planets and doing the same?

that the distinctions are real. Quine may simply announce that he does not care about the distinctions and go on to repeat his charge of bloating. All Meinong can do in response is to repeat his answer to that charge: that we genuinely commit ourselves to, and thus need be parsimonious about, only the Objects that we claim to find in *this* world, and not those which are merely objects of thought—thought is free, after all, and talk is cheap.

Contrary to what is suggested by the quoted passage, I believe Quine's real point has nothing to do with ordinary language: It is that anyone who actually makes theoretical use of a Meinongian apparatus in an appropriately regimented theory of modal semantics *quantifies over* nonexistent possibles in his official canonical idiom. Quine notoriously does not care what we say in casual speech; but the minute a semanticist such as Kripke or Richard Montague writes the backward **E**, the semanticist has got the nonexistents in his ontology and is stuck with them. Perhaps someone may find a way of doing modal semantics *without* genuinely (objectually) quantifying over mere possibilia; such a semantics would be welcome. But until it is produced, Quine contends, the modal theorist is committed to the presence of nonexistent possibles in his official ontology.

So much the worse, Jaakko Hintikka has remarked,[13] for Quine's much-touted criterion of ontological commitment.

> We have to distinguish between what we are committed to in the sense that we believe it to exist in the actual world or in some other possible world, and what we are committed to as a part of our ways of dealing with the world conceptually, committed to as a part of our conceptual system. The former constitute our ontology, the latter our 'ideology.' What I am suggesting is that the possible worlds we have to quantify over are a part of our ideology but not of our ontology. . . . Quantification over the members of one particular world is a measure of ontology, quantification that crosses possible worlds is often a measure of ideology. [Hintikka, "Semantics for Propositional Attitudes," p. 95]

Thus, an item's simply being the value of a bound variable is not sufficient for that item's being genuinely posited or for its being a member of our ontology. So, Hintikka concludes, Quine's criterion of ontological commitment should be rejected as incorrect and replaced by a suitably restricted criterion.

I believe this contention betrays a misunderstanding of Quine's use of

13. "Semantics for Propositional Attitudes," in Hintikka, *Models for Modalities* (Dordrecht: Reidel, 1969).

the backward-**E** test as revealing a theorist's commitments. Hintikka maintains that Quine's view, or his usage, is *wrong* and needs to be revised. But, as I understand him,[14] Quine never intended his "criterion" to be in any way substantive or controversial. Insofar as he regards it as true, he takes it to be trivial: writing the backward E is the logician's way of making an existence claim and officially adding something to his ontology. That is just what a quantifier *is*, at least on its ordinary interpretation. Thus, if Hintikka wishes to continue in this vein, he will have to show Quine some other, nonstandard way of understanding the quantifiers, and that would be precisely to concede Quine's point. Let us therefore return to our consideration of possibilia and parsimony.

It might be complained that Quine's objections to possibilia are purely *aesthetic* in character; Occam's Razor itself is an aesthetic principle. But, according to Quine, this feature of his reason for rejecting Meinong's ontology is shared by virtually every reason anyone ever has for rejecting or accepting any theory of anything, particularly when the subject matter is highly abstract. Meinongian quantification must therefore be justified on the basis of its explanatory value.

Robert Stalnaker, M. J. Cresswell, and others[15] have appreciated this and argued that possible worlds and their denizens are rich in explanatory utility. In fact, it seems, we have no idea of how to go about doing modal semantics, decision theory, Montague Grammar, or any such thing without quantifying over possibilia; it is hard even to imagine what a competing approach would be like. For now, therefore (it is said), we *must* quantify over possibilia no matter what further aesthetic objections Quine has to them. And we do not violate Occam's principle in doing so, for that principle only forbids our positing entities *beyond* explanatory necessity.

Quine surely sees the force of this argument but refuses to grant the premise, for any number of fundamental reasons: (i) He believes that most of the "data" for modal and for propositional-attitude semantics are unreal or negligible (e.g., his philosophical skepticism about "necessity" is well known). (ii) He has argued tirelessly that syntax and "semantics" are indeterminate; he holds that linguistic semantics of the sort that is currently

14. Cf. Gilbert Harman, "Quine on Meaning and Existence, II," *Review of Metaphysics* (1968), 348.

15. Stalnaker, "Propositions," in *Issues in the Philosophy of Language*, ed. by A. F. McKay and D. D. Merrill (New Haven: Yale University Press, 1976); Cresswell, "The World Is Everything That Is the Case," *Australasian Journal of Philosophy*, 50 (1972), 1–13, Chapter 6 of this anthology.

in favor is a pseudoscience and a pipe dream in any case.[16] (iii) He holds
that "explanations" of the sort provided by possible-world explications of
modalities are not explanations in any genuine sense. To say that "It is
possible for there to be pink elephants" is true in virtue of there being some
possible world in which there are pink elephants is to offer a pseudo or
"dormitive virtue" explanation.[17]

Here we soon arrive at a set of basic methodological differences between
Quine and the possibilia enthusiasts, having to do with the nature of science, the nature of explanation, and so on. Perhaps it is a fundamental
impasse in this area that explains the intractability of the dispute between
the friends and the foes of possibilia. And yet I do not think it is. I shall
now argue that the real problem lies elsewhere and has little or nothing to
do with Occam's Razor; in the rest of this essay, I shall try to make some
progress toward its resolution.

III. The Real Problem

It is maintained that, no matter how alien, ugly, and awkward nonexistent
possibles may seem, they satisfy an aching theoretical need and that we
have no real choice but to posit them as we have posited any other odd kind
of abstract entities for explanatory purposes. I believe that this represents a
bad misconception of the issue.

When we posited properties, some philosophers complained that properties were queer and obscure. When we posited sets, other philosophers
complained that sets were queer and obscure; and the same for propositions, negative facts, and so on. But in each of these cases it was fairly
clear what was being said, even if it was hard to imagine how an object
could be nonspatiotemporal and yet be apprehended by a human mind or
whatever; we understood the *quantificational* part of quantifying over
abstract entities, even if we did not understand the nature of the entities
themselves.[18] And this is what distinguishes nonexistent possibles from all

16. See, e.g., "Methodological Reflections on Current Linguistic Theory," in Davidson
and Harman, eds., *Semantics of Natural Language*, pp. 442–454. I discuss the impact of
Quine's views on linguistics in "Reality and Semantic Representation," *Monist* 59 (1976),
424–440.

17. Cf. Gilbert Harman, "Quine on Meaning and Existence, I," *Review of Metaphysics* 21
(1967), 124–151, on the positing of intensional entities in semantics.

18. Of course, there are philosophers whose revulsion for intensional entities Platonistically
understood is so great that they have tried to *reconstrue* such quantification as not having its
normal meaning. Rudolf Carnap is one; Wilfrid Sellars is another.

the foregoing kinds of posited abstract entities: A first try at quantifying over "things that do not exist" yields

(A) $(\exists x)-(\exists y)(y = x)$

(cf. Meinong's "paradoxical" formulation, "The Theory of Objects," p. 83). And this formula is a *contradiction*. The crux is that, unlike the notion of a property or a proposition, the notion of a *nonexistent* thing or world is not merely queer or obscure or marginally intelligible, but is an apparent overt self-inconsistency.

Of course, no friend of possibilia intends his view to be understood in this absurd way. It is at this point that many different moves can be made. I suggest that the best way of organizing the whole issue is to see the various contemporary metaphysical theories of possibility as being partially or wholly conflicting ways of resolving the prima facie contradictoriness of (A). For this is the first job to be done; I cannot see that any further talk of theoretical utility is germane for now.

IV. Continuing Hostilities

The obvious first move in this new direction is to disambiguate (A)'s quantifier. Meinong might therefore distinguish two different operators, one continuing to indicate actual existence and the other indicating some so far mysterious *secundum quid*. The former would be given the usual model-theoretic semantics; the latter would remain to be explained.

Meinong and other apologists for possibilia point out that this "mysterious" second operator already has a perfectly intelligible and straightforward English counterpart, viz., that which occurs in "There are things that don't exist," "There is a character in *Hamlet* who is smarter than anyone in our department," etc. Undeniably such constructions occur in English, and *almost* undeniably they occur in true sentences of English at that. The Meinongian may now say that insofar as we understand the casual use of such expressions, we can understand (A)'s leftmost quantifier—as a translation of this sort of thing. And this quantifier, introduced into our logical theory and into our semantical metalanguage for English, will bear the whole weight of our possiblistic apparatus. For our original, actuality-indicating quantifier can easily be defined in terms of our Meinongian quantifier, but not vice versa. "Actual" and "existent" figure as predicates in Meinongian English, and it is simple just to take this usage over into our logical theory. Thus, "There are things that don't exist" would be translated into Meinongian, not as (A), but as

$$(\exists x)_M - \text{Actual}(x)$$

or as

$$(\exists x)_M - (\exists y:\text{Actual}(y))(y = x),$$

neither of which is formally contradictory. And our original standard quantifier can now be introduced as a defined sign:

$$(\exists x)_A \ldots x \ldots = _{df} (\exists x)_M (\ldots x \ldots \& \text{Actual}(x));$$

or

$$= _{df} (\exists x:\text{Actual}(x))_M \ldots x. \ldots$$

(A), disambiguated accordingly, would be ruled satisfiable by whatever semantics the Meinongian intends to provide.

This last unspecific referring phrase was tokened in a smug and deprecating tone. It presupposes a demand on our part that the Meinongian search for, find, and offer "a semantics for" the quantifier "$(\exists x)_M$," and we have some fairly specific constraints in mind as to what is to be counted as success in this. In particular, what I am implicitly demanding is a *model-theoretic* semantics, done entirely in terms of actual objects and their properties—for what else *is there really?* I am allowing the Meinongian his funny operator only on the condition that he explain it to me in non-Meinongian terms.[19]

To this the Meinongian may reply that he will be happy to give us a model-theoretic semantics—one whose domains include nonactual objects, true enough, but that is all right, since *there are* nonactual objects, after all. And so it seems we have arrived at another impasse.

There is no formal circularity in this last Meinongian move. The Meinongian is explaining in the meta-metalanguage (English) how the expressions of his semantical metalanguage are to be understood, and so is not simply defining a linguistic item in terms of itself. But, clearly, anyone who *really needs* a semantics for "$(\exists x)_M$" (that is, anyone who needs a

---

19. In "On the Frame of Reference" (in Davidson and Harman, eds., *Semantics of Natural Language,* pp. 219–252), John Wallace seems to be proposing that we *can do no other* than to make such a demand vis-à-vis any canonical idiom if we are to understand that idiom.

semantical explanation in order to understand $``(\exists x)_M$'' *at all*) is not going to be relieved of his distress by an appeal to (or rather, by unexplained use of) a term of the meta-metalanguage of which it was introduced as a translation. The Meinongian evidently wants to take his "There is" *and* its canonical counterpart as *primitives* of their respective languages.

The difficulty that lies between Meinongians and philosophers who sport a "robust sense of reality" can thus be understood as being an intractable difference in what they are willing to take as primitives. Quine takes just his standard quantifier as primitive (and likewise talk of "existence," "actuality," etc. in English), and would seek some actualistic regimentation of Meinongian constructions in English. The point of such a regimentation would be to enable us to understand the Meinongian constructions, in terms of other constructions that we understand antecedently.[20] By contrast, the Meinongian takes his "There is" and $(\exists x)_M$'' as primitive and explains the actualistic usage in terms of them. These two competing choices of primitives may engender a pair of mutually incomprehensible conceptual schemes.

It should be noticed that the impasse is slightly lopsided: Though each of the participants has so far run up just one unexplained primitive, the Meinongian is in fact stuck with a second, viz., the predicate "Actual." I see no way of explicating "Actual" in terms of $``(\exists x)_M$'' plus notions accepted by both sides (that is, not without the use of further new primitives).[21] It is true that, so far as has been shown, attempts to explicate the Meinongian "There is" in terms of the actualistic notions already in play in reality-oriented semantical metalanguages may just fail and that we *may* therefore be forced to introduce a new primitive into the metalanguage

20. I am here glossing over Quine's insistence that "regimentation" (the replacement of an awkward or troublesome locution in a natural language by a formal construction of some chosen canonical idiom for technical purposes) does not do anything that might properly be regarded as displaying or even illuminating the *meaning* of the original locution. This denial falls trivially out of Quine's indeterminacy doctrine. So he would balk at my talk of offering an actualistic "semantics for" the Meinongian quantifier in the going sense of the term (cf. note 16 above). For purposes of this paper I shall waive this issue and continue to take semantical theories to be genuine theories *about* their target locutions. I discuss Quine's indeterminacy doctrine in Chapter 9 of a book I am preparing on methodology in linguistics.

21. In unpublished address delivered at the 1978 Australasian Association of Philosophy Conference, Richard Routley and Valerie Routley criticized a number of analyses that might be suggested. They also worked toward a positive proposal of their own, though their idea is not yet fully enough developed to be evaluated.

amounting to a Meinongian quantifier. But that is what remains to be seen. The recent literature contains the seeds of a surprisingly various array of theories of possibility, which I shall now begin to distinguish.

V. Approaches to Possibility

Again, I take the first task of any philosophical or semantical theory of possibility to be to resolve the prima facie contradictoriness of Meinongian formulations such as that translated by (A). I shall distinguish four basic approaches. They are not exclusive; some current views fall into more than one of the four categories. They may not turn out to be exhaustive either, though it is hard to imagine a further alternative.

1. The *Relentlessly Meinongian* approach. This is simply to leave our impasse as it is, embrace the Meinongian's two primitives, and dismiss Quinean-Russellian hostility as perverse. A Relentlessly Meinongian theory must be elaborated and ramified in something like the ways I have suggested in section I; such elaborations in fact have been carried out in some detail.[22]

2. The *Paraphrastic* approach. Some philosophers have believed that apparent reference to and "quantification over" nonexistent possibles could be eliminated by contextual definition, i.e., paraphrased away from whole sentences in which they occur. Possible individuals and possible worlds would then be treated as *façons de parler*.

3. The *Quantifier-Reinterpreting* approach. A practitioner of this method attempts to meet our Quinean challenge directly and provide a nonstandard semantics for the Meinongian quantifier which preserves its inferential properties but requires no nonactual entities.

4. The *Actualistic* approach. An actualist leaves his quantifiers standardly interpreted, but construes "possible worlds" etc. as being actual objects of some kind. The actualist ploy is to find some actual entities which are structurally analogous or isomorphic to an adequate system of possible objects and worlds, and which therefore can *do duty for* or *serve as* possibilia; he may then let his apparently Meinongian quantifiers range over these objects and define the Meinongian's "Actual" in terms of some property that some of them but not all of them have. Actualist positions

---

22. Lewis, *Counterfactuals*, sec. 4.1, and elsewhere; Terence Parsons, "A Prolegomenon to a Meinongian Semantics," *Journal of Philosophy*, 71 (1974), 561–581; Routley and Routley, "Rehabilitating Meinong's Theory of Objects," and elsewhere.

differ, naturally, according to what objects they take as world-surrogates or "ersatz" worlds.

In the next two sections I shall return to Relentless Meinongianism and consider the well-developed theory of David Lewis as a leading example of an articulated view of this type. I shall offer some reasons why I think we should avoid following Lewis' lead in the direction of extreme realism concerning Meinong's Objects. I shall then turn to the Paraphrastic and the Quantifier-Reinterpreting approaches and sketch my reasons for thinking that neither method offers a promising start toward the explication of possibilistic talk. The remaining sections of this paper will be devoted to exploring some versions of actualism.

VI. Lewis' "Extreme" Realism

Lewis' brand of Meinongianism is known for its distinctively extreme or radical air. In particular, he holds each of the following theses:

(i) There are nonactual possibles and possible worlds, and "there are" here needs no scare quotes; nonactual possibles and worlds exist, in exactly the same sense as that in which our world and its denizens exist.

(ii) Nonactual objects and worlds are of just the same respective *kinds* as are actual objects and the actual world. Nonactual tables are physical objects with physical uses; nonactual humans are made of flesh and blood, just as you and I are.

(iii) Nonactual objects and worlds are not *reducible* to items of less controversial sorts; worlds distinct from ours are not sets of sentences, or mental constructs of any sort, but blooming, buzzing *worlds*.

(iv) Quantifiers range over not all the actual individuals that there are but all the nonactual ones that there are as well, unless their ranges are explicitly or tacitly restricted in context.

(v) All individuals, actual or merely possible, are worldbound; there is no genuine identity across worlds. You and I are not world-lines, but merely have *counterparts* in other worlds who resemble us for certain purposes but are distinct individuals in their own right.

(vi) Expressions which distinguish actual individuals from among all the possible individuals, such as "real" and "actual," are really relational expressions holding between individuals and worlds; an

individual i is actual only "at" or with respect to some world w.
When we, in this (our) world, call some object "real" or "actual,"
these terms are abbreviations for the indexical "real (actual) at *our*
world"; every possible individual is real "at" the world it inhabits.

As Robert Stalnaker points out,[23] it is crucial to see that most of the
foregoing claims are independent of one another and that the discriminating
theorist might well accept some of them but disagree with Lewis over
others. (v) and (vi) are perhaps the most obviously expendable; Stalnaker
himself rejects (ii), while—interestingly—maintaining (iii).

On first hearing, in conversation anyway, philosophers have tended to
respond with delighted horror and loud forebodings of incoherence. Not
even Meinong dared to suggest that nonactual individuals *exist* in just the
same way as you and I do, or that somewhere out in logical space there are
flesh-and-blood counterparts of me who are leading admirable lives of their
own, sharing all of my virtues and none of my faults. In short, Lewis' view
seems just crazy (and unnecessarily so from the theoretician's point of
view).

I believe this response is based on a misunderstanding (one which Lewis
has rather charmingly avoided forestalling). The misunderstanding is a
very natural one, for we have no easy way of saying just what the core
claims (i) and (ii) come to. How should we express them in order to bring
out the said *extremeness* or craziness of Lewis' "extreme" realism?
"There *really are* possible worlds distinct from ours"? No. Lewis' other
possible worlds exist but do not *really* exist. "Other worlds have *just the
same ontological status* as ours"? No; our world is actual, while the others
are not (although ontological status is an indexical matter for Lewis, our
concern with individuals that inhabit the same world as *we* do is entirely
natural and legitimate).

I suggest that Lewis' view in fact is just Meinong's view, smoothly
elaborated in response to clever questions such as those raised in section I
above. To see this, notice first that Lewis' (ii) falls right out of Meinong's
doctrine of *Sosein*: just as (Meinong insists) the round square is both round
and square, the golden mountain is a *mountain*, and not another thing.
(Unlike Meinong's golden mountain, however, Lewis' individuals are not
"incomplete" in the sense of section I; for Lewis there are (indenumerably)
many golden mountains, each with its distinguishing maximally consistent
set of properties.)

23. "Possible Worlds," *Noûs*, 10 (1976), 65–75; Chapter 12 of this anthology.

Second, notice that what shocks us the most about Lewis' formulation of Meinongian realism is precisely his use of the *word* "exist" in (i). Meinong (or his translators) had shied away from this, evidently fearing to create the same horrified reaction to which Lewis is suavely impervious. But is not the difference merely terminological? Meinong distinguishes between "existing" and merely "subsisting," Lewis between "being actual" and merely "existing." But in this respect their theories are notational variants of each other; Lewis has just abjured Meinong's euphemism, co-opting "exists" and using it as his Meinongian quantifier. On this understanding, Meinong would accept Lewis' (i) as well as (ii).

(iii) seems to follow from (ii), and Meinong certainly would have accepted (iv). This leaves only (v) and (vi) as possible points of disagreement. I have already observed that (v) and (vi) are the least central or crucial components of Lewis' theory, in that they are less closely connected to the other four claims than those four claims are connected to each other. We cannot be sure exactly what attitude Meinong would have taken to (v) and (vi), since they concern worlds, and (so far as I am aware) Meinong did not think of grouping his Objects into worlds. The upshot is that, so far as we are able to say with confidence, Lewis' view is exactly as "extreme" as Meinong's own—no more so. Some readers will find Lewis' theory more palatable on this account; others will lose some of their naive tolerance of Meinong's view and come to regard *it* as radical or crazy.

Tom Richards and Susan Haack[24] have voiced the suspicion that Lewis actually is practicing a slightly more pernicious form of word magic. Haack writes,

> Lewis thinks that [a] critic must either beg the question by equating 'exists' and 'actually exists,' or else equivocate on these two senses. The critic might justifiably wonder what makes Lewis confident that 'exists' and 'actually exists' *have* distinct senses. The trouble, to put it bluntly, is that by 'exists' Lewis means 'is possible,' and by 'actually exists' he means 'exists', so that when he says that ('other') possible worlds exist, though they don't actually exist, this amounts only to saying that they are possible, though they don't exist. [pp. 419-420]

(Haack goes on to bolster this suggestion a bit.) We would be shortsighted to understand her as making a claim about the uses of English words in

24. Richards, "The Worlds of David Lewis," *Australasian Journal of Philosophy,* 53 (1975), 105-118. Haack, "Lewis' Ontological Slum," *Review of Metaphysics,* 33 (1977), 415-429.

ordinary speech (cf. my similar points about Quine and about Meinong in section II above). Haack could have made the same point against Lewis even if he had stuck with "subsist" and "exist" or used "bumble" and "stumble." And, as I understand it, that point is this: Lewis, she suspects, has merely taken ordinary talk of what is possible and worked a systematic but theoretically negligible orthographic permutation on it, just as if we were to translate it into Pig Latin. If this is so, then Lewis' view is even less "extreme," crazy, etc. than we have supposed. But it is also totally unilluminating; surely I would fail to illuminate or explain why physical bodies gravitationally attract each other by conjecturing that ysicalphay odiesbay avitationallygray attractay eachay otheray.

How might Lewis avoid this charge? He must show that his Meinongian quantification over "other" worlds is not just a trivial transcriptional exercise of this sort. By showing this he would not necessarily undercut the claim of his Meinongian explications to display the real truth-conditions of ordinary possibilistic talk (such is the lesson of the "Paradox of Analysis"). But if Lewis' Meinongian quantification is not just a respelling of ordinary alethic locutions, then we are correct in regarding him as bringing in novel theoretical appartus (and in taking its obscurity at face value); and so his claim to immediate naturalness and intuitiveness (like Meinong's) *is* undercut.

At the end of section IV above, we left the Relentless Meinongian and his reality-oriented opponent at an impasse regarding what they were respectively willing to take as primitives in philosophical discourse. Let us start again at this impasse and see what more might be said about it, now that we have distinguished Relentless Meinongianism from any softer or more tractable doctrine and hypothetically deprived ourselves of any tacit reparsings or reductive explications of quantification over nonexistent possibles.

I have to take my place among those who find *Relentlessly* (i.e., *genuinely* or *primitively*) Meinongian quantification simply unintelligible. However: in saying this, I am not using the term "unintelligible" in its sneering post-Wittgensteinian sense. So far as I am able to introspect, I am not expressing any tendentious philosophical *qualm*. (For this reason, my use of the term may be irrevocably misleading.) I mean that I really cannot understand Relentlessly Meinongian quantification at all; to me it is *literally* gibberish or mere noise.

Further, I hypothesize that most people who do profess to understand it are tacitly assuming that there *is* some paraphrastic program, some reinterpretation of the "Meinongian" quantifier, or possibly some actualist domain that will make sense of the quantifier. My evidence for this hypothesis is that professed Meinongians of my acquaintance, upon being pressed and confronted with suitably uncomprehending grimaces, typically are surprised that anyone would react in this way, infer that we must be talking past each other, and fall back on crude attempts at paraphrase or reinterpretation.

Yet I would quail at attributing any tacit assumption of this kind to Lewis himself. And, methodologically, I am not sure what argumentative force my unintelligibility claim has even if it is true for most people. For in some years' time a Relentlessly Meinongian scheme such as Lewis', or Richard Routley's and Valerie Routley's,[25] fully elaborated, may possibly have become quite fundamental to our semantical thinking, in such a way that younger philosophers will be taught it and work confidently within it without experiencing any difficulty of the sort I have forthrightly confessed to above. It may be that even I myself, if I follow developments and keep pace with the new generation, may come to share their linguistic facility and cease to have my now obdurate feeling of incomprehension. Should this prediction come true, how should we describe what it is that will have happened to me, or to the Meinongian quantifier, in the meantime?

It might be said (following Frege on the meaning of his term "sense") that during the interim the Meinongian quantifier will have taken on an indispensable role in the mechanics of a well-entrenched theory and that I will have come to grasp this role; this is why I will understand the quantifier then even though I genuinely do not understand it now. But this explanation will not do. For I already do grasp the explanatory role of the Meinongian quantifier, in the sense Frege intended: I already see and appreciate the functioning of the quantifier and its variables in semantical theories of the sort we all would like to bring to bear on the nasty philosophical problems they are designed to solve. So it is not understanding of the Meinongian quantifier's explanatory role that I lack now but will gradually acquire. Nor may we suppose that what I lack is knowledge of the real referents of the Meinongian variables, on the model of "gene" talk prior to the identification of "genes" as parts of DNA molecules: unreduced "gene" talk was understood (I presume) as placeholder talk, in that

25. Richard Routley has kindly let me see a large body of unpublished material in which he and Valerie Routley refute a number of standard objections to Meinongianism outright and clean up Meinong's view considerably in response to more trenchant objections. Their work is unsettlingly convincing.

"gene" did duty for "whatever physical things play such-and-such a causal role in the mechanics of heredity"; but to treat "possible-world" talk similarly would be to envision (in fact, to demand) a reduction of "worlds" to actual objects, and thus to forswear Relentless Meinongianism and opt for some unspecified form of actualism instead. So if it is true that the Meinongian quantifier somehow will subtly acquire meaning for me within the foreseeable future, I cannot easily describe this hypothetical process or find a model or precedent for it.

In any case, suppose that the Relentless Meinongian continues to take the strong line suggested above, insisting that his quantifier *is* primitive, and that he does understand it even if I do not, and that no truth serum or searching psychoanalysis would reveal any hidden explicative program that mediates this understanding. I believe that even if we go along with this and try to regard Lewis' view as a competing theory which I just do not understand very well (rather than as gibberish), we will find some theoretical drawbacks that I believe suffice to motivate our seeking some other approach to possibility.[26]

VII. Some Disadvantages of Lewis' Realism

Drawback 1: I have already pointed that the Relentless Meinongian is stuck with two primitives, while a practitioner of any of our other three approaches to modality deploys but one. This point is by no means decisive, but is not unimportant either. (It is closely connected to a more substantive theoretical problem that I shall bring out below.)

Drawback 2: The Relentless Meinongian leaves our impasse as it is, embraces the two primitives, and dismisses my Quinean hostility and incomprehension as slow-witted or perverse. This position may be tenable, but it does not illuminate what I have taken to be the fundamental problem. It resolves our contradiction (A), in effect, by announcing in a dramatic

26. Lewis offers a positive argument for his view, besides the theoretical advantages he claims for it. I shall omit discussion of the argument here, since I have criticized it elsewhere (Steven Boër and William Lycan, review of *Counterfactuals* in *Foundations of Language*, 13 [1975], 145-151) and since several other commentators and reviewers have criticized it as well, some more effectively than I. (See Donald Nute, "David Lewis and the Analysis of Counterfactuals," *Noûs*, 10 (1976), 353-362; Richards, "The Worlds of David Lewis"; Haack, "Lewis' Ontological Slum"; and Stalnaker, "Possible Worlds," Chapter 12 of this anthology.)

tone that the contradiction has been resolved and refusing further comment. (Compare the Cartesian Dualist on the subject of mind-body interaction.) Perhaps this is as it should be; perhaps Lewis' way of looking at things is on the whole a better way than any of the three more conciliatory ways, and perhaps I *am* being stupid and perverse in failing to see this and to understand the Meinongian quantifier. But it would be nice if this were not so and if there were some metaphysical theory of possibility that brought feelings of improved understanding to all concerned and did not instigate a wrenching cultural conflict.

Drawback 3: A Meinongian realism concerning worlds implies that other worlds contain individuals who are very different from me but who are in fact either identical with me or (as Lewis would have it) counterparts of me in their respective home worlds. And, since the Relentless Meinongian does not regard this consequence as metaphorical or as a *façon de parler,* he must suppose that there is some objective fact about these individuals in virtue of which they do bear this curiously intimate relation to me, that we can know there to be such a fact, and perhaps that we can come to know the fact itself by hypothetical inspection of the individuals and their properties, using an imaginary "telescope." It is this commitment on the realist's part that occasions all the traditional problems of transworld identity and their Lewisian counterparts concerning counterparts.[27] These problems, Kripke and Rescher have argued persuasively,[28] are pseudoproblems generated by the "telescope" view itself and not by anything in the actual nature of modality. It is possible for me to have been a purple chimpanzee with yellow spots; therefore, we are told, there is a nonactual world some inhabitant of which is a purple chimpanzee with yellow spots and is identical with (or is a counterpart of) me. Suppose this world contains many other chimpanzees of just the same type. Which one is, or is a counterpart of, me? The Relentless Meinongian must assume that there is a determinate, correct answer to this question rooted somewhere in transmundane reality. But, Kripke and Rescher point out, to accept this assumption is far less plausible than to say that worlds are something *we stipulate* in imagining ways in which *we* might have turned out differently

27. See Roderick M. Chisholm, "Identity through Possible Worlds: Some Questions," *Noûs,* 1 (1967), Chapter 3 of this anthology; and Fred Feldman, "Counterparts," *Journal of Philosophy,* 68 (1971), 406–409.

28. Saul Kripke, "Identity and Necessity," in *Identity and Individuation,* ed. by Milton Munitz (New York: New York University Press, 1971), pp. 135–164; Nicholas Rescher, *A Theory of Possibility* (Pittsburgh: University of Pittsburgh Press, 1975), chaps. 3 and 4.

and that one of the purple chimpanzees in the world I am imagining, to the exclusion of the other chimpanzees, is me or is my counterpart simply because I, who am doing the imagining, stipulate that it is and that the other chimpanzees are only its (my) casual acquaintances. So we should reject the "telescope" view, and therefore also the Meinongian realism that implies it.

Rescher and Richards have raised a closely related but more general epistemological point: How is it possible for us to know anything about other worlds, given that they are all "out there" independently of our mental activity and that they are causally and spatiotemporally inaccessible to us?

> [Lewis'] truth-conditions are such that, for any given [modal] statement, it is impossible in general to determine whether they are met and hence whether the statement is true. There is, however, a certain measure of agreement between people about the truth-value of certain modal statements. Insofar as there is agreement one must assume that if it is not catechised into the populace without any understanding of any truth-conditions for these statements, then there is some other account of truth-conditions for these modal statements, and these truth-conditions are such that we may with some degree of confidence determine whether or not they are met. [Richards, "Worlds of David Lewis," p. 109]

Richards seems to be assuming that I cannot know a statement S without *first* knowing a statement T_S which expresses S's truth-condition unless S has simply been "catechised" or drilled into me by rote. If "truth-condition" here means the fact in the world which ultimately makes S true, Richards' assumption is made doubtful by a number of standard cases of philosophical analysis. The *ordo cognoscendi*, contra "The Philosophy of Logical Atomism," need not coincide with the *ordo essendi*. But presumably Richards means "truth-condition" rather in the slightly different Davidsonian/Tarskian sense, in which a sentence's "truth-condition" is the core component of the sentence's locutionary *meaning*. Lewis intends his possible-world analyses of modal sentences to give those sentences' respective truth-conditions in this Davidsonian sense or something relevantly like it.[29] And it does seem we come to *know* a sentence in part by processing that sentence's Davidsonian truth-condition;[30] it is not so obvi-

---

29. "General Semantics."
30. I defend this claim in the manuscript cited in fn. 20 above.

ous that the *ordo cognoscendi* is independent of the *ordo veritatis*. So I am inclined to think Richards is right in challenging Lewis to provide an account of how humans can know things about "other" physical worlds.

Of course, the only statements about other worlds that we need to know for semantical purposes are *general* statements. But how (Richards asks on page 110) do we know whether there is a world in which Saul Kripke is the son of Rudolf Carnap? We cannot tell by inspecting worlds. We must know (if we do) independently, on the basis of some test. Richards suggests that whatever test we do use constitutes the *real* truth-condition of "Saul Kripke might have been the son of Rudolf Carnap." This is overhasty, since we ought not to suppose that verification-conditions are truth-conditions (that way lies Analytical Behaviorism and its ilk). The point remains, though, that Lewis' knowledge of what possible worlds there are and of other general truths about worlds is posterior, not prior, to his knowledge of what things are possible and what things are impossible. This raises the question of why Lewis needs to posit Relentlessly Meinongian worlds, if they provide no epistemic advantage. Doubtless he would reply that he needs these worlds for ontological and for semantical purposes, since (according to him) no conciliatory metaphysics of modality will work. But he has not examined the question of what test we do ultimately use in deciding which possible worlds there are, and so he has not shown that that test, whatever it may be, does not yield a conciliatory metaphysics that is acceptable.[31] Further, how could we even in principle have any independent evidence for the existence of *physical* worlds of particular kinds or even for the existence of any "other" physical worlds at all? I do not see that Lewis has any choice but to immunize his view against criticism by supposing that things must be the way he says they are because they would have to be in order for his views to be correct. In itself this supposition would not be particularly vicious, if his views have proved (as they have) to have systematic utility. The point of the present complaint is that the particular criticisms to which Lewis would be immunizing himself, if I am right, would be directed against the part of his modal metaphysics which far outruns the *formal* structure of semantical explanatory tasks, so far that a demand for independent evidence seems justified. A view such as Kripke's or Rescher's, according to which worlds are the way we say they

31. Harman makes a related (though less specifically epistemological) point in "Logical Form" in Donald Davidson and Gilbert Harman, eds., *The Logic of Grammar* (Encino, Calif: Dickenson, 1975), pp. 289–307.

are because they are simply products of stipulations by us, has a considerable advantage over Lewis' here.

Drawback 4: Lewis' (ii) raises an awkward question.[32] It follows from his realism that just in virtue of the logical possibility of my having climbed Mt. Everest and proved Gödel's Theorem upon reaching the top, there is, somewhere out in logical space, a flesh-and-blood person who is just like me except for having accomplished this *tour de force*. Now, if this person and other various counterparts of mine in other worlds *are* all flesh-and-blood people who resemble me in certain important respects, it would be fascinating for me to be able to meet some of them personally and talk about the interesting things we have in common. What prevents me from traveling to another world and meeting my counterpart at that world and discussing life with him? Of course there cannot be a logical spaceship that allows me to traverse logical space in this way. But why not?

True, worlds are causally and spatiotemporally disjoint from each other and may even differ in their physical laws; this fact suffices to explain why my counterparts in other worlds are forever cut off from me and why my visiting them is impossible "in principle." But I would like to say that the idea of "visiting one of my counterparts," *so far as this idea is occasioned by the mere possibility of* my having climbed Mt. Everest, etc., is not a pleasure which is *denied* me by scientific or even metascientific obstacles, but is rather nonsense. The impossibility of crossing causal or spatiotemporal dislocations, admittedly a very high *grade* of impossibility (stronger than physical, though weaker than logical), fails to do justice to my more nihilistic intuition to the effect that the mere possibilities of everyday life do not or should not occasion even an intelligible scenario of the sort at issue.[33]

Drawback 5: Lewis' (ii), (v), and (vi) get him into trouble of a related kind, pointed out by Richards:

32. I seem to remember that this point was suggested to me by Steven Boër.

33. Lewis himself has given a far more ingenious reply to the "logical spaceship" argument, in conversation. For fear of misrepresenting him I shall not try to reproduce it here in detail, but the general idea is that the personal continuity required for the duration of intermundane travel in turn requires a sustaining causal chain, which in turn requires the truth of certain counterfactual statements about worlds, which statements turn out to be undefined in Lewis' semantics for counterfactuals. If all this is correct, then my talk of "visiting one of my counterparts" ultimately is undefined, and this explains its perceived nonsensicalness. My only objection to this line of reasoning is that, for antecedent and independent reasons, I believe that the counterfactuals in question ought *not* to be left undefined by an adequate semantics for counterfactuals. (On this last point, see also Richards, "Worlds of David Lewis," p. 108.)

No criterion is provided for recognising [our] totality [of existents] as distinct from other totalities. The totalities are disjoint, but what divides them? Defining 'x actually exists' as 'x belongs to the same totality I do' presupposes an entirely unexplained principle of identity for these totalities. Their contents, for Lewis, are all equally real [*sic*] so 'our' world cannot be distinguished by appealing to a difference between existents and *possibilia*. ["Worlds of David Lewis," p. 107]

Richards and you and I are in our world @. Polonius is in another world w_H. The Wife of Bath is in still another world W_C, and so on. In virtue of what is Polonius in a world distinct from that enlivened by the Wife of Bath? In virtue of what is neither Polonius nor the Wife in *our* world? Since Lewis holds that all the worlds distinct from @ are physical and are out there independently of human imaginative or stipulative activity, he must seek some ontological ground for the grouping of possibilia into disjoint worlds. And there are not many possible sources (cf. the standard criticisms of Hume's "bundle" theory of the self). Richards pursues a couple of unpromising responses to this demand. Perhaps a more plausible suggestion, one that he does not address, is that possibilia are collected into worlds in virtue of causal or spatiotemporal interconnections; an object o_i is in the same world as a second object o_j iff o_i is causally or spatiotemporally reachable from o_j. But this criterion ignores nonphysical worlds of various kinds, worlds which themselves *contain* causal or spatiotemporal dislocations, and others.

The five drawbacks I have listed are neither individually nor jointly decisive against Lewis' position. I do not believe that it is possible to *refute* Lewis' position, unless the enormous cardinalities involved in a system of possible worlds should trigger some ingenious diagonal argument that is beyond my mathematical expertise to devise. I do think that the drawbacks are serious enough to provide strong motivation for seeking some alternative modal metaphysics. The remaining options are our three conciliatory ones: Paraphrastic, Quantifier-Reinterpreting, or Actualist.

VIII. The Meinongian Quantifier as Nonobjectual

The Paraphrastic and the Quantifier-Reinterpreting approaches share a tenet: that our Meinongian quantifier "$(\exists x)_M$" is not what at first it appears to be. On the former approach, the "quantifier" functions only as part of an idiom or *façon de parler* and is not really a quantifier at all. On the latter, "$(\exists x)_M$" remains a quantifier at least in the minimal sense of preserving "$(\exists x)$"'s standard implicational relations and receiving its own base clause in a Tarskian truth theory for the Meinongian language, but the truth theory in question characterizes it in other than its usual objectual way.

An obvious instance of the Paraphrastic strategy is Russell's own treatment of possible objects in "On Denoting," which falls cleanly out of his Theory of Descriptions. This version has well-known disadvantages. One is that virtually all the sentences "about" possibilia that Meinong would regard as straightforwardly true come out false on Russell's proposal, precisely because of the nonexistence of the possibilia in question. Another is that Russell's method of handling problems of intensionality generally has not proved to be powerful enough to yield a satisfactory systematic treatment of those problems.[34] Finally, the method offers no obvious way of eliminating talk of possible *worlds* from modal semantics, which would be our main task.

A more promising Paraphrastic program would be to understand "possible-world" talk counterfactually, as Kripke has proposed.[35] This is quite a natural suggestion and does much to make talk of possible worlds more homey. An antic sentence such as "In some possible world distinct from our own, Richard Nixon is a Black Panther" might be paraphrased as "If things had been otherwise, Richard Nixon might have been a Black Panther," a sentence which we all more or less understand or at least would not balk at in ordinary conversation.

The counterfactual approach is inadequate in two serious ways, I think. First: It is not enough to provide a sample paraphrase or two. The counterfactual theorist would have to work out a systematic and rigorous *formula* for paraphrasing formal, model-theoretic sentences concerning possible

---

34. A well-known attempt by A. F. Smullyan to extend Russell's theory in this way ("Modality and Description," *Journal of Symbolic Logic*, 13 [1948], 31–37) is criticized by Leonard Linsky in "Reference, Essentialism, and Modality," *Journal of Philosophy*, 66 (1968), 287–300. I have tried to push Russell's treatment in a slightly different way in sec. III of Steven Boër and William Lycan, "Knowing Who" (*Philosophical Studies*, 28 [1975]); in "Referential Opacity Explained Away" (in preparation) I go into the advantages and drawbacks of the Russell-Smullyan approach in considerable detail.

35. "Identity and Necessity"; "Naming and Necessity," in Harman and Davidson, eds., *Semantics of Natural Language*, pp. 253–355; and particularly in conversation. Nicholas Rescher shows considerable sympathy for the counterfactual approach (though he does not adopt it in the end) in *A Theory of Possibility*.

worlds, and in such a way as to preserve all the theorems of our logical theory and all the advantages of each of the modal logics or modal semantics under analysis. It is hard to imagine how this would go.[36] The difficulty becomes critical when we note that any adequate modal semantics will require many *sets of* possible worlds, sets of sets of worlds, and so on.[37] Intuitively, the counterfactual approach leaves set abstraction on worlds undefined. (This seems to me to be a crucial point, one that I have never heard a Paraphrastic theorist address.) Even if we have provided a satisfactory system of eliminative contextual definitions for *quantification* over nonexistent possibles, this system would have to be extrapolated to cover set abstraction as well, and no way of doing this in terms of counterfactuals comes to mind. (We might try invoking "ways things might have been" and abstracting on them, but to do that would be to reify the "*ways*" and leave us with all the same problems we had before.)

My second complaint about the counterfactual approach, which I have

36. The point I am making here is very easily overlooked by philosophers seeking paraphrastic eliminations of the metaphysically dubious entities assumed by some formal and highly technical theory. Consider a simple (and mythical) example: It seems that sentences of the form "$x \in \hat{y}(Fy)$" can be paraphrased simply as "Fx", as Quine has observed. Thus, some class abstracts may be regarded as *façons de parler*. A philosopher who lacked Quine's own mathematical sophistication might well come to think that nominalism had been achieved, in that Quine had hit upon a program whereby class abstraction and talk of classes could be paraphrased away. What this naive philosopher would be overlooking is that simple class abstraction is not the only technical operation that occurs essentially in set theory. In this case, as Quine points out, one would not even be able to explicate talk of classes of classes, since his "virtual class" device leaves undefined any construction in which a bound variable occurs immediately to the right of "$\in$." A nonmythical example of this optimistic sort of fallacy is some philosophers' reaction to Wilfrid Sellars' approach to abstract entities. Sellars, mobilizing his ingenious device of dot quotation, has offered some very plausible paraphrases for simple talk of properties, propositions, sets, and so on. Philosophers justly impressed by the cleverness and by the naturalness of these paraphrases have taken Sellars to have offered an acceptable nominalistic *theory of* abstract entities generally. But Sellars has given us no reason at all for thinking that the rarefied operations of (e.g.) graph theory, the integral calculus, or other areas of higher mathematics can be explicated in terms of dot quotation, since he has provided no directions in which his original paraphrases of simple and relatively nontechnical constructions are to be extrapolated. (Jeffrey Sicha has tried to provide at least one such direction in *A Metaphysics of Elementary Mathematics* [Amherst, Mass.: University of Massachusetts Press, 1974], but the mathematics he is able to treat is very elementary indeed.)

37. Perhaps the most elaborate set-theoretic world-encapsulating edifice to be found in the existing literature is that built up by M. J. Cresswell in *Logics and Languages* (London: Methuen, 1973).

made elsewhere,[38] is this: It is true that we "understand" counterfactuals in ordinary conversation, as I granted. But for purposes of serious philosophy they have proved to be among the most troublesome and elusive expressions there are. Their truth-conditions have remained genuinely (not just officially) mysterious; their well-known context-dependence has not been understood at all; and in a discussion or seminar on conditionals, people blank out or disagree even on very basic matters of data. Resting a philosophical theory on unexplicated counterfactuals is like hoping one may cross a freezing river by hopping across the heaving ice floes. Great progress has been made on the general understanding of counterfactuals in the last ten years, largely through the work of Stalnaker and Lewis; and the source of this progress is the considered, ingenious, and well-motivated use of possible-worlds semantics. Therefore we have extremely strong reason to analyze and understand counterfactuals in terms of possible worlds. But if we are to do so, we cannot without circularity turn back and paraphrase away talk of possible worlds in terms of unexplicated counterfactuals.[39]

I cannot say what other Paraphrastic programs might be devised concerning mere possibilia. But I think the kinds of considerations I have brought out so far give us substantial reason to look along still other lines. The same, I believe, can be said of the Quantifier-Reinterpreting approach, which has only one existing instance that I know of: Ruth Marcus has proposed[40] that Meinongian quantification be understood as *substitutional* quantification.

This suggestion has a good deal of intuitive appeal. It is quite plausible in the case of "There are things that don't exist": when I utter that sentence aloud, I feel a tendency to continue by listing *names* of things that don't

---

38. William Lycan and Ronald Nusenoff, review of Milton Munitz, ed., *Identity and Individuation, Synthese,* 28 (1974), 553–559.

39. Kripke has replied to this criticism (in conversation) that he regards the circularity as a trade-off; he does not believe that any analysis of counterfactuals will be found that is more acceptable than a possible-worlds analysis and does believe that unreduced possible-worlds analyses are unacceptable for more or less Quinean reasons similar to those I have presented above.

40. "Dispensing with Possibilia," *Proceedings and Addresses of the American Philosophical Association,* 44 (1975–1976), 39–51. Another option may emerge from Rantala's "urn" semantics; see Veikko Rantala, "Urn Models: A New Kind of Non-Standard Model for First-Order Languages," and Hintikka, "Impossible Possible Worlds Vindicated"; both are found in *Journal of Philosophical Logic,* 4 (1975), 455–474 and 475–483.

exist ("... you know, like the round square, Macbeth, the free lunch, and so on"). And there certainly is plenty of overt quantification in English that is substitutional. It might be thought that Marcus' proposal fails in the case of possible worlds on the grounds that worlds in general do not have names at all (the substitution class would be far too small); but we may easily generate a system of canonical names for possible worlds from existing resources: Each world, we may suppose, is correctly described by a maximally consistent set of sentences $\{P, Q, R, \ldots\}$; to obtain a name of a world in which $P, Q, R, \ldots$, simply form a definite description from the latter indefinite one: "$(\iota w)\mathrm{In}_w(P \ \& \ Q \ \& \ R \ \& \ldots)$."

This proposal will inherit the usual sorts of problems that philosophers have raised for substitution interpretations of more familiar quantifiers. The most obvious of these is the "not enough names" problem: First, given that almost any real-valued physical magnitude characterizing our world will have nondenumerably many nonactual worlds corresponding to it, the cardinality of the set of all worlds (if this notion is not undefined or paradoxical) will be inconceivably high. But there are only denumerably many names of the sort exemplified above; thus, it seems, universal quantifications over worlds will be verified more easily than we would like.[41] Second, a number of philosophers have argued that the substitution interpretation somehow collapses into the standard interpretation when incorporated into a full-scale truth theory. Kripke has recently refuted at least the most salient versions of this charge,[42] though I have argued elsewhere that there is a further, somewhat related difficulty which impugns the usefulness of the substitution interpretation for the truth-conditional analysis of *natural* languages.[43]

The main problem for Marcus' proposal, as I see it, is the same that arose for the counterfactual approach: How will Marcus reinterpret set abstraction and all the other operations that will need to be applied to names of "worlds"? (Certainly there have been attempts at metalinguistic

---

41. Several philosophers have recently claimed that the "not enough names" problem is soluble for the usual sorts of subject matters such as arithmetic. See (e.g.) Sicha, *Metaphysics*, and R. D. Gallie, "A. N. Prior and Substitutional Quantification," *Analysis*, 34 (1974), 65–69. I have not seen these purported solutions adjudicated in the literature, so I cannot say whether they could correctly be extended to cover the cardinalities involved in a system of nonexistent possibles.

42. "Is There a Problem about Substitutional Quantification?" in Gareth Evans and John McDowell, eds., *Truth and Meaning* (Oxford: Oxford University Press, 1976),

43. "Semantic Competence and Funny Functors," forthcoming in *The Monist*.

reinterpretations of set abstraction, but they have concentrated on reinterpreting the abstractor itself, not the variable it binds; that is, they have concentrated on detoxifying mention of the *sets* in question, not mention of the sets' members.)

If I am right in thinking that we should continue to look elsewhere for an understanding of possibilistic talk, only one option remains: to seek an actualist analysis.

IX. Potential World-Surrogates

The actualist's task is to find some system of actual objects that is structurally analogous or isomorphic to a system of possible worlds and therefore can *serve as* or *go proxy for* worlds. At least six sorts of systems come to mind:

LINGUISTIC ENTITIES.   Historically, the most popular "ersatz" worlds have been sentences or sets of sentences. Carnap's "state descriptions" functioned as possible worlds. Hintikka followed a similar practice in *Knowledge and Belief*[44] (though he dropped this in later works). If a "world" is understood as being a set of sentences, then possibility may be understood as *consistency,* and "actuality" neatly reinterpreted as *truth.* (Note that the metalinguistic approach fits nicely with metalinguistic theories of the propositional attitudes and provides handy objects for the attitudes.)

PROPOSITIONS.   One might move to sets of language-independent propositions, i.e., sets of abstract (but actual) objects having sentencelike semantical properties. This approach is defended by Robert Adams and nicely elaborated by Alvin Plantinga.[45]

PROPERTIES.   Castañeda, and subsequently Terry Parsons, have offered ways of construing Meinong's Objects as sets of properties.[46] Castañeda achieves a sort of fusing of Meinong with Frege and treats a number of

44. Ithaca, N.Y.: Cornell University Press, 1962.

45. Adams, "Theories of Actuality," *Nous,* 8 (1974), 211–231; Plantinga, *The Nature of Necessity* (Oxford: Clarendon Press, 1974). Plantinga actually talks of *states of affairs* which *obtain* or do not obtain and does not commit himself to identifying these respectively with true and false propositions (p. 45); I do not see that any fine distinctions here will be of importance to the metaphysics of modality.

46. Hector-Neri Castañeda, "Thinking and the Structure of the World," *Philosophia,* 4 (1974), 3–40; and Parsons, "A Prolegomenon to a Meinongian Semantics."

semantical issues quite neatly without any appeal to genuinely nonexistent possibles. A drawback here is that the approach requires the introduction of several new primitives.

COMBINATORIAL CONSTRUCTS. Quine has suggested, and Max Cresswell has elaborated, the idea of taking "worlds" to be set-theoretic combinatorial rearrangements of the posited basic atoms of which our own world is composed.[47] I shall explain and discuss this view in more detail below. below.

MENTAL ITEMS. An obvious but so far unattempted move would be to take mental entities of some sort as our "ersatz worlds." Rescher is tempted by this approach and points out a number of its advantages in *A Theory of Possibility,* but does not adopt it in the end (cf. pp. 216–217).

WAYS THINGS MIGHT HAVE BEEN. Stalnaker suggests taking "ways things might have been" as *sui generis* elements of our ontology;[48] thus, "ways things might have been" are actual abstract entities in their own right, not to be reduced to items of any more familiar kind. Stalnaker accepts Lewis' indexical analysis of "actual" (thesis (vi)), but regards it as metaphysically uninteresting, since there is only one *world* for entities to be actual "at."

I have argued that we have good reason to seek some such system of "ersatz worlds," giving up Lewis' Relentless Meinongianism but at least for now continuing to regard the Meinongian quantifier as a standard objectual one. And Actualism as a program has aesthetic attractions not unlike those of the analogous explications of number theory in terms of set theory. But any particular choice of a system of "ersatz worlds" may turn out to face philosophical difficulties of its own. For example, Lewis argues forcefully in *Counterfactuals* (p. 85) that the metalinguistic method of Carnap and Hintikka is circular, in that "consistency" of sentences cannot adequately be defined save in terms of possibility. In addition, more typically, a choice of a system of world-surrogates may be seen to be technically inadequate, in that the intended isomorphism between the system and the lattice of worlds for which it goes proxy falls short in some way that frustrates our purposes in using pseudo-Meinongian quantification in the

47. Quine, "Propositional Objects," in *Ontological Relativity and Other Essays* (New York: Columbia University Press, 1968); Cresswell, *Logics and Languages* and "The World Is Everything That Is the Case."
48. "Possible Worlds."

first place. A mentalistic approach, for example, is daunted by the paucity of *actual* mental events: the entire history of the universe will quite probably contain only finitely many mental entities, and it is hard to see how these might be parlayed into a system of proxies for all the multiply uncountable sets of worlds that must be posited for purposes of modal logic.

To illustrate some of the philosophical and technical limitations to which particular actualist programs are subject, I shall discuss the Quine-Cresswell combinatorial approach in some detail. I shall then conclude by making a tentative prognosis and drawing a moral.

X. *Combinatorialism*

To see the initial plausibility of combinatorialism, consider the familiar notion of a chess game. Many chess games have been played, but there are plenty of other chess games that never have actually been played, though they are permissible according to the rules of chess. We are little tempted, though, to assimilate unplayed chess games to the golden mountain or the present king of France. A *game* is quite naturally understood as being a sequence of moves. A *move* we may take to be a triple whose members are a chess piece, an initial square, and a destination square (castling would require a small refinement). *Pieces* and *squares* are types, which may be regarded as sets of tokens. A game is *played* when two people under appropriate circumstances make a series of physical motions using (physical) chessmen and a board, which series mimics the sequence of triples that *is* the game in question. Some allowable sequences are never in fact mimicked in this way, just as some grammatical sentences of English are never tokened. And there is nothing at all metaphysically mysterious about this, save perhaps to nominalists who have qualms about sets. Could we extrapolate our Actualist metaphysic of possible chess games to cover *all* "nonexistent" possibles, including "possible worlds"?

Suppose that there are some *metaphysically basic elements* out of which our universe is composed. Call them "atoms" (in the metaphysical rather than the chemical sense). Our world, we may say, consists of these atoms' being *arranged* in a certain fabulously complex way. The actual *arrangement* of the atoms could be taken to be, or to be represented by, a vastly complex *set* built up out of nothing but atoms and sets as members. Now let us construe "other possible worlds" as *alternative* arrangements of our atoms which mirror the ways our world might have been just as the actual arrangement mirrors the world as it is. These alternative arrangements are sets (actual entities), too, of course.

The "atoms" are the fundamental building blocks of our own world, whatever those may eventually be shown by science or philosophy to be. Hypothetically, we might take them to be little particles, or occupations of space-time points (Quine's preliminary choice), or Berkeleyan ideas, or whatever. As I shall now argue, however, our choice of "atoms" may ultimately affect the adequacy of our combinatorialist explication of nonactual worlds.

XI. Problems for Combinatorialism

Lewis has pointed out[49] that certain choices of atoms (certain decisions as to which actual things we ought to count as being the fundamental building blocks of the universe) commit the combinatorialist to strong modal theses which would better be left as open questions. Schematically: Any combinatorialist will end up ruling out some apparently imaginable states of affairs as holding in no possible world, on the grounds that these states of affairs cannot be construed as being arrangements of that particular combinatorialist's chosen atoms. This means that any combinatorialist's choice of atoms places substantive constraints on what states of affairs are to count as possible states of affairs.

Lewis does not really elaborate this point, but we can give some trenchant examples of what he is talking about, and we can also work the point up into a principled argument against combinatorialism which will be hard to resist. The examples:

(a) It would seem to be possible that the world should have contained either more or less fundamental stuff. It is easy to envision an arrangement involving fewer atoms, or even one which would serve as the null world (presumably the null set). But how might we construct an arrangement corresponding to an increase in the amount of fundamental matter? (One might think of representing new "atoms" by artificial means, such as pairing existing atoms with real numbers. This would be an appropriately Actualistic strategy, but would constitute an abandoning of the *combinatorial* approach, since these new artificial "atoms" would not be the very sorts of things—atoms in the strict sense—that physical things would be *physically made of* in the alternate world. To put the point slightly dif-

49. *Counterfactuals*, pp. 89-91.

ferently: our hypothesis is that there might exist *atoms* that do not already exist in this world; and atoms are not arrangements of atoms and so cannot be represented as alternative arrangements of atoms.) It seems, then, that any choice of a stock of atoms commits the combinatorialist to the *necessary* nonexistence of any more atoms, since there will be no arrangement and hence no possible world in which there exists an atom that is not one of our prechosen stock; any such extraneous atoms would be nonactual, and so shunned by the combinatorialist.

(b) In making remark (a), I was thinking of alternative physical worlds. But our world contains abstract objects too. ''Other'' worlds might contain fewer abstract objects (no problem), or more (same problem as in (a)), or possibly even strange abstract objects not found here in @. How could we hit upon an arrangement mirroring a world that is mathematically deviant in this way? Here, perhaps, it *might* help to resort to artificial means (cf. Philip Wiener's construction of ordered pairs out of ordinary sets), since abstract objects, unlike atoms, are not noncomposite by definition. But it is hard to imagine there being a way in which the abstract objects of this world might combine to form new composite abstract objects in another world, but in which they do *not* combine in this world.

(c) What about irreducibly spiritual objects? Very probably there are no ghosts, monads, or Cartesian egos in this world; but there could have been, at least if we are to take seriously the views of brilliant philosophers who have believed in them. What sort of arrangement of atoms and sets could mirror such a state of affairs?

(d) As Lewis points out, we want to leave open the possibility that our world could have operated according to an entirely different physics and even according to a radically different geometry. It follows that any combinatorialist who chooses either Euclidean space-time or Minkowskian space-time in which to locate his atoms will be oversimplifying at best. How might we allow for basic structural changes through worlds? It would be hard to motivate any further variegation of our procedures for forming wilder and more bizarre arrangements of the atoms of *this* world.

(e) I should think that *nonatomistic* worlds are also possible, such as one which consists of an undifferentiated miasma of Pure Spirit. A nonatomistic world can hardly be regarded as an arrangement of @'s stock of atoms.

Notice that in virtue of limitations such as (a)–(e), combinatorialism also constrains our accessibility relation in modal logic, and hence restricts the modal systems we may countenance.[50] For example, combinatorial accessibility will have to be asymmetric. A world having fewer atoms than @ is accessible from @, but @ cannot be accessible from it, since @ contains atoms that it does not contain and which therefore are nonactual relative to it. We are forced to conclude that S-5 is too strong a modal logic, since S-5 is based on a system of worlds whose accessibility relation is symmetric.

The obvious response for the combinatorialist to make to (a)–(e) is to bite the bullet and maintain that the apparent "possibilities" that I have imagined are simply *not* possible. But there are two crippling rejoinders to this. (1) When the combinatorialist says "not possible," he must mean this *in the strongest conceivable sense.* More atoms, spiritual objects, different physics, and so on must be impossible not merely in the physical sense, and *not merely in the metaphysical sense,* but in at least the sense in which overt contradictions are not possible. This is because otherwise there would have to be *logically* possible *worlds* in which such things obtained even if there were no physically or metaphysically possible worlds of that sort. And this is completely counterintuitive. It may be "impossible" for there to be Cartesian egos in some very strong sense or other, but not in as strong a sense as that in which it is impossible for 3 to be both prime and not prime. (2) Even if we collapse the distinctions between grades of possibility that I have just insisted on, the combinatorialist still cannot deny that bizarre situations of the kind we have been talking about are *believed in* by some people. Descartes, for example, believed that there were nonextended, irreducible egos. Now, one of the main functions of possible worlds is to provide semantics for propositional attitudes. E.g., *belief* is said to be a relation between a believer and a set of worlds (his doxastic alternatives). Thus, it should be true in each of Descartes' doxastic alternatives that there are nonextended egos—or else we shall have to rob the possible-worlds apparatus of much of its interest by finding a different semantics for propositional attitudes.[51]

A slightly more sophisticated combinatorialist ploy is that which Max Cresswell has taken in conversation.[52] This is to *refuse to make* a choice of

---

50. I owe this point to Phil Quinn.

51. This point is somewhat weakened by the fact, already brought out and illuminatingly discussed by Gail Stine in "Essentialism, Possible Worlds, and Propositional Attitudes" (*Philosophical Review,* 82 [1973], 471–482), that the failure of real people to be logical saints causes problems of this sort for possible-worlds semanticists in any case.

52. I am indebted to Cresswell for a number of helpful discussions on this topic.

particular items to serve as our atoms, and instead just to insist that there *are* basic objects in this world that play the modal role of atoms even though we shall never know or be able to say what they are. We are to find out what the atoms of our world are like by examining what is required to generate adequate modal semantics, and in no other way. This might seem to flout cherished principles of scientific realism, in that Cresswell's un-specifiable atoms are as inaccessible to physics as they are to the ordinary person, but Cresswell (I think) would respond that modal semantics *is* a science, and we are required by *it* to posit his unknowable atoms even if physics has no need of them and cannot discover them.

Further criticisms loom: (3) This Tractarian ploy is paradigmatically ad hoc. We posit the special, unknowable, subphysical atoms *solely* for the purpose of saving combinatorialism from refutation by entrenched modal intuitions. Accordingly, we render combinatorialism totally untestable. We also ignore the ineliminable *epistemic* possibility, given whatever objects are in fact the atoms of our world, that objects of that sort should have been composites and not atoms. (4) The ploy gets by some of our previous objections only at the cost of substantive metaphysical commitments. Take (c). Cresswell would have us believe that bodies and Cartesian egos (in such worlds as contain both) are just different kinds of composites out of more basic metaphysical objects; he is committed to "neutral monism" as a theory of the mental. Neutral monism might be true of minds and brains in this world, and it might be true even of Cartesian egos, but I doubt it, since *Cartesian* egos are supposed to be fundamentally different in kind from bodies. More to the point, we should not want our *semantics* to prejudge this venerable and complex metaphysical question if we can help it. (5) Cresswell's ploy fails even to address some of our objections, particularly (a) and (e). So if it helps at all, it does not help much.

A final criticism, one which applies to a number of other versions of actualism as well: In (a) and (b) above, I have mentioned the possibility of throwing together a system of set-theoretic objects that might *ape* the group of "nonactual" things or worlds we need, in the sense of being structurally isomorphic to that group of things (cf. again Wiener on ordered pairs). Suppose, to take another example, that our world contains only finitely many physical atoms out of which physical objects are made, but that we want to construct nonfinitely many physical variations on our world. We might easily allow for this by pairing existing atoms with numbers, or some such. The resulting set-theoretic objects might be quite arbitrarily chosen, and the objects themselves might well have nothing intuitively to do with the metaphysics of modality, even though they were carefully selected for their joint ability to play the desired combinatorial role. But why should we suppose that real *possibility* in this world has anything to do with pairs of atoms and numbers?

Frege would have rejected this question, and so do many of the intensional logicians who follow him on the methodology of positing abstract entities in semantics. ("*I* don't care what we let the quantifiers range over; the 'worlds' could be my dog, the Eiffel Tower, the real numbers, my grandmother's tricycle, and Bertrand Russell—just so long as the mathematics ends up dumping the right sentences into the right barrels.") This brings up Plantinga's distinction[53] between "pure semantics" and "applied semantics." A "pure" semantics does not interpret its quantifiers at all, and so does not commit itself to any particular domain. Its only adequacy-condition is that it predict the truth values of complex sentences given the truth and satisfaction values of their parts and that it capture the right sorts of felt implications. In effect, a "pure" semantics serves to axiomatize the predicate "valid modal formula" and nothing more. But any number of interpretations of such axiomatizations will be available, no one of them having any better claim to "correctness" than any other (compare now the alternative ways of reducing number theory to set theory). Plantinga points out that a "pure" semantics "does not give us a meaning for '□', or tell us under what condition a proposition is necessarily true, or what it is for an object to have a property essentially" (*Nature of Necessity*, p. 127; notice, incidentally, that the three tasks Plantinga mentions are mutually distinct). If our semantical theory is to *explain what it is* about our world that makes an alethic statement true in it, we must assign specific domains to its quantifiers, thus making it into an "applied" semantics.[54] (And if we are actualists, our domains must contain only actual objects.)

A serious qualification is needed here. Modal and intensional semantics have been employed in aid of many different sorts of jobs and projects, not just the few enterprises mentioned in the preceding paragraph. And many of these projects, though technically demanding, are not philosophically ambitious enough to require any very specific ontological choice of do-

53. *The Nature of Necessity*, chap. 7, sec. 4.

54. I do *not* believe a parallel argument would succeed regarding number theory and set theory. I have proposed an analysis of numerical terms that blocks it in William Lycan and George Pappas, "Quine's Materialism," *Philosophia*, 6 (1976), 109–110.

mains for the Meinongian quantifiers. A trivial and obvious example of a justifiably noncommittal appeal to "worlds" is the casual, everyday semantical computation we do in routinely checking the validity of complicated modal inferences in the process of carrying on philosophical arguments. Perhaps a less obvious example may be the use of "possible-worlds" semantics in obtaining consistency and completeness etc. results for modal systems.[55] Possibly we even learn something about the nature of necessity from "pure" semantics alone, though to articulate exactly what sort of illumination or understanding we gain here is much more difficult than most logicians admit. Then what uses of the "possible-worlds" apparatus do require a serious assignment of specific sorts of ranges to the Meinongian quantifiers?

I offer a paradigm case. Suppose someone were to argue as follows:[56] "Metaphysicians have always struggled with the problem of counterfactuals, wondering what fact it is in the world that makes a counterfactual true. Some have posited special dispositional facts; others have opted for what Quine calls an irresponsible metaphysic of unactualized potentials; still others have attempted deflationary but palpably inadequate metalinguistic accounts and such. Now, I can explain why metaphysicians have had such trouble with counterfactuals and have had to make such desperate lunges. The problem is that the metaphysicians have radically misconceived the issue: they have sought truth-makers[57] for counterfactuals *in the* (i.e., *this*) *world*. A counterfactual's truth-maker is not in the single world at which the counterfactual is true, but is transmundane, involving lots of worlds distinct from this one all at once. Once we see this, we can make great progress on the metaphysical problem of counterfactuals."

This argument seems very compelling, and so do similar arguments concerning the metaphysics of possibility and necessity. But notice that its *mainspring* is the metaphysical claim that our world is not the only world

55. Thus, in no way am I suggesting that modal semanticists should interrupt their work and wait for our ontological problems to be solved to everyone's satisfaction. I am a bit more doubtful, though, about linguistic semanticists, who base their theories of *natural* language on intensional formal systems; at least, the type of illumination that such theories yield needs very careful examination and sorting out, which to my knowledge it has not yet received.

56. Something like this is suggested, though not expressly claimed, by Stalnaker in "A Theory of Conditionals," in *Studies in Logical Theory,* ed. by Nicholas Rescher, *American Philosophical Quarterly* Monograph Series, No. 2 (Oxford: Blackwell, 1968), 98–112.

57. I borrow this term from David Armstrong.

and that other worlds and their histories figure just as crucially in determining the truth of a counterfactual "at" our world. This metaphysical claim, if it is genuinely to explain how earlier metaphysicians misconceived the problem of counterfactuals, must be understood in substance as well as in form—its proponent must be able to offer some account of what his "other worlds" are if it is to provide the kind of metaphysical illumination that is being claimed for it. (If we are actualists, of course, our "transmundane" facts will be reduced in turn to facts of our world; so for the actualist the foregoing account will not be literally correct, but will illuminate just in the way that a model does before it has been successfully demythologized.)

It is at this point that the arbitrariness of our choice among different methods of slapping together "arrangements" makes itself felt. No one way of pairing atoms or sets of atoms with real numbers is more intuitive or natural than all others, for example, and so none has a better claim than all others to tell us what fact it is that makes some counterfactual or alethic or doxastic statement true.

In fact, the arbitrariness goes a bit further down; we need not appeal to the indenumerability of worlds or to the need for bizarre worlds to be troubled by it. Take Quine's way of constructing "ersatz" worlds, in terms of occupations of space-time points. If a point is to be represented by a quadruple of numbers, what kind of set shall we choose to represent the occupation of a point? We might simply form the set of all the points that are occupied in a "world" and let that set be the "arrangement" that mirrors that "world." Or we might pair our quadruples with 1 and with 0 alternatively, representing occupation or vacancy respectively. Or the other way around. Or we might use the letters "O" and V," as is suggested by the examples of restrooms on passenger trains. The alternatives are limitless.[58] In light of this it is hard to see how a combinatorial interpretation of

58. Quine himself would reject this criticism and would reject the spirit of Plantinga's "pure"/"applied" distinction. In "Ontological Relativity" he argues in effect that any choice of an interpretation for *any* quantifier is arbitrary in this way, or at least that it is relative to an arbitrarily prechosen *scheme* of interpretation. Thus, he finds Plantinga's and my demand inherently unreasonable. The important thing to see, though, is that if they are successful, Quine's arguments for this indeterminacy of ontology also impugn the status of semantics as a science and the whole idea of giving determinate "truth-conditions" for modal sentences or any other sentences, not to mention the whole idea of any sentence's having a determinate "meaning." Quine is radically skeptical of all such enterprises (on this, see Harman's "Quine on Meaning and Existence, I, II," and my "Reality and Semantic Representation"). So appeal to Quine's doctrine of ontological relativity will not help the com-

modal semantics that has helped itself to artificial aids in this way could solve the problem of truth-makers even if it were technically adequate to lesser, merely computational tasks.

The case against combinatorialism seems serious. I have discussed it at such length partly just to illustrate the kinds of difficulties that an actualist can incur (for professed actualists often fail to notice these difficulties) and partly to urge combinatorialists to switch to some less troubled form of actualism. But to which one?

XII. Prognosis

I believe that the only promising choice of actual entities to serve as "worlds" is that of sets of intensional objects. Thus, I would fall in either with Adams and Plantinga and construct worlds directly out of propositions, or with Castañeda and Parsons and construct possible objects out of properties and then group the objects into worlds on the basis of their stipulated interrelations. My main reason for choosing familiar intensional entities is that actualist programs based on them do not seem to run into as serious difficulties of the kinds I have mentioned as do other actualist programs. I think this is largely because they are posits of *semantics* to begin with: so there are (or seem to be) enough of them; actuality can again be explained in terms of truth; set abstraction on worlds remains ordinary set abstraction; there is no arbitrariness problem of the sort raised in section XI, since properties and propositions are characteristically introduced as being the meanings of predicates and sentences in the first place; and for the same reason the connection between "possible worlds" and semantical notions and alethic notions becomes quite straightforward and intuitive. Plantinga in particular has proposed an actualist theory of this kind which seems to me quite promising and has defended it against a number of objections. I do not go along with all of Plantinga's choices on

---

binatorialist defend his own proposal for an applied semantics. Ironically, Quine himself (on pages 149–152 of "Propositional Objects") expends a fair bit of energy in trying to remove arbitrariness of this sort which infects spatial and temporal dimensions, apparently in an effort to get at the *real* (nonarbitrary) members of his domain of arrangements. This seems completely uncharacteristic of Quine and remains for me an exegetical paradox. A further mystery is that Quine seemingly invokes his "ersatz worlds" only to model the propositional attitudes of nonverbal creatures and does not seem to notice that his apparatus potentially generates a stock of arrangements adequate to deal with modal semantics generally.

matters of detail,[59] nor with all of Adams', but I would like to work out an account along their lines.

I predict it will be fruitful to allow real individuals to be constituents of propositions; a simple atomic proposition might be said to consist of a paired object and property. This policy would provide an obvious basis for transworld identity and hence for quantifying in. It would also obviate the "telescope" problem faced by the Relentless Meinongian. (In keeping with the policy, no "nonexistent individual" which by stipulation is not identical with any real individual could be treated as a genuine individual. Such an "object" might be reconstrued as a set of properties *simpliciter* or as the intersection of a number of maximally consistent sets of properties; or else apparent references to it might be paraphrased away à la the Theory of Descriptions.[60] This would effectively prevent our allowing that such "individuals" can have *de re* modal properties or be the objects of *de re* psychological attitudes, but I believe these things ought not to be allowed in any case.[61])

A very significant virtue of an actualist account based on sets of propositions, in my opinion, is that it makes room for *impossible* worlds as well as possible ones. So far as I can see, we have just as great a theoretical need for Meinongian quantification over impossible objects and worlds as we do for admitting possible but nonactual ones. Further, I can think of no direct argument for "nonexistents" that does not support impossibilia by parity of reasoning, and I have never been impressed by any of the objections that have been raised against impossible objects but do not hold with equal force against nonexistents of any sort.[62] On the propositional account, an impossible world is simply an inconsistent set of propositions. (Impossible worlds, unlike possible ones, need not be closed under deduction.) The propositional account also explains something that would otherwise be a bit paradoxical,[63] viz., how it is possible for a self-contradictory proposition to

59. For example, I do not preserve Plantinga's distinction between *worlds* and "world-*books*." I employ only the world-books, or, as Adams calls them, world-stories.

60. Rescher has elaborated and defended the idea of "supernumerary" individuals of this kind in *A Theory of Possibility*, chap. 3.

61. Cf. Robert Kraut, "Attitudes and Their Objects," *Journal of Philosophical Logic*, forthcoming.

62. For further defense of impossibilia see Richard and Valerie Routley, "Rehabilitating Meinong's Theory of Objects," p. 230; also Richard Routley, "The Durability of Impossible Objects," *Inquiry*, 19 (1976), 247–250.

63. The problem was put to me by Don Mannison.

be *true*, even "at" an impossible world: The account rejects Lewis' (vi) and does not analyze *truth* in terms of "truth at" our world. Rather, it analyzes "truth at" a nonactual "world" simply as set membership. The self-contradictory proposition is a member of the set of propositions constituting the impossible "world" in question; hence it is "true at" it.

A few objections need to be dealt with. First: Does the propositional account not run into the same problem of "too much necessity" that I raised for the combinatorialist? For if we construct our "worlds" out of properties and propositions, how could we then represent nominalistic worlds containing no properties or propositions?[64] Reply: A world *in which* there are no properties or propositions, though, like any "nonactual world," is largely *made of* properties and propositions, is just a set of propositions one member of which is the proposition that there are no properties or propositions. A Carnapian state description theorist would likewise represent a world containing no sentences or other linguistic entities as a set of sentences containing the sentence, "There are no sentences or other linguistic entities." I can write a story about people who never write stories; there is no inconsistency here.

Second objection: Does the propositional account not take *consistency* and *mutual compatibility* of propositions as primitive, thus forfeiting the crucial benefit of explaining these notions in terms of *possibility* of worlds or simply in terms of *worlds* (if we join Lewis in abjuring impossible worlds)?[65] Reply: Yes. But this is no defect. What makes some propositions compatible or incompatible with others is no more mysterious, ultimately, than what makes some worlds possible and others not, or than what makes some stories describe segments of worlds and others not. Any metaphysics of possibility is going to have to take some one of these easily interdefinable notions as primitive, and I see no lasting conceptual superiority in any one of the three approaches over the other two on this point.

Third objection: What difference is there, in the end, between a *false proposition* and a *nonexistent state of affairs*? I have claimed the preferability of quantifying over the former to "quantifying over" the latter, but is the difference not merely terminological? Are nonexistent states of

64. This objection was raised by Tom Richards. I am indebted to him and to his colleagues at LaTrobe University for helpful discussion of an earlier version of this paper.

65. Max Cresswell voiced this objection; it is also touched on by Stalnaker in "Possible Worlds."

affairs not just as familiar as false propositions, belying my crucial argument in section III above?[66] Reply: (i) The argument of section III shows
precisely why false propositions are preferable to "nonexistent" states of
affairs. "There exist states of affairs that do not exist" has to be disambiguated, and my invocation of *falsity* achieves this, assuming we have an
intuitive handle on what it is for a proposition to be false (or for a state of
affairs not to *obtain*) that is prior to, or at least independent of, considerations of modal metaphysics. (ii) We do have such an intuitive handle, plus
substantial grounds for expecting that it may be reinforced in a number of
technical ways. For *falsity* is a familiar semantical property; and propositions (as they have traditionally been conceived) have *structures* relevant
to the determination of their truth values. For example, a simple atomic
proposition would be false iff its individual constituent did not instantiate
its property constituent. Falsity for more complex propositions might be
explained in terms of a more elaborate picturing or mirroring relation,[67] or it
might be recursively defined à la Tarski. (In either case, care would have to
be taken to avoid the semantical paradoxes and other possible cardinality
problems.) (iii) The question of whether a proposition *exists* is a substantive and interesting question quite independent of whether the proposition
is *false*. A nominalist might admit that the sentence "Russell is a genius"
expresses a true proposition rather than a false one *if* there *exists* any
proposition at all for it to express; and we may debate whether (e.g.) the
proposition that quadruplicity drinks procrastination exists without doubt-
ing that if it does exist it is false.

   As usual, of course, we shall have to take the rough with the smooth;
there is a further objection to the propositional account that does reveal a
serious failing: the account sacrifices the wonderfully elegant practice of
explicating properties, propositions, and other Fregean intensions as being
functions from possible worlds to extensions. If we reduce "possible
worlds" to sets of propositions, for example, we cannot then reduce propositions to functions from possible worlds to truth values. This is an un-
pleasant price to pay, but I think a small one when compared to the

66. This point was raised by Phil Quinn; Stalnaker also hints at it in "Possible Worlds,"
but instead argues rather neatly that his Actualist world-surrogates, "ways things might have
been," are just as efficacious as sets of propositions and have a slight edge in economy. I
think his argument can be resisted, but I would be almost as happy with his candidates as I
would be with Plantinga's.

67. I have suggested this in "Could Propositions Explain Anything?" *Canadian Journal of
Philosophy*, 3 (1974), 427–435.

drawbacks that afflict other theories of modality. In any case, admittedly, more time will be needed to determine whether a program such as the one I have begun to sketch does not in fact face problems just as awful as those we have raised for its competitors.

XIII. Pointedly Unirenic Moral

It is only recently that our four basic approaches to the metaphysics of modality, and their various versions and subversions, have become as visibly distinct as I hope I have brought out in this essay. The primary point to grasp, and my main contention, is that anyone who needs to traffic in "nonactual" possible and/or possible worlds and who is concerned to use these notions in a philosophically self-conscious and responsible way must (eventually) choose between our alternative approaches and *face the conseqences*. I believe that much of the unconcern with which semanticists have countenanced possible-world talk has resulted from their having conflated two or more of our approaches and tacitly—but illicitly—helped themselves to the complementary advantages of each. (And perhaps some of the horror with which Quinean *anti*semanticists have reacted to intensional and modal semantics has resulted from their having conflated two or more of the approaches and likewise lumped together the *dis*advantages of each.) Logicians, who remain cautious in their explanatory claims, may put off the choice perhaps indefinitely; but it is time for philosophical semanticists and modal metaphysicians to get serious.

Bibliography

Abbreviations of Frequently Cited Journals

A   *Analysis*
AJP   *Australasian Journal of Philosophy*
APF   *Acta Philosophica Fennica*
APQ   *American Philosophical Quarterly*
ASP   *Aristotelian Society Proceedings*
ASSV   *Aristotelian Society Supplementary Volume*
CJP   *Canadian Journal of Philosophy*
JP   *Journal of Philosophy*
JPL   *Journal of Philosophical Logic*
JSL   *Journal of Symbolic Logic*
M   *Mind*
N   *Noûs*
NDJFL *Notre Dame Journal of Formal Logic*
PPR   *Philosophy and Phenomenological Research*
PQ   *Philosophical Quarterly*
PR   *Philosophical Review*
PS   *Philosophical Studies*
RM   *Review of Metaphysics*
S   *Synthese*
T   *Theoria*
ZML   *Zeitschrift für Mathematische Logic und Grundlagen der Mathematik*

ADAMS, ERNEST M. *The Logic of Conditionals*. Dordrecht: Reidel, 1975.

ADAMS, ROBERT M. "Critical Study of Plantinga's *Nature of Necessity*." *N*, 11 (1977), 175-191.

——. "The Logical Structure of Anselm's Arguments." *PR*, 80 (1971), 28-54.

——. "Middle Knowledge." *JP*, 70 (1973), 552-554.

——. "Must God Create the Best?" *PR*, 81 (1972), 317-332.

ANDERSON, ALAN R. "An Intensional Interpretation of the Truth Values." *M*, 81 (1972), 348-371.

——. "Modalities in Ackermann's 'Rigorous Implication.'" *JSL*, 24 (1959), 107-111.

——. "The Pure Calculus of Entailment." *JSL*, 27 (1962), 19-52.

——. "Some Open Problems Concerning the System E of Entailment." *APF*, 16 (1963), 7-18.

BACON, JOHN. "Ontological Commitment and Free Logic." *Monist*, 53 (1969), 310-319.

BALDWIN, TOM. "The Philosophical Significance of Intensional Logic." *ASSV*, 49 (1975), 45-65.

BELNAP, NUEL. "Entailment and Relevance." *JSL*, 25 (1960), 144-146.

BENFIELD, DAVID, AND EDWIN ERWIN. "Identity, Schmidentity—It's Not All the Same." *PS*, 28 (1975), 145-148.

BENNET, DANIEL. "Essential Properties." *JP*, 66 (1969), 487-499.

BENNETT, JONATHAN. "Counterfactuals and Possible Worlds." *CJP*, 4 (1974), 281-402.

——. "Entailment." *PR*, 78 (1969), 197-236.

——. "A Myth about Logical Necessity." *A*, 21 (1960), 59-63.

BERGMANN, GUSTAV. "Meaning." In Gustav Bergmann, *Logic and Reality*, pp. 84-97. Madison: University of Wisconsin Press, 1964.

——. "The Philosophical Significance of Modal Logic." *M*, 69 (1960), 466-485.

BETH, EVERT W. "Extension and Intension." *S*, 12 (1960), 375-379.

BIGELOW, JOHN C. "Possible Worlds Foundations for Probability." *JPL*, 5 (1976), 299-320.

BLACK, MAX. "Possibility." *JP*, 57 (1960), 117-126.

BLACKBURN, SIMON. *Meaning, Reference, and Necessity*. Cambridge: Cambridge University Press, 1977.

BLOCKER, H. GENE. "Back to Reality." *Metaphilosophy*, 5 (1974), 232-241.

BLUMFELD, DAVID. "Is the Best Possible World Possible?" *PR*, 84 (1975), 163-177.

BOSTOCK, DAVID. "Kripke on Identity and Necessity." *PQ*, 27 (1977), 313-324.

BRODY, BARUCH. "*De Re* and *De Dicto* Interpretations of Modal Logic or a Return to an Aristotelian Essentialism." *Philosophia*, 2 (1972), 117-136.

————. "Kripke on Proper Names." *Midwest Studies in Philosophy*, 3 (1977), 64–69.

————. "Natural Kinds and Real Essences." *JP*, 64 (1967), 431–446.

————. "Why Settle for Anything Less than Good Old Fashioned Aristotelian Essentialism?" *N*, 7 (1973), 351–365.

BUCHLER, JUSTUS. *Metaphysics of Natural Complexes*. New York: Columbia University Press, 1966.

BULL, R. A. "On Possible Worlds in Propositional Calculi." *T*, 34 (1968), 171–182.

BURDICK, HOWARD. "On Necessity *De Dicto*." *Philosophia*, 2 (1972), 85–116.

BURKS, ARTHUR. *Chance, Cause and Reason*. Chicago: University of Chicago Press, 1963.

————. "The Logic of Causal Propositions." *M*, 60 (1951), 363–382.

BUTCHVAROV, PANAYOT. "Identity." *Midwest Studies in Philosophy*, 3 (1977), 70–89.

CAMP, JOSEPH. "Plantinga on *De Dicto* and *De Re*." *N*, 5 (1971), 215–225.

CAMPBELL, RICHARD. "Modality *De Dicto* and *De Re*." *AJP*, 44 (1964), 345–359.

CANFIELD, J. V. "Anthropological Science Fiction and Logical Necessity." *CJP*, 5 (1975), 467–479.

CARGILE, JAMES. "On an Interpretation of T, S4, and S5." *Philosophia*, 2 (1972), 137–158.

————. "The Ontological Argument." *Philosophy*, 50 (1975), 69–80.

CARNAP, RUDOLF. *Introduction to Semantics*. Cambridge, Mass.: Harvard University Press, 1942.

————. *Logical Foundations of Probability*. Chicago: University of Chicago Press, 1950.

————. *Meaning and Necessity*. Chicago: University of Chicago Press, 1947.

————. "Meaning and Synonymy in Natural Languages." *PS*, 6 (1955), 33–47.

————. "Meaning Postulates." *PS*, 3 (1952), 65–72.

————. "Modalities and Quantification." *JSL*, 11 (1946), 33–64.

————. "Notes on Semantics." *Philosophia*, 2 (1972), 1–54.

CARTER, W. R. "Plantinga on Existing Necessarily." *CJP*, 6 (1976), 95–104.

CARTWRIGHT, RICHARD. "Identity and Substitutivity." In *Identity and Individuation*, edited by Milton Munitz, pp. 119–134. New York: New York University Press, 1971.

————. "Some Remarks on Essentialism." *JP*, 65 (1968), 615–626.

CASTAÑEDA, HECTOR-NERI. "On the Logic of Self-Knowledge." *N*, 1 (1967), 9–22.

————. "Thinking and the Structure of the World." *Philosophia*, 4 (1974), 3–40.

CHELLAS, BRIAN. "Basic Conditional Logic." *JPL*, 4 (1975), 133–154.

_____. "Notions of Relevance." *JPL*, 1 (1972), 287–293.

CHISHOLM, RODERICK. "Beyond Being and Non-Being." *PS*, 24 (1973), 245–255.

_____. "Events and Propositions." *N*, 4 (1970), 15–24.

_____. "The Logic of Knowing." *JP*, 60 (1963), 773–795.

_____. "On Mereological Essentialism." *RM*, 28 (1975), 468–476.

_____. "Parts as Essential to Their Wholes." *RM*, 26 (1973), 581–603.

_____. *Person and Object*. LaSalle, Ill.: Open Court, 1976.

_____. "Problems of Identity." In *Identity and Individuation*, edited by Milton Munitz, pp. 3–30. New York: New York University Press, 1971.

_____. "States of Affairs Again." *N*, 5 (1971), 179–189.

CHURCH, ALONZO. "A Formulation of the Logic of Sense and Denotation." In *Structure, Method, and Meaning: Essays in Honor of Henry M. Sheffer*, edited by Paul Henle, H. M. Kallen, and S. K. Langer, pp. 3–24. New York: Liberal Arts Press, 1951.

_____. *Introduction to Mathematical Logic*. Princeton, N.J.: Princeton University Press, 1956.

_____. "The Need for Abstract Entities in Semantic Analysis." *Proceedings of the American Academy of Arts and Sciences*, 1951, 100–112.

CLARK, MICHAEL. "The General Notion of Entailment." *PQ*, 17 (1967), 231–245.

COCCHIARELLA, NINO. "Logical Atomism, Nominalism, and Modal Logic." *S*, 30 (1975), 23–62.

CODE, ALAN. "Aristotle's Response to Quine's Objections to Modal Logic." *JPL*, 5 (1976), 159–186.

CORRADO, MICHAEL. "Proper Names and Necessary Properties." *PS*, 24 (1973), 112–118.

CRESSWELL, M. J. "Classical Intensional Logic." *T*, 36 (1970), 347–372.

_____. "Hamblin on Time." *N*, 9 (1975), 193–204.

_____. "Intensional Logic and Logical Truth." *JPL*. 1 (1972), 2–15.

_____. *Logics and Languages*. London: Methuen, 1973.

CURLEY, E. M. "Lewis and Entailment." *PS*, 23 (1972), 198–204.

CURRY, HASKELL. "The Interpretation of Formalized Implication." *T*, 25 (1959), 1–26.

DAVIDSON, DONALD. "The Method of Extension and Intension." In *The Philosophy of Rudolf Carnap*, edited by Paul Schilpp, LaSalle, Ill.: Open Court, 1964.

DAVIS, J. W., et al. *Philosophical Logic*. Dordrecht: Reidel, 1969.

DeSOUSA, R. B. "Kripke on Naming and Necessity." *CJP*, 3 (1974), 447–464.

DONNELLAN, KEITH. "The Contingent *A Priori* and Rigid Designation." *Midwest Studies in Philosophy*, 3 (1977), 12–27.

_____. "Reference and Definite Descriptions." *PR*, 75 (1966), 281–304.

_____. "Speaking of Nothing." *PR*, 83 (1974), 3–31.

DURRANT, MICHAEL. "Essence and Accident." *M*, 84 (1975), 595–600.

DUTHIE, G. D. "Intensional Propositional Logic." *PQ*, 20 (1970), 41–52.

ELLIS, BRIAN, FRANK JACKSON, AND ROBERT PARGETTER. "An Objection to Possible Worlds Semantics for Counterfactual Logics." *JPL*, 7 (1978), 355–358.

FELDMAN, FRED. "Counterparts." *JP*, 68 (1971), 406–409.

FEYS, R. "Carnap on Modalities." In *The Philosophy of Rudolf Carnap*, edited by Paul Schilpp, pp. 285–298. LaSalle, Ill.: Open Court, 1964.

FINE, KIT. "Models for Entailment." *JPL*, 3 (1974), 347–372.

––––––. "Properties, Propositions, and Sets." *JPL*, 7 (1978), 135–192.

––––––. "Propositional Quantifiers in Modal Logic." *T*, 36 (1970), 336–346.

––––––. "Vagueness, Truth, and Logic." *S*, 30 (1975), 265–300.

FISK, MILTON. "A Modal Analogue of Free Logic." In *The Logical Way of Doing Things*, edited by Karel Lambert. New Haven: Yale University Press, 1969.

––––––. *Nature and Necessity*. Bloomington: Indiana University Press, 1973.

FITCH, FREDERIC. "The Problem of the Morning Star and the Evening Star." *Philosophy of Science* (1949), 137–140.

––––––. "A Theory of Logical Essences." *The Monist*, 51 (1967), 104–109.

FØLLESDAL, DAGFINN. "Existence and Identity in Epistemic Contexts." *T*, 33 (1967), 138–147.

––––––. "Knowledge, Identity, and Existence." *T*, 33 (1967), 1–27.

––––––. "Quantification into Causal Contexts." In *Boston Studies in the Philosophy of Science*, II, pp. 263–274. New York: Humanities Press, 1965.

––––––. "Quine on Modality." *S*, 18 (1968), 147–157.

FREGE, GOTTLOB. *Translations from the Philosophical Writings of Gottlob Frege*. Translated and edited by Max Black and Peter Geach. Oxford: Basil Blackwell, 1952.

GABBAY, DOV M. *Investigations in Modal and Tense Logic with Applications to Problems in Philosophy and Linguistics*. Dordrecht: Reidel, 1976.

GEACH, PETER T. *Logic Matters*. Berkeley: University of California Press, 1972.

GIBBARD, ALLAN. "Contingent Identity." *JPL*, 4 (1975), 187–222.

GIBBS, BENJAMIN. "Real Possibility." *APQ*, 7 (1970), 340–348.

GOODMAN, NELSON. *Fact, Fiction, and Forecast*. 2d ed. Indianapolis: Bobbs-Merrill, 1965.

––––––. "The Problem of Counterfactual Conditionals." *JP*, 44 (1947), 113–128.

HAACK, SUSAN. *Deviant Logics*. Cambridge: Cambridge University Press, 1974.

––––––. "Some Preliminaries to Ontology." *JPL*, 5 (1976), 455–474.

HACKING, IAN. "All Kinds of Possibility." *PR*, 84 (1975), 321–337.

––––––. "The Leibniz-Carnap Program for Inductive Logic." *JP*, 68 (1971), 587–610.

––––––. "Possibility." *PR*, 76 (1967), 143–168.

HALLDÉN, SÖREN. "A Pragmatic Approach to Modal Theory." *APF*, 16 (1963), 53–62.

HAMBLIN, C. L. "Cresswell's Colleague TLM." *N*, 9 (1975), 205–210.
_____. "The Effect of When It's Said." *T*, 36 (1970), 249–263.
HANSON, N. R. "It's Actual So It's Possible." *PS*, 8 (1957), 69–80.
HARMAN, GILBERT. "Is Modal Logic Logic?" *Philosophia*, 2 (1972), 75–84.
_____. "A Non-Essential Property." *JP*, 67 (1970).
_____. "Quine on Meaning and Existence, I and II." *RM*, 21 (1967–1968), 124–151 and 343–368.
HARRÉ, ROM. "Surrogates for Necessity." *M*, 82 (1973), 358–380.
HARTSHORNE, CHARLES. *Anselm's Discovery.* LaSalle, Ill.: Open Court, 1965.
_____. "Necessity." *RM*, 21 (1967), 290–296.
_____. "Real Possibility." *JP*, 80 (1963), 593–606.
_____. "Rejoinder to Purtill." *RM*, 21 (1967), 308–309.
HAZEN, ALLEN. "Expressive Completeness in Modal Languages." *JPL*, 5 (1976), 25–46.
HINTIKKA, JAAKKO K. *Approaches to Natural Language.* Dordrecht: Reidel, 1973.
_____. "Are Logical Truths Analytic?" *PR*, 77 (1968), 178–203.
_____. "Carnap's Semantics in Retrospect." *S*, 25 (1973), 372–397.
_____. "Existential Presuppositions and Existential Commitments." *JP*, 56 (1959), 125–137.
_____. "Impossible Possible Worlds Vindicated." *JPL*, 4 (1975), 475–484.
_____. "Individuals, Possible Worlds, and Epistemic Logic." *N*, 1 (1967), 33–62.
_____. *The Intentions of Intentionality and Other New Models for the Modalities.* Dordrecht: Reidel, 1975.
_____. "'Knowing Oneself' and Other Problems in Epistemic Logic." *T*, 32 (1966), 1–13.
_____. *Knowledge and Belief: An Introduction to the Logic of the Two Notions.* Ithaca, N.Y.: Cornell University Press, 1962.
_____. *Logic, Language Games, and Information.* Oxford: Clarendon Press, 1973.
_____. "Modality and Quantification." *T*, 27 (1961), 119–128.
_____. "Modality as Referential Multiplicity." *Ajatus*, 20 (1957), 49–63.
_____. *Models for Modalities.* Dordrecht: Reidel, 1969.
_____. "Semantics for Propositional Attitudes." In *Philosophical Logic*, edited by J. W. Davis, pp. 21–45. Dordrecht: Reidel, 1969.
_____. "The Semantics of Modal Notions and the Indeterminacy of Ontology." In *Semantics of Natural Language*, edited by Gilbert Harman and Donald Davidson, pp. 398–414. Dordrecht: Reidel, 1973.
_____. "Studies in the Logic of Existence and Necessity." *Monist*, 50 (1966), 57–76.
HIRSCH, ELI. "Essence and Identity." In *Identity and Individuation*, edited by Milton Munitz, pp. 31–50. New York: New York University Press, 1971.

HUGHES, G. E., AND M. J. CRESSWELL. *An Introduction to Modal Logic.* London: Methuen, 1968.

JAGER, RONALD. "Realism and Necessity." *RM*, 18 (1965), 711–738.

JUBIEN, MICHAEL. "Essential Properties and Reduction." *JP*, 67 (1970), 1024–1046.

KAMP, HANS. "The Philosophical Significance of Intensional Logic." *ASSV*, 49 (1975), 21–44.

KANGER, STIG. "The Morning Star Paradox." *T*, 23 (1957), 7–11.

———. "A Note on Quantification and Modalities," *T*, 23 (1957), 133–134.

———. *Provability in Logic.* Stockholm: Almqvist and Wiksell, 1957.

KAPLAN, DAVID. "Quantifying In." In *Words and Objections,* edited by Donald Davidson and Jaakko Hintikka, pp. 178–214. Dordrecht: Reidel, 1969.

KATZ, FRED, AND JERROLD KATZ. "Is Necessity the Mother of Intension?" *PR*, 86 (1977), 70–96.

KNEALE, WILLIAM. "Intentionality and Intensionality." *ASSV*, 42 (1968), 73–90.

———. "Modality *De Dicto* and *De Re.*" In *Logic, Methodology, and the Philosophy of Science,* edited by Ernest Nagal, Patrick Suppes, and Alfred Tarski, pp. 622–633. Stanford, Calif.: Stanford University Press, 1962.

KORNER, STPHAN. *Conceptual Thinking.* New York: Dover, 1958.

———. "Individuals in Possible Worlds." In *Logic and Ontology,* edited by Milton Munitz, pp. 229–240. New York: New York University Press, 1973.

———. "On Entailment." *ASP* (1948), 143–162.

———. *Philosophy of Logic.* Berkeley: University of California Press, 1976.

KRIPKE, SAUL. "A Completeness Theorem in Modal Logic." *JSL*, 24 (1959), 1–14.

———. "Identity and Necessity." In *Identity and Individuation,* edited by Milton Munitz, pp. 135–164. New York: New York University Press, 1971.

———. "Naming and Necessity." In *Semantics of Natural Language,* edited by Donald Davidson and Gilbert Harmon, pp. 253–355. Dordrecht: Reidel, 1972.

———. "Semantical Analysis of Modal Logic, I." *ZML* (1963), 67–93.

———. "Semantical Analysis of Modal Logic, II." In *The Theory of Models,* edited by J. Addison, Leon Henkin, and Alfred Tarski, pp. 206–220. Amsterdam: North Holland, 1965.

———. "Semantical Considerations on Modal Logic." *APF*, 16 (1963), 83–94.

LAPARA, NICHOLAS. "Semantics for Logical and Nomic Modalities." *APQ*, 9 (1972), 39–48.

LEBLANC, HUGUES. "Matters of Relevance." *JPL*, 1 (1972), 269–287.

———. *Truth Value Semantics.* Amsterdam: North Holland, 1976.

———, AND T. HAILPEREN. "Non-designating Singular Terms." *PR*, 68 (1959), 239–243.

LEMON, E. J. "A Theory of Attributes Based on Modal Logic." *APF*, 16 (1963), 95–122.

LEWIS, C. I. "The Modes of Meaning." *PPR*, 4 (1944), 236–249.

———, AND CHARLES LANGFORD. *Symbolic Logic*. 2d ed. New York: Dover, 1951.

LEWIS, DAVID. "Anselm and Actuality." *N*, 4 (1970), 175–188.

———. *Convention*. Cambridge, Mass.: Harvard University Press, 1969.

———. *Counterfactuals*. Cambridge, Mass.: Harvard University Press, 1973.

———. "Counterparts, Persons, and Their Bodies." *JP*, 68 (1971), 203–211.

———. "General Semantics." In *Semantics of Natural Language*, edited by Gilbert Harman and Donald Davidson, pp. 169–218. Dordrecht: Reidel, 1973.

———. "Possible Worlds Semantics for Counterfactual Logics: A Rejoinder." *JPL*, 7 (1978), 359–363.

LEWY, CASIMIR. *Meaning and Modality*. Cambridge: Cambridge University Press, 1976.

LINSKY, LEONARD. *Reference and Modality*. Oxford: Clarendon Press, New York: Oxford University Press, 1971.

———. "Reference, Essentialism, and Modality." *JP*, 65 (1968), 287–300.

———. *Referring*. London: Routledge & Kegan Paul, 1967.

———. "Substitutivity and Descriptions." *JP*, 63 (1966), 673–683.

LOCKWOOD, MICHAEL. "Identity and Reference." In *Identity and Individuation*, edited by Milton Munitz, pp. 199–212. New York: New York University Press, 1971.

———. "On Predicating Proper Names." *PR*, 84 (1975), 471–498.

LONG, PETER. "Possibility and Actuality." *M*, 70 (1961), 187–200.

LOUX, MICHAEL J. "The Concept of a Kind," *PS*, 30 (1976), 53–61.

———. "Recent Work in Ontology." *APQ*, 9 (1972), 119–138.

———. *Substance and Attribute*. Dordrecht: Reidel, 1978.

———. *Universals and Particulars*. 2d ed. Notre Dame, Ind.: University of Notre Dame Press, 1976.

McKAY, THOMAS J. "Essentialism in Quantified Modal Logic." *JPL*, 4 (1975), 423–438.

MACKIE, J. L. *The Cement of the Universe*. Oxford: Clarendon Press, 1975.

———. "*De* What *Re* is *De Re* Modality?" *JP*, 71 (1974), 551–561.

———. *Truth, Probability, and Paradox*. Oxford: Clarendon Press, 1973.

MALCOLM, NORMAN. "Anselm's Ontological Arguments." *PR*, 69 (1960), 41–62.

MARCUS, RUTH BARCAN. "Classes and Attributes in Extended Modal Systems." *APF*, 16 (1963), 123–136.

———. "Dispensing with Possibilia." *Proceedings and Addresses of the American Philosophical Association, 1975–1976*, 44: 39–51.

———. "Essentialism in Modal Logic." *N*, 1 (1967), 91–96.

———. "Extensionality." *M*, 78 (1969), 55–62.

———. "A Functional Calculus of First Order Based on Strict Implication." *JSL*, 11 (1946), 1–16.

_____. "Interpreting Quantification." *Inquiry*, 5 (1962), 252–259.

_____. "Modalities and Intensional Languages." In *Contemporary Readings in Logical Theory*, edited by I. M. Copi and J. A. Gould, pp. 278–293. New York: Macmillan, 1966.

_____. "Modal Logic." In *Contemporary Philosophy*, edited by R. Klibansky, pp. 87–101. Florence: La Nuova Italia Editrice, 1968.

MATES, BENSON. "Leibniz on Possible Worlds." In *Logic, Methodology, and Philosophy of Science*. 3d ed. Amsterdam: Van Rootselaan and Staal, 1968.

MEINONG, ALEXIUS. "The Theory of Objects." In *Realism and the Background of Phenomenology*, edited by Roderick Chisholm, pp. 76–117. Glencoe, Ill.: Free Press, 1960.

MERRILL, G. H. "A Free Logic with Intensions as Possible Values of Terms." *JPL*, 4 (1975), 293–326.

MILLER, BARRY. "Making Sense of Necessary Existence." *APQ*, 11 (1974), 47–54.

MONTAGUE, RICHARD. *Formal Philosophy*. Edited by Richmond Thomason. New Haven: Yale University Press, 1974.

_____. "Syntactical Treatments of Modality with Corollaries on Reflexion Principles and Finite Axiomatizability." *APF*, 16 (1963), 153–168.

MORTON, ADAM. "On What Could Have Happened." *PR*, 77 (1968), 73–89.

_____. "The Possible in the Actual." *N*, 7 (1973), 394–406.

MUNITZ, MILTON. *Identity and Individuation*. New York: New York University Press, 1971.

_____. *Logic and Ontology*. New York: New York University Press, 1973.

MYHILL, JOHN. "Problems Arising in the Formalization of Intensional Logic." *Logique et Analyse*, 1 (1958), 78–83.

NELSON, JOHN O. "Modal Logic and the Ontological Proof for God's Existence." *RM*, 17 (1963), 235–242.

NORTON, BRYAN. "Is Counterpart Theory Inadequate?" *JPL*, 5 (1976), 79–90.

PAP, ARTHUR. *Semantics and Necessary Truth*. New Haven: Yale University Press, 1958.

_____. "Strict Implication, Entailment, and Modal Iteration." *PR*, 64 (1955), 604–613.

PARSONS, TERENCE. "Essentialism and Quantified Modal Logic." *PR*, 78 (1959), 35–72.

_____. "Grades of Essentialism in Quantified Modal Logic." *N*, 1 (1967), 181–200.

_____. "A Prolegomenon to Meinongian Semantics." *JP*, 71 (1974), 561–581.

PARTEE, BARBARA. "Possible Worlds Semantics and Linguistic Theory." *Monist*, 60 (1977), 303–326.

PLANTINGA, ALVIN. "*De Re et De Dicto*," *N*, 3 (1969), 235–258.

_____. "Existence, Necessity, and God." *New Scholasticism*, 50 (1976), 61–72.

_____. *God and Other Minds.* Ithaca, N.Y.: Cornell University Press, 1967.

_____. *God, Freedom, and Evil.* New York: Harper & Row, 1974.

_____. "Mereological Essentialism: Some Further Considerations." *RM*, 28 (1975), 477–484.

_____. *The Nature of Necessity.* Oxford: Clarendon Press, 1974.

_____. "Necessary Existence: A Reply to Carter." *CJP*, 6 (1976), 105–111.

_____. "Which Worlds Could God Have Created?" *JP*, 70 (1973), 539–552.

_____. "World and Essence." *PR*, 79 (1970), 461–492.

POLLOCK, JOHN. "Four Kinds of Conditionals." *APQ*, 12 (1975), 51–59.

_____. "Logical Validity in Modal Logic." *Monist*, 51 (1967), 128–135.

_____. *Subjunctive Reasoning.* Dordrecht: Reidel, 1976.

PRIOR, ARTHUR. *Formal Logic.* Oxford: Clarendon Press, 1955.

_____. "Intentionality and Intensionality." *ASSV*, 34 (1960), 91–106.

_____. "Is the Concept of Referential Transparency Really Necessary?" *APF*, 16 (1963), 189–200.

_____. *Objects of Thought.* Edited by Peter Geach and Anthony Kenny. Oxford: Clarendon Press, 1971.

_____. *Papers in Logic and Ethics.* London: Duckworth, 1976.

_____. *Papers on Time and Tense.* Oxford: Clarendon Press, 1968.

_____. *Past, Present and Future.* Oxford: Clarendon Press, 1967.

_____. "Possible Worlds." *PQ*, 12 (1962), 36–46.

_____. "The Possibly True and the Possible." *M*, 78 (1969), 481–492.

_____. *Time and Modality.* Oxford: Clarendon Press, 1957.

_____, AND KIT FINE. *Worlds, Times, and Selves.* London: Duckworth, 1977.

PURTILL, R. J. "About Identity through Possible Worlds." *N*, 2 (1968), 87–89.

_____. "Ontological Modalities." *RM*, 20 (1967), 297–307.

PUTNAM, HILARY. *Meaning and the Moral Sciences.* London: Routledge & Kegan Paul, 1978.

_____. *Mind, Language, and Reality: Philosophical Papers.* Cambridge: Cambridge University Press, 1975.

_____. *Philosophy of Logic.* New York: Harper & Row, 1971.

QUINE, W. V. O. "Carnap and Logical Truth." *S*, 12 (1960), 350–374.

_____. *From a Logical Point of View.* Cambridge, Mass.: Harvard University Press, 1953, 2d ed. 1961.

_____. "Intensions Revisited." *Midwest Studies in Philosophy*, 3 (1977), 5–11.

_____. "Notes on Existence and Necessity." In *Semantics and the Philosophy of Language,* edited by Leonard Linsky, pp. 77–91. Urbana: University of Illinois Press, 1952.

_____. *Ontological Relativity and Other Essays.* New York: Columbia University Press, 1969.

_____. *Philosophy of Logic.* Englewood Cliffs, N.J.: Prentice-Hall, 1970.

_____. "The Problem of Interpreting Modal Logic." *JSL*, 12 (1947), 43–48.

————. *The Ways of Paradox and Other Essays.* New York: Random House, 1966.

————. *Word and Object.* Cambridge, Mass.: MIT Press, 1960.

REICHENBACH, HANS. *Nomological Statements and Admissible Operations.* Amsterdam: North Holland, 1954.

REINHARDT, LLOYD. "Metaphysical Possibility." *M*, 87 (1978), 210–229.

RESCHER, NICHOLAS. "A Contribution to Modal Logic." *RM*, 12 (1958), 186–199.

————. "A Factual Analysis of Counterfactual Conditionals." *PS*, 11 (1960), 49–53.

————. *Essays in Philosophical Analysis.* Pittsburgh: University of Pittsburgh Press, 1969.

————. *Hypothetical Reasoning.* Amsterdam: North Holland, 1964.

————. *Studies in Modal Logic, American Philosophical Quarterly* Monograph Series, no. 2, 1975.

————. *A Theory of Possibility.* Pittsburgh: University of Pittsburgh Press, 1975.

————. *Topics in Philosophical Logic.* Dordrecht: Reidel, 1968.

————, AND ZANE PARKS. "Possible Individuals, Trans-World Identity, and Quantified Modal Logic." *N*, 7 (1973), 330–350.

RORTY. AMELIE O. "Essential Possibilities and the Actual World." *RM*, 25 (1972), 607–624.

ROSS, J. F. "Did God Create the Only Possible World?" *RM*, 16 (1962), 14–25.

ROUTLEY, RICHARD. "Some Things Do Not Exist." *NDJFL*, 7 (1966), 251–276.

————. "Semantics of Entailment, II." *JPL*, 1 (1972), 53–72.

————. "Semantics of Entailment, III." *JPL*, 1 (1972), 192–208.

————, AND L. GODDARD. *The Logic of Significance and the Content.* New York: Wiley, 1973.

————, AND R. K. MEYER. "Semantics of Entailment, I." In *Truth, Syntax, and Modality,* edited by Hugues LeBlanc, Amsterdam: North Holland,

————, AND VALERIE ROUTLEY. "A Fallacy of Modality." *N*, 2 (1969), 129–153.

ROWE, WILLIAM. "Plantinga on Possible Worlds and Evil." *JP*, 70 (1973), 554–555.

RUNDLE, BEDE. "Modality and Quantification." In *Analytical Philosophy,* 2d ser., edited by Ronald Butler, pp. 27–39. Oxford: Basil Blackwell, 1965.

RUSSELL, BERTRAND. "On Denoting." *M*, 14 (1905), 479–493.

————. "The Philosophy of Logical Atomism." In *Logic and Knowledge,* edited by R. C. Marsh, pp. 175–282. London: George Allen and Unwin, 1956.

SAGAL, PAUL. "Countering Counterpart Theory." *Metaphilosophy,* 5 (1974), 151–154.

SALMON, WESLEY. "Laws, Modalities, and Counterfactuals." *S*, 35 (1977), 191–229.

SCHOCK, ROLF. "A Note on Possible Object Logics." *AJP*, 48 (1970), 261–263.

SCOTT, DANA. "Advice on Modal Logic." In *Philosophical Problems in Logic*, edited by Karel Lambert, Dordrecht: Reidel, 1970.

SEARLE, JOHN R. "Proper Names." *M*, 67 (1958), 166–173.

SELLARS, WILFRID. "Counterfactuals, Dispositions, and Causal Modalities." In *Minnesota Studies in the Philosophy of Science II*, pp. 225–309. Minneapolis: University of Minnesota Press, 1956.

_____. *Philosophical Perspectives*. Springfield, Ill.: Charles C. Thomas, 1967.

_____. *Science and Metaphysics*. London: Routledge & Kegan Paul, 1967.

_____. *Science, Perception, and Reality*. London: Routledge & Kegan Paul, 1963.

SKYRMS, BRIAN. "Possible Worlds, Physics, and Metaphysics." *PS*, 30 (1976), 323–332.

SLEIGH, R. C. *Necessary Truth*. Englewood Cliffs, N.J.: Prentice-Hall, 1972.

SLOTE, MICHAEL. *Metaphysics and Essence*. New York: New York University Press, 1974.

_____. "Time in Counterfactuals." *PR*, 87 (1978), 3–27.

SMULLYAN, ARTHUR. "Modality and Description." *JSL*, 13 (1948), 31–37.

SNYDER, D. PAUL. *Modal Logic and Its Applications*. New York: Van Nostrand, 1971.

STALNAKER, ROBERT. "A Theory of Conditionals." In *Studies in Logical Theory*, edited by Nicholas Rescher, pp. 98–112. *American Philosophical Quarterly* Monograph Series, no. 2. Oxford: Blackwell, 1968.

_____. "Pragmatics." In *Semantics of Natural Language*, edited by Gilbert Harman and Donald Davidson, pp. 380–397. Dordrecht: Reidel, 1973.

_____. "Propositions." In *Issues in the Philosophy of Language*, edited by A. F. McKay and D. D. Merrill, pp. 79–91. New Haven: Yale University Press, 1976.

_____, AND RICHMOND THOMASON. "Modality and Reference." *N*, 2 (1968), 359–372.

_____. "A Semantic Analysis of Conditional Logic." *T*, 36 (1970), 23–42.

STINE, GAIL C. "Essentialism, Possible Worlds, and Propositional Attitudes." *PR*, 82 (1973), 471–482.

_____. "Intentional Inexistence." *JPL*, 5 (1976), 491–510.

STOOTHOFF, R. H. "What Actually Exists." *ASSV*, 42 (1968), 17–30.

STRAWSON, P. F. *Individuals*. London: Methuen, 1959.

_____. *Logico-Linguistic Papers*. London: Methuen, 1971.

TELLER, PAUL. "Essential Properties: Some Conjectures." *JP*, 72 (1975), 233–248.

THOMASON, RICHMOND. "Modal Logic and Metaphysics." In *The Logical Way of Doing Things*, edited by Karel Lambert, pp. 119–146. New Haven: Yale University Press, 1969.

Tichy, Pavel. "On *De Dicto* Modalities in Quantified S5." *JPL*, 2 (1973), 387-392.

_____. "Plantinga on Essence: A Few Questions." *PR*, 81 (1972), 82-93.

Tomberlin, James E. "Essentialism: Strong and Weak." *Metaphilosophy*, 2 (1971), 309-315.

van Fraasen, Bas. "Extension, Intension, and Comprehension." In *Logic and Ontology*, edited by Milton Munitz, pp. 101-132. New York: New York University Press, 1973.

_____. *Formal Semantics and Logic*. New Haven: Yale University Press, 1971.

_____. "Meaning Relations among Predicates." *N*, 1 (1967), 161-179.

_____. "Meaning Relations and Modalities." *N*, 3 (1969), 155-157.

_____. "The Only Necessity Is Verbal Necessity." *JP*, 74 (1977), 71-85.

_____. "Singular Terms, Truth-Value Gaps, and Free Logic." *JP*, 63 (1966), 481-495.

Vendler, Zeno. "The Possibility of Possible Worlds." *CJP*, 5 (1975), 57-72.

Vision, Gerald. "Essentialism and Proper Names." *APQ*, 7 (1970), 321-330.

von Wright, G. H. *An Essay on Modal Logic*. Amsterdam: North Holland, 1951.

_____. *Logical Studies*. London: Routledge & Kegan Paul, 1957.

Weiss, Paul. *The Modes of Being*. Carbondale, Ill.: Southern Illinois University Press, 1958.

Wiggins, David. "Essentialism, Continuity, and Identity." *S*, 29 (1974), 321-359.

_____. *Identity and Spatio-Temporal Continuity*. Oxford: Basil Blackwell, 1971.

Wilson, Margaret. "Possibility, Propensity and Chance: Some Doubts about the Hacking Thesis." *JP*, 68 (1971), 610-617.

Wilson, N. L. "Modality and Identity: A Defense." *JP*, 62 (1965), 471-477.

_____. "The Trouble with Meanings." *Dialogue*, 4 (1964), 52-64.

Wittgenstein, Ludwig. *Philosophical Investigations*. Translated by G. E. M. Anscombe. New York: Macmillan, 1953.

_____. *Remarks on the Foundations of Mathematics*. Translated by G. E. M. Anscombe. Oxford: Basil Blackwell, 1964.

_____. *Tractatus Logico-Philosophicus*. Translated by D. F. Pears and B. F. McGuinness. London: Routledge & Kegan Paul, 1961.

Woods, John. "Descriptions, Essences, and Quantified Modal Logic." *JPL*, 2 (1973), 304-321.

_____. "Essentialism, Self-Identity, and Quantifying In." In *Identity and Individuation*, edited by Milton Munitz, pp. 165-198. New York: New York University Press, 1971.

_____. "Relevance." *Logique et Analyse*, 29 (1964), 130-137.

_____. "Relevance Revisited." *Logique et Analyse*, 31 (1966), 364-371.

Zeman, J. Jay. *Modal Logic*. Oxford: Clarendon Press, 1973.

Index

331

The Possible
and the Actual

Designed by G. T. Whipple, Jr.
Composed by The Composing Room of Michigan, Inc.,
in 10 point VIP Times Roman, 2 points leaded,
with display lines in Times Roman.
Printed offset by Thomson-Shore, Inc.
on Warren's Number 66 text, 50 pound basis.